Federalism and Judicial Review
in West Germany

FEDERALISM AND JUDICIAL REVIEW IN WEST GERMANY

by
PHILIP M. BLAIR

CLARENDON PRESS · OXFORD,
1981

Oxford University Press, Walton Street, Oxford OX2 6DP

OXFORD LONDON GLASGOW
NEW YORK TORONTO MELBOURNE WELLINGTON
KUALA LUMPUR SINGAPORE JAKARTA HONG KONG TOKYO
DELHI BOMBAY CALCUTTA MADRAS KARACHI
NAIROBI DAR ES SALAAM CAPE TOWN

Published in the United States
by Oxford University Press, New York.

British Library Cataloguing in Publication Data
Blair, Philip M
    Federalism and judicial review
    in West Germany.
    1. Judicial review – Germany, West
    2. Germany, West – Politics and government
    I. Title
    354.4303'73   JN3971.A85   80–41334
    ISBN 0–19–827427–0

Phototypeset in V.I.P. Baskerville by
Western Printing Services Ltd, Bristol
Printed and bound in Great Britain
by Billing and Sons Limited
Guildford, London, Oxford, Worcester

TO ELISABETH

Preface

North American students of politics are accustomed to regard the study of federalism or of the role of the judiciary in politics as lying within the mainstream of their discipline. In the United Kingdom, on the other hand, for reasons which are not far to seek, less attention has traditionally been paid to these subjects than in many other countries. There are, of course, notable exceptions to this generalization. But even when scholars have devoted themselves to one of these topics, they have tended to concentrate primarily on the English-speaking world. Yet one of Britain's major European neighbours, the Federal Republic of Germany, provides noteworthy examples of both phenomena which differ in various ways from the Anglo-Saxon pattern. A study of the German experience may thus be of general comparative value; moreover, in the light of the evidence of an increasing British interest during the 1970s, for reasons of domestic politics, both in forms of federalism (or at least 'quasi-federalism') and in the possibilities of a broader controlling function for the courts, a closer understanding of the German system may prove useful and perhaps instructive. This book attempts to make a modest contribution to such a study by examining the role of the West German Federal Constitutional Court in relation to the federal system.

To the interest of the subject from a comparative point of view may be added its importance for an understanding of the German political system itself; particularly if, as the author believes, the institutional framework is itself a significant determinant of political behaviour. One of the striking characteristics of the governmental system of the Federal Republic, which is partly due to the 'new start' in 1949, is the degree to which the conditions for the exercise of political authority and the principles underlying political institutions are explicit. This phenomenon is connected with the marked predominance of law in German government and society as a basis of political action, a channeller of political expression and a criterion of political argument. It has consequences for attitudes to the basic rules of the political game and for the importance of those institutions whose role is to ensure observance of the rules. Foremost among such institutions is of course the Federal Constitutional Court.

In terms both of the constitution and of political reality, federalism must be accounted one of the most fundamental organizational principles of the West German state. Admittedly, in spite of its venerable traditions in Germany, it is not possible nowadays to regard federalism as a political 'way of life' in the same way as in Switzerland or the United States. It is certainly not the case, for example, that Germans find it hard to conceive of democracy except in conjunction with a federal structure. Some, indeed, consider the federal system as little more than a cumbersome nuisance. Yet it is scarcely an exaggeration to say that the whole of the West German political system, despite the various centralizing pressures at work within it, is imbued with a federal quality and a philosophy of decentralization. The federal structure has implications for the pattern of political activity, the mode of exercise of political authority and the form taken by administrative action. Above all, in a parliamentary democracy it is probably the most effective system of checks and balances. Since few things are more dangerous to federalism than lack of precision in the delimitation of powers and responsibilities, the political importance of the Constitutional Court's function as guardian and umpire of the federal system is evident.

These considerations must be my excuse for the presumptuousness of an undertaking whereby a British non-lawyer seeks to elucidate the role of a characteristically German judicial institution in a field which itself, given the comparatively legalistic environment of West German government, has tended to remain the preserve of scholars of public law. It must be hoped that the German reader will find the departures from traditional German methodology which result from this difference of perspective interesting rather than exasperating.

A book entitled 'Federalism and Judicial Review in West Germany' which concentrates on the influence of the Federal Constitutional Court on federal relations may call for a word of explanation. In particular, it should not be taken as implying that it is the only court concerned with the review of legal norms relating to the federal system. Most of the German Länder have constitutional courts of their own. But their task is to review the compatibility of legal norms with the constitution of the Land concerned; it is only indirectly that they may be entitled or obliged to adduce as criteria of decision-making certain provisions of the Federal constitution whose influence specifically extends into the constitutional sphere of the member states. The Länder constitutional courts are thus not of primary importance for a study which is principally concerned with the resolution of conflict between the Federation and its constituent states and the evolution of the federal relationship. Again, because the Federal Constitutional Court is not a supreme court of appeal but is responsible only for the adjudication of constitutional questions, jurisdiction over some kinds of cases of federal interest is reserved to other branches of the judiciary, and especially the administrative courts. But since the relationship between the Federal Government and the Länder is governed as a whole by constitutional law, it is the Federal Constitutional Court that occupies the strategic position of umpire of their respective powers, rights and obligations, with corresponding influence over the operation of the federal system in practice.

The text which follows is closely based on the thesis submitted in 1977 for the degree of Doctor of Philosophy in the University of Oxford under the title 'The influence of the Federal Constitutional Court on the evolution of federalism in West Germany'. Thanks are owed to many people for help and support in my research. I am grateful to the Warden and Fellows of Nuffield College for providing a congenial and stimulating environment in which to begin the work. The great benefit derived from being able to spend a year in Germany as Theodor Heuss Research Fellow and the kind assistance of the Alexander von Humboldt Foundation are also acknowledged with gratitude. My thanks are due to Professor Wilhelm Hennis of the University of Freiburg, both for enabling me to use his politics department as my base while in Germany and for his continuing interest and support. I am further indebted to several judges and former judges of the Constitutional Court, who generously consented to submit to interviews and conversations which were both cordial and candid. In addition, I wish to express my appreciation for being allowed to work for certain periods in the excellent library of the Court, and my gratitude to the deputy librarian, Herr Franz Schneider, for his ever friendly guidance. I am beholden to Professor Ulrich Scheuner for liberally giving of his time and for many useful comments both of detail and of principle.

My greatest academic debt, however, is to my former supervisor, Nevil Johnson, not only for his constructive criticism of the text but also for the stimulation of discussion ranging well beyond the bounds of this book.

Finally, I would not want to end without a reference to the unfailing support of my parents, a debt which cannot be repaid; and to the encouragement, inspiration and untiring help of my wife, in more ways than I can mention.

Strasbourg, June 1980 P.M.B.

Contents

Contents

Abbreviations and Explanations

Abs.	*Absatz* (Paragraph)
A.J.Comp. Law	*American Journal of Comparative Law*
Annexkompetenz	Incidental power
AöR	*Archiv des öffentlichen Rechts*
A.P.S.R.	*American Political Science Review*
Art.	*Artikel* (Article)
BayVBl	*Bayerische Verwaltungsblätter*
BGBl	*Bundesgesetzblatt* (Federal Law Gazette)
BT	Bundestag
Bundesbahn	Federal Railways
Bundespost	Federal Postal Service
Bundesrat	Council of Constituent States
Bundesstaat	Federal state, federation
Bundestreue	Federal comity
Bundeswehr	Federal Armed Forces
BVerfGE	*Entscheidungen des Bundesverfassungsgerichts* (Decisions of the Federal Constitutional Court)
BVerfGG	*Gesetz über das Bundesverfassungsgericht* (Federal Constitutional Court Act)
BVerwGE	*Entscheidungen des Bundesverwaltungsgerichts* (Decisions of the Federal Administrative Court)
CDU	Christlich-Demokratische Union (Christian Democratic Union)

CSU	Christlich-Soziale Union (Christian Social Union)
DÖV	*Die Öffentliche Verwaltung*
Drucksache	Printed paper, publication
EDC	European Defence Community
FAZ	*Frankfurter Allgemeine Zeitung*
FDP	Freie Demokratische Partei (Free Democratic Party)
GBl / GVBl	*Gesetzblatt / Gesetz- und Verordnungsblatt* (Law Gazette of a Land Government)
Gesamtstaat	'Overall state' (i.e. the Federation plus its member states)
GG	*Grundgesetz* (Basic Law)
JöR	*Jahrbuch des öffentlichen Rechts der Gegenwart*
Landtag	Parliament of a Land
Ministerpräsident	Prime Minister of a Land
Natur der Sache	Intrinsic nature of the matter concerned
NJW	*Neue Juristische Wochenschrift*
Norddeutscher Rundfunk	North German Radio
Nr.	*Nummer* (Number)
Rdnr.	*Randnummer* (Margin number)
Rechtsmissbrauch	Abuse of powers
Rechtsstaat	State based on the rule of law
Reichsgericht	Supreme Court (Weimar Republic)
Regierungsbezirk	Government district: administrative subdivision in several Länder
Regierungspräsident	Head of a government district
Sachzusammenhang	Association, affinity
Satz	Sentence
SPD	Sozialdemokratische Partei Deutschlands (Social Democratic Party of Germany)
Staatsgerichtshof	High Court of State (Weimar Republic)

Tz.	*Teilziffer* (Paragraph Number)
VVDStRL	*Veröffentlichungen der Vereinigung der Deutschen Staatsrechtslehrer*
Z.ausl.öff.R. u. VR.	*Zeitschrift für ausländisches öffentliches Recht und Völkerrecht*
ZParl	*Zeitschrift für Parlamentsfragen*
Zustimmungsgesetz	Law requiring the assent of the Bundesrat
Zweites Deutsches Fernsehen	Second German Television

The words 'federal', 'federation', etc. are written with a capital letter when they refer to the Federal authorities, i.e. the Bund as opposed to the Länder; without a capital letter when they denote federalism or the federal state in general.

All translations are the author's own, with the exception of most of those from the Basic Law, of which there is an English version published by the Press and Information Office of the Government of the Federal Republic of Germany.

CHAPTER 1

Introduction

1 West Germany as a Federal System

That the Federal Republic of Germany has a federal form of government is not merely implied by its name but asserted by its Basic Law[1] and universally assumed by German commentators on their own constitutional order. It is true that it is a markedly centralized federal system in terms of both its constitutional arrangements and its practical operation.[2] Indeed the designation 'federal' has been disputed by some Anglo-Saxon authors, notably Wheare, for whom West Germany has only a 'quasi-federal' constitution.[3] Moreover, perhaps the most celebrated German essay on the subject puts forward the paradox of a 'unitary federation'.[4] Yet to use the degree of centralization of political power as a criterion of federalism is by no means unproblematical.

Thus the powers possessed by the Government of Northern Ireland until 1972 were considerably in excess of those of the member states of some federations; yet it was seldom claimed that the Stormont Government was in a federal relationship with the Government at Westminster, and the ability of the latter to abolish it by simple legislative fiat would normally be accepted as conclusive proof that the relationship was not a federal one in the strict sense.

By the same token the fact that a federal system exists, though it may often be justified in terms of decentralization of power, in practice tells us very little about the distribution of power in the political system. This is true in both a formal and a less formal sense. In the first place, it seems possible to speak of a 'spectrum of federalism'[5] from quasi-unitary systems to those in which the bulk of the powers are assigned to the lower level of government (although there is admittedly room for dispute as to where the spectrum begins and ends). Secondly, the actual degree of political centralization in a society depends on a variety of factors other than the formal allocation of powers, most notably the character of the party system. The political basis of a federal system will crucially affect its vitality. Thus it would be usual to point to the much greater strength in the USA than in West Germany not only of the traditions of the States, but of a spirit of localism, of local party systems with distinct characteristics and concerns and distinct patterns of organized interests. Where Americans still accept considerable diversity as a necessary consequence of federalism, the Germans increasingly demand equality and uniformity in such fields as education and the social services. Moreover, within a single federal system (as I shall indicate with regard to Germany) great changes can take place in what might loosely be called the content of federalism as a result of economic, social, and political forces, while the federal framework remains essentially the same. Federalism may indeed be a hollow husk if strong political forces are working against its having a significant political effect. The Soviet Union is perhaps only an extreme example.

Yet if it is important to look beyond legal forms and adopt empirical criteria for the distribution of power in the political system, one should not then suppose that one is looking at the criteria of federalism itself. It is undoubtedly an accurate view of federalism-in-action when Vile declares that 'the foremost characteristic of American federalism . . . is the *inter*dependence of Federal and State governments, not their mutual independence.'[6] And when one looks at German federalism, such features as the nature of the 'Bundesrat' as a chamber of ambassadors of the State governments equipped with a power of veto over Federal legislation, and the arrangements for the Federal government to supervise the implementation of its legislation by the States, reveal a striking degree of formal institutionalization of such interdependence. Nevertheless such attributes are by nature necessarily secondary. The interdependence of Federal and State governments presupposes, and is interesting precisely in the light of, the presence of the classical 'legalistic' characteristics of federalism. These characteristics include a constitutional division of powers on a territorial basis between two levels of government such that each level has an autonomous right of decision in some areas of government, neither derives its authority from the other and neither can change the legal relationship between them unilaterally.[7] It is necessary that each of the political authorities should, within the sphere of responsibility assigned to it, possess the quality and the apparatus of a state. To these necessary formal conditions for the existence of a federal system must, indeed, be added the sufficient empirical conditions for it actually to exist in practice. But it is in virtue of the legal structures, whose influence on the empirical pattern of political power is in any case substantial, that one can claim to be talking about a federal form of government at all.

These basic criteria are met by the West German system. The Federation (or 'Bund') is divided into ten 'Länder' (excluding West Berlin, which necessarily has a special status), each of which has its own written constitution. The constitutional order in the Länder is subject only to certain general requirements in the Federal Constitution, in particular the stipulation in *Art.* 28 *GG* that it must conform to the principles of republican, democratic, and social government based on the rule of law. Indeed in most cases the Länder as constitutional entities actually pre-date the Federal Republic itself, which only came into being through the ratification of its Basic Law by the parliaments of more than two-thirds of the Länder.[8] So what has sometimes, though surely unnecessarily, been regarded as a further condition of a federal system is technically fulfilled. Admittedly, the Länder concerned, with the exception of Bavaria and the city-states of Hamburg and Bremen, were in no sense historical entities but rather fortuitous creations of the Western Powers within their zones of occupation and in many cases put together from what had formerly been parts of Prussia. But traditional identity can hardly be made a matter of definition, any more than the widely disparate size of the units concerned,[9] which is in any case not peculiar to West Germany.

Apart from the general principle enunciated in Article 20, the most vital guarantee of the West German federal system is to be found in *Art.* 79 *Abs.* 3 *GG.* This declares that any amendments of the Basic Law affecting the division of the Federation into Länder or their participation in legislation shall be inadmissible. Rather anomalously, this guarantee is not extended to the existence or territorial extent of the *particular* Länder forming the Federation in 1949 or acceding to it later. On the contrary, the three original south-western Länder were amalgamated in the early years and *Art.* 29 *GG* even laid an obligation on the Federal authorities to carry out a general reorganization of the federal territory. This provision, which was clearly motivated by the artificial nature of most of the existing Länder, is in stark contrast to the guarantees accorded to the member states in the United States or Switzerland. It has led the West German Constitutional Court to speak of the Federal Republic as an 'unstable federation' (*labiler Bundesstaat*), and one German-speaking author[10] to doubt if it is a genuine federation at all. However, the new Länder have taken root so firmly that the obligation to redraw the map of the Länder was reduced to a mere enablement in 1976, and such a reform can scarcely be regarded as still a practical possibility.

In addition to the immunity of the federal system itself from demolition by constitutional amendment, other amendments of the Basic Law require a two-thirds majority in both chambers of the Federal legislature, the second of which (the 'Bundesrat') consists of representatives of the governments of the Länder. As in the United States, Federal powers are of a delegated nature, the Länder possessing under *Art.* 30 *GG* the reserved or residual authority. The presence of all three branches of government, and especially of a sphere of exclusive legislative power, at Land level gives their public authorities the character of governments as opposed to subordinate agencies.

This element of vertical division of powers as in the USA is the backbone of the federal system. Of course Wheare is quite right when he points out that the powers given to the 'general legislature' in the exclusive list and potentially in the much longer concurrent list cover almost all subjects of importance. Moreover, almost exhaustive use has been made of the concurrent legislative powers, so that the amount of original Land legislation is relatively small. It may also be objected, despite what has been said above, that the actual distribution of formal powers between the two levels of government is relevant to some extent to the definition of federalism. Mackenzie and Chapman's hypothetical government possessing only the power to determine the shape of postmen's helmets springs to mind.[11] In other terms, such cases scarcely qualify for a place on the federal spectrum.

However, if emphasis is to be placed on the distribution of powers it becomes necessary to adduce the distinctive characteristic of central European federalism, namely the further horizontal division of powers whereby most Federal legislation is executed by the member states. Except for a restricted number of fields explicitly specified in the Basic Law—in particular the foreign service, defence, customs and excise, posts and telecommunications, railways, federal waterways and shipping administration—the Federal administration has no administrative substructures of its own. Here again Wheare stresses the Federal Government's extensive powers of direction and supervision of Länder administrative action. Yet, except where the Länder act as agents of the Federal Government, the latter does not normally have powers of direction but is restricted to the issuing of pertinent general administrative rules requiring the consent of the Länder governments as represented in the Bundesrat. The provision made for Federal supervision of the Länder's execution of Federal laws relates only to control of whether they have complied with their legal obligations and is itself hedged about with safeguards. In fact in many fields the executive discretion allowed to the Länder is wide enough for some supplementary Land legislation and administrative rule-making by which Federal policy can be adapted to regional circumstances and political predilections. Nor should it be forgotten that much modern administration lies outside the realm of the execution of laws in the strict sense.

Again, with regard to the financial provisions of West German federalism, it must be acknowledged that the Länder are left with no more than a minimum of original taxation, which would normally be regarded as the touchstone of fiscal autonomy. Yet the system of revenue-sharing which has been practised has protected them from financial exigency and dependence on the Federal Government by guaranteeing them fixed shares of the proceeds of major taxes and making the apportionment of a further block of taxation between Bund and

Länder subject to the assent of the Bundesrat. If, therefore, it is only over a very small area that the Länder are free to determine the rate of taxation, this is counterbalanced by their institutionalized say in the sharing out of the total fiscal cake. Certainly it is not apparent that the capacity of the member states of the Federal Republic to carry out their legitimate responsibilities has been impaired by lack of adequate resources to any greater extent than in other federations.

Finally, the adoption by the Basic Law of the 'Bundesrat principle' as the basis of the second legislative organ at Federal level has been considered by some German scholars to be a choice of the less federalist solution. Whereas the 'Senate principle' envisages a Federal second chamber directly elected by the population of each constituent state, the 'Bundesrat principle' provides for a legislative body composed of members of the governments of the Länder. But it seems clear that such a system, even if it might be claimed to be less, or less directly, democratic, is in reality not less federal in character but more so. Not only are the Bundesrat's forty-one members delegates of the Länder governments (which are allocated from three to five seats each, depending on their population), but each Land's delegation casts its votes *en bloc*. The political authorities of the Länder thus have an institutionalized role in the Federal legislative process which is unparalleled in the English-speaking federations and which, as will be seen, helps to compensate them for their own relatively meagre legislative powers.

In any case, whether a system of this kind, with its greater interpenetration and interdependence of the two levels of government, especially in the administrative sphere, as against the (at least theoretically) 'cleaner' division of powers in the Anglo-Saxon world, is to be regarded as warranting such designations as 'executive-legislative federalism',[12] or 'administrative federalism',[13] or as still not truly federal, is only a question of terminology. What matters for the present study is that the West German form of government, whether fully federal or not, shares an important characteristic with other federal states. One way of expressing this is to stress that since both levels of government have the rank of states the possibility is excluded of such unitary doctrines as the sovereignty of parliament: if the concept of sovereignty is not abandoned altogether, it must either be accepted that sovereignty can be divided or that sovereignty resides in some rather unilluminating way in the constitution-making power of 'the people'. Dicey was conveying the same point when he declared:

A federal state derives its existence from the constitution, just as a corporation derives its existence from the grant by which it is created. Hence, every power, executive, legislative, or judicial, whether it belong to the nation or to the individual States, is subordinate to and controlled by the constitution.[14]

Thus the nature of a federal system ensures that a large proportion of conflicts of interest between the different governments concerned are at the same time legal conflicts. Indeed it artificially creates potential disputes about alleged encroachment upon one another's sphere of jurisdiction or non-observance of mutual rights and duties. In these circumstances it must contribute to the stability of the whole if there is a mutually recognized arbiter to whom the parties can refer for authoritative decision a dispute which is not easily amenable to political negotiation. That arbiter is normally to be found in the institution of judicial review, and in this the Federal Republic of Germany is no exception.

2 Federalism and judicial decision

One of the major criticisms made of federalism by Dicey is that 'federalism means legalism.' It is certainly true that one of the first considerations of a government in a federal system with regard to a proposed course of action will be 'Have we the constitutional power?', and in the practical operation of federalism particular importance will attach to the question, which is first and foremost a question of constitutional law, as to where the dividing-line runs between the powers of the two levels of government. But the main part of Dicey's accusation of legalism was that in a federation '. . . the Bench of judges is not only the guardian but also at a given moment the master of the constitution.'[15] He recognized that the Supreme Court was definitely not the sovereign of the United States, but maintained that it could still pronounce a judgment which determined the working of the constitution. Even in Canada, where the Dominion Government had been given authority to disallow Provincial acts and there had been a careful and thorough definition of the powers of both levels of government, the courts had as in the United States become interpreters of the constitution. Dicey concluded, 'Federalism substitutes litigation for legislation, and none but a law-fearing people will be inclined to regard the decision of a suit as equivalent to the enactment of a law.'[16]

Does federalism lead to such a 'predominance of the judiciary in the constitution'? That it does not necessarily do so is suggested by the fact that some federations (including the Wilhelmine Reich and, as Dicey himself recognized, Switzerland) have got by with at most limited judicial review. But the question remains valid for those federations—and they are in a substantial majority—which have entrusted the issue of legislative and executive competence to the courts.

Granted the need, experienced by all federal systems, to adapt a comparatively legalistic governmental framework to changing circumstances, the question arises how the inevitable tensions between the constitutional provisions and new economic and social needs and pressures are to be resolved. In most established federations the answer would be: by judicial interpretation. The use which the United States Supreme Court has made of the concept of 'inter-state commerce' or the 'necessary and proper' clause to increase the powers of the Federal Government is well known. Similar 'expansive' interpretation is discernible in Australia, while in Canada the effect has been on the whole a restrictive interpretation of Federal powers. The observation of the consequences of interpretation of the constitution by the courts in these countries, combined with a realization that, far from being a mechanical process, judicial review provides the judges with wide discretion to select the line of legal reasoning leading to the conclusion which they regard as most desirable, provides support for Dicey's contention. Yet the opportunities open to the judiciary for influencing the development of a federal system may be severely limited, in many more ways than Dicey supposed.

It is the purpose of the present study to examine, in the light of its possibilities and limitations, the role of the West German Federal Constitutional Court (the Bundesverfassungsgericht) as arbiter of the federal system and to assess its influence on the evolution of federalism in Germany. Such an inquiry embraces a wide range of questions: What sort of cases come before the Federal Constitutional Court in the context of federal relations, and how? What criteria of constitutional interpretation are employed and how much discretion do they afford? How far can and do the judges have regard to the political circumstances in which their adjudication is set and the political consequences which it will have? To what extent does the Court endeavour to maintain a particular balance in the federal system (if necessary against deliberate attempts to shift it), or even to impose its own view of federalism? Or does it tend to see its role modestly as one of legitimation, bringing the constitution into line with changing political reality? Are most federal disputes, even those of a clearly constitutional nature, nowadays normally resolved by political means, with the development of co-operative practices within the federal system?

An investigation along these lines should shed light on how far the Court, in its role of guardian of the federal order, may be seen as having protected the interests of the Länder or alternatively as having facilitated greater centralization of power in the hands of the Bund. It can be expected to reveal whether in West Germany 'federalism means legalism' to the extent of justifying what D. R. Reich in 1963 called 'a new reckoning based on the contention that the character of West German federalism has become a function of the role which the Federal Constitutional Court has created for itself in presiding over federal relations'.[17]

3 The nature of the Federal Constitutional Court

Various relevant characteristics of the Federal Constitutional Court will emerge at the appropriate stage in later chapters. Here it is necessary only to make a few preliminary points.[18]

The assignment to a court of law of the task of adjudicating in constitutional disputes was by no means a new departure in German history. Thus, whereas under the Reich of 1871 the right of arbitration in constitutional disputes between Reich and Länder belonged to the political institution of the Bundesrat, the constitution of the Weimar Republic conferred on the newly established Staatsgerichtshof (High Court of State) jurisdiction *inter alia* over conflicts between the Reich and a Land or between individual Länder. However, it was not given responsibility for the general review of the constitutionality of legislation (although the Supreme Court or Reichsgericht, with which it was organically connected and which did have power to decide on the compatibility of Land law with Reich law, in fact began to arrogate such a right to itself). The Bundesverfassungsgericht established in Karlsruhe in 1951 is therefore the first instance of a German court endowed with fully fledged powers of judicial review.

The wide-ranging jurisdiction of the Constitutional Court has its basis in many different articles of the Basic Law, the relevant items being listed together in §13 of the detailed Federal Constitutional Court Act[19] by which it was established. The following are those with most relevance for the federal system:

6. Differences of opinion or doubts on the formal and material compatibility of Federal law or Land law with this Basic Law, or on the compatibility of Land law with other Federal law, at the request of the Federal Government, of a Land government, or of one-third of the members of the Bundestag (*Art. 93 Abs.* 1 *Nr.* 2 *GG*)

—the so-called abstract judicial review (*abstrakte Normenkontrolle*), which can be initiated directly by any of the parties mentioned without reference to any concrete case and therefore has no parallel in a system such as the American.

7. Differences of opinion on the rights and duties of the Federation and the Länder, particularly in the execution of Federal law by the Länder and in the exercise of federal supervision (*Art. 93 Abs.* 1 *Nr.* 3 and *Art. 84 Abs.* 4 *Satz* 2 *GG*)

—the so-called constitutional dispute (*Verfassungsstreit*), which may only be raised by one of the parties to the dispute, namely the Federal or a Land government.

8. Other disputes involving public law, between the Federation and the Länder, between different Länder or within a Land, unless recourse to another court exists. (*Art. 93 Abs.* 1 *Nr.* 4 *GG*)

11. The compatibility of a Federal or Land statute with the Basic Law or the compatibility of a Land statute or other Land law with a Federal statute, at the request of a court (*Art.* 100 *Abs.* 1 *GG*)

—the so-called concrete judicial review (*konkrete Normen-kontrolle*), which arises out of a specific case before another court. Although any judge may exercise judicial review in such a case, if he considers a norm to be unconstitutional he must stay the proceedings and refer the constitutional issue to the Bundesverfassungsgericht, which alone can make a declaration of unconstitutionality.

12. Differences of opinion regarding the continuance of law in force as Federal law (*Art.* 126 *GG*)

—the question of whether legal provisions dating from before the promulgation of the Basic Law in 1949 were, if still valid at all, to be treated as Federal or Land law.

The competence of the Bundesverfassungsgericht in federal matters is thus in some respects wider than that of the normal Anglo-Saxon-type Supreme Court. But in another respect its jurisdiction is much narrower. It is a *constitutional* court, designed to adjudicate upon all constitutional questions, but *only* upon constitutional questions: it is not a general court of final appeal.[20]

A further important jurisdictional and organizational point is the division of the Court into two Senates. These divide the workload between them and largely act independently of each other. There is a clear demarcation of responsibilities between the two Senates, which was originally based largely on the conception that the First Senate should be responsible for judicial review while the Second Senate was given the more traditional function of resolving disputes between governments or between governmental organs. However, serious disparities in the number of cases confronting the two Senates (caused largely by the unexpected eagerness of German citizens to exercise their new right of bringing individual constitutional complaints about alleged violation of their basic rights) made necessary several transfers of jurisdiction from the First Senate to the Second. The result has been that the First Senate retains jurisdiction in cases of concrete judicial review or constitutional complaints primarily concerning the interpretation of the first seventeen articles of the Basic Law (substantive basic rights), while all other cases—including all cases of abstract judicial review and those of concrete judicial review which are most likely to concern federal issues—go to the Second Senate.

Thus it is the Second Senate which is responsible for deciding the great majority of significant federal cases. But it should not be supposed that the First Senate is therefore excluded from any part in the definition and demarcation of the powers of Bund and Länder. On the one hand, there are the relevant cases dating from before the jurisdictional reforms. On the other hand, constitutional cases frequently raise more than one question of law, so that a case which *primarily* concerns, for example, an alleged violation of a basic right may also raise the issue of the entitlement under the federal allocation of powers to enact the legal provision concerned. The likelihood of this can be appreciated when it is borne in mind that, far from being restricted in Anglo-Saxon fashion to consideration of the issues and objections raised by the parties to a dispute, German judges are free to examine the compatibility of all the aspects of a legal provision with all the requirements of the constitution. In consequence, although the major federal cases, especially those arising from direct conflicts between the Federal and Länder governments, have fallen to the Second Senate, the number of decisions in which the First Senate has been able to clarify or determine the exact division of powers in the federal system is by no means insignificant. It is in some instances difficult to decide whether a case belongs to this category rather than to the large category of decisions in which no more than a perfunctory reference is made to the question of competence. But it is probably not an inaccurate estimate that the First Senate has been responsible for approximately 30 per cent of decisions which have had at least some impact on the federal system. A more precise classification is attempted in the following chapter.

Ideally, a court which is charged with adjudication in relation to the powers, rights and duties of the two levels of government should be independent of both. This is of course unattainable, except perhaps in post-colonial situations. But West Germany has gone further than most federations in the attempt to ensure that what is after all a Federal institution should not be unduly dependent on the Federal authorities. This it has done by providing that half of the judges of the Constitutional Court should be selected by the Bundesrat, and thus to that extent by the governments of the Länder (the other half being chosen by a special electoral committee of the Bundestag).[21] However, whether this has significantly increased federalist influence on the Court may be doubted.[22] It is worth noting that each electoral body selects half the judges for each senate.

Both the number and the tenure of the judges have been changed over time. Originally there were twelve judges in each senate; but by 1962 the number had been progressively reduced to eight. Until 1971 those judges (accounting for one-third of the total) who were recruited from the highest Federal courts held their position until they reached retirement age, whereas all the others were appointed for a term of eight years with the possibility of reappointment. It was awareness of the risk of judicial behaviour towards those with influence over the reselection process even appearing to be inhibited that led to the new regulation whereby in future all judges were to be appointed for a single non-renewable term of twelve years. On the other hand, it is arguable that if judges are appointed at a relatively early age their concern for a suitable position after their term of office could give rise to dangers just as great.

However that may be, it would be difficult in practice to find evidence of undue judicial deference. More apparent has been the Court's pride in its status and its independence, as revealed particularly by its early (and successful) campaign for recognition of its special status as an equal of the other supreme Federal organs, namely the Bundestag, Bundesrat, Federal President and Federal Government, with appropriate independence from external supervision (by the Minister of Justice) and budgetary and administrative autonomy.[23]

Such, then, is the character of the court which has been cast in the role *inter alia* of guardian and arbiter of the federal system. The present task is to examine how it has performed in this role and with what effect.

CHAPTER II

The Approach to the Inquiry

1 Definition

The task outlined in the previous chapter is a study of the influence of the Federal Constitutional Court on the evolution of federalism in West Germany. It is thus a study of the role of a strategically placed legal institution in relation to a significant aspect of the constitutional and political order. This nature of the subject as straddling the boundary between law and politics must necessarily have consequences for the approach to be adopted.

In particular, it is important to avoid the mistake, to which political studies of supreme courts sometimes incline, of assuming that one has to do with an actor in the political process which is basically similar to any other and actuated only by similar motives such as basic political preferences, public opinion and considerations of patronage. It must constantly be borne in mind that the Constitutional Court is a legal institution operating in what will be seen to be a relatively legalistic environment and bound by the inevitable constraints of the judicial process and the judicial method (even though these constraints will be shown to be rather less inhibiting than is sometimes assumed or implied). Reference must here be made to the substantial body of literature already existing in Germany both on the constitutional aspects of the federal system and on the practice of judicial review by the Constitutional Court.[1] For Germany has a prolific tradition of thorough, cumulative, and potentially exhaustive exegesis of the corpus of public law. Moreover, in a legal system which is not characterized by such principles as *stare decisis* the weight of academic opinion on points of law, including constitutional law, takes on an importance as a criterion of judicial decision which is unknown in common law systems. The Constitutional Court itself is by no means exempt from this tradition.

But if the existing stock of legal commentary is a more than adequate reminder of the fundamental nature of the Bundes-verfassungsgericht as an integral part of the judicial system working in accordance with recognized legal methods and principles, the conception of the present study nevertheless remains political. Rather than concentrate upon the relation-ship between the judgments of the Court and the development of theoretical constitutional exegesis, the aim is to examine the Federal Constitutional Court as a significant element in a living political system and to elucidate its role within and its influence over a particular aspect of that political system, namely its federal character. To that extent it will be moving in relatively uncharted territory. For, no doubt because of the pervasiveness of the law and a spirit of legalism in the German political system, the field has largely remained, in contrast to its American equivalent, the preserve of scholars of constitutional law.[2]

In attempting to steer the middle course just outlined, three lines of inquiry stand out amongst the rest. Firstly, a com-prehensive survey is required of the main areas of federal decision-making by the Court, for which the source is the published decisions of the Federal Constitutional Court, amounting to fifty-one volumes up to mid-1979.[3] Secondly, the author had the benefit of informal individual interviews with six judges of the Constitutional Court, all but one of them members of the Second Senate. Thirdly, it will be necessary to review the main developments in the West German federal system since 1949 in order to set the Court's decisions in their political context. By these means it should be possible to achieve the desired evaluation of judicial policy in a substantive field of constitutional law and an assessment of the extent to which the evolution of the federal order and federal relations has been shaped by the Constitutional Court. However, there are certain limitations to the evidence thus provided or caveats about the use that may be made of it, to which it is as well to draw attention at the start.

2 The quantification of cases

Prima facie perhaps one of the most obvious indicators of 'federalist' or 'unitarist' tendencies[4] in the decision-making of the Constitutional Court might be provided by a simple categorization of all relevant judgments into those in favour of the Bund and of the Länder. But such quantification of cases is highly unreliable for a number of reasons. It is not just that it fails to make any distinction between 'significant' and 'insignificant' cases (a distinction which is in any case less straightforward than might be supposed) or between cases where a question of powers is decided almost incidentally and those where it is the main point at issue. It also inevitably ignores the differentiation within individual judgments. Some review both Federal and Land norms or decide several related issues, and by no means all of them need go in favour of the same party. Indeed it is possible for the Court in a single judgment to ensure that a party wins the particular battle but suffers a serious setback in the on-going war. The decisions whereby Federal laws were upheld not on the ground that they had not required the assent of the Länder as represented in the Bundesrat, but because although such assent had indeed been required it was deemed to have been given,[5] are merely among the more obvious examples. Then there is the problem of how to classify cases of *verfassungskonforme Auslegung*, that is the validation of norms by specification of the one interpretation by which they are held to be in conformity with constitutional requirements.

To these misgivings about the practicability of neat classification of cases must be added the problem, which calls for even more value-judgments, of the nature of the issues confronting the Court. It is pointed out in Chapter IV, in relation to those cases raised directly by one of the levels of government via abstract review of norms or constitutional disputes, that the Bund is less likely to take issues to Karlsruhe. But if, in spite of the redressing of the balance by the larger number of cases reaching the Court by other means, a majority of the 'federal' cases concern the constitutionality of Federal norms or powers—and this does appear, though only to a moderate extent, to be the case—then any tendency when in doubt to presume constitutionality could create an apparent bias in the Bund's favour. In addition, and perhaps most difficult to assess, there is the possibility that there have been 'objectively' more infringements of the prerogatives of one of the levels of government than of the other, which might simply be reflected in the Court's judgments. Simple quantification does not take account of how far there may be an 'obvious' answer or how far in some cases particular considerations or methods of interpretation may have been employed to reach another conclusion than the prima-facie one. Finally—and increasingly, the more differentiation of cases is attempted to take account of some of the above objections—there is the problem of whether the number of relevant cases is sufficient to produce statistically significant results.

In the light of such misgivings the value of a simple classification must be regarded as highly questionable. For what it is worth, the performance of such an exercise on 'federal' or at least partially 'federal' decisions yields the result shown in the following table.

	Pro-Bund	Pro-Land	Ambivalent	Total
1st Senate	25	15	1	41
2nd Senate	41	47	6	94
Plenum	–	2	–	2
Total	66	64	7	137

This table includes all decisions relating to the allocation of legislative powers under *Art.* 70–5 *GG* and of administrative powers under *Art.* 83–7 *GG*, the financial arrangements between Bund and Länder as laid down in *Art.* 104a–109 *GG*, and the problem of whether old law has become Federal or Land law (*Art.* 124 and 125 *GG*). In so doing, it also covers applications of the basic residual powers clause of *Art.* 30 *GG*, as well as those judgments raising the issue of federal comity, as discussed in Ch. VII.[6] The figure of 137 decisions compares with a total of 1,640 decisions published in the first fifty-one volumes. Even among these 137 by no means all can be claimed to be primarily concerned with federal questions. On the other hand, the enumeration does not claim to be exhaustive, in that other articles of the Basic Law, and hence also Constitutional Court decisions based upon them, either are or can be of direct relevance to the federal order. But those sections of the constitution which have been selected permit a relatively systematic quantification encompassing the vast majority of cases which deal wholly or partly with federal issues.

However, apart from the inevitable exercise of personal judgment as to which cases qualify for inclusion and which categories they should be assigned to, and other objections already raised, the superficiality of such a table may be highlighted particularly by consideration of the incidence of cases in which a legal provision is declared null and void. Here too there are problems of classification, because of instances of partial invalidation (sometimes only in minor respects), invalidation on other than federal grounds, qualified confirmation, etc. But it is a striking fact that of the cases decided by the First Senate only two involve a clear invalidation for violation of the federal demarcation of powers,[7] whereas the rate of nullification of both Federal and Land norms by the Second Senate is much higher. Thus it could be argued (although this would run against the impressions of most judges interviewed) that the apparent pro-Federal bias in the decisions of the First Senate was simply a product of its greater reluctance to strike down legal provisions for lack of the necessary powers or on other federal grounds plus the fact that a majority of the cases confronting it have concerned Federal norms.

It is thus simplistic to suppose that such classification reveals anything about whether the Court has tended to promote the interests of the Länder or to facilitate greater centralization of power, beyond demonstrating perhaps that it has not pursued an extreme line in either direction. This study proceeds on the assumption that only a detailed examination of key areas of decision-making by the Bundesverfassungsgericht in relation to the federal system, and in particular of those areas in which the Court may have the means and the opportunity to develop or even manipulate the constitutional allocation of powers and prerogatives, can provide an accurate picture of the extent and direction of its influence.

3 Judicial values and the composition of the Constitutional Court

If it can be established that in general the Constitutional Court has taken an identifiable line in federal questions, it would be natural to ask why this should be the case. Thus, for example, if the Court, or at least its Second Senate, had been concerned to buttress the powers of the Länder rather than to accept an extensive interpretation of Federal powers, there would be several possible kinds of explanation. The simplest and most superficial would be that a majority of the Senate's members felt, or at any rate was open to persuasion by those who felt, that the constitutionally intended position of the Länder was threatened by persistent erosion and therefore required protection, or even that the federal system as established by the Basic Law was too unitarist in character and therefore ought where possible to be nudged in the other direction. It may be that one must be content with such an explanation, and it should not be supposed that there is any inherent unsatisfactoriness in an account which, after all, elucidates the role of a rather distinctive institution and the extent and nature of its influence upon a significant aspect of the political system.

A more thoroughgoing kind of explanation might try to probe the reasons why a substantial number of judges in the Second Senate had had federalist predispositions. It would attempt to delve into the background of the individual judges in order to identify factors which might have influenced their attitudes to federalism or the centralization of political power. This would clearly also raise the question whether such attitudes had been discernible at the time of their appointment and had played a part in their recruitment. If the latter point could be proved, it would be of obvious significance for an appreciation of the working of the political and constitutional system. If not, it must seriously be questioned what is to be gained by such research into judges' backgrounds. For if it were to be shown that certain judges simply happened incidentally to have come from backgrounds of regional loyalties or to have had experiences which persuaded them of the wisdom of dispersing political power, then this would be little more than could be inferred from the decisions themselves and so would scarcely reward the effort invested. And whatever the value of sociological inquiries into such questions as 'Are judges by nature conservative?', such an inquiry would certainly reach a dead end much more quickly if the question were changed to: 'Are judges by nature federalist?'

The evidence as to whether individual judges have federalist or unitarist sympathies is in reality very slender, as is the evidence as to the role of such considerations in judicial appointments.

At first sight, the observance of geographical ratios for the selection of judges might be regarded as a federalist concern. There are in fact unofficial Länder quotas for the recruitment of Federal judges in general. But the selection of Constitutional Court judges, half by the Bundestag and half by the Bundesrat, by qualified majorities, makes proportionality as between the Länder a very secondary consideration compared with party-political affiliations, agreement between the parties always being necessary to achieve the required majority. In any case any attempt to have strict regard to geographical origins would be bound to encounter great problems in the post-war Federal Republic, both because of the influx from the eastern territories of Germany (which have been strongly represented among the judges of the Court) and because of the high degree of mobility of the population, making it likely that residence at the time of appointment would not correspond to place of birth. In fact, however, a high proportion of those judges who were born within the territory now forming the Federal Republic were resident in approximately the same area immediately before taking up their appointment in Karlsruhe.

In general, north Germany appears to have been rather under-represented on the Court, perhaps partly because those judges who can be found to have links with the Christian Democrats appear to have come predominantly from southern Germany, while those with Social-Democratic connections came in greater measure from eastern Germany or Berlin or were based in Hesse, whose veteran Minister-President Georg-August Zinn took a particularly strong interest in the Constitutional Court. Although he admits that some Länder have as yet provided few or no judges (particularly Bremen and the Saar), Kommers[8] divides Germany into four sectors which he claims have had roughly equal distribution on the Court: (a) Bavaria, (b) the Rhineland and the Ruhr, (c) north Germany, Hesse, and Berlin, (d) the south-west. But the merits of such an artificial division, whereby, for example, Frankfurt (but not Düsseldorf) falls into the category containing north Germany, are open to serious doubt. It appears to be the case that in the selection of judges by the Bundesrat the larger Länder in particular informally share the places out amongst themselves. But the overall effect is far from one of strict proportionality. The question also remains whether such sharing is perhaps often less a matter of protecting the interests of individual Länder or regions than one of patronage.

At all events, in spite of the relative homogeneity of interests and culture in the Federal Republic, regional claims to representation have persisted. Commenting on the five new appointments made to the Court in November 1975, F. K. Fromme[9] pointed out that Bavaria's desire to be represented by a judge with a strong Bavarian background had been acceded to in the appointment of Niebler, while the north-German element, which had previously been under-represented, had been strengthened by the two Hamburg denizens Zeidler and Katzenstein.

The sheer geographical distribution of appointments, however, though possibly indicative of a concern for federalist sensibilities, is not in any way a guide to the attitudes of the judges towards the federal system or the distribution of interests within it. In view of the nature of the German public service and the pervasive influence of the political parties at Federal and Land level (Bavaria perhaps excepted), even those judges who come from the highest echelons of Länder administration cannot automatically be assumed to be convinced federalists. For the same reason the fact that the Länder via the Bundesrat are responsible for selecting half the judges is by no means a reliable indication of the sentiments of those judges with regard to federalism.

Given the predominant influence of party-political considerations in the negotiations both within the Bundesrat and between it and the Electoral Committee of the Bundestag, another approach might be to see whether attitudes to federalism could be deduced from party-political identification. However, even if general tendencies of the parties can be identified whereby the Christian Democrats (CDU/CSU) have on the whole been considerably more favourably disposed towards federalism than either the SPD, which in the early post-war years was particularly strongly unitarist,[10] or the highly centralist Free Democratic Party (FDP), and judges who conform to this pattern can easily be identified, nevertheless it would be rash indeed to assume that all the judges did so. Thus among the Christian Democrats, although such judges as Leusser, Geiger, Böhmer, and Scholtissek were known to be convinced federalists, Judge Rinck is a self-confessed unitarist (though it is perhaps significant that he is a north German).

In the early years some attempt does seem to have been made to create a balance between unitarist and federalist judges, just as approximate religious proportionality was also sought. Indeed in 1951 Bavaria voted against the selection of Katz as Vice-President on the ground, put forward by its Social-Democratic Minister of Justice, that in view of the well-known centralist views of the President, Höpker-Aschoff, this would put strong unitarists at the head of both Senates. But both kinds of proportionality have lost much of their significance and the number of the federalists has declined to the point where by the time he retired in 1977 Geiger was perhaps the only avowed federalist left on the Court.

However that may be, it must be admitted that in general there is little sign that Constitutional Court judges are chosen with an eye to their views on federalism. In consequence of this and of the relatively collegial and anonymous character of the Court, at least up to the introduction of dissenting opinions by the Second Senate in 1970, the views on federalism of most of the judges cannot be specified with certainty. There are of course those whose previous activities or associations are strongly suggestive of attitudes to federalism. Amongst these might be included both Wintrich, the second President of the Court, a Bavarian Roman Catholic who had even been associated with the Bavarian People's Party, and the third President, Gebhard Müller, who had long been prominent in the politics of south-west Germany, both as Staatspräsident of Württemberg-Hohenzollern and, after its amalgamation with its neighbours, as Minister-President of Baden-Württemberg;

as well as those such as Judge Roediger, whose party links with the Deutsche Partei and the FDP make federalist sympathies unlikely. In some instances weak circumstantial evidence may be buttressed by published remarks of the judges themselves. Thus Fabian von Schlabrendorff, a Protestant former member of the Prussian officer corps and active resistance fighter during the Third Reich, committed his view of that federal *cause célèbre*, the *Television Judgment*, to print in a newspaper article in 1971:

It must be conceded to your newspaper's critic that the Television Judgment of 1961 did not redound to the credit of the Federal Constitutional Court. To give television law to the Länder and practically deprive the Bund of this enormous potential for propaganda was the worst of all solutions.[11]

Others again, as already suggested, have made no secret of their federalist or anti-federalist views. Perhaps the extreme example was Leusser, who left the Court in order to become Bavaria's plenipotentiary in Bonn. His obituary in the *Süddeutsche Zeitung* even contained the assertion: 'In any future discussion about the federal character of our Basic Law, Claus Leusser must be mentioned as one of those persevering men who salvaged a minimum of federalist principles and ideas into our time.'[12] However, this still leaves many members of the Court whose views on federalism have not been publicly expressed and are simply not apparent. Much can be learned from conversations with the judges and their assistants, but here obligations of confidentiality apply. The general impression gained from interviewing some of the judges is that the attitude is often one of relative disinterest. But in any case, and particularly where views are not strongly held, the mere ability to count heads would not be sufficient. For it would ignore the effects both of personality and of judicial specialization on the decision which emerges from the Senate concerned. There is no need to elaborate upon the former, since the existence of opinion-leaders whose influence is based on talent, respect, good tactical skill, or general personality is well known. If such personalities amongst the judges feel strongly about federal issues, and particularly if some of their colleagues have no particular interest in them, then their influence is likely to be quite disproportionate. But the possibilities of identifying such influence from the outside are limited, especially so long as the Court's decisions are handed down in an impersonal institutional form which often represents the view of an unidentifiable majority with elements of compromise in the *ratio decidendi* to take account of the susceptibilities of the minority. It is only after the introduction of dissenting and concurring opinions by the Second Senate that any opportunity is afforded of identifying the attitudes of individuals and comparatively coherent groups.

As far as specialization is concerned, the practice is that each case is assigned to a *rapporteur* (*Berichterstatter*) who prepares an extensive survey (called a *Votum*) of the facts and issues of the case as well as the relevant views of legal writers and recommends a particular solution for consideration by his colleagues in session. He is also charged afterwards with writing a draft decision. Individual judges are assigned particular areas of law in which incoming cases normally go to them, though some cases may clearly belong to more than one category or distribution of work may require temporary reallocation, which gives the Senate President a certain amount of discretion. Inevitably the expertise built up by a judge in a particular field, the lack of time that his colleagues have to spend on a case for which he is *rapporteur*, and his opportunity to present the issues and arguments as he sees fit put the *rapporteur* at a considerable advantage. It can safely be assumed that the responsibility of Judge Geiger for many of the Second Senate's federal cases has not been without influence on the course they have taken.

This brief excursus into the realm of the values and the influence of individual judges should be sufficient to demonstrate the limitations of such an inquiry, in terms both of the incompleteness of the evidence and of the danger that its conclusions may have little more than gossip-value. For this reason the explanatory objectives of the present study are concentrated on the questions of how far the Constitutional Court is called upon to adjudicate on issues of doubt or dispute in the federal system, how it can and does go about this task, and how far and in what ways it has thereby affected the development of the federal relationship.

CHAPTER III

Judicial Discretion and Political Elements in the Judicial Resolution of Constitutional Disputes

1 The parameters of judicial decision-making

The political character of the Constitutional Court is logically implied by its preoccupation with constitutional law (or *Staatsrecht*, as it used to be called in Germany). As Heinrich Triepel said, 'Constitutional disputes are always political disputes. This fact sums up the problematical nature of the whole institution.'[1] This raises the basic question as to whether one ought to have a court of law to decide such 'political' disputes, or whether this constitutes an invasion of the domain of the legislature and executive by the judiciary. The introduction of comprehensive constitutional jurisdiction in Germany was delayed, partly by Bismarck's preference for arbitration by a political body which could be influenced more directly, partly by the fact that it did not easily fit into the German conception of the separation of powers. The dominant legal tradition, which emphasized the distinction and the antithesis between law and politics, was inimical to the prospect of a court overriding the will of the legislator as expressed in the law, along the lines of the American common-law tradition of judicial review. Thus Carl Schmitt feared that judicial review would lead either to a judicialization of politics or, more probably, to a politicization of justice.[2]

The political nature of a constitutional court is in essence the subjection of legislature and executive to the judgment of a court and the attendant rejection of the unrestricted rule of the majority limited only by its own self-restraint. That there was a new readiness to accept such subjection of the political to the judicial in post-war Germany is not surprising; more recently, voices have also been raised claiming that the respect enjoyed by the Constitutional Court is a corollary of distrust of the legislature, it being no longer believed that the political interests of the current majority are set aside when the constitution so requires.[3] However that may be, many have approved the aim, the practicability of which was doubted by Carl Schmitt, of withdrawing certain kinds of differences and conflicts concerning the permissible range and constraining framework of political action from the free interplay of political forces, of 'depoliticizing' them. It was often emphasized that a constitutional court was not a rival to the legislature and the executive since it was bound to decide by legal and not political criteria.

The fundamental question, beloved of older German scholars, of the theoretical relationship between law and politics, with inferences concerning the desirability of having a court for the decision of constitutional (and to that extent 'political') disputes, will here be left aside. For present purposes it is significant only that the Constitutional Court is not hampered in its activities by the existence of a substantial opposition to its functioning in the political system. The relevant questions are rather: given that such a court has been established, what opportunities does it have for exercising influence as an undoubted participant in the political arena? What are the limits of constitutional jurisdiction? What are the means by which the Court can develop the constitution? The answer will depend on

(i)   the extent of the Court's own jurisdiction;
(ii) doctrines and attitudes concerning judicial decision of certain kinds of political questions;
(iii) the prevailing philosophy as to the methods of legal interpretation;
(iv) the nature of the constitution which it is called upon to interpret.

The extent to which the possibilities of formative influence are realized depends, of course, on the judges themselves.

(i) *The extent of the Constitutional Court's jurisdiction*

Unlike the Staatsgerichtshof (High Court of State) of the Weimar period, which had much more limited jurisdiction, the Bundesverfassungsgericht, especially by means of the constitutional dispute (*Verfassungsstreit*), the review of norms (*Normenkontrollverfahren*) and the constitutional complaint (*Verfassungsbeschwerde*), has virtually comprehensive competence for all questions of constitutional law. It also has a monopoly of constitutional jurisdiction in so far as the other courts lack the right assumed by American Federal and State courts to invalidate, or at least refuse to apply, legislation on grounds of unconstitutionality; rather, in cases where they hold a rule of law relevant to their own decision to be in violation of the Basic Law they must obtain a ruling by the Constitutional Court (*konkrete Normenkontrolle*). Since such reference is on the court's own initiative and not in the hands of the parties to the dispute, it is important that the judges of other courts have been relatively willing to raise doubts about constitutionality: except in the field of basic rights the cases which reach the Constitutional Court by this means are much the most numerous.

Moreover, the Court's decisions are not merely binding upon the litigants in the actual concrete case, but in so far as they apply and interpret constitutional law they are generally held to bind all constitutional organs, courts, and authorities of the Bund and the Länder.[4] Perhaps partly for this reason, and in accordance with German custom whereby judges are more independent of the narrow issues raised by the litigants, the scope of the Court's decisions tends also to be considerably wider than is the case in the Anglo-Saxon world. As has already been noted, it does not consider itself restricted to an examination of the arguments advanced by the parties to the dispute, nor to those aspects of a legal provision against which specific objections were raised, but has regarded its task as a comprehensive review of the constitutionality of the legal provision in question. However, the Court seems to have come to recognize that there was a danger in the early years of too extensive and generalized decision-making, and there has more recently been a greater concentration on the concrete case.

(ii) *Judicial decision of 'political questions'*

Are there some disputes of constitutional law which despite its all-embracing jurisdiction the Constitutional Court nevertheless may not decide as being fundamentally 'political' questions?

In the first place, the Constitutional Court is clearly not in a position to decide political disputes for which there are no legal criteria, that is, disputes which are not covered by any constitutional norm. But even when a dispute could well be held to fall under a particular norm it might still be decided that its solution should be left to the political forum: the line of demarcation between *politische Rechtsstreitigkeiten* ('disputes about what the law is') and *rein politische Streitigkeiten* ('disputes as to what the law should be')[5] is not a clear one.

The problem is by no means a new one for German jurists, as can be seen, for example, from the perceptive discussion by Triepel of the assertion that the Staatsgerichtshof of the Weimar Republic ought never to pass judgment on political disputes.[6] Triepel rejected this view precisely on the grounds of the lack of a sharp antithesis between questions of expediency and legal questions, or between political questions and legal questions. With particular reference to the federal sphere, he maintained that all legal disputes between Reich and Länder, all disputes about the boundaries between Reich and Länder powers, all disputes concerning the Länder's obligations to or claims upon the Reich, were by nature always at the same time political disputes (though they varied in 'political significance'). In consequence, any attempt to eliminate 'political disputes' from the jurisdiction of the Staatsgerichtshof meant the exclusion of precisely the most important legal disputes.

Such considerations have not, however, prevented the development in the United States of a practice of identifying certain constitutional issues as fundamentally political and therefore not justiciable. Under the 'political questions' doctrine of the American Supreme Court, by means of which it has sometimes avoided being drawn into political controversy, all matters relating to sovereignty and to the essential core of political power and the manner of its exercise by the bodies designated for that purpose are held to be the exclusive domain of President and Congress, whose decisions are binding on the courts. These include such questions as what is to be understood by a 'republican form of government', the conduct of foreign relations, and whether a piece of legislation was properly enacted.

However, the 'political questions' doctrine seems to be based on expediency rather than on any well-developed theoretical distinction between cases which are and are not amenable to judicial methods of decision. In *Colegrove* v. *Green*[7] the Supreme Court refused to decide whether the failure of the legislature of the State of Illinois to redistribute the congressional districts during the previous fifty years was unconstitutional. Justifying this stance, Justice Frankfurter defined a 'political question' as one that 'brings courts in immediate and active relations with party contests' and argued that 'It is hostile to a democratic system to involve the judiciary in the politics of the people.' This ignores the fact that all constitutional cases involve the 'politics of the people' to a greater or lesser degree, and even a decision not to decide may have major consequences for the political balance of interests. The Court itself had no such inhibitions in the later electoral law case of *Baker* v. *Carr*.[8] Again, the Supreme Court did not take up an appeal which objected to the introduction of the referendum in individual States as an infringement of the 'republican form of government' on the grounds that it was a highly political matter which fell within the exclusive power of Congress.[9] Yet it would appear to be a legal question perfectly capable of decision according to the principles of constitutional interpretation, and one which a court entrusted by explicit constitutional provision with the judgment of all disputes of constitutional law could not refuse to decide. But the fact that the extent of American constitutional jurisdiction was developed by judicial practice gives it greater freedom to leave matters for political resolution.

Nothing corresponding to the doctrine of 'political questions' exists in West Germany. This may be because it is too vague and arbitrary for Continental legal reasoning, and it can certainly be partly explained by the fact that the jurisdiction of the Constitutional Court is much more clearly defined than that of the US Supreme Court, so that it is scarcely in a position to reject cases falling within its defined competence. But more generally, it is part of the Continental legal tradition that a judge may not refuse to give judgment and may even thereby become liable to punishment, as in *Art*. 4 of the French Civil Code: 'Le juge qui refusera de juger, sous prétexte du silence, de l'obscurité ou de l'insuffisance de la loi, pourra être poursuivi comme coupable de déni de justice.' Such a situation can lead to anomalies, as when in the dispute over West German rearmament in the context of the proposed European Defence Community the Constitutional Court found itself asked to decide whether it belonged to the 'essence of the state' that it should have an army:[10] if ever there was a 'political' question, this would seem to be it. Again, the appeals to Karlsruhe which led to the proscription of the right-wing Socialist Reich Party and the Communist Party of Germany (KPD) as unconstitutional political parties[11] were covered by explicit provision in the Basic Law; but are such highly problematical political questions really justiciable? That the feeling is growing among the politically aware that such judicial preoccupation with the political is not appropriate is apparent from the public discussion of the reference of the Basic Treaty with East Germany to the Constitutional Court which was eventually made by the Bavarian Government in 1973.[12] But so long as the parties entitled to do so continue to present it with such cases the Court has little choice but to produce a verdict.

On the other hand, the Court does find substitutes for the doctrine of political questions. Often an appeal can be rejected on procedural or technical grounds.[13] Otherwise matters which are politically highly embarrassing can simply be left in abeyance, a tactic which is possible because of the large number of cases always pending before the Court, even if it is limited by the Court's ultimate obligation to give judgment. In this way some disputes will solve themselves in the course of time, as did the issue of the treaty on the European Defence Community, though the question of the unconstitutionality of the KPD did in fact have to be decided despite a five-year procrastination. Finally, and above all, the Court's generous acknowledgement of a wide discretion of the legislature for questions of the expediency, necessity, or quality of legislative decisions, may not differ greatly in its effect from the designation of a matter as a 'political question'.[14] Moreover, just as with 'political questions' in the United States, a refusal to decide a question need not be neutral in its effects. It can be tantamount to giving a decision in favour of one of the parties.

(iii) *Methods of legal interpretation*

In view of the Constitutional Court's political character described above and its limited opportunities for avoiding judgment, how far can extra-legal considerations play a part in the decision of questions for which legal criteria *are* available? What interpretative possibilities are open to the Constitutional Court, set in the German legal tradition and like all courts bound by 'statute and law', for having regard to political considerations?

If a question of constitutional law is not open to doubt, in particular if the provisions of the constitution are unambiguous and clearly relevant, there is normally no room for the Court to allow other considerations to affect its decision. In such cases it is even an exaggeration to speak of 'interpretation'. However, in most cases which reach decision by the Court there are bound to be some aspects where doubt exists and interpretation is called for.

At the same time the German positivist tradition promoted the view that there is only one 'right' decision, the task of the Court being simply to 'discover' it by a process of logical deduction. If this were really so it would have major consequences for an inquiry into the role of the Constitutional Court in the political system. Interest would be restricted mainly to how far constitutional disputes were actually referred to the Court for decison and possibly to the question whether accepted methods of interpretation consistently tended to produce results favourable to particular groups or levels of government. For the role of the judges themselves would be reduced to a purely mechanical process without any possibility of contributing their own influence or preferences to the final result (unless by 'false' deduction).

Of course this view was never more than an illusion which was capable of masking the real grounds for decision, conscious or unconscious. In any case it lost its force during the twentieth century with the abandonment of the positivist conception of the law as exclusively embodying the will of the norm-setter, and more especially after 1945 in the face of general adoption of a doctrine of jurisprudence whereby positive law was to be tested against basic standards of justice and reason. This reaction in favour of the importation of ethical criteria into jurisprudence is well documented by E. Bodenheimer.[15] The natural law revival observed by him was in fact rather short-lived, partly no doubt owing to the danger to the predictability of the law seen in the possibility of appeal to such potentially subjective suprapositive principles, but perhaps primarily because the basic standards of justice concerned were enshrined in the constitution itself and thereby became 'positive' constitutional law against which ordinary law could be measured. A broader conception of the sources of law and the role of the judge remained, however, in particular the consideration of principles underlying the concrete norm and of the contingent circumstances of its application.[16]

Even in the heyday of positivism there had been a lack of agreement as to whether the criterion of judgment was the 'objective' meaning of the statute or the 'subjective' will of the legislator. Here the Constitutional Court has declared allegiance to 'objective statutory construction'[17] which looks to the 'objectivized' will of the statute itself. But the question remains how this will is to be determined. The Court claims to rely on traditional methods—'Interpretation based on the wording of the norm (grammatical interpretation), on its context (systematic interpretation), on its purpose (teleological interpretation) and on preliminary legislative materials and the history of the norm's genesis (historical interpretation)'[18]—although in practice it also sometimes resorts to other methods such as the comparative, drawing on other branches or systems of law. But the problem is that these aids to interpretation need not by any means all point to one single identifiable interpretation of the statute. If different results can be obtained by different methods, the way is opened up for choosing on a subjective basis. One way of trying to avoid this is to set up a hierarchy of interpretative methods whereby no method may be applied until those methods which take precedence over it have failed to produce a clear result or one compatible with the constitution in general.[19] The Constitutional Court has at

least made gestures in this direction, in particular by relegat-
ing recourse to the genesis of a provision to a confirmatory
role.[20]

In practice, however, the Court has sometimes given the
genesis of the norm considerably more prominence than this,
and indeed in the *Television Judgment* it even had recourse to
developments preceding the proper genesis of the norm.[21] The
decisions of the Court provide numerous examples of its free
use of the latitude afforded by the choice of methods of interpretation. This latitude is not without limitation. The actual text of
the norm obviously occupies a special position and the Court is
normally careful not to produce a solution which violates it or
transgresses the limits of its possible meaning. However, in the
Kehl Judgment[22] it did precisely this with regard to *Art.* 32 and
59 *GG*, which regulate the foreign affairs and treaty-making
power, by equating *staatsähnliche Subjekte des Völkerrechts* ('subjects of international law of a quasi-state character') with
auswärtige Staaten ('foreign states'). This was all the more
remarkable in view of its earlier decision[23] concerning the
Petersberg Agreement concluded by Adenauer with the representatives of the Western occupying powers. This agreement
was challenged by the SPD parliamentary party in the Bundestag on the ground that as an agreement which regulated the
political relations of the Bund it should have been laid before
the bodies responsible for legislation. But the Court upheld it
on the questionable ground that it was not a treaty with foreign
states within the meaning of *Art.* 59 *Abs.* 2 *GG*. Of course in both
cases one can detect a concern to find some legal justification,
even if not wholly convincing, for upholding the agreements in
order to avoid the embarrassing international consequences of
invalidating them.[24]

The general impression which emerges is one of a considerable degree of eclecticism with regard to judicial method. In
this connection it should also be recalled that the common law
principle of *stare decisis* does not apply, so that an elementary
form of pressure in favour of taking a consistent line is absent.
Thus although the judgments of the Bundesverfassungsgericht
retain a rather doctrinaire style, this may cloak an extensive
pragmatism on the part of the Court, which will be observable
in later chapters.

(iv) *The nature of the Basic Law*

Without actually doing violence to the text of the Basic Law or of the statute under review, the Constitutional Court gains considerable opportunity for a creative role from the fact that constitutional law is particularly rich in general concepts which require precision in the context of individual decisions. Many clauses of the Basic Law are to some extent 'open', i.e. contain concepts which are not strictly defined. This is true not only of obvious examples such as *Art. 20 Abs. 1 GG* ('The Federal Republic of Germany is a democratic and social federal state') but also of more detailed provisions. This is inevitable. A constitution which sought to regulate the framework of a country's political life in minute and inflexible detail, even if this were possible, would soon be found seriously to conflict with political reality and either require constant amendment or simply cease to be observed at least in its minor details. Either way it would quickly lose respect and observance as determining the context of political action. All branches of the law must have some degree of flexibility to cope with unforeseen cases, but constitutional law, given the dynamic nature of its subject-matter, must admit of more than one strict interpretation if it is to stand the test of time. The interplay of political forces leads inevitably to a development of constitutional law. Social, economic, or technological changes can bring about situations not provided for. Consequently, those judges who are called upon to interpret the constitution have not inconsiderable opportunities of influencing the development of the constitutional system.

On the other hand, the important function of the decisions of the Supreme Court of the United States as a means of adapting the constitution to changed circumstances is only weakly paralleled in West Germany. In part this is simply a result of the great difference in age of the two constitutions: a constitution drawn up in 1949 can be expected to require less adaptation to political realities than one framed in 1787. At the same time, there is far less sweeping generality and vagueness about the Basic Law. Though necessarily 'open' to some extent, it goes much more into detail and is less flexible. This deliberate attempt to provide a comprehensive regulation of the framework of political activity, leaving as little as possible to chance, partly resulted from and partly encouraged the German view that every aspect of the exercise of public powers and the interactions of political institutions should be covered at some point in the hierarchy of legal norms. A corollary of this view is the need for the constitution to be amended fairly frequently to conform to actual or generally demanded changes in political practice. And indeed, especially as compared with the American Constitution, the Basic Law is not particularly difficult to amend, requiring a two-thirds majority in both Bundestag and Bundesrat (apart from certain sections whose essential principles are declared inviolable). Moreover it has in practice undergone frequent amendments,[25] the majority of which have concerned the distribution of powers between Bund and Länder. New needs such as defence and nuclear energy have been satisfied by changing the catalogue of powers rather than subsuming them under already existing powers. The contrast with the United States, where the brief catalogue of powers has only once been the object of constitutional amendment,[26] is striking. This frequency of amendment, as in Switzerland, has meant that the Constitutional Court has been needed less in the process of adaptation (except with regard to the specially protected basic rights section), while it has not reached the point of threatening respect for the normative force of the constitution. However, it would be unrealistic to suppose that it had prevented real and supposed inconsistencies arising at many points between the letter of the Basic Law and what the Germans call *Verfassungswirklichkeit* ('constitutional reality'), and this has left ample room for control and influence by the decisions of the Constitutional Court.

To meet this situation the Court maintains that a constitutional provision can undergo a change of meaning if in its field new, unforeseen circumstances arise or known circumstances appear in a new light by virtue of their involvement in a general development.[27] In these circumstances the judges clearly enjoy a degree of freedom of interpretation, and it will often be necessary to have recourse to prevailing opinions as regards the value judgements embodied in the constitution and to sociological and political factors and contemporary needs. The scope for doing this is clearly more restricted in an area like the distribution of powers between Bund and Länder, where the Basic Law is comparatively detailed and concrete and therefore reacts less flexibly to political changes, but it remains considerable.

2 Political considerations in the decision-making of the Constitutional Court

If the opportunities and inducements to take account of more than purely legal factors are considerable, it may now be asked what the Court's reaction to this situation has been and how it is manifested in its judicial practice.[28]

Given the German tradition of a strict segregation of law and politics, acknowledgement of creative decision-making with regard for political realities has been much slower and more painful than in the Anglo-Saxon world, where it has long been taken for granted. The Staatsgerichtshof of the Weimar Republic took a narrow view of the issue, declaring in a judgment of 17 December 1927 that it was a court which had to decide constitutional disputes according to legal principles and to pronounce the conclusions it reached by the application of objective law without having regard to the political consequences of its verdict.[29] The Federal Constitutional Court has not always taken the same line, and it has in this respect been in advance of many more traditionalist legal commentators. In an early case concerning the 1951 electoral law of the Land of Schleswig-Holstein the Second Senate declared: 'The decisions of the Constitutional Court relate to political realities, and the Court must on no account disregard the political environment in which its decisions take effect.'[30] This was in accordance with the view expressed by the first President of the Court, H. Höpker-Aschoff, at the opening of the Court of 28 September 1951, that the Court must remain aware of the political consequences of its decisions, if only to weigh up its legal decisions the more carefully.[31] But another early decision, that on the European Defence Community Treaty, prompted the Second Senate to the observation: 'The political consequences which may arise from the rejection of the applications as inadmissible cannot be allowed to influence the Federal Constitutional Court. It must decide according to the law alone.'[32] Nevertheless, although some of the judges interviewed by the author were more reticent than others, there was a general opinion that the Constitutional Court must not take the view 'Fiat iustitia, pereat mundus', that political or social considerations were naturally always present, that the Constitutional Court, like all judges to a greater or lesser extent, was not immune to the force of public opinion.

In fact consideration of the political implications of a case has sometimes led the Court to depart altogether from the general rules of interpretation to decide a specific case.

One way of doing so is to recognize a political practice which endeavours to come as near as possible to the constitutional requirement when the full realization of the latter is unattainable. This line was followed in the 'Saar Judgment' in 1955.[33] The Constitutional Court did not deny that the Act ratifying the Saar Agreement of October 1954 violated provisions of the Basic Law including its guarantee of basic rights to all Germans. But it upheld the constitutionality of the Act, arguing that it must not lose sight of the political situation which gave rise to an international treaty and which it was intended to affect. This could justify the conclusion of agreements by the Federal Government and Parliament which, though not conforming fully to the Basic Law, strove to do so at least as far as was politically achievable. Otherwise, the Court maintained, one would be preventing the bad giving way to the better because the best was unattainable—something the constitution could not have intended. Thus the Court significantly did not maintain that an unconstitutional situation would have to be put up with in view of the political consequences, but that the situation was for special reasons not unconstitutional.[34]

Another possibility is to bow to the force of long-established political practice, provided that it is not quite clearly in violation of the constitution (an accepted principle in the United States). This is most easily justified in the area of assignment of powers, since an unchallenged exercise of a particular power over time may be regarded as having given an originally 'open' norm a specific sense and content, even if there are misgivings about the original exercise of the power. One example is the Court's confirmation of the constitutionality of §2 of the Prices Act of 1948 and the six Acts prolonging its validity, whose compatibility with the constitution had been hotly disputed.[35] There was considerable doubt, which the Court dispelled at length, as to whether the content, purpose and scope of the authorization to issue statutory orders was specified sufficiently in §2 of the Prices Act. Even before the case was decided there had been suggestions that the confirmation of the law's validity by the long-established political practice of its application could no longer be rebutted by newly arising theoretical misgivings, and that since the law had had very beneficial economic effects a belated discovery of its incompatibility with the Basic Law found no justification in political reality.[36] And the Court's judgment found both praise and blame for having by 'teleological decision-making' had regard to the need to avoid the confusion which would have followed upon an invalidation of the law.[37] The Court did not in fact argue at all in terms of the unacceptability of the consequences of invalidating the Prices Act but hammered out an interpretation in conformity with the constitution. However, it might well have decided differently if five years had not elapsed since the case was raised and ten since the law had been passed.[38]

An even clearer example is provided in the federal domain by the case of the responsibility for administering the turnover and transportation taxes, later replaced by the value added tax. Here it was made quite clear in *Art. 108 Abs. 1 GG* in its original form that the turnover and transportation taxes were to be administered by Federal revenue agencies. But the Federal agencies of financial administration—the general customs offices and their subsidiaries and the chief revenue boards (*Oberfinanzdirektionen*)—were not equipped for such a task and for this reason the administration of these taxes was carried out in practice by the tax inspectors' offices (*Finanzämter*), which were Land authorities. Since a legal basis for this apparent divergence from the requirements of the Basic Law had to be found, the Fiscal Administration Act of 1950 created the fiction that the chief revenue boards administered the turnover and transportation taxes with the tax inspectors' offices providing only 'administrative assistance'. The administrative order implementing the Act actually stated that this assistance consisted in the tax inspectors' offices raising the transportation tax for the chief revenue board![39]

This legal position was unchallenged for many years and so represented a shift in the constitution by governmental practice (until the amendment of 1969 omitted the turnover and transportation taxes from *Art.* 108 *Abs.* 1 *GG*, thereby assigning their administration to the Länder under *Art.* 108 *Abs.* 2–4 *GG*). In theory, of course, it remained an open question whether it was a case of what German constitutional lawyers would call *Verfassungsfortbildung* (development of the constitution) or simply one of violation of the constitution. But neither level of government had any interest in challenging it, so that the Constitutional Court did not become involved until 1971, when the Federal Finance Court (Bundesfinanzhof) questioned via the concrete review of norms whether the tax inspectors' offices as Land authorities had been entitled to issue certain disputed transportation tax rulings.

The reaction of the Bundesverfassungsgericht[40] was first to point out that no one had seriously disputed that any different solution would have required a very considerable and hardly defensible administrative outlay with attendant burdens on the taxpayers concerned. It also stressed that all administrations had acted in accordance with the relevant legal provisions for twenty years without any competent body challenging their validity. On this basis it then declared that it was possible to understand the wording of the clause in question as meaning that the entire legal responsibility for, and the basic decisions concerning, the administration of the turnover and transportation taxes lay with the (Federal) chief revenue boards. The constitutional objections related to the practical application of the provisions of the Fiscal Administration Act, not to the constitutionality of those provisions themselves, and this was a matter for the courts with the relevant jurisdiction. The Court further drew attention to peculiarities in the constitutional provisions for financial administration and pointed out other areas in which an equivalent interweaving of Federal and Länder functions occurred. It concluded that there was therefore no sufficient evidence of unconstitutionality.

These cases of the Constitutional Court finding ways of preserving legal provisions whose invalidation might have serious political consequences can be supplemented by even more

striking examples. Thus, although the report of the constituency boundary commission of 1 January 1962 established
that the population of thirty-seven parliamentary constituencies deviated by more than $33\frac{1}{3}$ per cent from the constituency
average, thereby violating the principle of electoral equality,
and although earlier reports had contained some similar findings, the Court refused to take the momentous step, almost two
years after the event, of declaring the Bundestag elections of 17
September 1961 invalid. Instead it took dubious refuge in the
argument that the shifts of population had not been sufficiently
obvious at the time.[41] With this may be compared the refusal
in 1966 to declare invalid the turnover tax in force at the
time, despite its admitted violation of the equality principle.
Invalidation would have had catastrophic consequences for
the Federal exchequer, so the Court maintained that the
temporary continuation of the injustice until the introduction of a new turnover tax system in conformity with the
equality principle was not entirely intolerable for the complainant.[42]

However, the main political element in the decision-making
of the Bundesverfassungsgericht is not the occasional willingness to let an otherwise obvious legal decision be overridden by
pressing political considerations, but rather the degree of
choice open to the Court within the normal ambit of legal
interpretation and deduction. The legal decision and its political implications are often intricately bound up together. The
decision is a political one, though in accordance with legal
criteria, and it is a real decision in view of the room for manoeuvre which, as has been demonstrated, is afforded to the
Court by the variety of legal criteria available. As one judge, no
doubt exaggerating slightly, put it when interviewed: 'One
never has a legal opinion because one has a supporting argument; rather, one has a supporting argument because one has a
legal opinion.'[43] It might well be asked where, in that case, the
legal opinion comes from, unless from inspiration or prejudice,
and whether it has not then lost much of its legal character.
Nevertheless as an exercise in candour it seems preferable to
the dubious rationalization offered by Bachof in an otherwise
admirable essay on political considerations in judicial
decision-making:

For the constitutional judge it cannot and must not be a matter of arguing from a preconceived conclusion and then subsequently putting a more or less violent legal construction upon this conclusion. However, the positive or negative evaluation of the compatibility with the general good of a conclusion which has already been reached by legal construction will indeed be an indication to the judge as to whether he may be content with this conclusion or whether he must review it again with the aim of discovering hitherto perhaps overlooked principles of law which correct it.[44]

The suspicion of humbug aroused by such a characterization is in stark contrast to the straightforward avowal by another of the judges interviewed that in 95 per cent of the cases decided there are also good arguments for the contrary conclusion to that adopted by the Constitutional Court: the political consequences are always weighed up first, whereupon the one chain of deduction looks more persuasive.

On the whole, although the Court's role has been far from passive, its use of such political discretion has been marked by self-restraint. Verdicts may vary according to the period considered[45] or the standpoint from which the Court is judged: thus Kommers asserts that the rate of invalidation of provisions of Federal and Land law via the process of 'concrete judicial review' has been by American standards 'judicial activism absolutely running wild'.[46] But although according to one of the members of the Court, Judge Rupp, writing in 1972, 'Since 1951 the Court has declared void—in toto or in part—one hundred and eleven federal and fifty-eight state statutes,'[47] and a substantial number of administrative regulations must be added to this sum, most of the legal provisions concerned lacked great political importance. Moreover, the Court has in general allowed wide scope for discretion on the part of the political authorities. It has explicitly acknowledged on many occasions that it is not entitled to examine whether the legislator has found the most expedient, reasonable or just solution, or to substitute its own substantive political judgement for that of government and parliament.[48]

A method to which the Court has had increasing recourse is that of *verfassungskonforme Auslegung*, i.e. specifying and adopting the one interpretation by which a particular measure would be constitutional.[49] This method, which amounts to a presumption that a law is compatible with the Basic Law, is often used to preserve laws which prima facie are unconstitutional. On the other hand, it may be for the Court a useful way of limiting what was bound to be a declaration of validity: instead of simply deciding that a legal provision does not conflict with the constitution, it may interpret the provision in a particular way and declare that it is therefore constitutional. This is the case with the controversial decision on the constitutionality of the Basic Treaty with East Germany,[50] where the verdict that it must be left to the discretion of the legislator to determine by what means German reunification may be most effectively pursued is tempered by the insistence of the Court that the Treaty is constitutional only in the interpretation given to it in the lengthy *ratio decidendi*. The latter includes assertions about the continued existence of the German Reich embracing both German states and the at least partial identification of the Federal Republic with this Reich, as well as about the legal nature of the border between the Federal Republic and the GDR. By such means the Court gains additional room for manoeuvre.

In general, therefore, considerable opportunities are open to the Constitutional Court for having regard to political considerations in its decision-making. Moreover it has been prepared, within a general framework of judicial self-restraint, to make use of these opportunities, occasionally quite adventurously, to frustrate the action of an organ of government. It remains to be seen, however, whether such generalizations hold good for the judgment of federal cases. Constitutional disputes arising from relations within the federal system have characteristics of their own, which must now be examined.

CHAPTER IV

The Nature of Conflicts between Bund and Länder

One of the most important effects of a federal system is the institutionalization of conflict. In some instances such institutionalization may help to contain existing regional conflicts and render them amenable to resolution by political compromise from positions of relative equality or even by impartial arbitration; in others it may exacerbate existing regional divisions and both legitimize and entrench irreconcilable standpoints.

Given the nature of German federalism, the constitutional demarcation between the two levels of government does not on the whole do either of these. Whereas in the history of the United States federalism has tended to represent as much unity as was politically acceptable, and in other federations, such as the Canadian, federalism has gone along with sharp ethnic or other cleavages in the population, there is no doubt that West German federalism represents as much *diversity* as is politically acceptable. The Federal Republic does not contain national minorities (apart from a minute Danish population in Schleswig-Holstein). Nor can the traditional 'tribal' consciousness of the German peoples be said to exist today in more than a very attenuated form, having been diminished still further by the truncation of Germany after the Second World War, the massive influx of refugees from the eastern territories and the greatly increased mobility of the population. Partly for the same reasons religious differences have also declined. In so far as the historical states and principalities which joined to form the German Reich in 1871 could be held to represent genuine cultural differences and be the focus of traditional loyalties, their replacement after 1945 (except for Bavaria and the Hanseatic city-states) by new Länder artificially created in the various zones of occupation, and not least the dismemberment of Prussia, largely effaced such regional political identity.

Admittedly, the old Länder did not in all cases go down without a fight. Thus in the 1950s popular initiatives calling for the re-establishment of former Länder were successfully carried out (i.e. received the support of at least 10 per cent of the electorate) in two parts of Lower Saxony and in Baden, which in 1951 had been submerged in the newly created Land of Baden-Württemberg against the expressed will of 52.5 per cent of the Baden population. There were also successful popular initiatives in three administrative districts of Rhineland Palatinate demanding their transfer to Hesse or, in one case, North Rhine Westphalia. Yet the referendums which thereby became obligatory were not held until the 1970s, by which time some of the movements had run out of steam, and it was only in the Lower Saxon districts of Oldenburg and Schaumburg-Lippe that the necessary majorities could be mustered.[1] Subsequent Federal legislation provided notwithstanding, mainly on grounds of economic viability, that these districts should remain part of Lower Saxony. The Constitutional Court afterwards refused to recognize the existence of any relationship in constitutional law between the Bund and the former Land of Oldenburg such as might confer justiciable rights on the latter and declared that individual citizens or elected representatives in Oldenburg had no standing to assert a right to implementation of the result of the relevant referendum. Meanwhile in 1976 a constitutional amendment to *Art. 29 GG* which finally transformed the Federal legislature's obligation to reorganize the federal territory into a mere enablement caused no public outcry.[2]

In spite of sporadic resistance, therefore, it is clear that the remodelled post-war West German federation has witnessed a probably irreversible decline in the political significance of traditional regional loyalties. Nevertheless, by establishing, however artificially, regional poles of attraction with distinctive regional patterns of interests, the federal system of itself creates the potential for all sorts of friction. Some of the frictions may prove to be creative, others are merely time-consuming, expensive, and perhaps frustrating. All of them are political in one sense or another, but because the political forces operate within a detailed constitutional framework, which essentially *is* the federal system, many of them also have legal aspects.

Since it is in the nature of federalism that one level of government may not simply override the other, those conflicts whose substance is not covered by a constitutional norm, or in whose case the constitution explicitly allows discretion or makes the action of one party conditional upon the consent of another, must normally[3] be settled in the process of political manoeuvring and negotiation between two sides which are legally equal though perhaps endowed with quite unequal political clout. A similar 'political' method of resolution may also often be preferred for disputes which have a substantial legal element, whether because the 'aggrieved' party regards his legal case as thin or because it is felt that confrontation before a court would be more damaging to relations than would negotiation (though in reality if there are no real negotiables a prolonged and fruitless process of negotiation may do more harm than a once-and-for-all judicial verdict).

In West Germany there has indeed from the start been some evidence of unwillingness to seek a judicial solution of disputes in the federal system. Thus the issue of whether amendments of laws which had required the assent of the Bundesrat themselves required such assent in order to become law had been disputed since 1951, but the Constitutional Court was not compelled to decide it until 1972.[4] This shows a pragmatic approach by Bund and Länder. Paradoxically, the *Television Case* of 1960–1, the most dramatic and bitter of all federal disputes, also illustrates the preference on the Länder side for political settlement as opposed to constitutional confrontation. They showed ample readiness to co-operate in negotiations, and it was only the uncompromising demands and ruthless behaviour of the Federal Government that drove them to legal action.[5]

The Federal Government, as the stronger party and the more likely to have its own way by other means, has seldom chosen to invoke the Constitutional Court; the *Concordat Case*, the issue of advisory referendums on the desirability of atomic weapons for the West German armed forces, and a number of cases concerning the salaries of public officials in the Länder are the only significant examples.[6] Indeed between 1958 and 1970 the Federal Government did not file a single suit against a Land government or a Land law. This can no doubt be attributed in part to the rap over the knuckles it received from the Court in the *Television Judgment* of 1961, as well as its lack of success in all its previous applications apart from the *Atomic Weapons Referendum Cases* of 1958.

In fact from 1962 until after the Social Democrat/Free Democrat Government came to power in Bonn in 1969 there is a remarkable dearth of federal cases from any quarter. As will be suggested below, it is not entirely a coincidence that this period was one of widespread coalition government, above all of grand coalitions of Christian Democrats and Social Democrats, in both Bund and Länder. Chapter VIII will also show that the mid- and late sixties were marked by increasing acceptance on the part of the Länder, in the face of financial and economic realities, of the need to transfer various powers to the Federal level and seek a new equilibrium in the federal system. This could scarcely be compatible with stubborn litigiousness in defence of every presumed constitutional prerogative. Similar considerations of the need to co-operate, and pressure on the Länder to co-ordinate their activities and present a common front *vis-à-vis* the Federal Government, no doubt also underlie the lack of constitutional disputes between different Länder in the federal system.[7]

An analysis of federal disputes also reveals that in the field of administration or execution of Federal legislation by the Länder, an aspect of German federalism which produces much more interpenetration of the two levels of government than in many other federations, recourse to Karlsruhe has been particularly rare.[8] Rather, the bureaucracies of Bund and Länder have developed close contacts and channels for the settlement of differences. Points of friction can be smoothed out in the multitudinous Bund–Länder committees, conferences, and commissions, and via the committees of the Bundesrat, the Länder legations (*Landesvertretungen*) in Bonn and in general the institutions of co-operative federalism discussed in Ch. VIII below.[9] Clearly a government will think twice before abandoning this environment of consultation and compromise, and perhaps sacrificing goodwill built up there, for the uncertain benefits to be derived from adversarial proceedings before the Constitutional Court.

If non-judicial solutions are often sought for disagreements involving questions of constitutional law, on the other hand those cases where appeal *is* made to the Constitutional Court are not necessarily 'straightforward' legal disagreements between the two levels of government. For if one side of a political dispute decides to seek a judicial solution, it is bound to adduce whatever legal arguments seem most likely to produce the desired end, even if its attitude to the legal issue concerned, if the latter were taken in isolation, would be one of indifference. To put it in terms of federalism: if conflicting political interests happen to occupy positions of power at different levels in the federal system and one of them appeals to the Constitutional Court for a decision in his favour, this appeal may be couched in terms of constitutional rights and obligations within the federal system as established by the Basic Law even if the real source of conflict is, say, different approaches to social policy. Where regional loyalties are not well developed, the championing or otherwise of Länder differences and Länder rights will often be prompted by considerations of expediency, particularly in the light of party-political configurations.

The Federal Republic is often labelled a *Parteienstaat*. It is characterized by party government, and the parties represented in Bonn have long been the major parties at Land level as well. (Even the Bavarian Christian Social Union (CSU), which has a separate identity at Federal level also, forms a joint parliamentary party with the CDU.) By creating additional centres of power (and patronage) in the Länder capitals and by the institution of 'Länder lists' for Bundestag elections the federal system has the effect of decentralizing the party system to a far greater extent than in unitary states. But the influence is reciprocal. Although the parties have more or less autonomous Länder-based substructures, their internal politics, the ever-increasing prominence of the national leadership, and the need to have regard to the party's interests at all levels of government and throughout most or all of the Federal Republic, together with the importance to Federal politics of the party-political composition of the Bundesrat, add a significant centralizing dimension to Land politics. The lines of division between the parties run straight across the division between Bund and Länder, and although Länder politics have retained a life of their own, it is not surprising if it sometimes appears that for the major parties the Länder capitals are merely another arena in which to carry on the same battle against their political opponents. In this way relations between Länder governments and the Federal Government can obviously be affected by their respective party-political complexions.

The question therefore arises as to the real nature of those disputes between the Federal Government and one or more Länder which are taken to Karlsruhe for decision by the Constitutional Court. Are they simply disagreements about powers, regardless of the use to which those powers are put, or controversies about the mutual rights and duties of Federal and Länder governments, irrespective of the party affiliations of those concerned? Or should one rather agree with Konrad Hesse, who as early as 1962 asserted: 'Disputes between Bund and Länder are today, as is well known, as a rule no longer true federal disputes but disputes between political alignments within the federal state, which are cast in the guise of federal disputes and settled by recourse to constitutional litigation.'[10]

Although it will be agreed that a considerable number of disputes between Bund and Länder are in fact at most superficially of a federal nature, the validity of the phrase 'as a rule' (*in aller Regel*) is open to serious doubt, both at the time when Hesse was writing and since. One of the problems is that cases do not necessarily fall neatly into one category or the other. Rather, there is a series of gradations from disputes where the desire to defend Land (or alternatively Federal) rights unites all political alignments or at least cuts across party lines, via cases where it is only party-political antitheses between the two levels of government that predispose one side to assert its rights where possible, to those where the federal dispute is simply a cover for, or a convenient means of conducting, a campaign on policy issues. Nevertheless a reasonably accurate classification can be undertaken at least into the following three categories:

(1) *Pure federal disputes.* Here the dispute is not merely superficially a matter of the powers, rights, or obligations of the two levels of government. There are no significant 'ulterior

motives', apart from the desire of those in power at either level to maintain a position of influence arising out of the federal division of powers itself.

(2) *Federal disputes with party-political implications* (federal/policy disputes). Here the argument is wholly or partly conducted in terms of the powers, rights, or obligations of the two levels of government, and such questions are in fact decided by the Constitutional Court. But the constitutional dispute masks and arises out of a different dispute between opposing political camps which happen to have power bases at the different levels of government. These cases are essentially party arguments about specific policy objectives in which federal arguments are largely only a means to an end.

(3) *Disputes between federal partners about non-federal issues* (quasi-federal disputes). In these cases the dispute is still between Länder and Federal authorities. But the argument is not merely in reality of a party nature but also relates to interpretation of the constitution on matters outside the federal sphere, such as basic rights, and often expresses ideological preferences about the purposes for which the constitution should be used. Thus the quasi-federal dispute is not conducted in federal terms at all. Rather, in circumstances of political competition or controversy one of the sides makes use of the rights it derives from being in government at Land (or, theoretically, Federal) level to appeal against a legislative act of the other side on whatever constitutional grounds seem most convincing.

There are two main ways in which either level of government may take a dispute to the Constitutional Court. First, and most obviously, there is the so-called constitutional dispute (*Verfassungsstreit*) or Bund–Länder dispute, which is a genuine adversarial process concerning the alleged rights or obligations of either party under the Basic Law.[11] Secondly, and in practice more commonly, the Constitutional Court may undertake abstract judicial review (*abstrakte Normenkontrolle*) at the request of the Federal Government or of a Land government, or even of one-third of the members of the Bundestag.[12] This consists in the determination of whether a norm of Federal or Land law is in conformity with the constitution, or whether Land law conforms with other Federal law. The judicial review is 'abstract' in that its initiators do not have to show that they have a direct, practical interest in its outcome; it can, however, result in an only too 'concrete' invalidation of an offending legal provision. The relevance of this latter procedure to the third category of disputes described above should be obvious.[13]

Only a minority of 'federal' applications made under these two heads could be said to have a significant ideological or party-political element, even if in certain instances the party-political affiliations of the Federal and Land governments were different or a particular political party had a greater interest in a particular outcome than its opponents.

1 Pure federal disputes

In the history of the Bundesverfassungsgericht only ten Bund–Länder constitutional disputes under *Art*. 93 *Abs*. 1 *Nr*. 3 *GG* had been decided up to the end of 1979.[14] Six of these cases can at once be shown to have no serious claim to be regarded as covert party-political disputes.[15]

(i) In the *South-West State Case*[16] the main issues were, firstly, the (successful) claim by the Government of Baden, one of the three small Länder originally created in south-west Germany by the Occupying Powers, that Federal legislation prolonging the life of its parliament pending the reorganization of the whole south-west area was unconstitutional; and secondly, its (unsuccessful) objections to the voting districts and method of evaluating the vote proposed for the forthcoming plebiscite. The context was one of resolute resistance in Baden to proposals for the amalgamation of the three south-western Länder, which was being actively promoted by the neighbouring government in Württemberg–Hohenzollern, which, being CDU-dominated, was of a similar political complexion. Thus the moving force was the loyalty of the 'Altbadener' to the tradition of a separate, united Land of Baden and their fear of domination by the more populous Württemberg with its powerful centre in Stuttgart.

(ii) The *Christmas Bonus Case* of 1953[17] was an (unsuccessful) attempt by the Federal Government, having decided that it could not afford to give a Christmas bonus to Federal civil servants, to secure temporary injunctions against the granting of such bonuses by the governments of Bavaria and Hesse because of the pressure this would put on the Federal Government and other Länder governments to do the same. Although Hesse had an SPD government, Bavaria was then governed by a grand coalition; but in any case this was hardly an essentially party-political issue.

(iii) The same goes for the *North Rhine Westphalian Salaries Case*,[18] in which the Federal Government tried in vain to prevent the largest of the Länder paying its officials at higher rates than the equivalent Federal officials. At the time North Rhine Westphalia was governed by a coalition on the Federal model.

(iv) The *Boiler Judgment* of 1960[19] upheld a claim by the Government of North Rhine Westphalia that the Federal Minister of Labour had violated its administrative rights by issuing licences to manufacturers of boilers. The CDU government in Düsseldorf was supported in its suit by the politically disparate governments of Hamburg, Bavaria, and Lower Saxony.

(v) The *Territorial Reorganization Case* was initiated by a complaint by the Government of Hesse that the Federal Government had failed to fulfil its obligation under *Art.* 29 *GG* to introduce a bill for the revision of existing Länder boundaries and if necessary the creation of new Länder. Hesse expected to gain territorially from such a redivision. Its appeal was accompanied by a plea on similar grounds by the *Heimatbünde* ('Homeland Leagues') of Hessen Nassau and Rheinhessen, which had been responsible for the holding of popular initiatives in the Montabaur and Rheinhessen government districts of Rhineland Palatinate demanding their transfer to Hesse. (Both popular initiatives obtained the support of over 20 per cent of the electorate, whereas only 10 per cent was required to instigate a plebiscite on the issue.) That the Social-Democratic Government of Hesse had no strong party-political reasons for wanting to regain the two areas can be seen from the table of results of the 1959 Landtag elections:[20]

	CDU %	SPD %	FDP %	Other %
Regierungsbezirk Montabaur	47.7	35.5	10.3	6.5
Regierungsbezirk Rheinhessen	37.2	43.7	10.2	9.0
(Rhineland Palatinate	48.4	34.9	9.7	7.0)

Even though Rheinhessen was the most strongly Social-Democratic district in Rhineland Palatinate, the evidence suggests that it was a matter of local patriotism in these areas and dissatisfaction with the new, artificial, and relatively poor unit of Rhineland Palatinate. Popular initiatives had also been carried out in the other parts of the Land: in the government districts of Trier and Koblenz for incorporation into North Rhine Westphalia, and in the government district of the Palatinate for transfer to Bavaria or Baden-Württemberg (the former also achieving more than the necessary 10 per cent). This case is therefore symptomatic of the persistence of historical territorial loyalties rather than of the strength of more recent party allegiances, even if the two are not mutually exclusive.[21]

(vi) In the *Hessian Water Law Case*[22] the Government of Hesse was challenging (with success) the issuing of licences by offices of the Federal Waterways Administration on the basis of the Hessian Water Act, which it claimed was an invasion of its administrative autonomy.

Even though in several of these disputes the Federal Government clashed with Länder governments of the opposite political persuasion, and no doubt friction was more likely in these circumstances, none of them by their nature deserve to be regarded as primarily 'disputes between political alignments'.

The cases of abstract judicial review have been more frequent, but many of them concern matters which could not be claimed to be objects of federal dispute. Thus they include applications by Länder governments or the Federal Government alleging the non-application of a legal norm by a court, challenges by one-third of the members of the Bundestag to Federal or alleged Federal legislation, and (ineligible) applications by political groupings outside the Bundestag. Of those cases which are of a federal nature the following can be regarded as 'pure' federal disputes.

(vii) The *Finance-Equalization Case*[23] concerned an objection by the Government of the then Land of Württemberg-Baden, supported by the Senate of Hamburg, to the Federal Finance-Equalization Act for the year 1950, whose redistribution of tax revenue from the richer to the poorer Länder it regarded as exceeding the constitutionally permitted limits. This was simply a case of two rich Länder (admittedly both SPD-governed) not liking being forced to subsidize their poorer neighbours. Three of the latter—Bavaria (with a grand coalition), Rhineland Palatinate and Schleswig-Holstein—sided with the Federal Government, which emerged victorious.

(viii) The challenge by the Bavarian Government to the validity of Federal laws for the temporary regulation of the establishment of chemists' shops[24] was based on the alleged lack of Federal legislative power and to some extent on special conditions obtaining in Bavaria. There is no obvious party-political element, and although the Bavarian Government was led by the SPD at the time of the judgment in 1956, the case had been initiated in 1953 by the Grand Coalition under the CSU Minister-President Ehard.

(ix) In the '*Article 131*' *Case*[25] Hamburg was seeking to set aside the Federal law in pursuance of the obligation under *Art.* 131 *GG* to regulate the legal position of former employees in the public service who had left it for such reasons as the disappearance after 1945 of central or local administrative bodies, expulsion or flight from eastern territories or dismissal on political grounds. This law obliged public employers, including the Länder, to reserve a certain proportion of vacant or new positions for such former public servants and to earmark at least 20 per cent of their salary expenditure for their employment; or failing that to pay a compensatory sum to the Bund to be used solely to promote the objectives of the law in question. Hamburg's objections, which were shared by its fellow CDU-led governments in Rhineland Palatinate and Baden-Württemberg, whereas the CDU Government of Schleswig-Holstein took the part of the Federal Government, were based primarily on the lack of Federal power to impose such a levy and the inability of any Land, and in particular Hamburg itself, to fulfil its quota in time and so avoid the levy. (The Court took the contrary view that *Art.* 131 *GG* was a *lex specialis* which took precedence over the general legislative and financial provisions and established a wide area of legislative discretion. It also held it to be equitable that a Land like Hamburg, whose administration had survived the débâcle of 1945 relatively intact and therefore could not absorb many 'displaced' public servants, should make a reasonable contribution in other ways to the solution of this general problem.)

(x) In the *First Federal Administrative Court Jurisdiction Case*, which was decided in 1958, the Government of North Rhine Westphalia objected to Federal legislation making the Federal Administrative Court in certain cases the court of first instance.[26] This it regarded as constitutionally admissible only where justified by the 'special character of the subject', such as non-constitutional disputes between Bund and Länder or between different Länder; otherwise the superior Federal courts could only act as final courts of appeal. Despite the different political affiliations of the Federal and Land governments concerned, there are no obvious grounds for asserting that this is not a 'true' federal dispute, with the Government of North Rhine Westphalia claiming such jurisdiction in the first instance for Länder courts. (The Constitutional Court held that the fact that the superior Federal courts were *principally* courts of last instance in their particular branch of the law did not mean that they could *only* be final courts of appeal. It was open to Federal legislation to give the Federal Administrative Court jurisdiction in the first instance for challenges against administrative acts of certain of the highest Federal authorities which were of supraregional or general importance or whose validity required speedy and definitive clarification.)

(xi) The case of the (successful) Bavarian application to set aside the Federal law on the settlement of the claims of banks against the state in compensation for the effects of the Economic Reform of 1948 is equally unequivocal.[27] The main plea was the lack of discretion for the Federal legislator under *Art.* 120 *GG* to determine which 'burdens caused as a consequence of the War' were transferred to the Bund, and his obligation in any case to assign any newly established burdens, such as the compensation payments, to the Bund and not to the Länder. The non-party-political nature of the case can also be seen from the fact that between the submission of the application to the Constitutional Court and the judgment of 16 November 1959 there was a change of government in Bavaria, whereby in the autumn of 1957 the CSU replaced the SPD as the leading coalition party; yet the request for abstract judicial review was not withdrawn. Moreover, the Bavarian case received an expression of support from Baden-Württemberg, which had had an all-party coalition under a CDU Minister-President since 1953.

(xii) The challenge by Baden-Württemberg, Hesse, and Lower Saxony to the Federal establishment in 1957 of a special foundation to administer the cultural property of the former Land of Prussia (some of which still stood on former Prussian territory in the Federal Republic but much of which had been evacuated from Berlin during the Second World War) was based on straight arguments of competence and on the assertion that the law should not have been passed without the consent of the Bundesrat. Only one of the governments was dominated by the SPD, the party in opposition at the Federal level, the other two being grand coalitions during the relevant period. The challenge is simply a matter of three of the Länder which included former Prussian territory trying to retain control of objects of cultural importance.[28]

(xiii) A further case of abstract judicial review relating to the jurisdiction of the Federal Administrative Court was initiated in 1958 by the Bavarian Government.[29] The plea was directed against a provision of the Federal Framework Law on the Legal Status of Public Officials (*Beamtenrechtsrahmengesetz*) of 1957, which established a right of appeal to the Federal Administrative Court even for those matters concerning the legal status of officials in which Land law was applicable. The Bavarian Government maintained that the Bund could exercise its legislative powers under *Art. 74 Nr. 1 GG* ('the organization and procedure of courts') only in such a way as was in conformity with the other constitutional provisions, but that according to *Art. 99 GG* only the Land legislator, and not the Federal legislator, had the power to assign jurisdiction in the last instance to the higher Federal courts in matters of Land law. In this dispute the Government of Hesse declared its support for its political opponents in Bavaria, thus underlining the truly federal nature of the case. (However, the Constitutional Court ruled that the Bund's power under *Art. 74 Nr. 1 GG* to regulate the organization and procedure, and hence the extent of the appellate jurisdiction, of administrative courts was restricted neither by *Art. 99 GG*, which merely created the exceptional possibility of jurisdictional attributions to *Federal* courts also being made by *Land* legislation, nor by general federal principles.[30])

(xiv) In the *Bank Lending Case* of 1962[31] four politically heterogeneous Länder (with the declared support of most of the others) challenged the establishment by Federal legislation of a Federal Bank Inspectorate (*Bundesaufsichtsamt für das Kreditwesen*) as an autonomous Federal higher authority under *Art.* 87 *Abs.* 3 *Satz* 1 *GG.* Both the multiplicity of the Länder Governments concerned and the nature of this in fact unsuccessful attempt to restrict the Bund's extensive use of the possibility of establishing such authorities as a substitute for its meagre administrative powers under *Art.* 83 ff. *GG* reveal that this was a genuine grievance of the Länder about an important feature of the operation of the federal system in practice.

(xv) The *Federal Waterways Case* of the same year was also intrinsically a federal dispute about powers.[32] Here again there was an alliance of politically disparate Länder—the CDU or CSU Länder of Bavaria, North Rhine Westphalia and Baden-Württemberg and Social-Democratic Hesse, with the SPD-led coalition in Lower Saxony and the Bundesrat expressing solidarity. The object of this general disapproval, which in the event was shared by the Constitutional Court, was the Federal Act for the Prevention of Pollution of the Federal Waterways, which was covered neither by the concurrent power under *Art.* 74 *Nr.* 21 *GG* for inland waterways used for general traffic, nor, in view of its detailed regulation, by the framework competence for water management under *Art.* 75 *Nr.* 4 *GG.*

(xvi) The *Railway Crossings Case* concerned a request by the Bavarian Government in 1964 for abstract judicial review of the Federal Railway Crossing Act, which was not complied with until 1969.[33] In a long and complex case the Bavarian Government was concerned fundamentally to challenge the assumption that the Bund's various powers in relation to traffic routes gave it the right to pass regulations, in connection with the construction of a railway or long-distance main road, which covered all its interactions with its environment; as well as to object to the requirement that the relevant Land bear a share of the costs of a project carried out at a railway intersection. In both respects it obtained substantial satisfaction from the Constitutional Court. But clearly there was no ideological issue between the CSU Government in Bavaria and the Erhard

Government in Bonn. This was merely the most individual of the Länder jealously guarding its rights against Federal encroachment.

(xvii) In the *Broadcasting Authorities Taxation Case*[34] the question at issue was the Federal Government's attempt to subject the broadcasting authorities to value added tax. The exclusive jurisdiction of the Länder over broadcasting, apart from the technical aspects of transmission, had already been confirmed by the *Television Judgment*.[35] The Government of Hesse now argued, with success, that the assignment by a Land to a broadcasting authority of the exercise of public powers was binding on the Bund, which had no right to turn such public functions by means of a fiction into commercial or professional ones for purposes of turnover tax. The radio and television licence fees, which were allocated to the broadcasting authorities by Land law, were resources of the Länder and the Federal attempt to tax them was tantamount to taxation of the Länder by the Bund. If it is possible to envisage party-political considerations which might conceivably underlie such a case, even though the application was made at the time of the Grand Coalition, such speculation is made redundant by the fact that the Hessian case was endorsed by the governments of Bavaria, Baden-Württemberg, North Rhine Westphalia and Rhineland Palatinate.

(xviii) The next two cases of abstract judicial review were initiated by the Federal Government in relation to salary provisions in Hesse. The *Hessian Judicial Salaries Case*[36] concerned a claim that the new Hessian salary provisions of 1970 did not observe the requirements of the Federal framework law and violated the duty of federal comity by causing a danger of fragmentation of public-service salary arrangements and an increased burden on the budgets of Bund, Länder, and local authorities. The Constitutional Court found only the provisions for new titles for judges to be incompatible with Federal law.

(xix) In the *Hessian Salary Adaptation Act Case* the Federal Government objected, with partial success, to revised and relatively more generous provisions for the payment of schoolteachers and government officials in Hesse, on the ground that the Federal legislation of 1971 passed on the basis of the new concurrent power under *Art.* 74a *GG* prohibited the Länder from further amendment of their existing salary provisions.[37] That these instances of independent-mindedness on the part of Hesse and the Federal reactions were not essentially party-political or ideological in character is suggested by the fact that both cases occurred after the SPD/FDP Coalition came to power in Bonn.

(xx) The most recent instance of a pure federal dispute via abstract judicial review looks at first glance unconvincing, since it is an application challenging the validity of a Federal law and lodged in 1972 by the Bavarian Government, which has shown a particular propensity to challenge the Social Democratic/Liberal Government in Bonn. Yet in this *Financial Subsidies Case* the issue is the eminently federal one of the limits to the Federal rights of granting financial assistance to the Länder for important investment projects.[38] The main ground of complaint was the right given to the Bund by the Act for the Promotion of Urban Building (*Städtebauförderungsgesetz*) to draw up a programme for urban redevelopment and allocate Federal subventions accordingly. Bavaria maintained that the requirement that this programme be based on consultation over the Länder's own programmes still left the Federal Minister in practice almost a free hand. Hints of party-political misgivings might be suspected in the assertions that the Federal Minister could select from the programmes of the Länder those projects which appeared to him, *for whatever reasons*, to be appropriate; and that he was not even prevented from going to the extreme of allocating all the Federal funds to one Land, giving bonuses for good conduct or imposing sanctions for Land behaviour of which the Bund did not approve and thereby influencing the whole of Land politics. Nevertheless the Federal influence gained via such grants-in-aid had long been a source of grievance to all the Länder, despite their legalization by constitutional amendment in 1969, although the poorer Länder, being most dependent on Federal subsidy, had generally been more restrained in their criticism.

(xxi) The same verdict must be passed on the Bund–Länder constitutional dispute initiated in the same field by Bavaria in 1974, in relation to an exceptional Federal programme for areas with special structural problems. This concerned the failure of the Bund to specify the arrangements adequately in an administrative agreement with the Länder and the illegitimacy of its dealing directly with the local authorities affected instead of via the Land government. It too was decided in the Bavarian Government's favour in February 1976.[39]

These twenty-one examples of 'pure federal disputes' no doubt include cases in which, although the argument is a genuine one about powers set within the federal framework, the motive of those involved is primarily to hold on to a position of influence or power: they might perhaps just as happily have used non-federal arguments had that been practicable. But their grouping into a single category seems justified in view of the evident lack of an ideological or party-political element. The vested interests concerned in the application to the Constitutional Court are simply those which are created by the very existence of the federal system. Taken together, these cases therefore demonstrate that constitutional controversies on federal issues which are in reality a cloak for ideological or party quarrels are by no means the norm. In fact such pure federal disputes are in a clear majority.

2 Federal disputes with party-political implications (federal/policy disputes)

The three remaining Bund–Länder constitutional disputes and four cases of abstract judicial review fall into the category of federal/policy disputes. In these cases the powers or obligations of the Bund or a Land are again at issue before the Constitutional Court. But the circumstances that give rise to the federal dispute are those of confrontation between different political groupings ensconced at Federal and Land level, or at least the underlying motivation is explicitly or implicitly ideological. Not surprisingly, these disputes aroused considerable public attention and are amongst the most famous cases to have come before the Court.

(i) The constitutional dispute known as the *Concordat Case*, which was decided in 1957,[40] arose out of a claim by the Federal Government that Lower Saxony, by passing its public education law of 1954, had violated the Concordat of 1933 between the Vatican and the German Reich and thereby infringed the

Bund's right to observance by the Länder of the international treaties by which it was bound. It therefore concerned the question of the foreign affairs power, which has been a bone of contention in several federal systems: can a state be bound by international obligations yet incapable, because of its federal structure, of ensuring respect for them internally; or, on the other hand, can a federal government, simply by concluding an international treaty, to that extent gain control over matters which are otherwise the exclusive responsibility of the member states?[41] But the subject concerned—the relations between church and state and the question of separate confessional education (which was guaranteed for all Roman Catholic schoolchildren by the Concordat)—was traditionally an explosive issue between the parties. The contention over the introduction of common, non-denominational state education for all children, except where a petition was made under strict conditions by a substantial number of parents, had dominated politics in Lower Saxony. The Christian Democrats in power in Bonn were inevitably opposed to such a measure, in common with their colleagues in Hanover who were in opposition until 1955 after the law had been passed. In the circumstances their swift but unsuccessful challenge to the Lower Saxon law, before this had even been requested by the Vatican, testifies to more than a concern for the letter of an international agreement concluded in 1933. Nor was it a coincidence that the two Länder which entered the lists on the side of Lower Saxony, namely Hesse and Bremen, were governed by the Social Democrats.

(ii) Even more obvious is the party-political foundation of the *Atomic Weapons Referendum Cases*. These must be seen against the background of the prolonged campaign waged by the SPD in the 1950s against German rearmament in the context of the Western Alliance. Condemned to opposition in Bonn and embittered by their lack of influence over the main directions which West German politics were to take, the Social Democrats sought to restrict the Adenauer Government's room for manoeuvre and secure their own participation by other means. Apart from invocation of the Constitutional Court,[42] these means included attempted recourse to the extra-parliamentary (and extra-constitutional) weapon of the referendum and exploitation of their position as governing party in several of the Länder.

After rejection by the Bundestag in 1958 of the SPD's proposal for a consultative referendum on the threatened arming of the Bundeswehr with atomic weapons, the SPD-controlled Länder of Hamburg and Bremen passed laws providing for the holding of such consultative referendums and several Social-Democratic local authorities in Hesse decided to put the same question to their electorates. The purpose of these measures was obviously to put pressure on the Federal Government to change its policy of nuclear armament, by demonstrating that public opinion was against it. The latter therefore reacted by requesting abstract judicial review of the Hanseatic cities' laws by the Constitutional Court and initiating a constitutional dispute against the Government of Hesse for failing in its duty to annul the resolutions of the local authorities under its supervision.[43] The Federal Government's main argument, which was accepted by the Constitutional Court, was that the proposed referendums concerned matters of defence and foreign policy, which belonged to the exclusive competence of the Bund, and were intended to exert illegitimate pressure on Federal decision-making in these fields. But although both cases were thus conducted in terms of constitutional powers and the duty of federal comity, this was entirely due to the misuse of the Länder governments concerned for purposes of Opposition politics at the Federal level.

(iii) Perhaps the most celebrated of all cases decided by the Bundesverfassungsgericht, the *Television Case* of 1961,[44] may also, without in any way detracting from its fundamental importance from a purely federal point of view, be placed in this category of federal disputes with party-political implications. The background to the judgment is related in detail in connection with the principle of federal comity in Chapter VII. Here it is sufficient to recall that although this was a Bund–Länder dispute about the Federal Government's infringement of Länder rights by its establishment of a second television channel and its breach of federal comity in the way it had gone about founding the so-called 'Deutschland-Fernsehen-GmbH' ('German Television Ltd.'), the quarrel was also a party-political one. All the SPD-led Länder governments were involved in the legal challenge to the Federal Government, whereas none of the CDU Länder took part. This came about not because of outright resistance by the SPD Länder to the succession of attempts by the Federal Government to secure its participation in a second television channel, nor because the CDU Länder had enthusiastically supported such moves. Rather, all the Länder had been willing to negotiate within reason, but when it finally became clear that Adenauer was not going to get all his own way with the Länder, he proceeded to exert his authority within his own party and, abandoning all consultation with the SPD Länder, put pressure on the Christian-Democratic Minister-Presidents to conclude a separate agreement. Fears were expressed, moreover, most notably by the distinguished political commentator Theodor Eschenburg,[45] that the limited television company created by administrative fiat of the Federal Government would be unilaterally controlled by it and abused for purposes of party propaganda. The *Television Case* had, accordingly, more than a purely federal dimension.

(iv) When several Länder challenge the validity of two Federal laws of 1961 on social services and the welfare of young people and use such arguments as lack of Federal powers under *Art. 74 Nr. 7 GG* (public welfare) and illegitimate interference in the administrative autonomy of the Länder, this looks very much like a case of abstract judicial review being used to settle a purely federal competence dispute. But again closer examination of the case reveals that the same four SPD-dominated Länder—Hesse, Hamburg, Bremen, and Lower Saxony— were concerned. Moreover, their main objection to the Federal laws was the prominent role assigned to the welfare efforts of private associations: public projects and institutions were in general only to be established or developed where the former were insufficient, and otherwise public funds were to be devoted to supporting and assisting the private organizations. Indeed the primary initiative for taking the issue to Karlsruhe (and a number of actual constitutional complaints) came from several cities with Social-Democratic town halls, which wanted to substitute municipal welfare facilities for those of the churches. Thus it is reasonable to conclude that this was a case of ideological antipathy towards a certain approach to social services, partially cloaked in the language of Länder rights.[46]

(v) The request for abstract judicial review of the Fourth

Pensions Insurance Amendment Act (*Rentenversicherungs–Änderungsgesetz*), which was made by Rhineland Palatinate and Bavaria in 1973,[47] was, in contrast to the latter's challenge to the Act for the Promotion of Urban Development in the previous year, a clear instance of a federal/policy dispute. For, although the case was basically concerned with clarification of the long-disputed veto powers of the Bundesrat, in which the views of the governments of the Länder are brought to bear on Federal politics, this disagreement between Federal Government and Bundesrat had flared up with renewed vigour after 1969 under the SPD/FDP Coalition Government, as the Christian Democrats continued to control a majority of the votes in the Bundesrat. Moreover, the pension reform which occasioned the request, having been passed in defiance of the Bundesrat's veto, had been the object of bitter party-political wrangling. During the parliamentary stalemate preceding the 1972 elections the parties had tried to outbid each other in their proposals on pensions, particularly on the right to a premature old-age pension and the so-called flexible age-limit. The law in question restored limits on permitted earnings which had been removed at that time at the insistence of the CDU/CSU.

Thus, if the Länder as a whole had an interest in preserving and extending their influence over Federal legislation via the Bundesrat, the interest of the Federal Opposition both in the Bundesrat's veto power in general and in the invalidation of the pension reform was at least as strong. This is illustrated by the fact that the application by Rhineland Palatinate and Bavaria was supported by their fellow Christian-Democratic governments in Baden-Württemberg and Schleswig-Holstein, as well as by the Bundesrat itself, whereas Hamburg, with a government of the same complexion as that in Bonn, took the view that the assent of the Bundesrat had not been required. Significant too is the welcome given to the Court's rejection of the plea by the SPD, whose leaders had frequently warned the Bundesrat majority against regarding themselves as a 'counter-government'. In its view Karlsruhe had made it clear that the Bundesrat 'may not be used as a blocking-instrument of the CDU/CSU Opposition against the reforming policies of the Social-Liberal Coalition with which it is out of sympathy'.[48]

(vi) The last case in this class of federal disputes with

party-political implications, the *Substitute Civilian Service Case* of 1978,[49] again concerns the Bundesrat's power of veto. And it is just as clear as in the *Pensions Insurance Amendment Case* that it is not an instance of a pure federal dispute. If the identity of the applicants—once again, the CSU Government of Bavaria and the CDU Governments of Rhineland Palatinate and Baden-Württemberg, as well as 215 (Christian-Democrat) members of the Bundestag—did not suffice to indicate the predominantly party-political motivation of this case, it need only be recalled that the law whose invalidation they sought, the 1977 Military Service Amendment Act, had been the subject of acute political controversy between Federal Government and Opposition. The latter objected strongly to its establishment of practically a free choice between military service and the alternative community service (or 'civilian service'). Their main arguments before the Constitutional Court accordingly concerned the compatibility of the new Act with basic rights and other constitutional provisions: the duty of the State to maintain viable armed forces; requirements of equality before the law; the general nature of the duty to perform military service as opposed to the exceptional nature of the substitute civilian service; the principle that to refuse a major obligation towards the general community required a genuine exercise of conscience such as was not guaranteed by a mere declaration paying lip-service to the right of conscientious objection but no longer subject to any scrutiny or vetting procedure. Furthermore, the decision of the Second Senate also bore primarily upon these aspects, and the law was declared null and void.

It might therefore be concluded that this case should rather be put into the third category of cases distinguished above, viz. disputes between federal actors about non-federal issues. However, the applicants had gone on to claim that the amending law had not been properly enacted, because the increase in the administrative responsibilities of the Federal Government which it entailed would have required, but had not received, the consent of the Länder governments in the Bundesrat. This federal issue is sufficiently prominent in the proceedings[50] to warrant including what is admittedly a border-line case among federal/policy disputes.

The foregoing examples exhaust the category of federal disputes with party-political implications. They illustrate *par excellence* the pervasive role of party politics in intergovernmental relations within the federal system and the extent to which ideological motivations may underlie the defence of Federal or Länder rights by appeal to the Constitutional Court.

3 Disputes between federal partners about non-federal issues (quasi-federal disputes)

Finally, a group of cases may be distinguished which also concern intergovernmental relations within the federal system but which do not revolve around the demarcation of powers or the obligations of one level of government to the other. They are all instances of the right bestowed by *Art. 93 Abs. 1 Nr. 2 GG* on Länder governments to apply to the Federal Constitutional Court in case of differences of opinion or doubts about the formal and material compatibility of Federal law with the Basic Law (though theoretically they could equally include Federal applications against Länder legislation). For this procedure of *abstrakte Normenkontrolle* there is no stipulation that a Land's interests must be at stake: the constitutional 'doubts' can be on any grounds. To this extent the provision is almost an invitation to Länder governments of the same political persuasion as the Federal Opposition to spring to the aid of the latter, whenever it has failed to secure the abandonment or substantial dilution of particularly objectionable legislation, by attempting to have the measure invalidated in Karlsruhe. (It is true that the same opportunity is open to one-third of the members of the Bundestag. But even assuming that the Federal Opposition has the required number of deputies, the challenging of a measure may be thought to come better from a body endowed with the title and authority of a government, or else one of the Länder governments may be less circumspect or more obstinate than its political friends in Bonn.) The Social-Democratic Government of Hesse gained something of a reputation for such a predisposition during the years of Christian-Democratic rule in Bonn, and the in any case rather individualistic Bavarian Government might be held to have inherited this role under the SPD/FDP Coalition. But in view of the potential political usefulness of such moves, even if excessive recourse to them might have undesired effects, what is remarkable is how few cases of this kind there have been.[51] Nevertheless the following five cases are undoubted examples of such 'quasi-federal disputes'.

(i) Two cases of abstract judicial review have been initiated by applications whereby the SPD Government of Hesse challenged the validity of Federal laws on the financing of political parties.[52] The first, in 1958, concerned an amendment of Federal income and corporation tax law whereby contributions to political parties were tax-deductible. The Land Government's submission, which was accepted by the Constitutional Court, was primarily on grounds of violation of the principle of equality of opportunity for political parties which the Court had derived from *Art.* 21 *GG*, in that the provision in practice worked to the advantage of political parties supported by wealthy individuals and private companies. Apart from the identity of its initiator, therefore,[53] this was in no sense a federal case, and the request for judicial review would have come at least as well from the SPD parliamentary party in Bonn as from its political friends in Wiesbaden.

(ii) The celebrated *Party Finance Case* of 1966, which was also the result of an application by the Government of Hesse, was no more a federal dispute than its predecessor. (This is not of course to deny that state subsidization of political parties would *also* have important effects in the Länder.) The Hessian objections to the method of party subvention via the Federal budget, the ensuing possibilities of state influence on political parties, and the lack of a law on political parties to provide safeguards found muted support from the SPD,[54] whose independent finances were healthiest, and determined opposition from the other parties represented in the Bundestag, as well as from the Länder governments of Bavaria, North Rhine Westphalia (now CDU/FDP again), Rhineland Palatinate, and the Saarland. The surprising decision of the Constitutional Court, which went further than the Government of Hesse had called for, was thus a victory not for the Länder or even one Land over the Bund, but for a particular party-political standpoint.

(iii) A similar verdict must be passed on the request made by Hesse in 1969 for abstract judicial review of the 17th

Amendment of the Basic Law and an ensuing Federal statute.[55] This amendment, passed in 1968, concerned the privacy of posts and telecommunications guaranteed by *Art.* 10 *GG* subject to legislative restriction, and it provided that the person affected need not be informed of such restriction if it served to protect the free democratic basic order or the security of the Federation or a Land, and that access to the courts could be replaced by parliamentary scrutiny. The (unsuccessful) Hessian plea, which was supported by the Senate of Bremen, was based on the fundamental prohibition in *Art.* 79 *Abs.* 3 *GG* of amendments affecting the basic principles of *Art.* 1 and 20 *GG*, in particular the inviolable dignity of man and the principle of the *Rechtsstaat* including the universal right of recourse to the courts. It was thus not a challenge on federalist grounds but symptomatic of relatively left-wing Social-Democratic misgivings about the extensive legislation on security and emergency powers passed by the Grand Coalition.

(iv) After the advent of the Social Democrat/Free Democrat Government in Bonn, it was the CDU and CSU Länder that began to make use of the opportunities provided by the procedure of abstract judicial review for party-political purposes. The two clear examples of such applications without significant federal content are the issues of the Basic Treaty with East Germany (the *Grundvertrag*) and the reform of §218 of the Penal Code legalizing abortion. In the former case the CSU Government of Bavaria conducted a concentrated legal campaign, including two applications (the second successful) for the exclusion of one of the judges on grounds of bias[56] and unsuccessful attempts to secure a temporary injunction first against ratification of the *Grundvertrag* and later against the exchange of the instruments of ratification.[57] On the substantive issue of the constitutionality of the treaty itself the Bavarian case was based especially on the call to achieve German unity in the preamble to the Basic Law, and on the Federal Republic's responsibility for Germans living in the GDR, but not on an intrusion upon the powers of the Länder or a violation of their rights. The legal action had been preceded by a prolonged political battle between Federal Government and Opposition and can be viewed realistically only against that background. The outcome was a very restrictive validation by the Constitutional Court.[58]

(v) The request for abstract judicial review of the abortion reform in 1974 was the culmination of a long campaign waged by the Opposition against this central pillar of the reform platform of the Social-Democratic and Liberal Coalition. It was made not only by the governments of all CDU or CSU Länder but also by 193 Christian-Democratic Bundestag deputies. It is true that one of their arguments was that because the law contained provisions relating to the administrative procedure of the Länder it had required the assent of the Bundesrat and, not having received it, was invalid. But it was obvious that the main ground on which the application was based was infringement of the constitutional guarantee in *Art.* 2 *GG* of the 'right to life and to inviolability of the person'. For this reason, and in view of the background to the case and the political allegiance of all the applicants, this case may also be placed in the quasi-federal category.[59]

There remains one case which is even more difficult to classify: the abstract judicial review initiated by Hesse concerning the measurement of the Länder quotas provided for in the Federal framework law on institutions of higher education (*Hochschulrahmengesetz*) for the selection of candidates in university subjects with restricted admission.[60] In common with the constitutional complaints and the request for concrete judicial review which came up for decision at the same time, the Hessian application was concerned partly with the basic rights of applicants for university places. But there was also a strong federal aspect to the case. The Government of Hesse objected to the basing of Länder quotas for university places primarily on each Land's proportion of the total numbers in the relevant age group, instead of on its share of the total number of university applicants. It maintained that this system discriminated against those Länder which had pursued a policy of providing access to higher education for as many as possible. And to back its case it invoked not only Federal obligations under *Art.* 12 *Abs.* 1 *GG*, the equality principle and the principle of the 'social state', but also the duty of federal comity. Although the Government of Hesse was of the same political colour as the Federal Government, it is clear that this case was far from being a pure federal dispute, since substantial issues of policy were at stake. What is not clear, however, is whether greater weight should be attached to the basic rights and *Sozialstaat* arguments in the Hessian application or rather to the aspects which bear upon the federal relationship. This case must therefore be regarded as being on the border-line dividing disputes between federal partners about non-federal issues from federal/policy disputes.

From this survey it emerges that those 'federal' cases which deserve to be characterized as 'disputes between political alignments within the federal state', whether in the sense of federal disputes with party-political implications or of quasi-federal disputes, are certainly both prominent and important but relatively few in number. Such cases show how, since German constitutional law envisages institutions as active agents in claiming rights and challenging legal norms, the various institutions concerned are bound to come into conflict not only on specifically federal issues but also on issues which relate to how, and to what end, powers are exercised and how the constitution is to be shaped in relation to specific problems; issues, that is, in respect of which federal arguments are necessarily subsidiary, if relevant at all. They illustrate how closely party politics and the federal system are interwoven and reveal the willingness of the political forces on occasion to pursue other political objectives by manipulation of the arrangements for the settlement of federal disputes. Indeed the instances of the Federal Opposition in particular availing itself of all the constitutional means and all the institutional vantage-points at its disposal for resisting Government policy bear eloquent testimony to one of the most important aspects of the complex federal structure. Such cases also present the Constitutional Court with some of its most difficult and delicate tasks, since it is operating in the glare of publicity and is required to apply convincing legal reasoning to controversial political issues.

However, the twenty-one cases of pure federal disputes cited in this chapter show that it would be a great mistake to regard constitutional litigation within the federal system as an adjunct of inter-party rivalry, or indeed to see the whole system of intergovernmental relations as merely one dimension of party politics in West Germany. They testify to the continuing tension between, on the one hand, the forces encouraging ever greater centralization or at least uniformity in German politics and, on the other hand, if not always the forces of regional loyalty, at any rate the interest of the political establishment at regional level in defending its autonomy and scope for distinctive regulation. The role of the Constitutional Court as arbiter of such genuine federal disputes as are susceptible to the application of constitutional norms is therefore at least as important.

CHAPTER V
Key Areas of Federal Adjudication

The federal disputes cited in the previous chapter include all the most celebrated and controversial federal cases decided by the Constitutional Court up to the end of 1975. This is only to be expected in view of the nature of the parties concerned and often of the questions at issue. However, although they are not few in number, it can hardly be said that they constitute the bread and butter of the Court even in the federal field. For the majority of cases which concern federal issues are not 'federal disputes' in the sense of the previous chapter at all. They are not initiated by one of the levels of government but reach the Constitutional Court by some other means.

Sometimes federal issues of legislative or executive authority are raised by constitutional complaints against alleged violation of basic rights;[1] and in any case the Court feels free, once the validity of a norm has been questioned, to review its constitutionality under other provisions of the Basic Law as well. But by far the most common sources of federal adjudication are the cases of 'concrete judicial review' (*konkrete Normenkontrolle*), in which a ruling on the validity of a Federal or Land norm is requested by another court.[2] In such cases an opportunity must then be given for the Federal Government or Parliament or a Land Government to submit its opinion on the matter. But the reference to the Constitutional Court is made neither on their initiative nor on that of the litigants in the original case, but at the discretion of the court concerned. Concrete judicial review accounts for a majority of the cases discussed in this chapter (and a very substantial majority of the cases relating to §§ 1 and 3).

The purpose of this chapter is to examine how the Constitutional Court has gone about its work in four of the most fertile areas of decision-making in relation to the federal system. The following chapters will then specifically consider possible methods of or aids to interpretation which the Court may use to develop constitutional provisions in the direction that seems appropriate or to create enough scope for judicial discretion and influence.

1 Concurrent legislation: Federal 'occupation of the field'

The vast bulk of the legislative powers in the Federal Republic belong to the 'concurrent' category and are enumerated in the catalogue of *Art. 74 GG*. Since it is the essence of concurrent powers that both levels of government have rights of legislation, the enforcement of the conditions under which either level of government may have recourse to such powers is likely to be an important part of the Constitutional Court's work in the federal sphere. The relevant conditions are to be found in the two paragraphs of *Art. 72 GG*, the second of which will be dealt with in the next section.

Art. 72 Abs. 1 GG provides that in the field of concurrent legislation the Länder have power to legislate in so far as the Federation does not exercise its right to do so. The general effect of this provision is clear: it is, as is normal in federal systems, the principle of Federal pre-eminence. Federal and Länder laws in the concurrent field do not meet on equal terms, nor are they in Germany strictly speaking concurrent; for, as soon as the Bund elects to legislate, the Länder are debarred from further legislative regulation and their existing legislation becomes permanently inoperative to the extent that the Bund has 'occupied the field'.[3] The scope for the Constitutional Court to exert decisive influence is therefore modest. Nevertheless a substantial number of cases have raised the question of how far Land legislation is excluded by Federal exercise of concurrent powers and have been decided with varying emphasis.

In early decisions relating to the rights of the Länder under *Art. 72 Abs. 1 GG* the Constitutional Court emphasized that they had power to legislate in the concurrent field 'as long as, *and to the extent that,*' the Bund did not exercise its right to legislate. Consequently the Court itself was obliged to determine in disputed cases whether existing Federal legislation constituted a comprehensive regulation of the subject. It was not sufficient that the Federal legislature should become active in a particular field: rather, the Court maintained that whether a Federal regulation was exhaustive was to be inferred from an assessment of the relevant complex of norms as a whole. It was thus a matter for judicial decision whether the Land legislation in question filled an identifiable gap left by Federal law and whether it concerned a question capable of separate regulation.

Using this concept of gaps in the legislative coverage of a theoretical total field open to regulation, the Court adopted from the start a rather exacting interpretation of what is required for the Federal legislator to have 'occupied the field'.[4] The effect was to protect the scope for Länder activity in the extensive area of concurrent powers.

Two judgments relating to the taxation powers of the Länder may serve to illustrate both the limits and the possibilities of the Court's interpretative approach.

The first case concerned the law of the former Land of Baden on the raising of funds for combating phylloxera.[5] The Court found that the so-called wine levy imposed on producers and importers into Baden of products of the grape exhibited all the necessary characteristics of a tax. It then determined that it could only be a tax on consumption or traffic, for which under *Art. 105 Abs. 2 Nr. 1 GG* in its then existing form the Bund had concurrent power. In answer to the question whether the Bund had made use of its right to legislate, the Court maintained that in the field of tax legislation it followed from the federal financial system as a whole that subjection of an object to taxation by the Bund must necessarily signify an exhaustive regulation as understood by *Art. 72 Abs. 1 GG.* Tax sources on which the Bund had already made claims could no longer be tapped by a Land (at least not with a similar kind of tax). This followed directly from *Art. 72 Abs. 1 GG.* But since the Baden wine levy was similar in kind to the general purchase tax and the latter must count as an exhaustive regulation of the taxation of proceeds from the sale of goods, Baden had not had the right to introduce such a levy. This ruling was in conformity with German legal tradition, although other federal systems show that it is quite possible for the same kind of tax to be levied by two different levels of government. However, it is difficult to see how the Court could have decided otherwise in the light of *Art. 72 Abs.* 1 *GG*. For if it had held that the mere imposition of a Federal tax did not necessarily amount to an exhaustive regulation of that source of revenue, it might have found itself compelled to assess how much tax a particular object could bear.

In another taxation case, initiated by a constitutional complaint against the imposition of a local tax on a licence to sell alcoholic liquor,[6] the situation was rather different. Recalling that the imposition of a tax by the Bund debarred the Länder from introducing a tax of a similar kind, the Court observed that the only tax which could possibly be regarded as similar was the *Gewerbesteuer* or tax paid for carrying on a trade. It then proceeded to demonstrate that the two taxes were basically different, the one attaching to an existing business, the other to the grant of a licence (even if no use were made of the licence). The *Gewerbesteuer* was a tax on economic performance, whereas the liquor-licence tax was a tax on the attainment of the right to make economic gain from the need of the population for conviviality, relaxation and the enjoyment of alcoholic beverages. Previous legislation had also recognized the distinction between the two. The Court therefore concluded that even if the liquor-licence tax were regarded not as a tax with purely local effect for which the Länder had exclusive authority under the then *Art.* 105 *Abs.* 2 *Nr.* 1 *GG*, but as belonging to the Federal concurrent power, the Bund had made no use of its prerogative since it had not established a 'similar' tax. The Länder had therefore been entitled under *Art.* 72 *Abs.* 1 *GG* to authorize local authorities to impose liquor-licence taxes. Here the objects of the two taxes were sufficiently different, and the legal tradition sufficiently favourable, to allow the Court to uphold the rights of the Länder.

A succession of judgments in the late 1960s and early 1970s served to discourage the tendency of some Länder to underestimate the extent to which they were disqualified from independent regulation by Federal exercise of concurrent powers. Thus in the case of Länder provisions establishing special appeal procedures within the system of administrative courts the relevant Federal law was shown to have undertaken a comprehensive regulation of the procedure of administrative courts, and the fact that it contained specific and detailed provisions reserving to the Länder the right to make certain supplementary or divergent provisions was held to confirm this. Therefore if a matter was not dealt with by the Federal law on administrative courts this could not be taken to signify that the Bund had to this extent made no use of its powers. The Länder were fundamentally prohibited under *Art. 72 Abs.* 1 *GG* from introducing new types of appeal in cases where the right to do so was not explicitly reserved to them by the Federal law.[7]

In two similar decisions striking down Länder provisions which extended the right of members of the press to refuse to reveal their sources[8] the Court took the opportunity of delivering the same little lecture to the Länder. It told them that they were not entitled to assume legislative powers in the field of concurrent legislation where they regarded an exhaustive Federal regulation as inadequate and therefore in need of reform. The Basic Law did not assign to them the task of 'improving' properly taken Federal decisions. If a comprehensive Federal regulation was inadequate in the light of higher constitutional guarantees, it was for the competent Federal legislator to remedy the situation. But as long as the Federal norm remained in existence the Länder were debarred from taking action.

Of rather more importance in relation to the exclusion of the Länder from legislation by *Art. 72 Abs.* 1 *GG* is the *Hessian Salary Adaptation Act Case* of 1972.[9] According to the Federal salary law of 1971,[10] passed under the authority of the new concurrent powers in *Art.* 74a *GG*, the existing Länder laws and ordinances concerning salaries and maintenance were, unless otherwise stipulated, to remain in force unchanged. The Federal Government argued that this exclusion of the Länder from further amendment of their salary provisions was necessary because the Bund could not establish uniformity in the salary law of Bund and Länder all at once and in one statute but needed a certain amount of time, during which the job should not be further complicated by Länder action. But the Court rejected this view. It maintained that under *Art. 72 Abs.* 1 *GG* the Bund could deprive the Länder of power to legislate in the concurrent field only by legislation which itself 'regulated' the subject (or provided that it should not be subjected to legal regulation at all), not by the attempt to impose a simple ban. This did not constitute 'regulation' of the subject but merely prevented such prompt regulation by the Länder as might become necessary until the Bund found time to regulate it itself. Viewed in isolation, therefore, the Federal provisions were considered to be in violation of *Art. 72 Abs. 1 GG*.

If this finding provided a significant and necessary safeguard against possible neutralization of Länder concurrent powers, the Court then took back with one hand much of what it had given with the other. It argued that the legislator could exercise the right to regulate a subject by accommodating the regulation, in accordance with an intrinsically necessary and declared general strategy, not in *one* law but in several successive and complementary laws. The circumstances indicated clearly, it maintained, that the Federal salary law of 1971 represented the beginning of such a project. Since the Bund had thus begun to make comprehensive use of its right of legislation in relation to the salary and maintenance of (Federal and) Land officials, *Art. 72 Abs. 1 GG* debarred the Länder from legislation throughout the entire field whose regulation the Bund had now undertaken. They could make laws only in so far as they were expressly authorized by the relevant Federal law. In several instances the Court found that this had not been the case with the new Hessian salary provisions.

This assorts strangely with the Court's earlier insistence that Land legislation is not excluded unless the Federal regulation is exhaustive. Whereas the Court had previously maintained that whether a Federal regulation was exhaustive could only be determined by an evaluation of the relevant norm-complex in its entirety, there was in this case no entire norm-complex but only an inference that existing and future legislation was intended to effect a comprehensive regulation.

However, not all the more recent judgments relating to how far there is room for independent Land regulation alongside Federal legislation are unfavourable to the Länder. In its decision of a constitutional complaint in 1972[11] the First Senate harked back to the earlier decisions relating to *Art. 72 Abs. 1*

GG. At issue was the question whether the Federal regulations regarding the prohibition of outdoor advertising in built-up areas, enacted under the concurrent jurisdiction for road traffic (*Art.* 74 *Nr.* 22 *GG*), were definitive or whether they left room for the application of Land law. The Court first determined that the road traffic power necessarily included the averting of external dangers to traffic and that even though the erection of advertising hoardings was a matter of building law for which the Länder were competent this did not rule out their prohibition by Federal law if it were purely in the interests of traffic. It then observed that the mere fact that, unlike the wide-ranging restrictions outside built-up areas, the provisions for built-up areas related only to possible confusion with, or prejudice to the efficacy of, road signs was not conclusive evidence that the latter area was open to regulation by Land law. For (in a reference to the *Bavarian Public Holiday Law Judgment*) the Land legislator must not act in contradiction to a discernible Federal intention not to permit Land legislation. Since the Bund had comprehensive legislative power, the law's silence in relation to built-up areas could simply mean that in the context of a regulation which was intended to be exhaustive there were to be no further restrictions. However, from an evaluation of the not entirely unequivocal evidence the Court concluded that the Bund had not intended a definitive regulation of advertising in connection with road traffic and therefore the relevant provisions of North Rhine Westphalian building law were not *ultra vires*.

This upholding of the Land's regulations was the only reasonable conclusion. The exercise of the Federal concurrent power for advertising in connection with road traffic could hardly be allowed to exclude Land provisions relating to advertising from the point of view of public safety in general or the appearance of a street or locality. What is not clear is why the Court concentrates on the question whether the Federal regulation was intended to be exhaustive, instead of simply maintaining that the right of the Länder to prohibit advertising on grounds other than the safety and free flow of traffic was in any case untouched by *Art.* 74 *Nr.* 22 *GG*. This is particularly surprising since the path chosen by the Court involves a return to the rather exacting interpretation, characteristic of some of the earliest judgments, of when the Bund may be deemed to have 'occupied the field'.

The Bundesverfassungsgericht has thus been able to decide the question of the exclusion of the Länder by Federal exercise of concurrent powers over a wide field. The picture is far from uniform or consistent, but in view of the comparatively un-equivocal nature of some of the cases which went against the Länder it may be maintained that the Court was often con-cerned to protect the Länder's scope for independent regula-tion alongside Federal legislation.[12] Yet the limitations upon the Court must again be emphasized. The resolution of such questions as what constitutes exhaustive regulation, or whether Land provisions have *yet* been overtaken by Federal regulation, is on the whole a tidying-up operation. It has little influence on how far the Federal Government in fact chooses to legislate in the vast concurrent field. And here there is no doubt: in almost all important respects the Bund has made extensive use of its concurrent powers and so squeezed the Länder out.[13]

2 Concurrent legislation: the 'need' for Federal regulation

At first sight, *Art. 72 Abs. 2 GG* provides a much more effective basis for controlling the activities of the Bund in the concurrent field. The paragraph runs as follows:

The Federation shall have the right to legislate in these matters to the extent that a need for regulation by Federal legislation exists because:
1. a matter cannot be effectively regulated by the legislation of indi-vidual Länder, or
2. the regulation of a matter by a Land law might prejudice the interests of other Länder or of the people as a whole, or
3. the maintenance of legal or economic unity, especially the main-tenance of uniformity of living conditions beyond the territory of any one Land, necessitates such regulation.

Potentially, aggressive judicial application of the weapon thus provided could substantially restrict the range of Federal legislation. This was the expectation of the Western Military Governors, at whose insistence such a clause was inserted in the Basic Law, as they were concerned that the new federal system should not be too lop-sided in favour of the Federation. However, partly no doubt because of the origin of the provision, it was from the start widely[14] interpreted as a non-justiciable guideline for the Federal legislator. This interpretation was quickly adopted by the Constitutional Court.

The question of the prerequisites stipulated by *Art. 72 Abs.* 2 *GG* for the exercise of a Federal concurrent power first arose in the very early *South-West State Case*.[15] However, it did not appear in the main decision whereby the Court denied the Bund the right to prolong the life of the parliaments of Baden and Württemberg-Hohenzollern so long as these Länder still existed. Rather, in a supporting *obiter dictum* it was argued that even if the special territorial reorganization provisions of *Art.* 118 *GG* did give the Bund the power to extend the life of the Landtage in question, this would necessarily be a concurrent, not an exclusive, power and therefore subject to the prerequisite of a need for regulation by Federal legislation. Given the nature of the measure concerned, the only one of the reasons enumerated in *Art. 72 Abs.* 2 *GG* which could possibly apply was *Nr.* 1, that the 'matter cannot be effectively regulated by the legislation of individual Länder'. Yet even after the enactment of the Territorial Reorganization Law the Länder were quite capable of putting the measure through effectively, and indeed both had initiated the necessary procedures. Therefore, the Court concluded, regulation by a Federal law was not necessary and the law would have been in violation of *Art. 72 Abs. 2 Nr. 1 GG.*

If this first major decision of the Constitutional Court displayed a willingness to examine whether the conditions of *Art. 72 Abs. 2 GG* are met, even when this was strictly superfluous to the resolution of the matter at issue, the Court soon began to draw in its horns.

The First Senate evinced a much more restrictive approach when it touched on the question of the need for regulation by Federal law in two cases in 1952.[16] It was then squarely confronted by the issue the following year in relation to the Federal Amnesty Act of 1949.[17]. Having decided that the Bund's concurrent powers for court procedure and the execution of sentences under *Art. 74 Nr.* 1 *GG* gave it the right to declare an amnesty even for offences which in the first instance fell within

the jurisdiction of Länder courts, the Bundesverfassungsgericht declined to review the question whether the prerequisites of *Art. 72 Abs. 2 GG* were fulfilled. It now confirmed the
view adumbrated in its previous judgments that the decision as
to whether a need for regulation by Federal legislation existed
was a matter for the conscientious discretion of the Federal
legislator, which by its nature was not justiciable and was
therefore fundamentally excluded from verification by the
Constitutional Court. It conceded that in contrast to the equivalent provision in the Weimar Constitution (*Art.* 9) the prerequisites for the exercise of the right of concurrent legislation by
the Bund were individually specified in *Art. 72 Abs. 2 GG.* But
although this limited the Bund's freedom of discretion it did not
affect the essentially discretionary nature of the decision. The
question as to how far the decision was subject to review by the
Constitutional Court if the Federal legislator had mistaken the
limits of his discretion or abused it was left open on the ground
that with regard to the enactment of the Amnesty Act there was
no basis whatever for supposing that this discretion had been
exceeded or abused.

This terse statement virtually abandoning control over the
conditions under which the Bund may exercise its wide-
ranging concurrent powers is cited by the Second Senate in the
North Rhine Westphalian Salaries Case[18] and in a second amnesty-
law judgment,[19] where the Court simply declares, without
further substantiation, that it is 'not evident' that the Federal
legislator mistook the limits of his discretion or abused it.

The First Senate went into slightly more detail and subtly
modified its position in two judgments in 1961 on constitutional
complaints by customers and a shop-keeper against the provisions of the Shop-Closing Act.[20] As far as the third possible
basis for a 'need' for Federal regulation was concerned, namely
that 'the maintenance of legal or economic unity, especially the
maintenance of uniformity of living conditions beyond the
territory of any one Land, necessitates such regulation', it held
that the Bund was not restricted to legislation which merely
conformed to an already existing uniformity of living conditions. Rather, it must be permitted to strive after the degree of
uniformity in social life which it felt to be desirable. This the
Court declared to be a pre-emptive political decision which the

Bundesverfassungsgericht had in principle to respect, since it was the job of every legislator, especially in the economic field, to shape and determine living conditions. However, the Federal legislator had then to consider whether the uniformity of living conditions to which it aspired required it to take action itself. The Court accepted that the maintenance of legal or economic unity and the maintenance of the uniformity of living conditions were legal concepts (which would in principle make them now justiciable), but found them so indeterminate that their closer specification in itself went a long way towards deciding whether a Federal law was necessary to achieve them. For this reason the Constitutional Court was confined to reviewing whether the Federal legislator had in principle interpreted the terms correctly and kept within the compass defined by them.

This time the Court does not content itself with a simple assertion that the Bund has not exceeded or abused its discretion. This conclusion is reached only after enumeration of the considerations in favour of a need for Federal legislation which the Federal Government had put forward in the oral hearings. These had included the uniformity of living conditions throughout the Federal Republic, uniform economic regions extending across Länder boundaries, and the connection between shop-closing and the Federally regulated restriction of working hours. The fact that the Länder Ministers of Labour had urged Federal action had also been taken as evidence that an 'effective' regulation by the Länder as understood by *Art.* 72 *Abs.* 2 *Nr.* 1 *GG* was not possible. In the circumstances the Court had no material misgivings as to the Bund's interpretation and observance of the conditions of *Art.* 72 *Abs.* 2 *GG*.

These judgments discuss the question of Federal discretion at rather greater length and represent a doctrinal shift by abandoning all talk of non-justiciability. Yet in practice they could scarcely be said to narrow the Bund's room for manoeuvre much more than before. Indeed, with the acceptance of a need for regulation by Federal law when the latter is intended not merely to maintain but to advance or create uniformity of living conditions, it is not easy to imagine circumstances in which *Art.* 72 *Abs.* 2 *GG* could deprive the Bund of the right to legislate.

It must be recognized that this expansive approach to the criterion of uniformity of living conditions is in line with a marked tendency of West German public opinion, in contrast to that of most federal states, to object to any significant local deviation from uniform conditions, not only in the economic, taxation, or social-welfare fields but even in the archetypal Länder preserve of primary and secondary education. In these circumstances it became difficult to dispute the alleged demands of legal or economic unity and uniformity of living conditions; indeed in the eyes of many these criteria of *Art. 72 Abs. 2 Nr.* 3 took on something of the character of a positive requirement justifying most kinds of unitarist intervention.[21] However, a more restrictive interpretation in defence of the Länder's sphere of legislative action could still perfectly well have been opted for by the Court.

With regard to a possible attempt to derive a virtual *carte blanche* for the Bund from the criteria of *Art. 72 Abs. 2 GG*, what seemed a rather self-evident limitation had indeed been pointed out in the early *Building Law Case*.[22] The Court here remarked in an aside that the much emphasized need for uniform Federal regulation of the whole of building law could not in itself confer upon the Bund the necessary legislative authority; rather, such a need was an additional requirement in accordance with *Art. 72 Abs. 2 GG* when a Federal power had already been accepted in principle on other grounds.

This interpretation of 1954 appears to follow necessarily from the wording of *Art. 72 Abs. 2 GG*, which was clearly not intended as a general competence clause establishing new Federal legislative powers wherever a need for uniform regulation could be claimed. Quite different, however, are the implications in this connection of the *Federal Waterways Judgment* of 1962,[23] less than a year after the shop-closing cases. Having decided on other grounds that the Federal responsibility under *Art. 74 Nr. 1 GG* for inland waterways used for general traffic covered these waterways only *qua* traffic routes, the Court found that this followed also from the purpose of the clause concerned. It held that for the legal regulation of shipping the conditions of *Art. 72 Abs. 2 GG* for uniform regulation were met in that shipping took place on waterways which repeatedly crossed Länder frontiers and it would have intolerable consequences if the regulation of shipping differed from one stretch of water to another. The maintenance of the inland waterways used for general traffic was a necessary prerequisite for shipping traffic. But whereas the purpose of *Art. 74 Nr. 21 GG* was therefore to enable uniform regulation of shipping and shipping routes in the interest of efficient traffic, this purpose did not require uniform Federal regulation of other water-management functions of the waterways. This passage appears to reverse the otherwise undisputed rule that the assignment of a field of concurrent power comes first and only then is *Art. 72 Abs. 2 GG* applied in relation to individual cases of proposed exercise of the power. However, its import seems to have been quietly forgotten.

The general picture remains one of extreme self-restraint on the part of the Court and willingness to leave almost entirely to the discretion of the Federal Government and Parliament the question of how far they have the right to legislate in the wide field of concurrent powers.[24] This is explicitly confirmed in the *Hessian Salary Adaptation Act Case* in 1972.[25] Here the Court, while stressing the full justiciability of the duty of federal comity which it derives from the federal principle, makes a gratuitous contrast with *Art. 72 Abs. 2 GG*, the observance of whose limits cannot be reviewed by the Constitutional Court (a particularly strong formulation). Nor is it sufficient evidence of a fundamental volte-face when later in the same judgment[26] the Court declares that if the Bund forbade Hesse to adjust the emoluments of its three remaining state musicians with the status of public official (*Beamte*) to the level of the other state-employed musicians in Hesse, it would be evident and manifest that it was exceeding the discretion allowed to it in *Art. 72 Abs. 2 GG*!

In taking up this stance the Court has had the support of a substantial body of literature,[27] and there is no doubt that it is also supported by some common sense considerations. The Federal Government and Parliament are indeed better placed than a court to exercise the fundamentally political judgement as to whether a matter can be effectively regulated by individual Länder, whether this might have harmful consequences for other Länder or the population as a whole, and what is necessary for the maintenance of uniformity of living conditions. Yet although the formulation of *Art. 72 Abs. 2 GG* perhaps invites a doctrine of non-justiciability, it is not obvious that its contents are less amenable to judicial application than other imprecise yet indisputably justiciable clauses of the constitution, both inside and outside the catalogue of basic rights, not to mention 'unwritten' principles like that of federal comity.[28] In other fields the Court has not shrunk from an assessment of the presumed effects of legislation, and it is not otherwise noted for its inclination to allow the legislative bodies areas of unrestricted discretion. Doubts could be entertained, in the light of what was said earlier about political questions, as to how far the Constitutional Court was entitled to refuse judgment under an explicit if imprecise constitutional norm. Moreover, the concurrent category encompassed the bulk of legislative powers; therefore demarcation between Bund and Länder was especially important in this field. To leave the Länder, who might at least theoretically all disagree with the Bund on the question of a need for regulation by Federal legislation, with no means of redress (except in quite blatant cases) was to discard a notable instrument offered by the Basic Law for controlling an expansionist approach to Federal powers.

That there is felt in consequence to be an undue lack of restraint upon Federal legislative ardour in the broad concurrent field is shown by the final report submitted at the end of 1976 by the commission of inquiry into the constitution set up by the Bundestag in 1973.[29] It recommended a revision of *Art. 72 GG* which would permit Federal legislative action on such matters only in so far as either the legal unity necessary for bringing about equivalent living conditions within the federal territory, or economic unity or the ordered development of the federal territory cannot be achieved except by Federal legislative regulation.[30] (The expression 'maintenance of uniformity of living conditions' was discarded by the commission on the ground that neither were there uniform living conditions which could be maintained nor was their uniformity or homogeneity a realistic or even desirable goal: the criterion could therefore only be the *creation* of *equivalent*—not homogeneous—living conditions.) The express purpose of the suggested new formulation was to tighten up the existing requirement of a 'need' for Federal regulation and so make it more justiciable. Indeed it was backed up by the proposal of an explicit stipulation that on application by the Bundesrat or by a Land the Federal Constitutional Court should decide whether a Federal law conformed to these prerequisites—this despite an acknowledgement of the political nature of such a decision in view of the still necessarily indeterminate nature of the legal concepts involved.[31]

In default of such encouragement to judicial activism, the reluctance of the Constitutional Court even to attempt to define the boundaries of the Federal legislator's discretion in relation to *Art. 72 Abs. 2 GG* is perhaps understandable. But this reticence on the part of the judges has surely contributed to the fact that the Federal Government rarely wastes much time justifying legislative proposals in the light of its provisions beyond simple reference to the text. *Art. 72 Abs. 2 GG* has had practically no influence on the federal system.

3 The framework power

Another part of the legislative field which presents particular difficulties of interpretation is the right of the Bund under *Art. 75 GG* to enact 'framework' or 'skeleton' provisions (*Rahmenvorschriften*) in certain fields. The purpose of this article is clear enough. It is to enable the Bund to ensure a minimum of legal uniformity throughout the Federal Republic while leaving the Länder room within this general outline to shape the legislation in accordance with their particular needs or political predilections. The number of fields for which this arrangement is prescribed is far smaller than in the case of the concurrent power, but taken together they are by no means insignificant:

1. the legal status of persons in the public service of the Länder, communes or other corporate bodies under public law . . .;

1a. the general principles governing higher education;

2. the general legal status of the press and the film industry;

3. hunting, protection of nature, and care of the countryside;

4. land distribution, regional planning, and water management;

5. matters relating to the registration of changes of residence or domicile (*Meldewesen*) and to identity cards.
The problem is that the Basic Law offers no definition or explanation of the bald expression 'framework provisions'. It was therefore inevitable that the Constitutional Court should find itself confronted by the question of what is to be understood by framework provisions and how far they may go into detail. The line it took could have significant consequences for the federal balance of power in this area; above all, to leave the question to the free discretion of the Federal Government and Parliament, as with *Art. 72 Abs. 2 GG*, might have reduced the framework power virtually to equivalence with the concurrent power.

The problem of defining the permissible compass of framework legislation was the main issue in the dispute between the Federal Government and the Government of North Rhine Westphalia in 1954[32] as to whether the latter had had the right to pass a law fixing the salaries of its officials more favourably than those of the corresponding Federal officials. This had been explicitly forbidden in a Federal law of 1951, which had been passed under the framework responsibility for 'the legal status of persons in the public service of the Länder, communes or other corporate bodies under public law' (*Art. 75 Nr. 1 GG*, original version). But the Land Government denied the constitutionality of such framework provisions in the light of *Art. 75 Nr. 1 GG*, arguing that they left the Länder no free scope but went into detail such as could only be justified by exclusive legislative authority.

The Court took the opportunity of undertaking a closer definition of the framework power, which it emphasized was not a matter of discretion like the conditions laid down by *Art. 72 Abs. 2 GG* but a legal question to be decided by the Bundesverfassungsgericht. Yet—perhaps because of the nature of the question—it could hardly be said that it established unequivocal criteria for future application. Thus it begins with the scarcely clarificatory observation that regulation of a subject by framework provisions must not be of the same 'intensity' as in the case of concurrent legislation. However, it later proceeds to distinguish the two on the basis that when the Bund makes use of its concurrent power the Länder are to this extent debarred from the right to legislate, whereas Federal framework legislation under *Art.* 75 not merely preserves the right of the Länder to legislate but positively presupposes future Land legislation. Thus the Federal law cannot stand on its own but must be designed to be 'filled in' (*ausgefüllt*) by Land laws; it may not exhaust the subject or go into all the details, but must leave to the Länder an area which is of substance (*von substantiellem Gewicht*). In a difficult balancing act the Court argues that the Land legislation must fit into the Federal framework but must be left free to take account of the particular conditions of the Land concerned; that the Federal framework provisions need not be restricted to fundamental principles yet must not exceed their declared purpose of forming a boundary for discretionary regulation by the Länder nor confine the latter to a choice between predetermined legal alternatives. This requirement that framework laws should in content and purpose be capable of and in need of completion by Land legislation is said to obtain for two different kinds of Federal framework legislation, that consisting of guidelines for the Land legislator and that containing legal provisions directly binding on all concerned.

On turning to consider the compatibility with these criteria of the Federal provisions concerning the salaries of Land officials, the Court had first to go into the problem that the relevant Federal laws were merely amendments of the Reich salary law, which had become partly Federal and partly Land law, and to elucidate the relationship to this law of the new category of framework provisions. It then decided that the Federal guidelines imposed on the Länder's freedom of action under *Art.* 75 *Nr.* 1 *GG* might be permitted to prescribe a specific salary system but not to lay down maximum figures. There follows a noteworthy instance of the Court interpreting the provisions of the Basic Law in the light of what it regards as fundamental federal principles, since it postulates distinctions between the items of the catalogue of framework powers as to how narrowly the limits may be drawn. It recognizes in the federal state an especially strong and legitimate interest of the Länder as employers to regulate the legal status of Land officials themselves and a consequent presumption that they have freedom of decision in relation to so important an element of their individual state organization: in so far as a federal

constitution restricts this freedom, its provisions are to be interpreted narrowly, and this especially in the case of the Basic Law
with its strong federalist emphasis. In the light of this presumption the Court maintains that framework provisions must leave
the Länder room to suit the salaries of their officials to their
financial resources and to the general living standards in the
Land, as well as to evaluate jobs and determine the resulting
salary groups according to their own criteria which may differ
from those of other Länder or of the Bund. The Federal law of
1951 and the later qualifications made to it did not meet these
requirements, in particular by their stipulation that every Land
official has a corresponding Federal official whose salary is
automatically the maximum that can be paid to the Land
official. In the Court's view the possibility left to the Land of
fixing its salaries *below* the Federal maximum figures did not
realistically constitute the necessary free scope to 'fill in' the
framework provisions.

Quite apart from the theoretical possibility which had
existed of denying the justiciability of the issue, it seems not
unreasonable to suggest that if the Court had chosen to emphasize not the implications of Länder sovereignty but the need to
preserve pay equilibrium and financial stability throughout the
Federal Republic, it could have shifted the balance of the
framework power in a more unitarist direction. That it rele-
gated the latter considerations to the realm of federal comity[33]
seems indicative of a concern to protect the legislative sphere of
the Länder. Meanwhile the Court's exposition of the
framework power had left it considerable room for manoeuvre
in the future.

This thorough discussion of the framework power formed the
basis for all the Court's later decisions in this field.

One of the problems inevitably thrown up by the new federal
division of powers under the Basic Law was that of the status of
legal provisions pre-dating the foundation of the Federal
Republic. If they fell within the field of exclusive powers of
either Bund or Länder, the answer was clear enough, while *Art.*
125 *GG* laid down that old law affecting matters subject to the
concurrent legislative power of the Federation was to become
Federal law under certain conditions. But this left the technical
problem of whether the objects of the framework power were

covered by *Art.* 125 *GG*, that is whether Reich law continued in force as Federal or Land law if its content belonged to the new sphere of framework legislation. On this point the Basic Law was silent. The question was raised in two applications to the Constitutional Court in 1957 and 1958 concerning respectively provisions of the Reich Press Act and the Reich Nature Conservancy Act of 1935.[34] In neither case did the Court decide the general issue. But it referred to the *North Rhine Westphalian Salaries Case* to support the assertion that even if *Art.* 125 *GG* did extend to framework powers only a Reich regulation which as a whole had the character of a framework or general principle could have become Federal law. Neither law in question met the requirement of being designed as a whole to be 'filled in' by Land legislation. And the Court refused to pick out individual parts of the older laws as continuing in force as Federal framework provisions, on the ground that this would amount to an illegitimate judicial exercise of legislative discretion.

Decisions such as these helped substantially to preserve the Länder's room for independent action in the field of the Federal framework power.

The same is true, despite their upholding of Federal framework provisions, of two judgments which concerned, like the *North Rhine Westphalian Salaries Case*, the question of the scope left to the Länder, under Federal provisions, for adapting the law on the pay scales of public servants to local circumstances and priorities. In 1964[35] it was held that the provisions of the Federal Salary Law kept within the limits of framework legislation: although, as was the nature of framework provisions, they led to greater basic uniformity in Bund and Länder, they still left the Länder sufficient scope, for example, for increasing the number of salary groups, independent regulation of the local bonus or allowance and determination of the level of the basic salary. The Court emphasized that the Federal provisions were necessarily based on the categories of official and career existing in the Federal administration. Given that there were more such categories in the Länder, especially in the field of education, they must be assumed to be allowed the latitude to insert these sensibly and fairly into the Federal structure and to make consequent adjustments to the age-scale in the interests of equity while remaining within the spirit of the

Federal framework provisions. This conclusion upholding the relevant portion of the Salaries Act of Schleswig-Holstein was all the easier to reach because the Federal Government, in contradiction to the Schleswig-Holstein Administrative Court, explicitly accepted the constitutionality of the Land salary provisions. A similar case in 1971 concerning salary provisions in Hamburg was given similar treatment.[36]

The question of the discretion left to the Länder by Federal framework provisions was further refined by the Constitutional Court in 1969.[37] The case concerned widows of state officials who married again and the restoration, after the ending of their second marriage, of their former right to a widow's allowance deriving from their first marriage. The Federal Framework Law on State Officials provided *inter alia* that maintenance rights from the second marriage were to be set against those from the first marriage. The Court accepted the right of North Rhine Westphalia to amplify this provision by stipulating that pension rights were also to be counted against them. It was true that the mere fact that a Federal *framework* law was concerned did not necessarily mean that this particular provision must be capable of supplementation by Land legislation; for within the general regulation of a matter for which it had framework powers the Bund could make individual definitive provisions provided that the whole remained open to completion by Land legislation (this having been established in the *North Rhine Westphalian Salaries Judgment*). But in case of doubt a framework provision was by its nature to be interpreted as designed to be 'filled in'; in other words, this did not have to be stated explicitly but was to be inferred from the spirit of the individual provision, its position in the context of the statute and the development of the law relating to the subject in question. In this instance the Court saw the intention of the framework provision as enabling the widow to marry again with an easier mind yet avoiding the possibility of her receiving double maintenance on the basis of the two marriages. It therefore concluded that it made good sense not to regard the provisions for setting new maintenance rights against the former ones as definitive, particularly in a period when pensions from the statutory pension insurance normally fully guaranteed the means of subsistence and could reasonably be taken into account. This corresponded in any case to the tendency of framework provisions in the field of salary law to put upper limits on the payments or services of the Länder but to leave them free to provide less than this maximum (in this case by counting further claims against the widow's allowance). This last point is rather surprising in view of the Court's rejection of such Federally determined upper limits in relation to the salaries of Land officials, though it does not affect the tenor of the judgment here. The main point of interest is the 'in case of doubt, open to supplementation' ruling in favour of the Länder.

If a clear policy appears to emerge from this succession of decisions, a more recent judgment on the framework power can scarcely be made to conform to the trend. In the constitutional complaints of various judges against the Federal law of 1972 which altered the judges' official titles[38] one of the grounds of complaint was that the Bund did not have the power to pass a law on this subject. In particular a possible authorization under *Art. 74 Nr. 1 GG* was ruled out by *Art. 98 Abs. 3 GG*, according to which the legal status of the judges in the Länder was to be regulated by special Länder laws and the Federation was restricted to the enactment of framework provisions. Openly departing from its previous view propounded at a time when there had been no law devoted to a comprehensive regulation of official titles, the Court agreed that a question of status was concerned and not a matter of the organization and procedure of courts (*Art. 74 Nr. 1 GG*) or pay scales and pensions of members of the public service (*Art. 74a GG*). But although the Bund could enact only framework provisions concerning the status of Land judges, the Court found it had not exceeded the limits of framework regulation. Recalling its previous statements on the subject, it conceded that the Bund had made complete and definitive regulation of the official titles of Land judges, leaving the Länder no room for detailed arrangements of their own, but insisted that it had not nearly undertaken a definitive regulation of the whole subject-area of the legal status of Länder judges. Thus the Land legislator still had room for regulations of his own. The Court added in support of definitive Federal regulation of the official titles of judges in Bund and Länder that there was a 'manifest interest' in uniform regulation 'from the nature of the subject' (*von der*

Sache her)—an observation of interest in relation to the derivation of Federal powers according to the doctrine of *Natur der Sache*.[39]

There is not much sign in this decision of the principles of the *North Rhine Westphalian Salaries Case* whereby in the field of framework powers a Federal law cannot stand on its own but should in content and purpose be capable of and in need of completion by Land legislation. Moreover, the Court could have taken as its model its decisions under *Art*. 72 *Abs*. 1 *GG* as to when in the concurrent sphere the Bund could be taken to have 'occupied the field' and thereby debarred the Länder from further legislation: it had at that time divided the items of the catalogue of powers into component parts and applied *Art*. 72 *Abs*. 1 *GG* to these individual subject-areas. Here, however, it took a very substantial area of *Art*. 75 *Nr*. 1 *GG*, namely the legal status of judges in the Länder and local authorities, and accepted that a Federal law which went into exhaustive detail was a true framework law because it did not cover every aspect of the wider area.

Apart from this case, however, the consistent tendency is for the Court to protect the freedom of action of the Länder in the area of the framework power.[40] It is true that its sanctioning of individual definitive regulations within a Federal framework law, however justified on practical grounds, may have encouraged the Bund to stretch the concept of a framework perhaps unduly, for example in the Water Management Act of 1957[41] and the Act for the Standardization of the Law relating to Public Officials as revised in 1971.[42] But the disqualification of both old and new law as framework law in the earlier cases and the latitude allowed to the Länder in the later decisions for adaptation in conformity with the general spirit of the framework provisions testify to a desire to preserve for the Länder an area of real legislative, as opposed to purely executive, discretion.

4 The powers of the Bundesrat

The governments of the Länder are given a direct say in the Federal legislative process by their representation in the Bundesrat. Parallel to the unmistakable shift of power from

Länder to Bund which has taken place since 1949, this 'federalist' element in the central governmental process has come to assume an importance and exercise an influence far beyond what was originally envisaged. Its chief strength lies in its power of veto, and here attention is primarily focused not on the general right of suspensive veto which can be overridden by an equivalent majority in the Bundestag, but on the range of primary and subordinate legislation which is subject to absolute veto or, in the terms of the Basic Law, 'requires the consent of the Bundesrat'. When the individual cases where such consent is specifically required are added up, they amount to all legislation affecting the legal status of the Länder or the relationship between them and the Bund, most notably where subsequent executive action by the Länder is involved. This category of legislation has proved to be unexpectedly large and has in fact accounted for just over half of all laws since 1949. The main reason for this is that most modern legislation requires an administrative follow-up. *Art. 84 Abs.* 1 *GG* stipulates that where the Länder execute Federal laws as matters of their own concern, they shall provide for the establishment of the requisite authorities and the regulation of administrative procedures in so far as Federal laws consented to by the Bundesrat do not otherwise provide. But the need for a coordinated approach to the implementation of Federal legislation has led to the exception here provided for becoming the norm. Moreover, the increase of Federal powers has meant that the Bundesrat's influence grew correspondingly, because the exercise of a new responsibility was generally made conditional on the Bundesrat's assent. This is true, for example, of all the new powers of the Bund in the taxation and budgetary field and of the wider Federal competence for salaries in the public service created by *Art. 74a GG.*

However, it is also true to say that the Bundesrat has taken a very expansionist approach to the question of *Zustimmungs-bedürftigkeit* (the requirement of consent). This has been possible partly because the Basic Law is surprisingly cursory in its references to the role of Bundesrat consent in the legislative process and unclear as to what precisely it means for its consent to be necessary for a bill to become law. In particular, the framers of the constitution can hardly have foreseen the development whereby the inclusion in a bill of one or two minor provisions requiring Bundesrat assent was taken to entitle the Bundesrat to throw out the whole bill because it disagreed with its main tenor. Whether everything which the Bundesrat claimed to belong to administrative procedure really did so was also seriously open to doubt.

Although their activities and influence in the Bundesrat were by no means an adequate compensation for their loss of power elsewhere—after all, the federal principle requires the possibility of individual independent action, whereas the Bundesrat operates by majority decision—the opportunities which it offered the Länder were considerable. Since the extent of its power of absolute veto was also a matter of dispute between it and the Federal Government, there was clearly scope here for the Constitutional Court to exert a significant influence on the balance of power.[43]

The Bundesverfassungsgericht was confronted by the question of the powers of the Bundesrat in the first year of its existence when, in a procedure still permissible at that time, the Federal President requested an advisory opinion from the Plenum of the Court on whether the law passed by the Bundestag in execution of *Art. 108 Abs. 2 GG* required the assent of the Bundesrat.[44] The law in question concerned the administration of the income and corporation taxes, part of the revenue from which accrued to the Bund. The administration of the Federal share of these taxes had already been entrusted to the Länder revenue authorities as agents of the Federation; but this law's provisions also covered the independent administration of the Länder's share.

The Court first took the opportunity of emphasizing that against bills passed by the Bundestag the Bundesrat 'in general' possessed only a suspensive veto which could be overridden; however, in *certain* cases, where the interests of the Länder were particularly strongly affected, it had the right of absolute veto, these cases being specifically enumerated in the Basic Law. (The effectiveness of this formulation of a 'general' principle with enumerated exceptions may seem questionable in the light of the balance of enumerated and residual legislative powers between Bund and Länder.) The Court found such a right of absolute veto in the then *Art. 108 Abs. 3 Satz 2 GG* (corresponding to the present *Art.* 108 *Abs.* 2 *Satz* 2 *GG*), which prescribed that the Bund could by legislation requiring the consent of the Bundesrat lay down the procedure to be followed by the Länder revenue authorities. Several provisions of the law under consideration did precisely this. In the Court's opinion it was immaterial, as far as the Bundesrat's right of veto was concerned, who had legislative power over the taxes or to whom the revenue accrued. What mattered was only who was responsible for the administration of the taxes: if it was the *Länder* revenue authorities, then Federal legislation about the procedure they were to follow required the consent of the Bundesrat regardless of whether these authorities were performing independent Land administration or acting as agents of the Bund.

This early opinion of the Court thus gave no great comfort to those who would have liked, by narrow interpretation of the kind of law which was subject to the Bundesrat's consent, to restrict the influence of the Länder governments on the Federal legislative process. On the other hand it did indicate, for what it was worth, that the right of absolute veto was technically the exception, and it specifically left unresolved the Bundesrat's own contention, significant for future developments, that the mere fact that the law contained in effect an amendment of the earlier Fiscal Administration Act, which itself had required Bundesrat consent, sufficed to make it in turn subject to absolute veto. It could hardly be said, therefore, that it had opened the way for wholesale arrogation to itself by the Bundesrat of the right of absolute veto.

The most significant utterances of the Constitutional Court in the early years on the subject of which laws require the assent of the Bundesrat are to be found in the Second Senate's judgment of 1958 on the constitutionality of the succession of laws extending the life of the Prices Act of 1948.[45] The Prices Act, having become Federal law as from 1949, was an example of a Federal law which the Länder executed 'as a matter of their own concern' (*als eigene Angelegenheit: Art.* 83 *GG*). In these circumstances *Art.* 84 *Abs.* 1 *GG* stated that they were to provide for the establishment of the requisite authorities and the regulation of administrative procedures in so far as Federal laws consented to by the Bundesrat did not otherwise provide.

Without determining what in general might count as regulation of administrative procedures, the Court was in no doubt that the clause of the Prices Act which stipulated the method of delivery of orders made under the Act did regulate administrative procedure of the Länder and so required the consent of the Bundesrat. But in that case, the Court maintained, it was not merely the individual provision relating to administrative procedure but the whole Act that required the Bundesrat's consent. It was the law as a technical unity that under the terms of *Art.* 78 *GG* only came into being if the Bundesrat assented. If only those provisions relating to procedure were regarded as subject to absolute veto, this would give rise to virtually insuperable difficulties in the legislative process and the promulgation of laws.[46] The Court added that it had been the consistent practice of Bundestag, Bundesrat, and Federal Government to regard the whole law as requiring assent.

Having thus ruled that the administrative character of a single clause was sufficient to give the Bundesrat an absolute veto over the whole law, the Court decided that the laws which simply extended the period of validity of the Prices Act also required Bundesrat consent. The prolongation of the life of the Prices Act was equivalent to the enactment of new laws with the same content and the Court saw no reason to suppose that the life of the administrative provision should not also have been thereby prolonged.

The need for the Bundesrat's assent having been established, the problem remained that in the case of the fourth, fifth and sixth extending Acts, although the Bundesrat had voted to refrain from demanding the convening of the Mediation Committee for joint consideration of legislation (*Vermittlungsausschuss*), it had not explicitly given its consent in the usual manner. However, the Court deduced this consent from the attendant circumstances.

If, therefore, the concrete result was the upholding of the legislation in question, this judgment nevertheless gave the Court's blessing in two respects to an extensive interpretation of the circumstances in which the Bundesrat had an absolute veto. This can only have encouraged the tendency of the Bundesrat to claim that an increasingly wide range of bills was subject to its consent, so that contrary to all original expectations they came to outweigh those bills liable merely to a suspensive veto in both number and importance.[47]

It may have been awareness of this development that caused the Constitutional Court to adopt a more cautious approach during the years that followed. If the broad principle had been confirmed that any law which contained provisions governing the establishment of Länder administrative authorities or the administrative procedure of the Länder required as a whole the consent of the Bundesrat, it was still possible to be restrictive as to what provisions fulfilled this criterion. When Baden-Württemberg, Hesse, and Lower Saxony appealed against the Federal law establishing a special foundation to look after the cultural property of the former Land of Prussia,[48] they not only maintained that it transgressed the limits of Federal legislative competence but also complained that the law had been enacted without the consent of the Bundesrat, even though this had been required on several counts. But the latter argument was as unsuccessful as the former. The Court denied any requirement of Bundesrat consent under *Art. 84 Abs. 1 GG*, on the ground that the Federal legislation regulated neither the establishment of a Land authority nor administrative procedure. Rather, it merely *ended* the administrative activity of the Länder in a particular field; but this was not an encroachment upon their right, protected by *Art. 84 Abs. 1 GG*, to organize their own administration within their own sphere. Equally little sympathy was shown with the claim by the Länder that the Federal law established a Federal authority with administrative infrastructure and so under the terms of *Art. 87 Abs. 3 Satz 2 GG* required the consent of the Bundesrat. Here the Court simply declared that the organization of the new Foundation was not comparable to a direct Federal Administration with intermediate and lower-level authorities.

The Court took a similar line in the *Bank Lending Case* of 1962, in which several Länder challenged the constitutionality of the Federal Bank Lending Act.[49] Apart from their main plea on grounds of lack of legislative competence, which was also rejected by the Court, they maintained that the Act had required, but not received, the consent of the Bundesrat. However, the Court felt able to deal with their arguments in as summary a fashion as in the *Prussian Cultural Property Case*.

Thus, although the law provided for action to be taken by the recorder's courts, which were Länder institutions, these were not administrative authorities, but courts, and were therefore not covered by the requirement in *Art.* 84 *Abs.* 1 *GG* of Bundesrat consent for a Federal law regulating the procedure of Land administrative authorities. Similarly, provisions about the observance of confidentiality by those in the bank inspectorate *vis-à-vis* the Länder revenue authorities were held to belong to 'substantive' administrative law rather than to regulate the administrative procedure of the Länder revenue authorities. Again, and with specific reference to the *Prussian Cultural Property Case*, the mere repeal by the Bank Lending Act of regulations relating to the administrative procedure of Länder authorities within the meaning of *Art.* 84 *Abs.* 1 *GG* was not itself such a regulation but simply ended the Länder's administrative activity in the field of bank supervision: for this the Bundesrat's assent was not necessary. This judgment thus shows the Constitutional Court continuing to circumscribe the possibilities of claiming a right of absolute veto for the Bundesrat on the basis that a law affects in some way the administration of the Länder.

What is interesting about these cases, therefore, is not so much general pronouncements on the scope of the absolute veto as the fact that, although presented with so many arguments (some admittedly not very plausible), the Court did not seize upon any of them to establish a requirement for the consent of the Länder through the Bundesrat. Not that this more cautious approach appears to have had much influence on the tide of events. Nor did constitutional litigation on the Bundesrat's power of veto become common. It is true that the Federal authorities had no need to appeal to Karlsruhe on the question provided that the Federal President was prepared to sign a law from which the Bundesrat had withheld its consent: a challenge would have to come from the Länder. But in fact the proportion of laws passed as *Zustimmungsgesetze* ('laws carrying assent') is far from being in decline in this period.

The tide of judicial decision seemed to be beginning to turn again in favour of the Länder when in 1968 the Bundesrat itself brought an action against the Federal Government in relation to its ordinance on the certification of the authenticity of documents for foreign use under the 1961 Hague Convention.[50] The relevant clause of the Basic Law was *Art.* 80 *Abs.* 2 *GG,* according to which the consent of the Bundesrat was required, unless otherwise provided by Federal legislation, for ordinances issued pursuant to Federal laws that themselves required the consent of the Bundesrat. In the end the Court rejected the Bundesrat's case (though only by five votes to three) on the ground that the law on which the ordinance was based had indeed 'otherwise provided' for ordinances which the Federal Government was authorized to issue 'for its own sphere of business', and therefore the need for Bundesrat consent had been removed. Before this, however, it spent some time considering the arguments of the parties to the dispute and upholding the views of the Bundesrat. First of all the Court reiterated its finding in the *Price Law Case* that the Bundesrat's right of absolute veto extended not merely to the individual provisions requiring assent but to the law as a whole and again interpreted the term *Bundesgesetz* ('Federal law') as denoting a conceptual unity. From this it was inferred that all ordinances issued pursuant to such a law must also obtain the Bundesrat's assent. The Court saw the purpose of *Art.* 80 *Abs.* 2 *GG* as being to give the Bundesrat decisive influence over all norms issued in execution or supplementation of the statutory provisions whose passage had been subject to its consent. The possibility of omitting parts of a subject from the statute and leaving them to be regulated by the executive should not in its view lead to a curtailment of the Bundesrat's participation in law-making. If the Federal authorities had decided to combine norms in one law, this was at the same time a decision as to the *Zustimmungsbedürftigkeit* ('assent-requiring character') of all the norms contained in the law; it followed that all ordinances issued on the authorization of a law which required Bundesrat assent themselves required assent, regardless of whether or not it was the norms containing the authorization that had made the statute subject to the Bundesrat's assent in the first place.

The Court continued to hark back to its earlier and bolder approach to the veto power of the Bundesrat in the *Telephone Charges Case* of 1970.[51] *Art.* 80 *Abs.* 2 *GG* was again concerned, in so far as it stipulated that the consent of the Bundesrat was required, unless otherwise provided by Federal legislation, for ordinances issued by the Federal Government or a Federal Minister concerning basic rules for the use of postal and tele-communication services or charges therefor. The initiators of the relevant constitutional complaints claimed that an ordi-nance of the Federal Minister of Posts raising telephone charges offended against this article because it had been issued without the assent of the Bundesrat. It was true that the Fed-eral Postal Administration Act, which contained the necessary authorization, explicitly stated that ordinances based on it did not require the consent of the Bundesrat. But the proviso in *Art.* 80 *Abs.* 2 *GG* that Federal legislation could provide otherwise did not in the opinion of the complainants mean that the explicitly stated requirement of consent could be set aside without the consent of the Bundesrat; yet the Federal Postal Administration Act had been passed without such consent. In reply, the Federal Government maintained that the clause 'providing otherwise' did not need the assent of the Bundesrat because the cases where such assent was required had been exhaustively enumerated in the Basic Law (as the Court itself had argued in its first decision on the subject), and there was no mention in *Art.* 80 *Abs.* 2 *GG* of a requirement of Bundesrat assent in instances where Federal legislation 'provided other-wise'.

In taking the side of the complainants the Court pointed to the traditionally recognized legitimate interest of the Länder in the fares and charges for railways and postal and telecommuni-cation services: given that some allowance had been made for this in the more centralist Weimar Republic, it would run counter to the federal principle as more strongly embodied in the Basic Law, if a right of absolute veto specifically established for the Bundesrat for ordinances concerning the use of postal and railway facilities could be removed by simple Federal law without its consent. Such an interpretation, it suggested, would make the right of veto largely redundant. Moreover, the pro-viso in *Art.* 80 *Abs.* 2 *GG* about Federal legislation providing otherwise applied equally to 'ordinances issued in pursuance of Federal laws that require the consent of the Bundesrat'; but here the absurdity of allowing a later Federal law without Bundesrat assent to cancel the requirement of consent was even more manifest.

If this decision appealed convincingly to common sense, the Court still had to answer the Federal Government's case. It admitted that in its 1951 Advisory Opinion it had itself asserted that the cases in which a law needed the consent of the Bundesrat were individually explicitly enumerated in the Basic Law. It then contented itself, however, with pointing out that this was not the first time that it had accepted the necessity of Bundesrat consent where this was not explicitly laid down in the Constitution. Rather, in the *Railway Crossings Judgment*[52] it had found that while *Art.* 84 *Abs.* 2 and *Art.* 85 *Abs.* 2 *GG* authorized the *Federal Government*, with Bundesrat consent, to issue general administrative rules, they contained no prohibition(!) against a Federal law authorizing a departmental minister to issue general administrative rules; but it had concluded on federal grounds and by analogy that such an authorization could likewise only be made by a law with Bundesrat consent. With this reference to a rather weak parallel case the Court (or rather five-eighths of the Second Senate) apparently felt that it had disposed of the Federal Government's case.

The Constitutional Court thus appeared to have edged back to a position more in line with the extensive interpretation of the constitutional clauses requiring the consent of the Bundesrat which had prevailed in political practice. The need to secure the co-operation of the Länder in the implementation of legislation meant that in practice the Federal Government and Bundestag had generally not found it worth challenging the Bundesrat's claims but had preferred where necessary to come to political understandings. Indeed this flexibility had worked both ways: the Constitutional Court itself in the *Legalization of Documents Case*[53] noted that the Federal Government had issued ordinances without the Bundesrat's consent, which in the Bundesrat's opinion required it, without the latter doing anything about it; while on the other hand the Federal Government had also laid ordinances before the Bundesrat to receive its assent even when it regarded such assent as unnecessary.

Such a situation remained viable so long as the Bundesrat largely confined its role to feeding the administrative expertise of the Länder into the Federal legislative process and where necessary defending general Länder interests. It was inevitable that it should begin to break down when, after the advent of the Social Democrat/Free Democrat Coalition in 1969, the Opposition parties for the first time had a majority of the votes in the Bundesrat. Increasingly the Bundesrat became dominated by party-political considerations as the Christian Democrats began to exploit their advantage there in order to compel major concessions from the Government if it hoped to get its legislation through at all.[54] In these circumstances the question of which bills were subject to the Bundesrat's absolute veto took on a new urgency.

In the event the dissension crystallized around the issue of whether a later amendment of a law passed only with Bundesrat assent, even if it did not affect any provision which in itself required assent, nevertheless was subject to absolute veto. This was a long-standing claim of the Bundesrat, disputed by the Federal Government from the start, and legal commentators had been equally divided on the subject. The Constitutional Court had never been directly confronted by the question and even in the judgments that were most favourable to the Länder had refused to concede this claim, preferring to maintain that resolution of the issue was unnecessary for the case in hand. However, when in 1973 the Bundesrat chose to apply its absolute veto to the Fourth Pensions Insurance Amendment Act (*Rentenversicherungs–Änderungsgesetz*) and the Federal Government, denying that it required the Bundesrat's consent, proceeded with its enactment, the CDU Government of Rhineland Palatinate and the CSU Government of Bavaria appealed directly to Karlsruhe.

In this politically highly charged case,[55] therefore, the Court was not just reviewing the constitutionality of a statute but clarifying the extent of the power of the Bundesrat (and to that extent of the Opposition). In the circumstances the judges were very evenly divided. By a majority of five votes to three it was decided that not every amendment of a law that had required Bundesrat assent was for that reason alone itself in need of assent. The majority saw the purpose of the power of absolute veto as being the protection of the constitutional allocation of powers between Bund and Länder against 'systemic shifts' (*Systemverschiebungen*) which might otherwise be effected by simple legislation such as the regulation of administrative procedure under *Art.* 84 *Abs.* 1 *GG.* Thus the Pension Reform Act, whose amendment was now under dispute, had by regulating the procedure of Länder administrative authorities made an 'inroad' into the field of Länder powers which had been 'sanctioned' by Bundesrat consent. If a later amendment made no *new* inroad into the Länder preserve, i.e. no further 'systemic shift', then it did not require similar approval. Moreover, in reconversion to the Advisory Opinion of 1951, according to which the requirement of Bundesrat assent was the exception, being restricted to specifically enumerated cases where Länder interests were *particularly strongly* affected, the majority argued that the fact that most Federal laws affected Länder interests *in some way* could not be allowed to establish a general right of disallowance for the Bundesrat. This would not correspond to the constitutional arrangement whereby the Bundesrat was not a second chamber participating in the legislative process on equal terms with the 'first chamber' (a statement no doubt made with an eye to the current political situation and in fact immediately seized upon by the governing coalition).[56] The considerable increase in the number of bills requiring Bundesrat consent which would result from acceptance of the Bundesrat's claims would, the majority later declared, be contrary to the Basic Law's intention of an equilibrium between all the bodies participating in the legislative process. The view that, because the assent of the Bundesrat covered the whole law as a technical unity, every amendment also required its assent, was rejected on the basis that the Basic Law gave no grounds for supposing that a requirement of assent 'outlived' the law to which it applied and had a long-distance effect on every future amending law. Finally, the majority referred to the possibility (in fact latterly often invoked by the Federal Government) of singling out those provisions concerning the procedure of Land administration which required consent and putting them in a separate law; it pointed to the absurdity of treating the question of the veto on later amendments differently just because they happened to be included in the same law.

Most of the objections which can be raised against this judgment, which represented a victory for the Federal Government Coalition, are made unsparingly in the detailed dissenting opinion of Judges von Schlabrendorff, Geiger, and

Rinck. They rejected attempts to establish general constitutional principles—like that on 'systemic shift'—based on imputed motives of the framers of the constitution. The content of the relevant clauses of the constitution was not to be derived from a postulated general principle about the federal structure or the balance between Bund and Länder. (This despite the Court's appeal on various earlier occasions to 'the federal principle'.)[57] The current dispute in any case related only to the demarcation of the powers of two Federal organs. The dissenting opinion then pointed out that the argument that acceptance of a need for Bundesrat consent would alter the balance between the legislative bodies of the Bund depended on an arbitrary view of where that balance lay and could equally be applied vice versa. Moreover, the rule/exception relationship obtaining between bills which were subject to suspensive or to absolute veto was dismissed as being no more than an effective means of demarcation between two categories of object, as with the catalogue of legislative powers, without implying any assumptions about the number of cases belonging to either group: it therefore in no way justified the conclusion that the constitutional provisions should be interpreted in such a way as to keep the number of bills requiring Bundesrat assent as low as possible. Again, the minority opinion maintained that the amending law was not a wholly independent self-sufficient unit but had its *raison d'être* in the insertion of new law into the old statute so as to create a single new unit: the old law did not cease to exist or lose its need for Bundesrat consent, so that it was misleading to speak of a 'long-distance effect'. In the view of these three judges, to allow a 'simple' law to amend one which had required and received Bundesrat consent would be to sanction an undermining of the position of the Bundesrat and so indeed effect a shift in the balance of power between Bundesrat and Bundestag. It would enable the Bundestag majority to reach a compromise with the Bundesrat and afterwards to remould that compromise to its own advantage by amendment of those provisions which did not require Bundesrat consent.

The minority opinion further claimed to have the Court's previous judgments on its side. With reference to the *Price Law Judgment*,[58] the extension of the period of validity of a law which had required assent was seen as a special instance of amendment of the original law to create a single new unit; yet this had been judged to require the Bundesrat's assent. The dissenting judges also convincingly demonstrated that the formulation of the *Legalization of Documents Case*[59] prefigured their own view, and asserted that what went for ordinances supplementing a law that had required the Bundesrat's assent must also be valid for legislative amendments. Finally, reference was made to the *Telephone Charges Case*:[60] there it had been insisted that where *Art.* 80 *Abs.* 2 *GG* laid down a requirement of Bundesrat consent for ordinances issued in pursuance of Federal laws that had themselves required consent, it was absurd to allow a later law amending the authorization in the original law (by cancelling the requirement of Bundesrat consent) to pass without consent. But, it was now argued, if this applied to one sort of amendment it should apply to all.

At the end, the dissenting opinion in effect (though perhaps unintentionally) takes back most of what it has given to the Bundesrat in a passage rejecting the majority verdict's claim that it was absurd to assess the veto power on amendments differently according to whether procedural provisions were included in the same law as material provisions or put in a separate law. In agreeing with the majority verdict (as against the Bundesrat's own view) that the Federal legislator is free to choose whether or not to enact the procedural provisions separately, but accepting that he must reckon with greater obstacles in the one case than in the other, the dissenting judges are extending an open invitation to make a general practice of treating the necessary procedural aspects in a separate law in order to reduce the Bundesrat's control over substantive provisions. This is logical, as the dissenting judges insist, but it could erode the Bundesrat's power even more than the majority verdict.[61]

Having ruled that the Fourth Pensions Insurance Amendment Act was not unconstitutional just because it amended a law which had required the consent of the Bundesrat, the Court had to decide whether the amending law itself contained provisions relating to the procedure of Land administration. Here it was again divided, this time straight down the middle. Four judges took the view in particular that the clause providing for a restoration of the right to a premature old-age pension, after cessation of employment or appropriate reduction of earnings, *upon the filing of an application*, did not constitute a regulation of the administrative procedure of the Länder. The other four judges thought that both this and other provisions were of an at least partly administrative nature; but under the rules of the Federal Constitutional Court Act in a stalemate the disputed norm or norms received the benefit of the doubt.

On one part of the judgment unanimity did prevail, namely the Court's list of cases in which amendments of *Zustimmungsgesetze* required Bundesrat assent.[62] This included the two obvious and unchallenged cases where the amendment itself contained new provisions requiring assent or where it affected regulations of the original law which had given rise to the requirement of assent. To these the Court added the case of an amendment which, though not explicitly affecting those provisions relating to administrative procedure, nevertheless made innovations which substantially altered their significance and range. This bow in the direction of the four judges who had held the Pensions Insurance Amendment Act to require Bundesrat assent in its own right is no doubt justified in its aim of preventing covert modification of administrative provisions without the Bundesrat's approval. But it opens up the prospect of a further range of disputes about how 'substantial' particular alterations are.

On the whole, however, the Court had, despite internal dissensions, effectively resolved this aspect of the long-standing dispute about the powers of the Bundesrat. It had done so in a way that was perhaps not wholly in line with its (again reiterated) older theory that a law containing only some norms requiring consent in themselves was nevertheless subject in its entirety to absolute veto. The decision may also have opened up the possibility of the Bundestag majority outflanking a compromise forged with the Bundesrat by later veto-free amendment. But the Court's solution was probably politically necessary. It is true that the increase in the number of laws requiring Bundesrat consent was regarded by some as a (scarcely adequate) *quid pro quo* for the relentless expansion of Federal regulation at the expense of the Länder, especially in the administrative field. But in view of the Opposition's majority in the Bundesrat an excessive expansion of the opportunity for absolute veto might create a situation in which the Government could apparently act only by leave of the Opposition. The decision of the Constitutional Court was no more than a partial pruning of the growth of the power of absolute veto. But its significance was far from being largely psychological. For with the passage of time an increasing proportion of laws are amendments of former legislation, and the increasing complexity of the law may mean that a new statute in fact amends a large number of laws; so that, had the Constitutional Court decided otherwise, a subsidiary administrative provision in one of these would have sufficed to subject the amendment of all the rest to the Bundesrat's absolute veto. To this extent the Court, in deciding 'against the Länder', was in fact acting to protect the viability of the Federal Government and the efficient functioning of the political process.[63]

Not long afterwards, in the even more controversial *Abortion Case*,[64] the issue of the Bundesrat's power of veto again played a minor role. The CDU-governed Länder got short shrift with their request that the First Senate reconsider the Second Senate's majority verdict on the circumstances in which amendment laws require consent. But several other arguments were also advanced, though without success. The Court rejected the view that the reform law in question itself contained provisions subject to absolute veto in that it made a prior visit to an authorized advice centre a condition of termination of pregnancy. This was held not to constitute a regulation of the establishment of administrative authorities or of administrative procedure: rather, the establishment and operation of the advice centres was left entirely in the hands of the Länder. Nor would the Court accept the argument based on its affirmation in the *Pensions Insurance Amendment Case* that Bundesrat assent was required for an amendment which, though not explicitly affecting administrative provisions, nevertheless made innovations which substantially altered their significance and range. This was in no way pertinent, since the Länder in this case retained considerable administrative freedom of action. Finally, in response to the complaint that allocating the abolition of criminal penalties for abortion and the provisions relating to advice to two separate laws was an artificial and illegitimate ploy to elude a Bundesrat veto of the former, the Court referred to its previous practice of assuming the legitimacy of such partition of a legislative project into several statutes.

In this case, therefore, which signalized some of the question-marks left by the *Pensions Insurance Amendment Judgment*, the judges of the First Senate staunchly defended their colleagues' restriction of the powers of the Bundesrat. They thus confirmed the re-emergent inclination of the Constitutional Court, after several oscillations, to discourage undue expansion of the opportunity for the majority of the Länder governments acting together to frustrate Federal legislative intentions.

The most recent decision on the powers of the Bundesrat, however, demonstrates a renewed determination on the part of the Second Senate to uphold its veto rights. The case in question is the *Substitute Civilian Service Case* of 1978.[65] It was initiated by a request for abstract judicial review of the controversial Military Service Amendment Act of July 1977, which had put the alternative community (or 'civilian') service virtually on an equal footing with traditional military service. As has already been seen,[66] the proceedings mainly revolved around the issue of the law's incompatibility with basic rights and other constitutional provisions. But the applicants had also submitted that the Military Service Amendment Act as a technical legislative unity had not been enacted in accordance with the provisions of the Basic Law because the Bundesrat had not given its assent. The Constitutional Court agreed.

The relevant constitutional provision was *Art.* 87b *Abs.* 2 *GG*, which concerns the general execution of laws concerning defence including recruitment for military service and protection of the civilian population. In its first sentence it authorizes ordinary Federal laws with the consent of the Bundesrat to depart from the general principle of *Art.* 83 *GG* ('The Länder shall execute federal laws as matters of their own concern in so far as this Basic Law does not otherwise provide or permit') and to provide that they shall be carried out, wholly or in part, either by means of direct Federal administration having its own administrative substructure or by the Länder acting as agents of the Federation. In accordance with this clause the original Civilian Service Act had, with the blessing of the Bundesrat, assigned its execution to direct Federal administration. But the question was: could this earlier consent by the Bundesrat be held to cover the administration of the civilian service in its new scope and character? Or did the new regulations on the recognition of conscientious objectors entail its expansion into an alternative form of service on a par with military service and thereby effect a new shift of administrative powers to the detriment of the Länder which required fresh Bundesrat assent? For in that case the Bundesrat's veto could not have been overridden.

The Court pointed out that the first sentence of *Art.* 87b *Abs.* 2 *GG* contained one of the instances explicitly and exhaustively enumerated in the Basic Law in which the Bundesrat was given an absolute veto because the sphere of interest of the Länder was particularly strongly affected. It then went on to declare that under this provision the assent of the Bundesrat was required not only for a Federal law by which such a departure from the general rule of the executive prerogative of the Länder was authorized for a particular subject-matter for the first time: the requirement of Bundesrat assent also arose when an administrative responsibility previously transferred with the consent of the Bundesrat to direct Federal administration or to administration by the Länder as agents of the Bund was altered or extended by an amending law to such a degree that in the light of the principle of *Art.* 83 *GG* it was equivalent to a fresh transfer of executive responsibilities to the Federation. The Court cited its doctrine expounded in the *Pensions Insurance Amendment Case* that if a later amendment to a law passed with the consent of the Bundesrat made no new inroad into the administrative preserve of the Länder, i.e. no new 'systemic shift', then it did not itself require assent. By development of that doctrine, it said, such a new inroad was made when an amendment of substantive provisions fundamentally transformed the legal quality of the responsibility conferred on the Federation by the original legislation and thereby substantially altered the significance and scope of the provisions concerning the administrative responsibilities of the Federation from that which had been sanctioned by the original Bundesrat assent.

That was, in the Court's view, the situation in the case in hand. The previous legislation on the substitute civilian service, which had been passed and several times amended with the consent of the Bundesrat, had provided for direct Federal administration by an autonomous Federal higher authority and a Federal Civilian Service Commissioner and for delegation of some administrative tasks to administrative units of the Länder acting as agents of the Federation. This arrangement was not changed by the new Military Service Act. But the transformation of civilian service into what amounted to an independent form of community service alongside military service was held to entail a much larger intake and to widen the scope of the work both of the Federal Office for Civilian Service and of the Länder agency administration. This was found to be equivalent to a fresh transfer of powers for implementing the Civilian Service Act. The new law thus effected a new systemic shift in the federal structure which was inadmissible without renewed assent by the Bundesrat.

That the Constitutional Court was not bound to reach this decision is shown by the dissenting opinion of Judge Hirsch. He maintained that the amending law altered nothing in the sphere of Länder jurisdiction and effected no systemic shift to their detriment: it merely caused a temporary quantitative shift in the burden of work between the Länder agencies and the vetting offices which were in any case under direct Federal administration. Making the substitute service accessible to a different but still unknown number of 'non-genuine' conscientious objectors did not amount to a fundamental transformation of the civilian service and thus could not justify the finding that without Bundesrat assent the law was *ultra vires*.

This dissenting opinion reveals the scope for dispute and hence for genuine judicial choice which had been left by the *Pensions Insurance Amendment Case* and in particular by the Court's acceptance that Bundesrat assent was necessary for amendments which did not explicitly affect administrative provisions but yet indirectly brought about a substantial alteration of their significance and range. The *Civilian Service Judgment*, indeed, extended this doctrine to cover not only amendments by which Länder administrative procedures or authorities were indirectly affected (as under *Art. 84 Abs.* 1 *GG*), but also changes in the scope of a matter for which executive responsibility had already been wholly or partially transferred to the Federation. The Second Senate reapplied its not uncontroversial concept of 'systemic shift' and showed that it was capable of wide interpretation. And by this means it in turn substantially mitigated the effect of its own previous decision circumscribing the rights of the Bundesrat. In the process, the ability of the Federal Opposition to thwart the governing coalition on a major political issue was upheld.

The major political importance of these judgments does not lie in their response to a situation in which legislation initiated by the Federal Government is consistently thrown out by an Opposition-dominated Bundesrat. In fact very few laws have totally come to grief at the hands of the Bundesrat.[67] Much more frequently an accommodation is reached in the Mediation Committee (*Vermittlungsausschuss*), which is usually convened at the Bundesrat's instigation.[68] But it is precisely via the joint deliberations and enforced compromises in the Mediation Committee (even though the results are not binding on either legislative organ) that the Opposition is able to modify and water down substantial parts of the Federal Government's programme, and its power to do so depends on the ultimate possibility of the refusal of assent to a bill. For this reason the general question of the proper extent of the Bundesrat's power of absolute veto seems likely, despite its partial clarification by the Constitutional Court, to remain a thorny political and legal issue.

This chapter has concentrated primarily on legislative, as opposed to administrative, powers. That does not mean, however, that the Constitutional Court has hardly been concerned with the latter. It has been seen that several problems about what constitutes regulation of administrative procedure have confronted the Court in the guise of the question whether the assent of the Bundesrat was required for Federal legislation. Moreover, other aspects of the demarcation of administrative powers arise in the following chapters in relation to the so-called presumption in favour of Länder jurisdiction, the recognition of tacit Federal powers and the principle of federal comity.

Nevertheless it must be admitted that the decisions of the Court with regard to administrative powers are markedly less prolific than in the legislative sphere and a number of substantial issues have barely been touched upon.[69] One example is the possibility of so-called 'mixed administration' (*Mischverwaltung*), which is generally assumed to be ruled out by the fact that the Basic Law provides for quite separate, even if in some respects dovetailing, Federal and Länder administrations. In the *Transportation Tax Administration Case* the Court states that the constitution prohibits 'mixed administration' in so far as it does not explicitly permit it, but it is accepted that in individual cases such an arrangement is permissible under the terms of the Basic Law.[70] An earlier judgment on the administration of family allowances describes as 'inadmissible mixed administration' a situation in which a Federal authority is set over a Land authority in a relationship of hierarchical superiority (*übergeordnet*) or collaboration between Federal and Länder authorities takes place by means of requirements of assent.[71] The judgment in the *Financial Subsidies Case* appears to restrict further the scope of any permissible 'mixed administration',[72] but it could hardly be said that the Court had established a clear dividing-line between legitimate co-operation on the part of Federal and Länder administrative authorities and inadmissible mixed administration.

A separate treatment of the Constitutional Court's adjudication in matters relating to administrative powers is thus rendered superfluous on the one hand by the fact that a number of such issues are covered in the examination of the various aspects of the Court's decision-making in this and succeeding chapters and on the other hand by the paucity of judgments dealing with other problems in this field.[73]

The present chapter has examined the decision-making of the Constitutional Court in four important areas of uncertainty or controversy within the federal order: the extent to which the Länder may be excluded from legislation by Federal 'occupation of the field'; the degree of constraint upon Federal exercise of concurrent legislative powers exerted by the requirement of a 'need' for Federal regulation; the compass of the framework legislative power, and the veto rights of the Bundesrat. It has shown that much of its work is of a relatively nit-picking, or at least 'interstitial' nature, but that cumulatively it can have a substantial impact on constitutional practice and the scope of political action, while sometimes individual judgments are of immediate political significance. The picture which emerges of the Court's influence on the development of the federal system is not a uniform one, since although the decisions on Federal 'occupation of the field' and the requirement of Bundesrat assent may be judged on the whole, and those on the framework power quite clearly, to have promoted the interests of the Länder, the contrary is true of the question of the 'need' for Federal regulation. The advisability of a carefully qualified assessment has thus been confirmed.

The survey also confirms the impression of a fundamentally pragmatic approach on the part of the Constitutional Court. It often appears to be better disposed to casuistic exercises on points of detail than to the elaboration of a firm and consistent doctrinal position. It may indeed be that in the absence of a dependence on the rule of precedent, and in the context of a detailed constitution, a rather messy and unpredictable pragmatism represents a shrewd assessment of the most effective way for a court to clear a path through the 'political thicket'. However, it remains in the next two chapters to examine the Court's recourse to special interpretative methods, sources, and principles which might enable it to pursue a relatively steady line in federal judgments.

CHAPTER VI

The Admission of Unwritten Powers and the Presumption in Favour of the Länder

1 Introduction

A glance at the federal systems of the English-speaking world suggests that perhaps the most important means by which Supreme Courts can develop or indeed manipulate the constitutional provisions allocating powers to the two levels of government is the doctrine of implied powers. The most obvious example is the wide use which has been made by the United States Supreme Court, particularly in the field of interstate commerce, of the clause authorizing Congress 'to make all Laws which shall be necessary and proper for carrying into Execution the foregoing powers. . . .'[1] But Australia has also, in addition to a favourable common law tradition, an explicit provision[2] for a Commonwealth 'incidental power', which is freely invoked though with rather more self-restraint than in the United States.[3] And even in Canada, where there is no such explicit provision and the British North America Act attempted an exhaustive distribution of powers between Dominion and Provinces, inevitably some subjects have been found to be incidental to a Dominion power in one respect and to a Provincial power in another.[4]

In West Germany there is no explicit provision for implied or incidental powers, but the Constitutional Court has not thereby been prevented from their consideration.

Although there may theoretically be a distinction between 'broad construction' of explicitly assigned powers and recognition of implied or incidental powers, in practice the latter may be simply a convenient legal guise in which to cloak the former.

Sometimes it may be more convincing to attach one field of competence to another as being a necessary means to an end or standing in some other inseparable relationship with it, than baldly to define the one power as including the other. The possibilities of either are likely to be affected by the general provisions of the constitution, its precision, detail, and flexibility, and other considerations already suggested in relation to 'creative' decision-making. It will therefore be necessary to place the discussion of implied or 'unwritten' powers in the context of the general approach to broad construction.

Some doubt could be cast on the right of the Federation to claim unwritten powers by *Art.* 30 *GG* which declares the Länder to be competent in so far as the Basic Law has not assigned the exercise of governmental powers and the discharge of governmental functions to the Bund. The equivalent provision in the 10th Amendment of the US Constitution did not prevent either broad construction or extensive recognition of implied powers, but the Basic Law, apart from its more detailed and exhaustive allocation of powers, has no 'necessary and proper' clause and is not set in a tradition of judge-made law. Moreover, there is a difference in the formulation of the Federal powers in the two constitutions. The American constitution gives Congress the power to *do* certain things—'to lay and collect taxes', 'to regulate commerce with foreign nations', etc.—a formulation which positively invites invocation of the 'necessary and proper' clause and the kind of argument put forward in the *Federalist Papers:* 'No axiom is more clearly established in law, or in reason, than that wherever the end is required, the means are authorized; wherever a general power to do a thing is given, every particular power necessary for doing it is included.'[5] The same form of reasoning is taken up by Chief Justice Marshall in *McCulloch* v. *Maryland:*[6]

The power of creating a corporation, though appertaining to sovereignty is not, like the power of making war, or levying taxes, or of regulating commerce, a great substantive and independent power, which cannot be implied as incidental to other powers, or used as a means of executing them. It is never the end for which other powers are exercised, but a means by which other objects are accomplished. (at 407).

Let the end be legitimate, let it be within the scope of the constitution, and all means which are appropriate, which are plainly adapted to that end, which are not prohibited, but consist with the letter and spirit of the constitution, are constitutional. (at 421)

This style of reasoning comes much less naturally to German constitutional lawyers, not only for the general reasons already mentioned, but also because the Federal powers are cast in terms of subject-matters or areas:

The Federation shall have exclusive legislative power over: . . . (foreign affairs as well as defence including the protection of the civilian population. . . currency, money and coinage . . . the unity of the customs and commercial territory . . . the freedom of movement of goods, etc.)[7]

Concurrent legislative powers shall extend to the following matters: [—e.g.] the law relating to economic matters (mining, industry, supply of power, crafts, trades, commerce, banking, stock exchanges, and private insurance).[8]

On the one hand this allocation of areas of competence already includes much of what would have to be inferred as 'implied' or 'resulting' powers in the United States, and the means/end question is far less likely to arise. On the other hand the horizontal division of powers in German federalism, whereby executive authority is generally assigned to the Länder, places greater restrictions on what can be read into an explicit Federal power as necessary and proper to its execution.

2 The presumption in favour of the Länder

The implications of *Art.* 30 *GG*, and of the restatement of its basic principle with respect to legislative power in *Art.* 70 *GG* and execution of Federal laws in *Art.* 83 *GG*, are raised in several judgments of the Bundesverfassungsgericht.

(i) The so-called *Boiler Judgment*[9] concerned a claim by the Land of North Rhine Westphalia that the Federal Minister of Labour had violated its rights under *Art.* 30 and 83 *GG* by issuing licences to manufacturers of boilers under former Reich regulations which had become Federal law. The Court agreed that under the articles in question the power to grant licences, being an administrative act, fell to the Länder and not to the Bund unless the Basic Law provided or permitted otherwise. Since the matter in question was not an object of direct Federal administration under *Art.* 86 ff. *GG,* the only question was whether the Basic Law 'tacitly' permitted otherwise. But the Court could only accept this in exceptional cases where full execution of a Federal law could not be achieved, or its full purpose could not be realized, by Länder administration. A right to execute Federal laws could not be claimed by the Federal Government merely on the ground that this would be more expedient in the particular case or execution by the Länder would not lead to uniform administrative practice. The Court recognized that the uniform validity of legal provisions must not be rendered illusory by implementation which varied substantially from Land to Land. But it preferred to refer the Federal Government to its written powers: before it started claiming a right to implement Federal laws, it must first exhaust the possibility, provided by *Art.* 84 *Abs.* 2 *GG,* of securing uniform Länder administrative practice by issuing general administrative rules. This judgment thus recognized the possibility of tacit or implied Federal administrative powers, but defined the conditions so strictly as to make it unlikely that they could be met.

(ii) In the *Television Judgment,* with reference to the disputed broadcasting power, the Court emphasized that 'as a general rule' (*in der Regel*) Federal legislative powers could be based only on explicit conferment by the Basic Law and in case of doubt there was no presumption in favour of a Federal power; rather, the taxonomy (*Systematik*) of the Basic Law demanded a strict interpretation of *Art.* 73 ff. *GG.* In any case, the Court argued, broadcasting was also a cultural phenomenon and in view of what it saw as the basic federalist decision of the constitution whereby cultural affairs belonged to the domain of the Länder, it was particularly inadmissible in that sphere, in default of a sufficiently clear exceptional provision in the constitution, to assume that the Bund was competent. Later it made clear that *Art.* 30 *GG* covered every governmental activity in discharge of public functions, regardless of whether it made use of public or private law and whether it took the form of implementation of legislation (*gesetzesakzessorisch*) or purely executive action (*gesetzesfrei*). In both respects, therefore, the Federal Government's claim that its establishment by executive agreement of the private-law limited television company 'Deutschland-Fernsehen-GmbH' did not fall foul of provisions of *Art.* 30 *GG* was rejected.[10]

(iii) The comments of the *Television Judgment* on the presumption in favour of the Länder are repeated in the judgment on the validity of the 1960 Federal Act for the Prevention of Pollution of the Federal Waterways.[11] On the basis of this presumption the Court held that apart from the Federal framework power in respect of water management (*Art.* 75 *GG*) the Länder were responsible for the passing of regulations in the field of water law. It had already shown that the Federal concurrent authority under *Art.* 74 *Nr.* 21 *GG* for 'inland waterways used for general traffic' could not be extended to cover questions of the water supply with regard to the inland waterways; yet otherwise there was no sufficiently clear provision in the catalogues of powers in the Basic Law such as would be necessary to create an exception to the basic rule of Länder competence. Essentially the Court was saying that the proof required for a Federal power could only come from the constitutional text itself.

(iv) In a decision on the constitutionality of a residence tax levied by local authorities on the basis of an enabling regulation of the former Land of Württemberg-Hohenzollern[12] the Court rejected the view of the Federal Government, of the Federal Administrative Court and of a substantial body of literature[13] that the catalogue of Federal and Länder taxes in *Art.* 105 *GG* (in its then existing form) contained an exhaustive enumeration of classes of taxation and to this extent restricted the powers of the Länder. The Federal Government had argued on this basis that any new tax must be attributed to that class of taxation with which it showed most affinity. The Constitutional Court, however, maintained that not only would this require a manipulation of categories to accommodate existing local taxes; it also overlooked the fact that *Art.* 105 *GG* intended only to determine and delimit the Bund's exclusive legislative responsibility for customs matters and fiscal monopolies and its concurrent authority for taxation, whereas it did not mention the Länder's legislative powers in the taxation field but rather assumed them as self-evident. This was natural in view of *Art.*

70 *Abs.* 1 *GG,* which was the fundamental rule of the federal constitution for every kind of legislation, including tax law. The reasons why the demarcation of jurisdiction between Bund and Länder in the latter field was dealt with in Section X of the Basic Law, whereas *Art.* 70 *GG* stood at the beginning of Section VII, were purely editorial. For Section X too was based on the principle that in the field of legislation the Bund had only the powers assigned to it and otherwise the Länder were responsible. If therefore *Art.* 105 *GG,* contrary to *Art.* 70 *Abs.* 1 *GG,* had wished to leave the Länder, apart from concurrent powers, only the right to levy taxes on consumption and traffic which had purely local effect, this would have to be plainly inferable from the text. Yet apart from providing that taxes on consumption and traffic did not fall within the Federal concurrent competence if they had only local validity, the article had nothing to say about Länder powers of legislation. When taken in conjuction with *Art.* 70 *GG, Art.* 105 *GG* thus left the Länder free to invent and regulate such taxes as it did not assign to the sphere of Federal legislation. This obdurate defence of Länder powers in the face of prevailing legal opinion by reference to the principle of *Art.* 70 *Abs.* 1 *GG* forms an interesting contrast to some of the Court's applications of the concept of powers implied by association or affinity.[14]

(v) In the course of the judgment on the constitutionality of the Federal Youth Welfare Act,[15] the latter's authorization of the Federal Government to *promote* efforts in the field of welfare, interpreted as meaning the provision of Federal funds, was construed as covering a governmental function within the meaning of *Art.* 30 *GG.* This made it a matter for the Länder in so far as the Basic Law did not otherwise provide or permit. Since it did not explicitly do so the only question was whether it tacitly permitted otherwise. The Court repeated its comments from the *Boiler Judgment* about the admissibility of such an assumption only in the exceptional case where full execution of a law could not be achieved through Land administration. This would be an instance of a Federal responsibility deriving 'from the intrinsic nature of the matter concerned'.[16] In the case of the Youth Welfare Act these strict conditions would be fulfilled only where the Federal Government promoted measures of a clearly supraregional character, such as by their very nature could not be promoted effectively by one Land alone. This would apply to central institutions covering the Federal territory as a whole or to all-German or international ventures, but such Federal competence could not extend to the promotion of regional or local measures.

(vi) In 1969 a constitutional complaint was made against a Federal law for the protection of the professional title of *Ingenieur*. [17] One of the main grounds of appeal was the lack of Federal power to enact a statute which, it was claimed, only marginally affected the law relating to economic matters for which the Bund was responsible under *Art. 74 Nr.* 11 *GG* but rather merely laid down conditions for assuming a title and indirectly regulated the educational system for engineers, a matter of Länder responsibility. Again the Bundesverfassungsgericht took the opportunity to stress that in contrast to the Reich Constitution of 1871 and the Weimar Constitution a generous interpretation of the Federal powers listed in the Basic Law in *Art.* 73 to 75 was ruled out by the general primacy of the Länder established by *Art.* 30 and 70 *Abs.* 1 *GG*. From this starting-point the Court was able to determine that the Federal law in question was not concerned primarily with clarity in commercial intercourse and confidence in the training of a business partner calling himself 'engineer', since it permitted all those who had formerly conducted business under the title to continue to do so on the simple condition of registration. Nor had the law attempted to define the substance of the professional activity of the engineer; yet only in this context, not in isolation, could its provisions concerning the use of the title *Ingenieur* be seen as covered by the Bund's right under *Art.* 74 *Nr.* 11 *GG* to regulate the practice of professions 'in economic life'. There can be little doubt that if the Court had not taken the residual power of the Länder so seriously as demanding a restrictive interpretation of Federal powers, it could easily have come to the opposite conclusion. [18]

(vii) The Court's insistence on the presumption in favour of the Länder and the need for a strict interpretation of Federal legislative powers was given another airing in the same year in a concrete review of norms concerning the right of the Land of Baden-Württemberg to exact dues from the Federal Railways and Federal Post Office. [19] Land law specifically excepted these bodies from the general exemption accorded to Federal authorities, yet Federal laws relating to the Bundesbahn and Bundespost expressly provided that for purposes of payments to Bund, Länder, or local authorities they should be treated no differently from other Federal authorities. The question of the compatibility of the Land law with the Federal laws was left aside by the Court as relevant only if the Federal laws were themselves judged to be compatible with the Constitution. But this was found not to be the case. Adverting again to *Art.* 70 *Abs.* 1 *GG*, the need for Federal powers to be individually included in the definitive catalogue of *Art.* 73 ff. *GG*, and the need for a strict interpretation of this catalogue in the light of the basic principle of Länder competence, the Court pointed out that the Basic Law did not explicitly confer on the Bund the right to issue directions as to when and under what circumstances the Länder could impose administrative charges. Rather, the general right of the Länder to determine the procedure of their own administrative authorities must be taken to include the right to differentiate on pertinent grounds between those who occasioned administrative action as to whether or not they should be granted general exemption from administrative charges. In particular, the exclusive Federal legislative responsibility under *Art.* 73 *Nr.* 6 and 7 *GG* for federal railways and postal services did not cover the right to determine their liability to pay administrative dues to the Länder. This responsibility encompassed all questions which were essential to the maintenance and performance of the traditional services of the Bundesbahn and Bundespost. But whether they had to pay dues for administrative action by Länder authorities did not directly affect the operation of these traditional services. Once again, therefore, though in a rather more unequivocal case, the presumption in favour of the Länder was adduced against an extensive interpretation of a Federal power.[20]

Such uncompromising application of the basic principle of *Art.* 30 *GG* is by no means universally regarded as incumbent upon the Court. Some constitutional lawyers have pointed to the wording of *Art.* 30 *GG*, 'The exercise of governmental powers and the discharge of governmental functions shall be the responsibility of the Länder in so far as this Basic Law does not otherwise prescribe or permit', and have argued that the word 'permit' (*zulässt*) leaves a loophole for tacit or unwritten Federal powers, though others[21] see it as referring only to explicit authorizations for the Bund to exercise a particular power or function. The foregoing examples show how cautious the Constitutional Court has been on the whole in its approach to this loophole. There is in any case no mention of 'permitting' when the principle is reiterated with respect to legislative power in *Art.* 70 *GG*: 'The Länder shall have the right to legislate in so far as this Basic Law does not confer legislative power on the Federation.' In view of the clear intention to provide an exhaustive enumeration of Federal powers it is only reasonable to take *Art.* 30, 70, and 83 *GG* as meaning that the burden of proof is on the Bund; the question is what may legitimately count as proof. Thus, for example, authors such as Maunz[22] argue that the Federal powers are conceived by the Basic Law as exceptions which must be construed narrowly. Others[23] countered that in practice they had never been the exception, and even if they were technically the exception this was not an automatic reason for assuming that they must be interpreted narrowly. In the light of such divergent views the Bundesverfassungsgericht was plainly not bound to take the presumption in favour of the Länder to mean that a Federal power could be based only on narrow textual criticism of the catalogue of powers. It need not rule out other traditional aids to interpretation such as consideration of the general context and coherence of the constitution, the origin and development of the constitutional provision concerned, and even teleological considerations of the means by which fulfilment of the recognized purpose of the provision is possible. Thus one might argue that the effect of *Art.* 30 *GG* is only that if in the light of all these considerations there is still doubt, then the competence belongs to the Länder. But all these methods open up much greater possibilities of broad construction of Federal powers to cover aspects which the wording of the Basic Law does not at first sight suggest, and the Court may have seen this as sufficient reason for trying to shield the area of Länder powers by taking a strict view of *Art.* 30 *GG*.

The line taken by the Constitutional Court on the question of a broad construction of Federal rights or tacit Federal powers is, admittedly, not always consistent with the picture given by

the above examples. Thus only a fortnight after the *Federal
Waterways Judgment* (15 November 1962) the Court is to be
found saying: 'It is also in the interests of the Länder that the
interpretation of Federal powers should not be as narrow as
possible but should do justice to their meaning.'[24] This occurs
in a judgment whereby 'Reich property', which under *Art.* 134
Abs. 1 *GG* became on principle Federal property, was to be
taken as including not merely the assets but also the liabilities
of the former German Reich. Such a view is taken on the basis of
pragmatic and common-sense arguments such as a presumed
desire to avoid uncertainties and risks for the future financial
position of Bund and Länder and arguments of equity towards
the creditors of the Reich. The Court argues that this extensive
interpretation of Federal responsibility according to the sense
and purpose of *Art.* 134 *Abs.* 1 *GG* in default of any other
constitutional provision concerning the Reich's liabilities is in
the interests of the Länder. In particular if—as in the case of
Art. 134 *Abs.* 4 *GG*, by which details are to be regulated by a
Federal law requiring the consent of the Bundesrat—the Basic
Law contains as well as a reference to the simple legislator a
regulation in the Bund's favour, the compass of the Federal
responsibility cannot be construed more narrowly just because
the legislative power of the Länder is thereby correspondingly
restricted. The Court admitted that in the case in question this
issue presented no problem since it could not seriously be
maintained that the liabilities of the Reich could be regulated
by Land laws.

One can also discern a willingness, in the case of major
Federal powers which are broadly formulated and relatively
free from qualifications, to recognize marginal or peripheral
areas of governmental activity as being covered by them.
Perhaps the most obvious example is the law relating to
economic matters.[25] Here a broad construction could seriously
erode the powers of the Länder. Yet in its early decision on the
Federal Law on Investment Assistance[26] the First Senate ruled
that the legislative power of the Bund was not limited to regulation of those branches of the economy specifically enumerated
in the relevant paragraph. (Rather, it extended also to laws
which intervened to manage and direct economic life; and the
Investment Assistance Act was such a law, since its aim was to

divert capital from one area of the economy to another for purposes of investment.) In the light of the Court's invocation elsewhere of *Art.* 30 and 70 *GG* it could perfectly well have insisted on a narrow interpretation and argued that otherwise there would have been no point in including the list of branches of economic activity in *Art.* 74 *Nr.* 11 *GG* at all. Then in its judgment on the validity of Federal laws for the temporary regulation of the establishment of chemists' shops[27] the Court went so far as to declare that it was the demonstrable intention of the framers of the Constitution to give the Bund as wide an economic power as possible. This was then used to underpin the finding that there was no indication that the subcategory 'trades' (*Gewerbe*) in *Art.* 74 *Nr.* 11 *GG* was to be denied its traditional wide interpretation, which included pharmacies, notwithstanding their special medical characteristics.

An even earlier example of generous interpretation of the Federal economic power occurred in 1952 in the consideration of the constitutional complaint against the Federal Law on Chimney-Sweeps.[28] Here the Court convincingly demonstrated that chimney-sweeping had traditionally been regarded as a craft or trade and the law relating to it fell under *Handwerkrecht*, which is one of the subcategories of *Art.* 74 *Nr.* 11 *GG*. This was not invalidated by the fact that for reasons of police concern with buildings and the risk of fire chimney-sweeping was subject to more intensive public-law intervention than was normal with 'free' crafts and trades. The Court rejected the submission of the complainants that the Bund could only make regulations concerning chimney-sweeping as a craft or trade and this did not include the introduction of an age-limit or old-age pension arrangements. *Art.* 74 *Nr.* 11 *GG* covered every kind of craft, each with its own distinctive characteristics, and if the latter included an age-limit and an old-age pension scheme appropriate to it, then these could also be regulated by the Bund. It was also generally agreed that the provisions of the Federal law formed an integrated whole which would lose its coherence if the provisions relating to pensions were removed: the law was therefore covered in its entirety by *Art.* 74 *Nr.* 11 *GG*.

Further evidence of this generosity in relation to the Federal economic power may be seen in the *Small-Arms Case*[29] and, more recently, in the *Lift Safety Regulations Case*.[30] In the latter instance the Court again declared that 'trade' as part of the law relating to economic matters under *Art. 74 Nr.* 11 *GG* was to be interpreted 'comprehensively': the makers of the constitution had wanted to avoid a situation whereby special areas relating to trade would be beyond the reach of Federal legislation. It then cited constitutional precedents from the 1871 Reich and the Weimar Republic to justify assigning responsibility for the technical safety of installations which are used not for the exercise of a trade but nevertheless in enterprises with an economic purpose (in this case lifts in rented blocks of flats) to the Federal economic power rather than to the Länder domain of public safety and order.

A second such broad and potentially far-reaching Federal power is that relating to criminal law;[31] however, as will appear from the discussion of various cases concerning the doctrine of *Sachzusammenhang*, the Court's practice here has been much less unequivocal

Nevertheless these exceptions are not sufficient to necessitate a revision of the picture so far obtained of a fairly consistent emphasis of the presumption in favour of the Länder. *Art.* 30 *GG* assumes a much greater significance in the federal order than its American counterpart, the 10th Amendment.

3 The concept of implied powers

In view of the general readiness of the Constitutional Court to invoke *Art.* 30, 70, and 83 *GG* in order to protect the preserve of the Länder against expansive interpretation of Federal powers, it might be expected that there would be no place in the Court's conception of the constitutional apportionment of responsibilities for a special category of implied or incidental powers. Yet its decisions not infrequently contain consideration of the possibility of precisely such powers, namely those implied by association or affinity with an existing explicit power (*Kompetenzen kraft Sachzusammenhangs*) and those based on the intrinsic nature of the function concerned and the overall import of the federal constitution (*Kompetenzen aus der Natur der Sache*).[32]

The discussion so far has already raised the issue of implied powers at several points, and what follows will continue to have a bearing on the question of broad or narrow construction. This is in itself an indication of the difficulty of totally disentangling the two issues. The problem is further complicated by the lack of unanimity as to what precisely is entailed by the two kinds of incidental power. Thus for some the concept of *Sachzusammenhang* is an aid to interpretation enabling established powers (in practice normally the enumerated Federal powers) to be exploited up to the limits of the sense and purpose of the constitutional provision concerned, and therefore it is precisely an instrument of broad construction after the fashion of implied powers in the USA and the unwritten powers of the Reich which had been widely recognized under the pre-1933 German constitutions. Others, however, have seen it as a justification, over and above the normal process of interpretation of the competence clauses, for expansion into a sphere of alien jurisdiction (in most cases only to deny either its legitimacy in principle or its admissibility for most practical purposes). The Constitutional Court appears to start with something akin to the latter conception of *Sachzusammenhang* and to shift markedly towards the former.

Finally, there is yet another type of incidental power recognized by the Constitutional Court under the name of *Annexkompetenz*,[33] whose nature is also subject to dispute. Maunz–Dürig–Herzog[34] see it as a separate type of competence, less questionable than *Sachzusammenhang*, because the original power is extended not in breadth but in depth, that is into the stages of preparation and execution. Thus they compare the *Annexkompetenz* to the American doctrine of implied powers, according to which tacit powers are only admissible for implementing already existing powers, not on the basis of the existence of some affinity (or *Sachzusammenhang*); the right to take measures *kraft Sachzusammenhangs* constitutes on the contrary a real invasion of the preserve of the Länder.[35] Others[36] see no real distinction between *Annex* and *Sachzusammenhang*, at least in the former of the two conceptions of *Sachzusammenhang*. However, for present purposes this form of incidental power may be accepted as a subspecies of power implied by association.

4 Powers implied by association (*kraft Sachzusammenhangs*)

The first major appearance of the doctrine of *Sachzusammenhang* comes in the *Building Law Opinion*.[37] The Federal Government argued that if its view were rejected that a Federal responsibility for building law as a whole followed from the individual powers relating to land law, housing, etc., which were listed in *Art. 74 Nr.* 18 *GG*, then at least it followed from their totality with the aid of the 'corrective aspect of *Sachzusammenhang*'. In support of its invocation of the concept it produced the graphic image of several partially overlapping circles forming a whole whose outer boundary contained a number of angles that needed to be rounded off—by means of the concept of *Sachzusammenhang*. The Court, however, held that the mere consideration that it was expedient to deal with some related subject along with a subject expressly assigned to the Bund did not suffice to establish a Federal right of legislation. In a much-quoted, if clumsy, sentence it declared:

A so-called 'association' could sustain a competence only if a subject assigned to the Bund cannot reasonably be regulated without another not explicitly assigned subject being regulated along with it, that is if an encroachment upon not explicitly assigned subjects is the indispensable prerequisite for the regulation of a subject assigned to Federal legislation.[38]

The Court refused to accept, however, that land law etc. could not sensibly be regulated without regulation of the whole of building law.

This formulation of *Sachzusammenhang* in terms of 'inroads' (*Übergreifen*) into matters not explicitly assigned to the Bund (which would thus normally, on the basis of *Art. 30, 70,* and *83 GG*, be the responsibility of the Länder) is the main indication that the Court is thinking in terms of something beyond the normal interpretative process. Confirmation is provided by the fact that after authority for Federal action has been found to be lacking by the normal rules of interpretation the Court then raises the question whether such authority can nevertheless be implied 'by association'. The same procedure is followed in the *Television Judgment*,[39] where, after careful exposition of the limitation of the Federal powers concerning telecommunication services[40] to the technical aspects of transmission, it is asserted that more extensive powers for broadcasting do not attach to the Bund 'by virtue of association' either. Bullinger[41] has pointed out that in such cases the invocation of the concept of *Sachzusammenhang* always results in confirmation of the conclusion already reached, namely rejection of Federal jurisdiction, since no new criteria are really adduced. Indeed the examination of powers from the point of view of association or affinity can sometimes assume a very perfunctory character.[42] One of the reasons for this must be that in such cases where explicit reference is made to the formula of the *Building Law Opinion* the Court is understandably very wary of arguing that a function assigned to the Bund cannot reasonably be carried out unless it reaches over into an area not explicitly assigned to it. In the *Television Judgment*, once the premiss of the formula of the *Building Law Case* is accepted, the Court's conclusion is inevitable that the general management of broadcasting studios or production of programmes is not an 'indispensable prerequisite' for the regulation of the technical aspects of transmission; rather, the two fields are quite capable of separate and independent regulation. Similarly, in the judgment on the liability of the Federal Railways and Post Office to pay Länder administrative dues it is quite obvious, on the basis of the reiterated formula of the *Building Law Opinion*, that (Federal) regulations relating to the Länder law on administrative charges are not 'indispensable prerequisites' for sensible provisions concerning the operation of the traditional rail and postal services.[43]

This is a much more restrictive application of the doctrine of *Sachzusammenhang* than prevailed under the Wilhelmine Reich or the Weimar Republic, where in case of doubt the Reich was assumed to have all powers necessary for the full and effective exercise of explicitly granted powers.[44] That it was motivated, like the frequent insistence on the implications of *Art.* 30 *GG*, by the perceived need to protect the domain of the Länder against expansion of the already wide-ranging enumerated powers of the Bund need not seriously be doubted. Yet despite the intention of the framers of the Basic Law to achieve an exhaustive allocation of responsibilities, this view of *Sachzusammenhang* appears to have been too demanding for the needs of flexible constitutional interpretation. At any rate there are ample instances where the Constitutional Court does not invoke the *Building Law Opinion* as the basis of its judgment or else has recourse to the different terminology of the *Annexkompetenz*.

Instead of 'indispensable' expansion of Federal powers into areas of Länder responsibility it is a question of recognizing peripheral areas of governmental activity as incidental to a field for which responsibility is undisputed. The implications of this conception are more modest, but precisely because the conditions are less demanding this kind of 'association' with a Federal power can more readily be admitted, especially since there is no longer any requirement of indispensability for acknowledgement of Federal competence. Clearly, however, it could in practice lead to substantial erosion of Länder powers, as tended to happen under previous German constitutions, if it were sufficient to establish some connection, however tenuous, with an individual item of Federal jurisdiction considered in isolation. The association of such peripheral areas with the Federal power in question will not merely have to be demanded by considerations of the effective exercise of that power; their connection with it will have to be stronger than with any recognized Länder power. This is by no means always simple to establish, though undoubtedly the issue leaves a certain latitude for considerations of preference or expediency. But the crucial point is that Länder powers are also weighed in the balance in the consideration of possible Federal powers *kraft Sachzusammenhangs*. This does more than merely reduce the danger of potentially unlimited attachment of different aspects of a field to a core item of Federal jurisdiction; it also opens up the possibility of giving the Länder the benefit of the doctrine of incidental powers.

The relatively pragmatic or common-sense reasoning promoted by this allocation of items to a particular subject-area according to their 'centre of gravity' can be seen at work in several decisions of the Bundesverfassungsgericht.

(i) A start is made in the *Building Law Opinion* itself[45] when the Court comes to consider the right to determine *Baupolizeirecht*, i.e. what is traditionally recognized as the responsibility of the police concerning the erection and maintenance of buildings, in particular the averting of dangers to the general public or the individual. This is held by the Court to be part of police law in general, which is a Länder responsibility, especially since 'building law' as such had not been assigned to the Bund. The police power to protect public safety and order is declared to be an 'adjunct' (or *Annex*) of the subject-area in which it is exercised and therefore to be covered by the relevant legislative power. But since the Bund had not received jurisdiction over 'building' in general, it did not possess the ensuing authority to issue particular po'ice regulations in this field, except in so far as this could be derived from the responsibility for 'housing' under *Art.* 74 *Nr.* 18 *GG*. Otherwise 'building police law' was a separate field of law and a Federal right of legislation could not be established by interpretation of the individual subject-areas which bore some relation to it.

(ii) In the dispute as to whether the Act of 1939 on the Testing of Small-Arms and Ammunition (*Beschussgesetz*) had become Federal law in accordance with *Art.* 125 *Nr.* 1 *GG*,[46] the Bavarian Government argued that its provisions were predominantly concerned with safety considerations. Therefore, since the Bund had no competence in the field of general public safety, the Act continued in force as Land law, and the regulation of charges for the testing of small-arms made by the Federal Minister of Economics on the basis of an authorization by the Act was illegitimate.

The Constitutional Court found that the Small-Arms Act had two main objectives, the economic one of regulating manufacture and guaranteeing quality, and the maintenance of public safety and order. But this did not prevent it from assigning it to the law relating to economic matters for which the Bund had concurrent power under *Art.* 74 *Nr.* 11 *GG*. It took this category to cover all regulations relating to the production and distribution of economic goods, including small-arms. Recognizing that a clear boundary could not be drawn between what belongs to the law of the economy and regulations pertaining to the maintenance of public safety and order, the Court pointed to various provisions of economic and business law which contained measures promoting public safety and order without thereby being beyond the legitimate reach of Federal legislation. This was because the totality of norms pertaining to the maintenance of public safety and order did not constitute an autonomous subject-area in the distribution of powers between Bund and Länder. Rather, the stipulation of the *Building Law Opinion* that this police power is an 'adjunct' of the area of jurisdiction in relation to which it is exercised worked in this case in favour of the Federation. The power to issue regulations for the maintenance of public safety and order was in the Court's view to be ascribed to that field of competence with which such regulations had a 'necessary connection'. Only such regulations as had the maintenance of public safety and order as their sole and direct purpose could be attributed to an independent subject-area which was designated police law in the narrower sense and was the responsibility of Länder legislation. But this was not the case with the Small-Arms Act.

(iii) A similar case arose in relation to the Reich law on traffic in base metals, which had become Federal law under *Art.* 125 *GG*, its subject-matter belonging to the law of the economy under *Art.* 74 *Nr.* 11 *GG*.[47] Some provisions which were concerned exclusively with administrative procedure were held to stand in direct 'relationship' (*Zusammenhang*) with the substantive economic regulations and had validity only in this narrow connection. They were therefore held to be 'law affecting matters subject to the concurrent legislative power of the Federation' within the meaning of *Art.* 125 *GG*.

(iv) In its review of the validity of Bavarian provisions concerning the subjection of press offences (dissemination of printed matter with punishable content) to the statute of limitations[48] the Bundesverfassungsgericht rejected the view that the Reich law on the subject had become Federal law as belonging to the concurrent powers for either 'court procedure' or 'criminal law' under *Art.* 74 *Nr.* 1 *GG*. Rather, because of the special nature of offences committed by the press it must continue, as in the past, to be assigned to the category of 'press law', for which the Länder were responsible, restricted only by a Federal framework power under *Art.* 75 *Nr.* 2 *GG*. The Court decided that the short period before press offences lapsed resulted from the peculiar way in which offences were committed by the press. Because of this 'inner connection' the regulation of the lapsing of such offences was linked more closely and strongly with press law than with general criminal law—a connection reflected in the traditional location of such provisions in special press laws. Here, then, was a significant innovation by which, even though the powers of the Länder were residual and not enumerated, a particular matter could be assigned to them on the basis of *Sachzusammenhang* with a recognized subject of Länder responsibility.

(v) In the judgment on the right of members of the press to refuse to give evidence[49] the Bundesverfassungsgericht faced conflicting attempts by the Federal Code of Criminal Procedure[50] and the Hessian Act concerning the Freedom and Law of the Press to specify who might refuse to reveal sources and under what conditions. It ruled that the right to enact such legislation was to be attributed to the Federal concurrent responsibility for court procedure in *Art. 74 Nr.* 1 *GG* and not to the legislative power of the Länder for the law of the press. The Court emphasized that if a provision exhibited a recognizable connection with more than one subject-area—in this case law of the press and court procedure—this did not remove the necessity to assign it to one or the other. A 'double competence', on the basis of which Bund and Länder could make different regulations concerning the same object, was alien to the system of norms governing constitutional powers and would be incompatible with its demarcation function.[51] Then the Court referred to its previous criteria for deciding to which of two rival fields a subject was to be ascribed, namely its intrinsic and historical association, as in the case of the lapsing of press offences.[52] By their intrinsic nature regulations concerning the right of refusal to give evidence belonged to the law of evidence in court procedure. Their purpose might in the case of members of the press be the preservation of a free and effective press, but the only connection (*Sachzusammenhang*) in which they protected these aspects of the press and had any direct effects was the procedure in a court of law. The Court recognized that this ruling might appear to conflict with the *Press Offences Judgment* and was at pains to stress their compatibility. It demonstrated that traditionally the right of journalists to refuse to give evidence had been attached to the law of court procedure, and argued that it would be improper and contrary to the need for legal unity to destroy the uniform regulation of court procedure which had in general existed since 1877. Since the Bund had clearly occupied the field, the Hessian provisions were automatically rendered null and void by *Art. 72 Abs.* 1 *GG.*

(vi) A similar case in the same field came before the Constitutional Court in 1978 in the wake of the deaths in

Stuttgart-Stammheim Prison of leading members of the Baader–Meinhof terrorist group. Posters distributed in Frankfurt by Communist groups were confiscated as being defamatory of the Prime Minister of Baden-Württemberg, Herr Filbinger, and complaints against this confiscation were rejected by the competent Regional Court (*Landgericht*). Appeal was then made to the Higher Regional Court (*Oberlandesgericht*) in accordance with the provisions of the Hessian Press Act concerning complaints against the confiscation of printed matter. But because the Federal code of criminal procedure (*Strafprozessordnung*) provided that no further challenge to decisions of a *Landgericht* in cases of complaint should normally be possible, the Higher Regional Court referred the question of the constitutionality of the Hessian provisions to the Federal Constitutional Court.

The latter agreed[53] with the *Oberlandesgericht* that Hesse was not entitled to allow further complaint in cases of confiscation of printed matter since this was not a matter of press law but of court procedure in criminal cases, which had been exhaustively regulated by the Federal legislator under *Art. 74 Nr. 1 GG*. The determining factor, the Court said, was not the 'connection' (*Sachbezug*) with press matters—which certainly existed—but the fact that the subject in question belonged intrinsically and historically to one field or the other. And it cited the earlier *Press Offences Case* and *Hessian* and *Hamburg Press Law Cases* in support of this position.

Even if in the press law cases there is also some emphasis on the traditional definition of powers, there remains an uneasy coexistence between the Bundesverfassungsgericht's concern for a narrow construction of Federal powers in the light of *Art. 30 GG* and the tendency revealed by the above examples to regard *Sachzusammenhang* as simply a matter of closer affinity or stronger connection. For the advantage derived by the Länder from the fact that their acknowledged powers are also considered in relation to *Sachzusammenhang* still leaves possibilities of an extensive interpretation of Federal powers which are largely excluded by an uncompromising insistence, on the basis of *Art. 30 GG*, that what is not explicitly taken away from them must belong to the Länder. A glance back at the *Residence Tax Case*[54] indicates how a quite different result in favour of the

Bund could have been obtained by assessment of stronger association or affinity. The availability of either approach sometimes adds to the Court's room for manoeuvre. However, it could hardly be said that it had been bold in its exploitation of the possibilities of inferring incidental Federal powers.

The decisions of the Constitutional Court in which the concept of *Sachzusammenhang* appears do not, however, fall neatly into the two contrasting categories outlined above. Thus an early decision on disciplinary tribunals in the medical profession[55] makes no reference to the formula of the *Building Law Opinion* but is no less uncompromising for that in its refusal to admit any Federal competence by virtue of association. The fact that the revoking of a licence to practise, which belonged to the Bund's power to license doctors and other health practitioners under *Art.* 74 *Nr.* 19 *GG*, was compulsorily linked to ascertainment in the professional judicial process of unworthiness to practise the profession was recognized to constitute a close connection but not such as made it necessary to ascribe the latter legislative complex to the former. The Court here argued in a strict and almost pedantic way that the professional tribunal did not itself decide about the granting or revocation of licence to practise but only punished derelictions of professional duty; its declaration of unworthiness to practise the profession was only a factual prerequisite for revocation of appointment by the competent state authorities.

On the other hand, the *Federal Waterways Judgment,* which faithfully recites the demanding formula of the *Building Law Case*, proceeds to ignore it in its consideration of the possibility of an incidental power.[56] Instead the Court argues pragmatically that the acceptance of a *Sachzusammenhang* which would extend powers of regulation of the transport functions of waterways to include the right to determine all questions of water supply is ruled out by the fact that in this way a sensible arrangement could not be achieved. Amongst other considerations, an incidental power with respect to water management functions inferred from *Art.* 74 *Nr.* 21 *GG* would cover only the navigable parts, not the non-navigable upper reaches or tributaries where the cause of pollution of the waterways could equally lie. In fact, the Court maintained, if one really wanted to infer a power by virtue of association, the only relevant connection would be that between the waterways and the water supply of their whole catchment and precipitation area and the interrelation between water economy and land use. The legislative competence of the Länder for the management of their waters would thus lead to similar powers in relation to the internal waterways if they did not already possess such powers anyway. In this case, therefore, payment of lip-service to the strict formula of indispensable inroads into powers not explicitly assigned did not prevent a highly pragmatic assessment of what solution would be more sensible, along with recognition of a possible *Sachzusammenhang* with a Länder rather than a Federal sphere of responsibility.

The conclusion from the cases already cited must be that, although it became more flexible in its approach, the Constitutional Court has not been over-eager to use the concept of *Sachzusammenhang* to make adjustments to the constitutional distribution of powers or even very often to give the benefit of the doubt to the Bund. Something of an exception can be found in the period of the late 1960s, when two judgments seem to be clearly weighted in the Bund's favour: The disputed Federal Youth Welfare Act of 1961 had contained measures relating not only to young people who were at risk or already in trouble (*Jugendfürsorge*) but also to the general physical, mental, and moral well-being of all young people (*Jugendpflege*), for example by the promotion of youth clubs or of institutions for leisure activities, political education and international contacts. In their appeal to Karlsruhe in 1967 several Länder argued that these general measures of *Jugendpflege* were not covered by the Federal responsibility for public welfare (*öffentliche Fürsorge*) under *Art. 74 Nr. 7 GG*. But the Court rejected this view on the ground that the boundaries between the welfare of young people directly at risk and provision for well-adjusted youth were fluid; the various difficulties which many young people had in adjusting to society, without thereby being necessarily at risk, could sometimes be partially overcome by contact with other young people in the local context of a youth club or at regional or international level in a youth camp or on holidays for young people, so that potential problems were averted and future welfare measures made unnecessary. According to the Court the same was true of arrangements for political education designed to make young people realize that the individual in a democracy cannot isolate himself from society but must actively help to mould it and its political form. It concluded that the two fields were so closely interconnected that considerations of *Sachzusammenhang* would by themselves suffice to bring *Jugendpflege* under the concept of *öffentliche Fürsorge* in *Art. 74 Nr. 7 GG*.[57] Whatever one may think of the Court's expectations of education for democracy, it is clear that there is here not merely no question of 'indispensable prerequisites', but not even any consideration of whether at least some aspects might be more closely 'interconnected' with Länder powers. The contrast with, for example, the refusal to countenance a perhaps more obvious link between the disciplinary process in the medical profession and the power to revoke licence to practise is striking.

In the following year came a decision[58] concerning police powers in relation to buildings, which had been declared in the *Building Law Opinion* to be an adjunct of the subject-area in which they were exercised. This time the Constitutional Court refused to agree with the court which referred the issue that the relevant provisions of the Reich Criminal Code had not continued in force as Federal law but belonged to the traditional Länder sphere of 'building police law' and had a necessary connection with building law. For its finding to the contrary the Court relied purely on the historically comprehensive compass of the Federal criminal law power and the argument that there was no indication that *Art. 74 Nr. 1 GG* wished to give 'criminal law' a more restricted meaning. It consequently accorded the Bund the right to establish punishable offences within the field of subjects traditionally covered by the Criminal Code without being bound by the limitations otherwise imposed upon it by the catalogue of powers. The regulations in question were blanket provisions requiring closer specification by 'building police law', which the Court still accepted as belonging to the Länder domain of police law. But it rejected the argument of some commentators that the enactment of so-called dependent norms of criminal law which serve to protect regulations from other branches of law belongs by *Sachzusammenhang* to the relevant jurisdiction for the latter: there was no objection to the Bund protecting Land law with a criminal penalty, because the right of the Länder to determine the content of the Land law in question was in no way prejudiced. Again there is a marked contrast with, for example, the *Press Offences Judgment*, where the regulation of the lapsing of press offences had been regarded as more closely linked with press law than with general criminal law (though admittedly in that case historical arguments were on the other side). Instead of weighing up the possibility of a closer affinity with the relevant Länder powers, or indeed stressing the presumption in favour of the Länder, the Court prefers the argument of historical continuity with a former constitution under which Federal powers had in any case been very broadly construed.

It is interesting in this connection that the Bundesverfassungsgericht seems in the *'Ingenieur' Judgment* to have taken the opportunity to tidy up its position.[59] In rejecting the possibility of a Federal right to regulate the assumption of the title of *Ingenieur* under *Art.* 74 *Nr.* 1 *GG* on the basis of the penal sanctions which the law contained, the Court stressed that, despite the validity of its decision in the *Building Police Law Case*, it was not admissible for the Bund to use its power to lay down penal sanctions as a backdoor means of determining the content of such Länder provisions as were to receive the protection of criminal law: this would violate the principle of *Art.* 30 and 70 *GG*. In this way it re-established a yardstick for preventing abuse of the possibilities of extensive interpretation to the detriment of the Länder.

The timing of the *Youth Welfare* and *Building Police Law Judgments* may well be significant. The late sixties were the period of the Grand Coalition, the Troeger Report on financial reform, and a spate of constitutional amendments of the catalogue of powers. The inference seems plausible that the Court was moving with the tide of increased Federal powers and perhaps even wishing to show that the necessary constitutional flexibility could be achieved by judicial interpretation without recourse to constitutional overhaul.

5 Intrinsically implicit powers (*aus der Natur der Sache*)

The possibility of deriving Federal powers *aus der Natur der Sache* (i.e. 'from the intrinsic nature of the matter concerned') plays a considerably less prominent role in the decisions of the Constitutional Court than the doctrine of *Sachzusammenhang*. This is perhaps hardly surprising when one considers that by comparison with it even the concept of *Sachzusammenhang* is a model of unequivocal precision. There is not even unanimity as to whether it is an aid to interpretation in the light of the basic federal provisions of the constitution, or a basis on which appeal may be made beyond the written text to the essential nature of a federal system for the establishment of unwritten Federal powers.[60] A court which is concerned to protect the powers of the Länder against Federal encroachment is bound to be wary of such a potentially radical instrument. Indeed, in view of the principles of *Art.* 70 *Abs.* 1 and 2 *GG*, whereby the Länder are the recipients of all residual power and the division of responsibility between Bund and Länder is to be determined 'by the provisions of this Basic Law concerning exclusive and concurrent legislative powers', the recognition of unwritten Federal powers as being intrinsically implicit can scarcely be undertaken lightly.

Yet the Constitutional Court, having raised the issue in the *Building Law Opinion*, declares in 1960 in the *Bremen Holiday Law Judgment*[61] that it is 'undisputed' that in the federal state there are unwritten legislative powers *aus der Natur der Sache*. The case was a rather esoteric one concerning whether certain provisions of the 1948 Holiday Law of the Land of Bremen which related to postal workers had become Federal law upon the establishment of the Federal Republic. The issue turned partly on whether the power to regulate the holiday claims of its employees in the postal service had belonged *exclusively* to the Bizonal Economic Administration (which had preceded the establishment of the Federal Republic), thus making the Bremen provisions invalid; and the Court decided that such an exclusive power could not be ascribed to the Bizonal Economic Administration simply 'by the nature of the matter'. But what is significant here is that, although the Court refused to base a jurisdictional allocation on the doctrine, it not only declared the existence of such unwritten powers to be 'undisputed' but explicitly embraced the bold formulation of Anschütz in relation to the Weimar Constitution, whereby jurisdiction *aus der Natur der Sache* is established by the '. . . unwritten legal maxim,

founded on the nature of things and therefore not requiring
explicit recognition by the Reich Constitution, whereby certain
subject-areas, because by their nature they represent inherent
Reich matters which are *a priori* removed from particularist
legislative competence, can be regulated by the Reich and only
by the Reich.'[62]

It is true that it could be a sovereignty notion that lay behind
Anschütz's remark. It is also true that the Court added that
inferences from the intrinsic nature of the matter concerned
must be logically necessary and cogently demand a particular
solution to the exclusion of other possibilities of appropriate
solution, and that arguments based on intrinsicality break
down if an acceptable case can be made out for another solution. Nevertheless, with the invoking of an essential concept of a
federation having certain fundamental jurisdictional arrangements, a whiff of suprapositive law remains.

In practice, however, the Court has virtually never accepted
Federal powers based on the intrinsic nature of the subject.
This is true not only of the *Bremen Holiday Law Judgment* (where
although regulation of the holiday rights of Federal employees
could have been claimed to be a 'domestic' Federal matter of
administrative organization, it is found to fall foul of the Anschütz conditions), but also of the *Building Law Opinion*.[63] Here
the view was taken that even if *Art.* 30 and 70 *GG* did not
exclude recognition of a Federal responsibility for those functions which arose directly out of the nature and constitutional
organization of the Federation ('natural Federal tasks'), the
regulation of building law was not one of them. Just as it was
not possible for the seat of the Federal Government or the
symbols of the Federation to be determined by the Länder,
whether in identical or divergent laws, so it was perfectly
conceivable that building law should be regulated by Länder
laws. That disparate regulation by the Länder might appear
inappropriate did not make the regulation of building law a
natural Federal task such as could establish a Federal right of
legislation.

The same also applies to the *Television Judgment*,[64] where the
Court ruled that the physical 'supraregionality' of broadcasting did not make it a natural Federal responsibility, nor did the
fact that in view of the high costs involved a television channel

was bound to be a supraregional, co-operative venture. It equally rejected the idea that a natural Federal prerogative could be derived from the acknowledged need for national representation internally or to foster tradition in the interests of continuity: such tasks were incapable of closer definition and were in any case served by many cultural institutions, even perhaps the whole educational system. With reference to the conditions it had laid down in the *Bremen Holiday Law Case*, the Court observed that the Bund would be empowered to organize such broadcasting *aus der Natur der Sache* only if it were a question of inherent Federal matters which were *a priori* removed from the competence of the Länder and could only be undertaken by the Bund. This was not the case. From the nature of the tasks of 'national representation internally' and 'fostering tradition in the interests of continuity' it did *not* follow logically that their promotion by *Federal* broadcasts was cogently required (especially in view of the limitations imposed on governmental influence by *Art. 5 Abs. 1 GG*).

In the *Federal Waterways Judgment* there is a particularly unceremonious rejection of the view that since the prevention of pollution of the federal waterways required a legal basis extending beyond the boundaries of the Länder the nature of the matter thus demanded uniform regulation by the Bund. The Court declared that such Federal powers could not be considered when the interpretation of the jurisdictional provisions of the Basic Law indicated unequivocally that the Länder were competent.[65] Similarly in the *'Ingenieur' Case* the Court cited the Anschütz conditions again and remarked that protection of the professional title of *Ingenieur* by no means required a Federal law: uniform regulation by Länder laws of similar content was perfectly conceivable and practicable.[66]

An unexpected instance of derivation of Federal powers from the intrinsic nature of the matter concerned crops up in the *Building Law Opinion* itself. Having distinguished 'town planning', which falls under Federal concurrent powers for land law in *Art. 74 Nr. 18 GG*, from 'regional planning' (*Raumordnung*), for which the Bund can issue only framework provisions under *Art. 75 Nr. 4 GG*, the Constitutional Court perhaps rather gratuitously adds that regional planning cannot stop at the frontiers of the Länder; if regional planning is recognized as a necessary task of the modern state, then the largest region to be planned is the whole state territory, and for this the Federation must have full and exclusive powers *aus der Natur der Sache*.[67] This is in noticeable contrast to the refusal in the *Federal Waterways Judgment* to draw equivalent conclusions from the fact that the problem of pollution did not stop at the frontiers of the Länder. Nor is it obviously consonant with the Court's general emphasis upon the presumption in favour of the Länder, when one considers that the Basic Law had explicitly given the Bund only framework responsibility for regional planning.

If this conclusion, perhaps pragmatically justifiable, though methodologically adventurous and in its import imprecise, can by one means or another be squared with the insistence in the *Television Judgment* that mere supraregionality does not suffice to create a 'natural' Federal prerogative, the same is not true of the *Youth Welfare Judgment*.[68] Here the Court quoted at length not merely its conditions laid down in the *Bremen Holiday Law Case* but its acceptance in the *Boiler Judgment* that there could conceivably be laws (other than those falling under *Art.* 86 ff. *GG*) whose purpose could not be achieved by administrative action on the part of a Land and whose execution by the Bund could therefore be taken to be tacitly permitted.[69] In applying these principles to youth welfare measures and recognizing Federal responsibility for those of clearly supraregional character such as 'by their very nature cannot be promoted by one Land alone', the Court does not this time stop to consider whether uniform regulation by harmonized Länder legislation is not perfectly conceivable. Here, then, is an isolated instance of acknowledgement of the inherent nature of a Federal power which would otherwise by no means be self-evident.[70]

In conclusion, it may be remarked in relation to the interpretative principles of *Sachzusammenhang* and *Natur der Sache* that both are vague and neither gives clear criteria for assigning one field of competence to another as necessarily implied by, resulting from or incidental to it. Nor has the Constitutional Court hammered them into consistent systematic principles. Inevitably there is an element of judicial discretion and personal political preferences can come into play. As in other federal systems, the judges' attitude to unwritten Federal powers is in reality determined partly by unitarist or federalist prejudices. Certainly the reasons for the comparatively restrictive approach to recognizing such powers in West Germany will to some extent be those which have already been put forward with regard to other aspects of 'creative' decision-making, such as the nature of the catalogue of powers and the ease of constitutional amendment. But the Court is bound to have been influenced by the consideration that to open the already extensive enumerated powers of the Federation to expansion by implication was to risk leaving nothing of substance to the Länder.

6 The possibilities of broad construction

Finally, it is worth remembering that the Constitutional Court may achieve similar results in terms of expansion or amplification of powers without reference to *Sachzusammenhang* or *Natur der Sache*. This may be briefly illustrated by reference to three judgments, two of them by now familiar.

In the *Building Law Opinion*, after rejecting a general Federal responsibility for building law, the Court went on to confirm that the category of 'land law' covered not only town planning, in so far as the latter defined the permissible use of land, and therefore the right to draw up a binding plan for building development, but also the right to draw up preparatory plans which undertake broad area allocation and define general building intentions. For this it relied on the assertion that such plans can be a necessary prerequisite for the proper fulfilment of the local administrative responsibility of conducting the building process systematically, and drew attention also to the inseparable connection between them and the final plan. Yet it maintained that these Federal powers were not established by *Sachzusammenhang*, but rather the category of 'land law' was specifically interpreted as extending to planning law. Similarly, as far as land evaluation was concerned, the Court viewed this as necessarily a subsidiary activity required for a wide variety of purposes, so that it was within the Federal competence in so far as it had a connection with subjects for which the Bund had authority to legislate.

Again, the *Federal Waterways Judgment*, after ruling out a

general power of the Bund to enact provisions relating to water economy based on *Sachzusammenhang* with its responsibility for inland waterways, then blandly allows it the right to make specific regulations in the interests of shipping even when they inevitably affect general water management.[71]

Finally, an instance of the derivation of a kind of natural Federal competence from the supraregional character of a problem occurs at the end of the *Numerus Clausus Judgment* of 1972,[72] which is otherwise not a federal case at all. In relation to Bavarian provisions giving preferential treatment to residents of Bavaria in the allocation of university places, the First Senate had maintained that if a matter 'by its nature' transcended Länder boundaries and concerned a legal position guaranteed equally for all citizens of the Federal Republic in all the Länder (such as the right of free choice of one's place of training under *Art.* 12 *Abs.* 1 *GG*), preferential treatment for residents of the Land could impair the rights of other citizens. Universal restrictions on the number of student admissions in a particular subject were held to turn the problem of preserving a balance between universities and of the selection of applicants into a 'federal-wide task'. However, in view of the difficulties encountered in co-ordinating the different systems and provisions of the Länder, the Court then declared that it was primarily a matter for the Bund, exploiting the legislative and administrative possibilities at its disposal, to take the necessary action. Measures by the Länder in the form of inter-Länder treaties were envisaged only if the Federal authorities failed to act. And such measures were seen as based on the Länder's 'co-responsibility' for the protection of basic rights—not, as would normally have been expected, on their powers in the field of education. Thus, although this *obiter dictum* makes no reference to the doctrine of *Natur der Sache*, its rather remarkable inference of a Federal power from the need to maintain equal rights throughout the Federal Republic is similar in its effect.

When it seems necessary, therefore, the Court is quite capable of giving a broad construction to powers which it regards as too narrow, without worrying about the requirements of *Art.* 30 and 70 *GG*. One of the types of incidental or inherent power may be adduced or not as appears appropriate. Room for manoeuvre is provided especially by the variety of aspects under which many subjects can be considered with regard to jurisdiction, the overlapping of economic and cultural questions or economic and law-and-order objectives being prominent examples. Here the stronger or intrinsic connection may be assessed, or alternatively reference may be made to constitutional tradition and historical practice.[73] Indeed, where the designation of a particular power in the Basic Law is identical with that in the Weimar Constitution (or even in the 1871 Constitution of the German Reich), the Court commonly prefers, if there is no evident reason to the contrary, to assume that the scope of the power is also equivalent to that of its predecessor as illuminated at the time by legislative and judicial practice. Thus it has been seen that in the *Lift Safety Regulations Case* the Court traced the concept of 'trades' (*Gewerbe*) as far back as the 1871 Constitution in order to show that traditionally the law governing trades had been understood as extending to safety regulations for installations even where these were not used in pursuit of a trade but merely in the context of an economic enterprise.[74] Such a presumption of continuity in the definition of powers may often be convenient and indeed desirable. But, apart from the risk of producing inappropriate results in cases where technical or social developments have substantially widened the scope of public responsibility, reference to former constitutions, one of which was markedly more unitary than the Basic Law and both of which tended to be interpreted in a centralizing manner, must be likely to favour the broad construction of Federal powers.

However that may be, the possibility of invoking historical practice or associations or alternatively the presumed intentions of the framers of the constitution considerably increases the Court's room for manoeuvre in the interpretation of the powers of the Federation and the Länder: thus it has already been demonstrated how the Court assumes as comprehensive an economic power as possible, whereas, in view of what it regards as a basic constitutional decision whereby cultural affairs belong to the domain of the Länder, a restrictive approach is found particularly necessary in such cases as the *Concordat* and *Television Judgments* and implied powers generally get short shrift.

This leads us back to the view that implied powers must be

seen in the context of the general approach to broad construction. Although some signs of increasing flexibility may be detected, the Court never had a closed mind with regard to generous interpretation, nor on the other hand could it be said more recently to have become adventurous: the presumption in favour of the Länder still receives emphasis. Within the possibilities of broad construction the concepts of incidental or implied powers have by the standards of the English-speaking world played a minor and undramatic part. This can be attributed not only to the constraining characteristics of German constitutional law, but above all to the fact that their invocation must necessarily benefit the holder of enumerated powers, and to the perceptions of the judges as to whose powers were most in need of protection.

CHAPTER VII
The Federal Principle and the Doctrine of Federal Comity

1 Introduction

When considering the extent to which the Federal Constitutional Court tends to develop the Constitution by its own decisions or affect the balance in the federal system it is important to ask: How far does it act from 'positive law' assumptions and try to interpret the provisions of the Basic Law fairly restrictively? Or is it the case that the Court regards the Constitution rather as a more or less deliberate concretization of general principles and interprets it relatively freely in the light of its own conception of those principles?

It seems to be only in the field of basic rights that the Court has shown an inclination in any grand way to interpret in accordance with its own view of general principles; and indeed there this role is virtually forced upon it by the exceedingly general formulation of some of the concepts concerned. In the delineation of the powers of Bund and Länder there is, as the nature of the task, the German legal tradition and the detailed provisions of the Basic Law would lead us to expect, a much more positivist approach, and indeed a fairly restrictive interpretative practice, as has already been seen from the modest use of the possibilities of recognizing powers 'by association' or 'from the intrinsic nature of the matter'. Nevertheless it was remarked by some of the judges interviewed that in the federal as in the basic rights field most of the members of the Constitutional Court are far from being strict constructionists. Moreover, there are in fact certain general principles which can be regarded as underlying the constitution and appealed to as the basis of a specific ruling. The most obvious are the concepts *Bundesstaat* and 'federalism'; but there is also the unwritten principle of federal comity (*Bundestreue* or *bundesfreundliches Verhalten*), which the Constitutional Court inherited from Germany's federal tradition. Here the Court seems to have considerable room for imposing its own views or predilections. Has it done so?

2 'Federalism' and the *Bundesstaat*

The Basic Law proclaims at *Art. 20 Abs. 1 GG:* 'The Federal Republic of Germany is a democratic and social *federal state*.'[1] Thus the federal principle appears to be singled out as one of the main foundations of the constitutional order. However, it is embarrassing for the Court that the Basic Law contains no definition of what federalism is, apart from its detailed dispositions with regard to the allocation of powers. One natural recourse is therefore to look to the historical conception of federalism in Germany. But this almost inevitably involves a simplification of the past, since even then there were controversies—a fact sometimes conveniently overlooked by contemporary jurisprudence. A brief glance at the tradition of federal doctrine in Germany will reveal some of the problems.[2]

One of the significant points about the German federal tradition is the distinction frequently made between *Föderalismus* and the concept of the *Bundesstaat*. This despite the fact that *Bundesstaat* clearly denotes what is normally referred to in English as a 'federal state' or 'federation'. The *Bundesstaat* is generally described as lying between the unitary state and the *Staatenbund* or confederation. The latter is, literally, a league of states. It is therefore not itself a state but merely a legal relationship between states. The essence of the *Bundesstaat*, on the other hand, is that the statehood of both the whole and the parts is recognized.

However, this concept of the *Bundesstaat* is a very flexible one (in much the same way as Livingston's 'spectrum of federalism'[3]). Depending on the distribution of powers between the two levels of government it can tend towards either the unitary state or the confederation. It is by its nature destined to be a permanent battle-ground between two countervailing tendencies, the centrifugal and the centripetal. Triepel described it as a *forma mixta*, an attempt to find a compromise between the two principles of federalism and unitarism.[4] The latter principle is clearly that which tends or strives towards a unitary state, whereas 'federalism' strives towards the autonomy of the member states in a system of confederation or a league of states (but not their complete separation). Both are regarded as in some sense presupposing the *Bundesstaat*, as concerned with the balance which should be struck within it. Similarly, individual institutions within the *Bundesstaat* can in themselves be federalist (such as, in Triepel's view, the Bundesrat under the Reich Constitution of 1871) or unitary (the Reichstag and the Kaiser). Triepel concluded: 'One can thus conceive of *Bundesstaaten* which are predominantly unitary or predominantly federalist in character.'[5] He admitted that the terms *föderativ* and *föderalistisch* were sometimes used interchangeably as equivalent to *bundesstaatlich*, but he did not regard this as the proper usage.

To the extent that this influential work of Triepel's represents the German legal tradition, the consequences for recourse to traditional principles by the Constitutional Court are clear. If it appeals to the principle of the *Bundesstaat*, enshrined in *Art. 20 GG*, it is appealing to a concept which is too vague to be useful, one which can accommodate both the unitarist and the federalist principles. Perhaps all it would really demand would be the requirements of *Art. 79 Abs. 3 GG*: the Federal Republic must consist of *some* states and they must have some part in the legislative process. On the other hand, if the Court appeals to the principle of 'federalism', which makes no appearance in the written text of the constitution, it is using a term which in the German tradition suggests a degree of political partisanship such as a constitutional court could scarcely afford to profess.[6] However, in both political and academic circles the term *föderalistisch* appears nowadays to be used regularly in the general sense of the English word 'federal', and even *Föderalismus* is frequently recognized by less than avowed 'federalists' as one of the principles on which the constitution is based.

Of the 'federal', as opposed to 'federalist', principle even the broadest characteristics and requirements were the subject of dispute. Thus as early as 1872 Max von Seydel[7] took issue with the concept of the *Bundesstaat* put forward by Georg Waitz, and in particular with the contention that the *Bundesstaat* was a state whose parts were also states. Explicitly appealing to the arguments of Calhoun, von Seydel declared this claim to be logically impossible, since sovereignty was by nature indivisible and unlimited: thus the concept of the *Bundesstaat* was legally untenable in that it conflicted with the concept of the state. He concluded that the German Reich (and, for that matter, the United States and Switzerland) was in reality a confederation. Its constitution was a treaty of sovereign states, and there was no indication that they intended to renounce their sovereignty.

Von Seydel's position never became generally accepted. Others tried to proclaim that sovereignty was in fact divisible, or else that the member states were not states in the strict sense because they were not sovereign.[8] The doctrine that sovereignty attached only to the totality in fact became the prevailing one. There was general acceptance of Laband's view that the *Kompetenz-Kompetenz* confers sovereignty, i.e. that to be sovereign the state need not possess all the powers but must only be able to appropriate them to itself at will. However, Laband preserved the statehood of the Länder by arguing that sovereignty was not essential to a state; the sole criterion of the state was public law authority in its own right (that is, not subject to any control). Thus in those fields in which the member states establish the norms and have powers in their own right, not conferred by the Reich, Laband speaks of their being subordinate to the Reich as autonomous (not sovereign) states.[9]

Yet despite the general endorsement of Laband's position contrary views persisted. Otto Mayer, for example, while accepting that in circumstances of popular sovereignty a union of states produced a new sovereign in the shape of the *Gesamtvolk* ('We the people of the United States'), denied that this was possible with a monarchical *Bundesstaat*: the sum of several monarchical sovereigns was not a new sovereign but a 'league of monarchs' (*Monarchenbund*).[10] Even after promulgation of the more unitary Weimar Constitution Nawiasky took up again the view that sovereignty was a necessary characteristic of state power and so revived the idea of dual sovereignty.[11]

In reality the academic conflict over the nature of the Reich was a reflection of the political struggle between federalism and unitarism, which on the whole went steadily in favour of the latter. Indisputably, Prussian hegemony was a crucial factor here. The close organic connection between Prussia (which accounted for approximately three-fifths of Germany) and the Reich was a highly unitarizing influence despite the strong federal elements in the constitution. The relatively laconic 1871 constitution was filled in and amended by political practice in the direction of greater legislative and especially administrative powers for the Reich. Nevertheless the 'monarchical' federation had its own peculiar backbone in the ruling dynasties of the member states (and in the key role of 'their' legislative organ at Federal level, the Bundesrat). With the disappearance of this element under the Weimar Constitution the federal characteristics of the political order were also weakened considerably, with the Reich in possession of the vast bulk of legislative powers, dominant financial and taxation powers, and extensive rights of supervision over the Länder.

The Bonn Constitution, on the other hand, created Länder of less disparate size and influence, with somewhat greater residual powers (especially in the cultural field), stronger administrative and financial autonomy, and the protection of judicial review by the Constitutional Court. In view of this deliberate redressing of the balance after 1945 the political reality of previous German federal systems can scarcely form a touchstone for the general interpretation of the federal aspects of the Basic Law. It may be, and is, used for example to clarify the content of specific terms and concepts inherited from earlier constitutional usage. But for assistance in handling the concept of the *Bundesstaat* it is to legal doctrine that the Court must look, and here it has been shown that the federal tradition is by no means unequivocal even in its most fundamental aspects.

Some modern legal scholars have tended to jettison much of the legacy of the older *Staatstheorie* and to dismiss as sterile such issues as the divisibility of sovereignty or the 'derivative' nature of one of the levels of government. Thus for Scheuner in particular such preoccupations stem from an obsolete monarchical notion of the state as a kind of overlord rather than as an institutionally ordered association of its citizens.[12] However, it could scarcely be said that post-war jurisprudence in Germany had devised a generally accepted replacement for traditional conceptions and theories of federalism,[13] and elements of the latter persist.[14] Indeed the lack of a theory of the contemporary federal state is the point of departure of Hesse's book, *Der unitarische Bundesstaat*.[15] In common with other authors Hesse sees the *raison d'être* of the modern federal state in the decentralization of political initiative and the institutionalization of an additional form of separation of powers. Scheuner, on the other hand, rejects the attempt to explain federalism from the national perspective alone as simply an expedient organizational form, on the ground that it is a violation of the basic federal principle to ignore the existence of the individual members as centres of political decision-making in their own right. He puts the emphasis not on the mere division of powers but on the balanced interplay of the whole and the parts, defining the essence of the *Bundesstaat* as consisting in the historical experience by which its structure was created, the continuing consensus of its citizens and the spirit of co-operation, accommodation, and compromise.[16] The deliberations of the Conference of German Constitutional Lawyers in Münster in 1962 provide a convenient collation of the differing views of the nature of federalism.[17]

The lack of a consistent tradition of federal doctrine does not preclude the Federal Constitutional Court from borrowing from the literature of *Staatstheorie* and seeking out what is appropriate for the concrete situation. But any attempt to amplify the detailed federal provisions of the Basic Law by this method is bound to be a fairly arbitrary, or at least pragmatic, process.

Some of the early decisions of the Court on federal matters were indeed overlaid with the language of general principles and on occasion it explicitly derived its findings from 'the federal principle' or 'the essence of the *Bundesstaat*'. Three examples of its doing so may be cited.

(i) The first instance is provided by the decision on the South-West State: 'A further basis of the constitution is the *federal* principle (*Art.* 20, 28, 30 *GG*). As members of the Bund the Länder are states with their own supreme state power, which—even if limited in its field of application—is not derived from the Bund but recognized by it.'[18] From this rather 'federalist' formulation—it is not clear how far a distinction can convincingly be drawn between *Hoheit* and 'sovereignty'—the Court draws the conclusion that the shaping of the constitutional order in each Land falls within its own legitimate sphere, provided it remains within the framework of *Art. 28 Abs.* 1 *GG* which requires it to conform to the principles of a republican, democratic, and social state based on law. In particular the determination of the rules for the formation of the constitutional organs of the Land, their functions and their powers, including provisions as to how often and on what occasions the citizen may exercise his franchise and when and under what circumstances an elected Land parliament is dissolved, is exclusively a matter for the individual Land. So long as the Länder exist and their constitutional order conforms to *Art. 28 Abs.* 1 *GG*, the Bund cannot intervene without violation of the federal principle guaranteed in the Basic Law. The Court used this statement of general federalist principle to conclude that although the Bund had the power under *Art.* 118 *GG* to 'dismantle' the Länder of Baden, Württemberg-Baden and Württemberg-Hohenzollern in order to make possible a redivision of the federal territory, it did not have the right in anticipation of such redivision to prolong the life of their parliaments while they still existed.

(ii) The second instance of the Court basing a specific decision on the federal principle was the case concerning the constitutionality of 'horizontal financial adjustment'.[19]

Although economic development is, by international standards, spread relatively evenly across the Federal Republic, there are inevitably imbalances in the financial capacity of the individual Länder. To prevent this leading to unacceptable differences in the level of services provided, a particularly thorough financial equalization procedure was devised. Within the context of 'vertical financial equalization' between Bund and Länder, part of the latter's share of joint tax revenues (i.e. income and corporation tax, plus turnover tax since 1969) is used to compensate those Länder whose per capita tax receipts are below the average.[20] A further system of 'horizontal equalization' was instituted by *Art.* 106 *Abs.* 4 *GG* (original version), which provided for direct subsidies from the richer to the poorer Länder using funds taken from certain Länder taxes.[21] However, the Federal law of 1951 regulating the details of this redistribution was referred to the Constitutional Court by the Governments of Württemberg-Baden (then still in existence) and Hamburg, as being unconstitutional on the grounds of unfair discrimination against the wealthier Länder.

The Court in its decision first acknowledged that the federal system of the Basic Law guaranteed the budgetary independence of the Länder, but then argued that the federal principle established not only rights but also duties. It thus proceeded to justify the financial-equalization provisions on the basis of the duty of mutual support incumbent on Bund and Länder in a federal system, accepting that this 'duty relationship' necessarily involved some limitation of the financial autonomy of the Länder. However, it hastened to derive limits to this duty from the same federal principle. Equalization may not be used to achieve a financial 'levelling' of the Länder (which was clearly not the import of the 1951 legislation), but may aim only at a relative improvement of the financial capacities of the weak Länder. Due account must be taken of the financial requirements of the Länder obliged to provide equalization payments and the practice must not serve to prop up intrinsically unviable Länder.

This derivation from the federal principle of a duty of solidarity towards financially weaker Länder is remarkable, considering that *Art. 106 Abs. 4 GG* as then in force already created a positive right of the Bund to take Land funds for purposes of financial equalization: 'In order to ensure the viability of Länder with a weaker tax base and to equalize the disparate burdens of expenditure falling on the different Länder, the Federation may make grants using funds taken for this purpose from certain taxes accruing to the Länder. . .' In the light of these provisions it is strange that the Court should first have resorted to the duties implied by the federal principle to justify the financial measures. For such an examination presumably carries with it the theoretical possibility of arriving not merely at the contrary conclusion, viz. that the federal principle does *not* require horizontal financial equalization, but even at the contradictory one that it does not even permit it, which would have the embarrassing result that *Art. 106 Abs. 4 GG* itself was contrary to the federal principle. Given a concrete constitutional ruling, the only sensible use of general principles of federalism is as a guide to the interpretation of that ruling. Thus they could be used to define more closely the circumstances under which the Bund 'can' make grants, or the permissible proportions in which the funds may be distributed, or to introduce discussion of economic and social factors determining the degree of redistribution necessary to enable the financially weak Länder to carry out their functions.

Even this is a very major role for the federal principle and allows considerable freedom of manoeuvre. But a simple derivation from the 'essence' of the federal principle of a duty of the stronger Länder to contribute resources to the weaker is here not merely unnecessary but also arbitrary. For traditionally the federal principle would seem to point on the contrary to dependence of member states on their own local revenues with at most certain taxes being shared on a uniform basis with the Federal government. Yet equally, in view of the co-operative element of federalism, it could hardly be held to exclude financial equalization as provided for by the Basic Law. This is an illustration of the problems arising from the lack of clarity as to what federalism consists in. In such circumstances the only wise course is to conclude that the federal principle neither prohibits nor demands horizontal financial adjustment and to rely on the black letter of the constitution. It looks as if the Court may have considered that its recourse to general obligations in a federal state provided a neat balance with its subsequent use of the federal principle to set limits to what can be required of the financially stronger Länder—limits which it admitted were not exceeded by the law of 1951. Since its decision in this case could on purely positive law grounds hardly have been otherwise, it was thus preparing the way unobtrusively and in comparatively uncontroversial circumstances for a more adventurous application of the principle in future.

(iii) When in 1952 Federal provisions for allocating resources for housing construction to the various Länder were challenged by the Bavarian Government, the Court's judgment again testified to an expansive approach to invocation of the federal principle.[22]

In so far as the Bavarian application asserted a claim to a

specific proportion of the available funds on the basis of an earlier agreement, the Court found the agreement in question not to have been legally binding. It focused its attention rather on the stipulation in §14 of the First Housing Construction Act that the resources earmarked by the Federal budget for social housing construction should be distributed by the Federal Minister of Housing by agreement with the Länder. In practice, however, the objections of a minority of the Länder, including Bavaria, were simply ignored, and the Federal Minister announced his intention of implementing his proposals as approved by the majority of the Länder.

The Court first made use of the federal principle for the purpose of confirming the legitimacy of a provision which made action by a Federal Minister dependent on agreement with the Länder.[23] It maintained that, in so far as the Länder did not already participate in Federal legislation and administration through the Bundesrat, there was nothing to prevent an ordinary Federal statute from introducing other forms of Länder influence on Federal policy-making, provided that this did not clash with explicit constitutional provisions or affect matters which must by their nature be the responsibility of the Bund alone. In support of this position the Court declared that it was in accordance with 'the federal structure' (*der föderalistischen Struktur*) of the Bund that it should grant the Länder a right of participation in certain administrative measures. However, it quickly backed up this general reasoning from the federal structure with the observation that co-operation by Bund and Länder in the field of administration was not foreign to the Basic Law either, as when the Länder executed Federal laws 'as agents of the Federation' (*Art. 85 GG*).

This recourse to the general nature of federalism is taken up again to support the conclusion (already reached from the wording of the relevant provision and confirmed by the history of its genesis) that the requirement of agreement with the Länder can only mean the consent of each and every Land. In the Court's view,[24] the participation of the Länder in the allocation of Federal funds is an expression 'of the federal principle' (*des föderalistischen Prinzips*), which along with other principles shapes the constitution of the Federal Republic of Germany. As members of the Federation, the Länder are equal in status and rights, in so far as positive constitutional provisions do not determine otherwise; they are not subject to the rule of majority decision-making which obtains in the sphere of the democratic principle, but rather to the principle of unanimity, viz. that no Land can be overruled by the other Länder. Finally, to counteract the potential ill effects of such a conclusion on the cohesion of the political system, the Court derived from the 'principle of federalism' the duty of federal comity incumbent on both Bund and Länder.[25]

From these early cases there emerges an evident enthusiasm on the part of the Court for using the concept of federalism to justify specific rulings concerning both the need to respect the independent status of the Länder and the requirements of solidarity within the federal structure.[26] Judge Geiger, in a lecture delivered in 1961,[27] declared, on the basis of various quotations of such generalizing statements by the Court, that there could be no doubt that the Constitutional Court's abstract concept of the federal state was a significant background influence on the interpretation of the specific constitutional order created by the Basic Law. He went on to emphasize the differences between this concept and the concept of the *Bundesstaat* which prevailed during the Weimar Republic. In contrast to Anschütz's conception of the potentially unlimited subjection of the Länder within the federal state, Smend's similar assessment of the republican, as opposed to the monarchical, *Bundesstaat,* and Triepel's view of the *Bundesstaat* as naturally developing towards the unitary, Geiger saw the conception of the *Bundesstaat* held by the Federal Constitutional Court as having lost this 'list' in favour of the Bund.

The contrast between these different concepts of the federal state was seen by Geiger as lying particularly in the issue of whether the Länder were in a subordinate or co-ordinate relationship with the Bund. This issue usually took the form of a dispute about whether the *Bundesstaat* was 'two-tiered' (*zweigliedrig*) or 'three-tiered' (*dreigliedrig*). On the two-tier theory, the Länder as member states are subordinate to the Bund as the *Gesamtstaat* or totality. The three-tier concept, on the other hand, views the *Bundesstaat* (or *Gesamtstaat*) as the sum of the Bund (or *Zentralstaat*) and the Länder. In the latter case it was natural to regard Bund and Länder as standing in a relationship of fundamental equality.

If the two-tiered conception of the federal state was the prevailing view of German jurisprudence, the concept of *Dreigliedrigkeit* had nevertheless found protagonists in such scholars as Kelsen[28] (who saw it as a mere historical accident that the authorities of the *Gesamtstaat* and the *Zentralstaat* were in practice always identical), Nawiasky[29] and Maunz.[30] It was clearly a 'federalist' view, in that by distinguishing between *Bund* and *Bundesstaat* (or *Gesamtstaat* or *Bundesrepublik Deutschland*) it assumed, as Geiger put it, that the interests of the Bund in relation to the Länder (the other 'parts' of the whole) by no means necessarily coincided with the interests of the whole.

The Constitutional Court went through some vacillations before reaching a definitive stance on this issue. The *South-West State Judgment* made a passing reference to the 'hierarchical relationship' (*Überordnungsverhältnis*) of Bund and Land which seemed entirely in accordance with the traditional doctrine.[31] By the time of the *Concordat Judgment*, however, the Court had dissociated itself from this position to the extent of specifying that the successor to the German Reich as party to the Concordat was 'the Federal Republic of Germany—that is in constitutional law the Bund and the Länder as a whole'. Later in the same judgment it referred to the Federal Republic, 'whose members are the Bund and the Länder'. On this basis it argued that since education belonged to the Länder's sphere of responsibility the Bund had no constitutional possibility of enforcing its external obligations on the Länder and concluded that in the case of conflict between Federal and Land interests it must be left to negotiation between Bund and Länder on the basis of equality (*Gleichordnung*) to produce a compromise.[32]

If proof were still needed that this theoretical issue of primacy in the federal state and of its dual or triple nature could have significant practical implications, it was provided by the *Territorial Reorganization Case* in 1961.[33] And here the Constitutional Court was to make another striking volte-face. Since several of the Länder were rather artificial and fortuitous constructions arising out of the zones of the occupying powers, *Art.* 29 *GG* laid down that the federal territory was to be reorganized by Federal legislation with due regard to regional ties, historical and cultural connections, economic expediency and social structure, to create Länder which by their size and capacity would be able effectively to fulfil the functions incumbent upon them. But although partial reorganizations were made by the creation of Baden-Württemberg and by the accession of the Saarland (with full effect from June 1959), and popular initiatives for a change of Land affiliation as provided for in *Art.* 29 *GG* had been successfully carried out in several areas,[34] the Federal Government was understandably reluctant to grasp such a political nettle. It announced its intention of postponing territorial reorganization on the ground that *Art.* 29 *Abs.* 6 *Satz* 2 *GG*, which set a time-limit expiring on 5 May 1958, was only a *Sollvorschrift* (i.e. an 'ought' rather than a 'must') and that due regard must be had to the problems of the re-establishment of German unity and the reintegration of the Saarland.

But when by 5 May 1958 no bill had been introduced for the reorganization of the federal territory, the Government of Hesse, one of the Länder which could hope to gain from such reorganization, charged the Federal Government before the Constitutional Court with dereliction of its constitutional obligations. It argued that the right of the Länder under *Art.* 29 *Abs.* 1 *GG* to a strengthening of the federal structure by means of territorial reorganization was being ignored by the Bund. This contention was then backed up by an explicit appeal to the concept of *Dreigliedrigkeit*. According to the Government of Hesse, in the three-tiered federal state presupposed by the Basic Law the reorganization of the federal territory, as a piece of supplementary constitution-making, was the responsibility of the Federal Republic of Germany as the *Gesamtstaat*. By *Art.* 29 *GG* the Bund as *Zentralstaat* was both authorized by the *Gesamtstaat* and put under obligation to it to fulfil this responsibility by means of Federal legislation. It was up to the Länder as guardians of the federal constitution to vindicate this duty of the Bund to the *Gesamtstaat* by recourse to the Constitutional Court.

In its decision the Court first agreed with the submission of the Federal Government that the Government of Hesse had no standing to raise the dispute, on the ground that disputes under *Art.* 93 *Abs.* 1 *Nr.* 3 *GG* presupposed the assertion of claims arising from a relationship existing in constitutional law between Bund and Länder. Such a legal relationship was lacking in the present case, the Bund having neither encroached upon the Land's jurisdiction nor disregarded a constitutional norm which safeguarded the rights of the Land. *Art.* 29 *GG* made territorial reorganization exclusively a concern of the Bund, not even requiring the assent of the Bundesrat as the organ whereby the Länder could influence the legislation and administration of the Bund. Moreover, an article calling on the Bund to create new Länder could not create a legal relationship between the Bund and the existing Länder; while a reorganization which could lead to a loss of identity by the present Länder was not provided for in the interests of the existing Länder but only in the interests of the whole.

The Court then explicitly rejected the conception of a three-tiered federal state as a basis for Hesse's case. True, in the *Concordat Judgment* it had referred to the Federal Republic of Germany as the *Bundesstaat* whose members were the Bund and the Länder. But this, the Court now maintained, was only intended to indicate that the internal partition of state powers within the federal state between the organs of the Bund and the organs of the Länder had no effect externally: rather, all organs which internally exercised state powers represented the Federal Republic of Germany in its external relations. It could not be deduced from this that in addition to the *Bundesstaat* as *Gesamtstaat* there was a separate *Zentralstaat;* there was only a 'central organization' which together with the 'member-state organizations' carried out as *Bundesstaat* all the state responsibilities which in a unitary state would fall to a centralized state organization. Such a formulation might appear still to hanker after a threefold division of the federal state. But the Court also declares that the 'Bund' as understood by the Basic Law is the *Gesamtstaat* created by the union of the Länder. The additional novel designation of the Bund as the *oberstaatliche Organisation*, which 'at the same time represents the *Bundesstaat* in relation to the member states . . .', and as the '*Oberstaat* which is brought about by the amalgamation of the Länder into a *Bundesstaat*', perhaps betrays further signs of discomfort. However, the Court rules out the possibility of a further alliance between this *Oberstaat* and the member states which would give rise to a so-called *Gesamtstaat*. It also expressly quotes its remark in the *South-West State Case* in support of its assertion that the *Oberstaat* is in principle 'superior in status' (*übergeordnet*) to the Länder; only in those fields which have not been regulated by the federal constitution is there equality of status. As evidence of this superiority the Court cites the so-called *Kompetenz-Kompetenz* of *Art.* 79 and 24 *GG*, whereby the power to amend the constitution or to transfer sovereign powers to intergovernmental institutions is vested solely in the Federal legislative organs. Moreover, the preservation of the federal constitution is in principle entrusted to the authorities of the Bund alone, and it is only where it obtrudes directly and with binding force upon the constitutions of the Länder that the latter may appear in relation to the central authorities as guardians of the constitution of the whole (but not as spokesmen of a hypothetical *Gesamtstaat* to which the *Zentralstaat* might be conceived as being under obligation).

With this verdict of the Court, for all the no doubt deliberate complexity of its formulation, little remains of the assertions by Geiger in the very same year[35] about the increasingly clear differentiation between *Bund* and *Bundesstaat* and about Bund and Länder alike being members of the whole with no room for a preponderance or legal superiority of the one over the other. How far this retreat from the Court's previously more federalist position is due simply to developments in the Court's internal politics, and how far to embarrassment over academic assaults on the three-tier theory,[36] is difficult to determine.

The disowning of the theory of the three-tiered federal state is in fact symptomatic of the role of the general concept of the *Bundesstaat* or the principle of federalism in the resolution of federal issues. Despite the auspicious beginnings indicated above, they have in later years seldom played a prominent part in the decisions of the Constitutional Court, and then mostly only in moral support of a more specific provision of the Basic Law or a conclusion already arrived at by other methods of interpretation.[37] Their generality and vagueness, together with the detailed dispositions of the Basic Law, may have rendered it difficult to make them do more.

The Court itself seems to acknowledge the intrinsic difficulties of appeal to such general principles in the *Second Federal Administrative Court Jurisdiction Case*.[38] Here 'general principles of

the federal state' were found not to prohibit the assignment to
Federal courts by Federal legislation of jurisdiction in matters
involving the application of Land law. In amplification the
Court observed that the federal constitutional order could take
very different forms. The strict separation of Federal and State
powers which distinguished the Constitution of the United
States was foreign to the Basic Law, which linked Länder and
Federal courts in hierarchies of appeal. It was self-evident that
Länder courts applied Federal law. This being the case, the
Court maintained, general federal principles could not be used
to deduce, with reference to the constitutional order of the Basic
Law and the interpretation of its relevant articles, that the
application of Land law by Federal courts was permissible only
when sanctioned by Land legislation. In this instance, therefore, the Constitutional Court recognizes that general federal
principles, if indeed there is any basis for ascertaining them in
view of the diversity of actual manifestations of federalism,
have no standing alongside the specific federal order established by the Basic Law.

In the light of such considerations, the Court is on comparatively safe ground when its finding is an extrapolation from the
written constitutional text. A good example of this occurs in
relation to the dispute about whether the school provisions of
the 1933 Concordat, which in 1949 had become Federal law
under the terms of *Art. 123 Abs. 2 GG,* were binding on the Land
legislator.[39] The Court maintained that such a verdict would be
particularly questionable in this instance because it would
result in a major inroad into the 'cultural sovereignty' (*Kulturhoheit*) of the Länder: this would be contrary to the federal
structure of the Federal Republic of Germany, in which cultural sovereignty, especially sovereignty in the field of education, was the kernel of the statehood of the Länder. Although
the Basic Law makes no reference to *Kulturhoheit,* an analysis of
those fields of government which are and are not assigned to the
legislative power of the Bund does indeed reveal that culture
(interpreted as including education) is the most substantial
field left in the hands of the Länder. From this it is but a short
(even if 'federalist') step to the discernment of an intended
'cultural sovereignty' of the Länder.

Such appeal, which is not uncommon,[40] to the characteristics and implications of the particular federal order established by the Basic Law continues to reveal a fundamentally federalist attitude on the part of the Constitutional Court. But it does not alter the conclusion that the Constitutional Court's use of the general principle of federalism in the adjudication of federal cases has, after its initial burst of enthusiasm, been relatively modest.[41] Much more prominent is the role allotted to its 'offspring', the doctrine of federal comity.

3 The principle of federal comity

The concept of 'federal comity'[42] appears to have its origins in the federalist view of the constitution of the German Reich. It turns up first in the language of politics where a 'treaty basis' of the German Reich is assumed, and hence the term *Bundestreue* is used interchangeably with *Vertragstreue* ('fidelity to the treaty'). Thus the Bundesrat declared unanimously on 5 April 1884: 'The governments are determined to uphold and maintain in inviolable fidelity (*Treue*) the treaties on which our Reich institutions are based.' A year later, moreover, Bismarck asserted explicitly before the Bundesrat: 'The Reich has its firm foundation in the federal fidelity of the Princes.'[43]

It has already been indicated that such a 'treaty basis', also called a 'federal basis', of the Reich constitution was rejected by most constitutional lawyers. Thus Triepel found the appeal to the treaties untenable as a lasting explanation because the treaties had been fulfilled and thereby extinguished. They had been replaced by the Reich Constitution. For Triepel the 'federal basis' was simply the historical fact that the constitution came into being by the will of all the member states: from this was derived the loyalty of those member states to the Reich.[44] It was therefore not until Rudolf Smend that *Bundestreue* was conceived as a genuine legal principle.

Smend[45] gives several examples of accepted duties of Reich and Länder which are not found in the constitution of the Reich. He rejects the Seydelian theory of the Reich as a confederation, but sees the emphasis of the historical basis of the constitution on a treaty as a justified emphasis on the mutual duties of *Bundes-* or *Vertrags-Treue* encompassing the exercise of explicit constitutional rights or duties. In other words, the

Reich and the member states are not simply in a relationship of subordination but also at the same time in the relationship of confederates: the special position of Prussia *vis-à-vis* the Reich executive seems to be used to require the Reich also to act towards the other member states in this spirit. Pointing to the analogy with the general principle of good faith (*Treu und Glauben*) in civil law, Smend finds that *Bundestreue* is not merely a political tradition or convention but an important unwritten legal principle inherent in the federal basis of the Reich Constitution.

Smend admittedly shows that the idea of the unwritten law behind the explicit constitutional provisions tended in the Bismarckian Reich to be used to undermine those provisions, provided that their spirit was allegedly observed. However, he speaks of a deliberate incompleteness of the Reich Constitution which is partly due to the technical difficulty of translating the import of unwritten law into precise constitutional provisions. As examples he cites the problem of stipulating how far the Reich is obliged to inform the individual states or even to reach an accommodation with them, or how far the latter may pursue foreign policy without trespassing upon the rights of the Reich. The unwritten principle of *Bundestreue*, Smend feels, preserves the necessary elasticity.

It must be borne in mind, however, that Smend was developing the principle of federal comity in the circumstances of the monarchical, as opposed to the republican, federal state. This is highlighted, for example, by a further proffered justification of the comity principle which he sums up as 'federal politeness': one could not speak in an overbearing way to the crowned heads of the individual states about their duties to the Reich. He was also writing in the absence of a developed system of judicial resolution of constitutional disputes. The concept of *Bundestreue* was taken up on occasion under the Weimar Republic by both legal scholars and courts. But it was only with the advent of comprehensive judicial interpretation of the constitution in the Federal Republic that the Constitutional Court developed the principle, which still found no explicit expression in the Basic Law, into a fully justiciable norm of federal relations.

The adoption of such an indeterminate unwritten principle

inevitably leaves open many questions, which have to be clarified in the course of the Court's decision-making. Thus Bayer points out that it is not clear how far the requirement of *Bundestreue* can itself independently create rights or duties of Bund or Länder, or whether it is merely a duty to have regard to the general interest in the exercise of a power; whether it can serve to ascertain the content of constitutional provisions (as Smend and Geiger are quoted as suggesting), or whether it is no more than a limitation on the permissible exercise of an undoubted constitutional right (the more generally accepted view).[46] It is evident that the concept opens up at least an opportunity for the development by the Court of a range of implied duties to correspond to the implied powers potentially deducible *kraft Sachzusammenhangs* or *aus der Natur der Sache*. But how has the Constitutional Court used the discretion thus afforded to it?

The question how far the doctrine of federal comity, indeterminate and conducive to judicial discretion as it necessarily is, has been used by the Constitutional Court to influence the shape of the West German federal system can be answered only by an extended analysis of those cases where it makes an appearance. This analysis will serve at the same time as a 'barometer' of the Court's role as arbiter of federal relations.

(i) The first explicit invocation of the principle of federal comity by the Constitutional Court came in the *Housing Funds Case*.[47] As has already been recounted, the Court here had no problem in finding that a legislative requirement that Federal resources be distributed by agreement with the Länder could only mean that all the Länder must have consented to the proposed allocation. However, recognizing the political reality of the risk of deadlock in cases where the law demands that an understanding be reached between Bund and Länder, the Court tried to modify its ruling by recourse to the duty of federal comity. This duty is derived directly and explicitly from the notion of federalism. The federal principle is held to establish for the Länder in their relations with each other and with the 'greater whole', and for the Bund in its relations with the Länder, a duty in constitutional law to keep 'faith' (*Treue*) and reach a common understanding. All the participants in the constitutional federation[48] are bound to co-operate in the spirit of this federation and to promote its consolidation and the well-understood interests of its members.[49] Rather gratuitously, but most revealingly in that it is quite contrary to the application of the principle in this case, the Court adds that it is above all the duty of federal comity that sets firm limits to the predominance of the *Gesamtstaat* in the interest of its members.

If the obligation to co-operate sincerely and reach a common understanding thus expounded by the Court sounds so vague and sweeping as to risk either being impossible to enforce or opening up possibilities of wholesale and unjustifiable interference with the political bargaining process and power relations (it is said to justify, in the interests of a general agreement, the disregarding of opposition on the part of one or more Länder on grounds not pertinent to the case), there is a hint that the Court itself felt some reservations about it: 'The compulsion to reach an accommodation entailed by this duty does not operate so automatically as the democratic majority principle: however, it is strong enough to bring about the necessary common decisions in an appropriate way.' In the case in hand, the Court decided that the Bavarian objections were indeed pertinent and could not be construed as a violation of the duty of federal comity. But in the process it had taken the opportunity to expound the principle of *Bundestreue* in a way which amply demonstrated its future possibilities. This was not the last time that the Court was to derive from the duty of federal comity such indeterminate but potentially far-reaching consequences for the character of negotiations between Bund and Länder.[50]

(ii) Two disputes concerning the permissibility of divergences of the remuneration of public servants in the Länder from that of their Federal counterparts both produced references, albeit rather less controversial references, by the Constitutional Court to the principle of federal comity.

The first case, a comparatively minor one, arose in 1953[51] when the Federal Government decided in view of its serious budgetary position not to give its civil servants a Christmas bonus that year. The governments and parliaments of Bavaria and Hesse, on the other hand, proposed to pay such a bonus as they had done the year before. This prompted the Bund to apply to the Constitutional Court for temporary injunctions to prohibit the execution of these decisions, on the gound that if they went ahead both the Federal Government and the other Länder Governments would be exposed to strong pressure to do the same despite their financial situation. Apart from holding that the actions of Bavaria and Hesse could not produce a *legal* duty for the other governments, which must be able in the fulfilment of their political responsibility to cope with 'moral' pressure, the Court decided that the strict conditions for the granting of temporary injunctions were not met. But it did add a warning that the Länder Governments must answer for their further decisions about Christmas bonuses themselves, that in doing so they must show federal comity and consider the balancing of their budgets in the context of the total financial structure of Bund and Länder.

This recognition of constitutional limitations upon the rights of financially strong Länder to grant remunerations which may be beyond the resources of the less affluent Länder (and the Bund) has obvious affinities with the *Finance-Equalization Decision*[52] discussed above, with its derivation from the federal principle of a duty of mutual financial support. Although the decision is not in itself of major importance, the brief, almost incidental, reference to the demands of federal comity does seem to open the way for the possibility of more general restrictions of Länder spending policies which run counter to the current economic needs of the Federal Republic as a whole. But such a case has not in fact been brought before the Court.[53]

(iii) In the following year the Court was confronted by a more major case in the same field, the *North Rhine Westphalian Salaries Case*.[54] It has already been shown how the Court found that the Federal framework regulations on civil servants' salaries, which the North Rhine Westphalian law in question had been alleged to contravene, were themselves invalid, thus leaving the Länder fundamentally free in the determination of the salaries of their officials.[55] But the Court then stressed that this did not mean that the Länder could proceed arbitrarily. It pointed to the general legal limitation upon the exercise of legislative powers in a federal state—by both Bund and Länder—arising out of the unwritten constitutional principle of federal comity: if the effects of legislation extend beyond the area of a Land's jurisdiction, then it must have regard to the interests of the Bund and of the other Länder. In determining the salaries of their officials the Länder must bear in mind that, in spite of the independent budgetary powers of Bund and Länder guaranteed in *Art.* 109 *GG,* there is a single overall financial structure in a federal state. In particular, since the Bund and the other Länder also have civil servants, the Länder are required by the principle of *Bundestreue* to take the general salary situation in Bund and Länder sufficiently into consideration, so that the whole financial structure is not shaken and the risks are minimized of variations in the attractiveness of the public service from Land to Land or dissatisfaction within the civil service, especially where Federal and Land officials work side by side.

Apparently aware that the principle of federal comity as formulated above could, if actively pursued, wipe out all the benefits gained by the Länder from the rejection of the Federal Government's case, the Court pointed out that in practice a Land law can be invalidated on the basis of violation of the obligations of *Bundestreue* only in cases of obvious misuse of legislative discretion. It also recognized that the Länder have a particular interest in giving their bureaucracies a distinctive image; complete uniformity in the payment of officials as obviously striven for by the Federal Government is demanded neither by the nature of the federal state nor by the constitutional order of the Federal Republic. By these criteria, the Court found no obvious misuse of its freedom on the part of North Rhine Westphalia. It regarded individual regulations indirectly leading to a higher salary for individual officials, such as a more favourable ordering of seniority, as immaterial, and declared that even the average raising of civil servants' incomes was not of such an extent that it could in its effects shake the finances of Bund and Länder. To this no doubt necessary political judgement it added the interesting assertion that it was very significant that in the opinion of the Federal organs themselves the Federal salary law which was taken by the Bund to be a binding standard was in need of reform. Considering the delay in introducing any reform, the Court said, behaviour of a Land which met some of the generally recognized requirements of a salary reform could not violate the principle of federal comity.

This argument, which could easily be omitted without altering the essence of the decision, is remarkable for its adducing the mere expression of a political opinion at Federal level as a justification of Land action. For the nullity of the Federal framework provisions, the Court's main finding, alone provided the Länder with freedom to determine general salary regulations. Thus in the case of validity of the Federal framework provisions, legislation of a Land incorporating reform of these would not be justified by the fact that reform was generally recognized to be necessary; while in the (actual) case of invalidity of the framework provisions, the only limitations imposed upon the legislative freedom of the Länder by the principle of *Bundestreue* were those of 'obvious misuse', and within those broad limits the opinion of the Federal authorities was irrelevant.

If, as seems probable, the Court's reasoning is only intended to be that if the Bund is generally in favour of such reform it cannot be a case of obvious misuse, this is also unsatisfactory. For the desirability in principle of reform of the Federal salary law would be compatible with its delay on all sorts of grounds such as practicality, expediency, timing, balancing of priorities, etc., all such considerations (which are often decisive) being the prerogative of the Federal authorities. There might be circumstances in which it would then be desirable for the Länder to undertake some of the necessary reforms, but, under the federal provisions of the Basic Law, once the Bund had occupied the field in virtue of its power to enact framework legislation they would have the right to do so only if explicitly authorized by the Bund—something the Bund clearly had no intention of doing. This argument by the Court thus makes most sense not as a legal but as a political argument directed at the Federal Government: How can you object to a Land doing something you yourselves admit needs to be done? It thus gratuitously adds, even if in a negative direction, a political dimension to thinking about federal comity which the Court was later at pains to deny.[56]

(iv) The *Concordat Case* of 1957 came as the climax of a struggle between the conflicting claims of the foreign affairs power of the Federation and the 'cultural sovereignty' of the Länder.[57] The Constitutional Court found that the Concordat concluded by the German Reich with the Vatican in 1933, which among other things guaranteed separate church-controlled schools for all Roman Catholic children in Germany, was still valid and binding. Yet under the Basic Law education came within the exclusive powers of the Länder. For this reason the Court refused the Federal Government's request that it should set aside a law of Lower Saxony which virtually did away with confessional education, ruling instead that an international obligation of the Federal Government arising from a treaty with a foreign power could not in itself furnish it with the right to regulate the subject in question if it otherwise fell within the jurisdiction of the Länder.

This decision amounted to a judicial confirmation of the conflict-ridden status quo and thus protected the position of the Länder for want of any legal means for the Bund to constrain them. In taking this line the Constitutional Court declined to follow the example set in equivalent cases by the United States Supreme Court and the High Court of Australia, both of which had adopted a broad construction of the foreign affairs power whereby the national government was entitled both to conclude and to implement treaties on subjects which would otherwise fall outside its enumerated powers in the constitution. Such rulings have the virtue of preserving the credibility of the Federal Government as a treaty-partner; but in an age in which international agreements cover an ever wider range of state activities, including those which in federal systems are normally the responsibility of the member states, they clearly provide an opening for substantial inroads into the jurisdiction of the latter by the expedient of concluding a treaty. Presumably it was for this reason that the German Court eschewed this path. Rather, as McWhinney points out,[58] the *Concordat Judgment* accords not only with the end-result but also with much of the reasoning of the Judicial Committee of the Privy Council in the controversial Canadian *Labour Conventions Case* of 1937.[59] However, it also shares the inherent unsatisfactoriness of the latter, in that it fails to provide any guidance as to how in such cases the gulf between the Federal Republic's international treaty obligations and its constitutional inability to implement them internally is to be overcome.

The Court suggested some basis for bridging this gulf by resorting to the principle of *Bundestreue*. From a brief review of its previous applications of the principle it drew the general conclusion that in the federal state nothing may happen which injures the whole or one of the members. Federal comity therefore demands special consideration by the members for the external interests of the Federation: 'It must be inferred from this that especially in the field of foreign relations, where the presumption is in favour of a Federal power, the duty of comity (*Treuepflicht*) on the part of the Länder towards the Bund is to be taken particularly seriously.'[60] Yet despite this admonition the Karlsruhe judges were not inclined to draw practical consequences from the doctrine. In view of both the decision of the Basic Law that in determining the confessional nature of the school system the Länder were restricted constitutionally only by *Art. 7 GG* (basic rights in relation to the school system) and the fact that for concordats, unlike treaties, the Länder had since 1949 full rights of regulating foreign relations in their fields of exclusive legislative power without Federal influence, it was concluded that in the present case there could be no question of the principle of federal comity establishing a constitutional duty of the Länder to the Bund to observe the school provisions of the Concordat. Thus, as in the foregoing *North Rhine Westphalian Salaries Case,* the Constitutional Court was restrictive in its use of the weapon of federal comity against the Länder. For in this case there seems little doubt that, had it so wished, the Court could have decided that the Länder had a duty in federal comity at the very least to abide by valid international obligations of the Federal Republic originating before the distribution of powers by the Basic Law. That it did not do so suggests that its paramount concern was to protect Länder control of education.

As for the practical solution of this and potential future deadlocks, the Court only had this to say: 'In the case of tension between Federal and Land interests, it must be left to an accommodation between Bund and Länder on a basis of equality to reach an acceptable settlement'.[61] It should be noted that the Constitutional Court is not here applying the principle of *Bundestreue* as requiring accommodation (though no doubt a refusal to attempt to reach an accommodation could be construed as a violation of federal comity). For the essence of *Bundestreue* is that it establishes concrete, if unwritten, legal obligations. The remark is more reminiscent of the old distinction of Smend (no longer made today) between *Bundestreue* and *bundesfreundliches Verhalten*, the latter being merely a mode of behaviour which is not constitutionally demanded yet practised in fact out of prudent regard for the sensitivities of the members of the federation.[62] That is to say, though not a constitutional (or *legal*) obligation, it is a political (or *moral*) one.

This can no doubt be regarded as a prudent exercise of judicial self-restraint, especially given that the Court had never before had to apply the doctrine of federal comity to such a highly charged political dispute, involving as it did not merely important powers of both Bund and Länder but also the interests of the Roman Catholic Church and a major source of inter-party hostility. Nevertheless it leaves a suspicion of being a helpless recognition by the Court that it has not solved the fundamental problem.[63] It is interesting, however, that a successful *modus vivendi* between Bund and Länder on the wider issue of the treaty-making power was worked out in the very same year as the *Concordat Judgment*, in the form of the 'Lindau Agreement'. This agreement made the contracting of international obligations by the Federal Government in fields of exclusive Länder powers conditional on the prior assent of the Länder; at the same time it provided that they should be informed at an early stage about prospective treaties affecting their interests even outside their exclusive competence, to enable them to press their point of view, and that a permanent Länder commission should be established for this purpose. The success of these arrangements can be seen in the proposal of the Commission on Constitutional Reform to codify them in the Basic Law while establishing an explicit obligation on the Länder to transform international obligations in their sphere of competence into domestic law.[64] To this extent, the Constitutional Court's decision could be argued to have been vindicated by political practice. But it is significant that the Commission expressly rejected a reference to the principle of *Bundestreue* as an adequate means of ensuring implementation by the Länder, citing the *Concordat Judgment* as evidence.

An examination of the cases so far cited in which the Court applied the principle of comity to Bund–Länder relations shows that in every case it is used not as the main basis of its judgment or even in support of its basic decision, but rather to restore something of a balance by mitigating the impact of the decision. Since all the decisions in question are basically in favour of the Länder, this means that the principle of *Bundestreue* is being used as a warning to the Länder not to become carried away by their legal victories to the point of actions contrary to the spirit of a federation and prejudicial to the needs of the whole. The next case, however, harks back rather to the use of the federal principle in the *Finance-Equalization Case* and shows that the Court was prepared to make more adventurous use of the doctrine of federal comity to impress upon the Länder the limits of permissible unco-operativeness and to reduce an otherwise existing power of discretion.

(v) The *Atomic Weapons Referendum Case*[65] demonstrated how far the Constitutional Court's strictures on federal comity had taken root in the federal consciousness, since for the first time the principle became the basis of an application to the Court.

In the course of the heated conflict between the political parties on the issue of German rearmament,[66] measures were passed in Hamburg and Bremen for the holding of advisory referendums on the question of support for or opposition to the Federal Government's policy of arming the Bundeswehr with nuclear weapons; this led to a case before the Constitutional Court,[67] which established that although such referendums would not be binding on any government, they would constitute undue pressure on the Bund in a field within its exclusive competence. A similar bill was introduced in the Landtag of Hesse, but when it ran into difficulties, some local authorities, including those of Frankfurt, Darmstadt, Kassel, and Offenbach, decided to go ahead on their own initiative. After unsuccessful attempts to persuade Hesse's Minister of the Interior to annul these decisions, the Federal Government took the matter to the Constitutional Court, with the claim that the local authorities had invaded the exclusive jurisdiction of the Bund over defence matters and that, in the absence of Federal powers of control over local government, the Land Government was violating its duty of federal comity by failing to exercise its constitutional supervision of the observance of the Basic Law by local authorities.

The Government of Hesse contended *inter alia* that encroachment on Federal powers could be effected only by laws or administrative acts, but not by taking up a political stance as indeed the Länder parliaments often did with regard to Federal affairs, and as had already happened in consultative referendums in the communes without objection by the Federal Government. The issue of *Bundestreue* it dismissed with the argument that it could not in itself establish any independent obligation on the Land but at most set an unwritten limit to the exercise of the Land's powers; besides, not merely the question whether the local authorities had violated the law but also the decision whether it wished to intervene lay within the discretion of the Land concerned.

The Court proceeded to demolish this narrow interpretation of *Bundestreue*: the principle was not something to be administered by the Länder 'as their own affair' as under *Art. 84 Abs.* 1 *GG*, but could only be 'observed'; it was indeed to be observed by Bund and Länder with regard to every governmental act of whatever kind. Most important: the Court indicated that it was possible to offend against the comity principle by sins of omission as well as of commission.[68]

Armed with this new statement of the multi-purpose nature of its tool of federal interpretation, the Court set about using it to confirm the arguments of the Federal Government. It laid down that local authorities might concern themselves with matters beyond those of purely local impact only in so far as they affected them in some special way (such as a specific intention to erect installations for atomic weapons on their territory). But general policy questions such as that to be asked in Frankfurt—'Should military forces be armed with atomic explosive devices, and atomic missile bases be installed, on German soil?'—clearly transgressed the municipal domain. The Court laid particular emphasis on the political background of the actions of the local authorities as the crucial element transforming a simple transgression of the limits of their powers into an 'invasion' of an exclusive Federal preserve: far from being individual local initiatives, the referendums represented a concerted nation-wide attempt to achieve the political effect which a consultation of the Federal electorate might have had and thereby to force a reversal of specific political decisions in the field of defence. As evidence of this it referred to the similarity of all the attempts at all the levels of the federal state to institute such referendums, as well as many utterances of opposition politicians.

The Court thus seems to have been attaching at least as much importance to the motives of the participants as to the objective facts. In this connection it also recognized that the local authorities' power of decision and willingness to shoulder responsibility were protected by the fact that the Land supervisory authorities in Hesse were not bound to intervene in every case of measures which conflicted with the law. But in a crucial passage it argued: 'That which according to Land law in relation to the municipality is a *power* lying in the discretion of the Land government, can under federal constitutional law become a *duty* of the Land in relation to the Bund'.[69] In the federal state Bund and Länder had a common duty to maintain the constitutional order, and where the Bund could not do so directly but was dependent upon Land co-operation, the Land was bound in federal comity to give such co-operation. Such an obligation was declared to be in the same vein as the Court's previous derivation from the principle of federal comity of a duty of the financially stronger to assist the financially weaker Länder[70] and a duty of all the Länder to reach an agreement on the distribution of Federal funds between them where their assent is legally required.[71]

As if shrinking from the anticipated impact of its finding in the context of the political battle between CDU and SPD, the Court ended by emphasizing the strictly legal nature of its decision. The ascertainment of a violation of the duty of federal comity, it said, did not presuppose evidence of 'faithlessness' or malevolence on the part of the Land; it implied no reproach. The only concern was with clarification of an objective concept of constitutional law and its application to circumstances in which it could be presumed that the participants were convinced of the constitutionality of their actions. The Government of Hesse had further claimed that it could only have violated its duty if it had acted contrary to the real interests of the Bund; while the question whether the Federal Government's policy with regard to atomic weapons was in the interests of the Federal Republic was precisely the subject of dispute, a dispute which was not justiciable. The Court replied that the violation of *Bundestreue* was not to be found in Hesse's political campaign against the policy of the Federal Government but in its refusal to intervene against an unconstitutional measure of the local authorities, a matter which was eminently capable of judicial examination. The trouble with this necessary attempt to define the proper concern of judicial decision and in particular of the doctrine of *Bundestreue* is that the Court had earlier put forward the political character of the local authorities' intentions as decisive in giving their actions the character of an 'invasion' of Federal powers; and it is in such circumstances that the context of the constitutional order of the Basic Law overrides the Land's normal discretion under its own constitution and changes a 'can' into a 'must'. Yet the Court clearly regards this political assessment as coming within its jurisdiction.

The inevitability of constitutional decisions being concerned with the political background of a case (compare the Court's comment that other local authorities would follow suit with referendums of their own if the present ones were declared legally admissible) means that the line between legal and political judgement cannot be clearly drawn. Indeed the cases so far studied suggest that one of the major purposes of development of the principle of federal comity was the avoidance of 'undesirable' consequences of decisions based narrowly on the letter of the constitution—consequences which are necessarily of a political nature.

In the present case it is difficult not to agree with Konrad Hesse[72] that the same result follows directly from the validity of the general constitutional order. Thus the Court itself states: 'In the *Bundesstaat* Bund and Länder have a common duty to preserve and establish the constitutional order in all parts and at all levels of the federal state (*Gesamtstaat*).' It is not clear why the principle of federal comity must be adduced in support of this sentence to procure a duty of the Land Government to intervene. But this would not remove the Court's need or temptation to make political judgements. Moreover, in the next case involving application of the principle of *Bundestreue* the Court was to reveal much more clearly that this was what it was doing.

Up to this point the principle of federal comity had been applied (apart from a secondary warning against a 'levelling' of the Länder in the *Housing Funds Case*) to restrict the freedom of the Länder in their relations with the Federal authorities. Since the principle is to a large extent the Court's own development this appears to give the lie to allegations that the judges were concerned only to support the claims of the Länder; though it must be admitted that some of the decisions reveal an evident reluctance to deduce from it any specific, practical, and immediately binding consequences for Länder conduct. But potentially the duties established by the principle of respect, consideration, and co-operation in the exercise of powers could equally be imposed upon the Bund, and in 1961 the *Television Case* showed that the Court was prepared to do this in a new and dramatic way.

(vi) The momentous *Television Judgment* of 1961[73] made clear for the first time in no uncertain manner that *Bundestreue* did not simply mean 'loyalty to the Bund', but rather that for the Federal authorities *Bundestreue* meant *Ländertreue*: it was not merely in theory that comity was required as much of the Bund as of the Länder.

For an appreciation of the judgment's application of the principle of federal comity it is necessary to recall some of the political background to the case. The first television channel had been organized by agreement between the Länder and various private associations without any Federal attempt to interfere. But the Federal Government revealed from an early stage that it intended to exercise more influence over broadcasting, intentions strongly resisted by the Länder as an encroachment on what they saw as part of their cultural sovereignty. The Länder reacted by increasing co-operation among themselves, but nevertheless protracted negotiations were held with the Federal Government on its broadcasting claims. These remained fruitless, however, and in 1959 a Federal broadcasting bill providing for a commercial television network was introduced unilaterally. When the Länder unanimously rejected this bill in the Bundesrat, Chancellor Adenauer's response was to use his massive influence in the CDU to erode the intransigence of those Länder with Christian-Democratic governments. This produced a compromise whereby a law providing for Federal Government influence over foreign short-wave radio broadcasting and a share in a new broadcasting authority was passed against SPD opposition.

But as soon as Adenauer had this behind him, he produced a plan for a purely administrative agreement creating a limited company to run the second television channel under joint Federal and Länder control. This plan was discussed in two meetings on 8 and 15 July 1960, at which apart from the Federal Government only the CDU and CSU Länder Prime Ministers and CDU and CSU members of the Bundestag were represented. It was proposed that the agreement establishing the television company be signed on 25 July. The first the heads of government of the SPD Länder heard of this plan was a letter of 16 July from Herr Altmeier, the Prime Minister of Rhineland Palatinate, inviting them to a discussion of the outcome of the negotiations on 22 July. In the event, astonishingly, even the SPD governments did not reject the proposal, but certain reservations and counter-proposals were attached. However, in a letter dated 23 July Adenauer replied that he could not answer for further postponement of the foundation of the company, but that the agreement would be so formulated that the accession of the Länder would be possible at any time. On the 24th he hastily recalled Schäffer, his Minister of Justice, from holiday and appointed him trustee for the interests of the Länder until they should join the company. The following day the 'Deutschland-Fernsehen-GmbH' was established in Cologne. A month later, by which time it was clear that none of the Länder was prepared to participate, Schäffer transferred his share of the company to the Federal Republic.

Meanwhile all four SPD Länder (Hamburg, Bremen, Hesse, and Lower Saxony) challenged the Federal Government's action before the Federal Constitutional Court on the grounds of infringement of the guarantee of 'freedom of reporting by broadcasting' contained in *Art. 5 GG*, of the residual powers of the Länder under *Art. 30 GG*, and of the duty of federal comity.

The Court's decision made use of the principle of federal comity at several points. In the first place it provided a further example of the duty of *Bundestreue* modifying an existing freedom of discretion (as in the *Atomic Weapons Referendum Case*) and in particular establishing limits for both Länder and Bund in the exercise of their powers (as in the *Christmas Bonus Case*). Having already decided that the Bund's power over 'postal and telecommunication services' encompassed only the technical sphere of transmission but not broadcasting as a whole, which fell within the 'cultural sovereignty' of the Länder,[74] the Court was concerned to prevent the Bund's exercise even of this limited power from having too far-reaching effects which might prejudice the organization of broadcasting by the Länder. The principle of federal comity would be violated, it said, if the Bund made such use of its powers as amounted to removing from the existing broadcasting stations their right of disposing of their own transmitting equipment. This would be the case if Federal legislation were to deprive these stations of the wavelengths they used and in its distribution of presently available or prospective frequencies failed to show them due consideration in accordance with the arrangements of Länder legislation for broadcasters.[75]

This application of the principle of *Bundestreue* lies well within the Court's previous practice, except for the novel aspects of its being used against the Federal Government and not to mitigate the impact of a favourable decision but rather to restrict further an already restricted power. It may therefore be vulnerable to the charge that the situation could be catered for as well by the more conventional concept of *Rechtsmissbrauch* ('abuse of powers'), but not to that of being an instrument designed to enable an unprecedented intrusion to be made into the political process. But the Court was not content to leave matters there. After a brief sketch of its use of the doctrine hitherto it summed up:

Rulings of the Court hitherto reveal both the possibility of developing from this principle specific additional duties of the Länder towards the Bund and of the Bund towards the Länder, such as go beyond the duties in constitutional law explicitly established in the federal constitution, and also that it gives rise to specific restrictions in the exercise of the powers granted to Bund and Länder in the Basic Law.[76]

The present case, it continued, gave occasion to develop the principle further in another direction. It then launched into a massive attack on the whole of the Federal Government's conduct of the negotiations and its treatment of the Länder throughout the affair, using for its purpose the principle of federal comity: 'The conduct and the style of such negotiations as may become necessary in constitutional practice between the Federation and its members and between the Länder are also subject to the requirement of federal comity.'[77] First the Court emphasized that all the Länder enjoyed the same constitutional status and had a right to equal treatment by the Bund. That being so, whenever the Bund sought an agreement on a matter with which the Länder were constitutionally concerned, it was prohibited by the duty of federal comity from acting on the principle of *divide et impera*, in other words from aiming to split the Länder, seeking an agreement with only some of them and leaving the others with no choice but to participate in a *fait accompli*. The Federal Government was not allowed to treat Land governments differently according to their party-political complexion, in particular to call to the decisive discussions only representatives of those Länder governments which it found politically congenial. The Court recognized that politicians belonging to a single party at the two levels of government had every right to clarify and harmonize their views on the solution of problems concerning the Bund and all the Länder both before and during the official negotiations. But this did not remove the obligation to hold intergovernmental negotiations with all the Länder on equal terms.

The Court then singled out the Federal Government's treatment of the Länder in the last few days before its establishment of the limited company. It pointed to an anomaly in the Federal Chancellor's final communication to the Prime Minister of Rhineland Palatinate, in which he declared that there could be no further delay and the agreement setting up the Deutschland-Fernsehen-GmbH would be signed on 25 July in the form envisaged by the Federal Government. Although the letter was dated 23 July 1960, it was not dispatched in Bonn until 5 p.m. the following day and did not reach Herr Altmeier until 4.15 p.m. on 25 July, by which time the company had been formally established. Such behaviour was in the Court's view simply incompatible with the requirement of federal comity, even if the Federal Government had reason to be annoyed at the way in which the Länder, or some Länder governments, were dragging their feet. It was not a question of whether the Federal Government could regard the negotiations with the Länder as having broken down and so take what it thought to be the quite constitutional step of establishing the company without participation by the Länder; but rather that every Land government had the right to expect from the Federal Government that it would not simply answer new counter-proposals of the Länder with a *fait accompli*—and at improperly short notice at that.

In addition, the way in which the company was actually set up was found to conflict with the duty of federal comity. The Court accepted that there could be situations in which the Bund might establish an association in the interests of the Länder and appoint as a partner a 'trustee' for the Länder. But when as in this case it was clear that the Länder were not willing to participate, it was a breach of federal comity if the Bund found some 'trustee' for the Länder and with his help established the company to which the Länder had objected.

Not surprisingly, this point by point sermon to the Federal Government on its breaches of a code of acceptable political conduct caused a sensation. The indignant reaction of the Federal Government itself and in particular Adenauer's announcement to the Bundestag that in the unanimous view of his Cabinet the judgment was 'false' is, if constitutionally disturbing, nevertheless understandable, suggesting as it does that the Court's remarks had struck home. There can after all be no doubt that the Federal Government, and particularly Adenauer himself, fully deserved such criticism. Admittedly, there could be some justification for a charge of one-sidedness in the fact that the years of obstructive delay by the Länder, which no doubt severely tested the Federal Government's patience, receive no more than a parenthetic reference. Nor can such an omission simply be explained away on the ground that obstruction was within the rights of the Länder because the broadcasting power was theirs. For the Court made it clear that its criticism of the Federal Government's behaviour held good even under the latter's presumption of the constitutionality of its objectives. Geiger[78] claims that the sole reason why only the Federal Government's behaviour was measured against the requirements of *Bundestreue* was that the legal representatives of the Bund, unlike those of the Länder, had not made accusations of violation of federal comity. But in view of the Court's previous enthusiasm for applying the principle regardless of the fact that the litigants themselves did not raise it until the *Atomic Weapons Referendum Case*, this is not very convincing. Nevertheless it can scarcely be denied that the Federal Government's 'misdemeanours' had been much more glaring and more detrimental to federal relations and to the balance of the federal system.

But what caused such public controversy, and indeed criticism even in quarters not generally sympathetic to Adenauer, was rather the highly political argumentation and severity of tone of a rebuke which was purely incidental to the decision of a fairly clear-cut question of legislative and administrative powers under the Basic Law. There were many complaints that the Court had invaded the realm of the political, that it had obscured the boundary between constitutional judgment and political criticism by its lecture to the Federal Government on the tactics it employed to reach its political objectives, that condemnation of the style of negotiations between Bund and Länder constituted a judicialization of politics.[79] Sometimes such complaints were provoked simply by shock at the first major instance of the Constitutional Court thwarting Adenauer's Government in an issue where its prestige was at stake (and in an election year at that). But it was the dramatically extended use of the weapon of *Bundestreue* that enabled the Court to humiliate the Federal Government, whereas a more sober technical approach restricted to the jurisdictional provisions of the Basic Law, such as is to be found in the first half of the judgment, would have achieved the required results for control of the second television channel without causing anything like such a stir.

Thus although the Court said in a revealing sentence that the issue 'gave occasion' (it might almost have said 'opportunity') to develop the principle of federal comity further, it is not clear that this was either necessary or felicitous. It is true that it had the instigation of the SPD lawyer Adolf Arndt, who on behalf of the Länder had stressed the relationship between the mode of procedure of the Federal Government and the duty of federal comity, so that the *obiter dictum* was not purely gratuitous. But

though it was highly desirable that it should be brought home
to the Adenauer Government that such high-handed conduct
towards the Länder was inadmissible, it was very doubtful
whether this reprimand should come in pseudo-legal terms
from a court of law, even the Constitutional Court, prestigious
and inevitably concerned with the political though it was. It is
indeed ironic to recall at this point the protestations of the
Court in the *Atomic Weapons Referendum Case* that the ascertainment of a violation of the principle of federal comity does not
presuppose evidence of 'faithlessness' or malevolence nor imply
any reproach.

There is in fact some doubt as to the logical relationship of
the *obiter dicta* on procedure and style to the main body of the
decision. Karl Zeidler[80] argues plausibly that strictly speaking
non-observance of the rules of procedure derived by the Constitutional Court from the principle of federal comity would
lead to even a constitutionally permissible outcome of the
negotiations being null and void. This view finds confirmation
from one of the judges responsible for the decision, Willi
Geiger,[81] who wishes to show thereby that a finding of unconstitutionality of procedure or style is not purely theoretical or
vacuous. But such a power of disallowance of arrangements
which in themselves are constitutionally unobjectionable looks
like an unwarranted restriction of the freedom of political decision of Bund and Länder.[82]

Finally, the Court hinted at another possible far-reaching
innovation in the use of the principle of federal comity, namely
that it could justify a constitutional claim of a Land upon the
Bund that the latter should not disregard the common constitutional order in such a way as to damage the interests of the
Länder as member states of the federation. It did not feel
obliged to decide this general question. But with reference to
the case in hand it did conclude that the constitutional guarantee of the freedom of broadcasting contained in *Art.* 5 *GG* was at
all events of such fundamental importance for the whole of
public, political, and constitutional life in the Länder that they
could require of the Bund that it leave this freedom intact. Since
on the face of it at least most of the basic rights of *Art.* 1-19 *GG*
could just as plausibly be claimed to be 'of fundamental importance for the whole public, political, and constitutional life in

the Länder', Zeidler suggests that this is indicative of a 'compact theory of federalism' by which any violation of the constitution is necessarily a violation of the compact and thereby of the rights of all the parties to it.

With the *Television Case* we have reached the high-point of the doctrine of federal comity. It now looked as if this indeterminate norm developed by the Constitutional Court might be capable of almost unlimited extension over every aspect of the political relations between Bund and Länder. It was at this point that Geiger declared enthusiastically that through the decisions of the Constitutional Court the principle had gained 'a fundamental, comprehensive significance which profoundly shapes the whole constitutional structure'.[83] And some time later Reich concluded: 'Where the development of Bonn federalism is concerned we are in the realm of judicial supremacy, and the principal instrument the Court has evolved for exercising its right is its doctrine of federal comity.'[84] But those who hoped for increasing judicial supervision of the fair play and good manners of the partners in the federal state, or who feared increasing judicial constraints upon the natural give and take of a dynamic federal system, were to be proved mistaken over the following years.

(vii) The first sign of the Court pulling in its horns on the issue of federal comity came in the same year as the *Television Judgment,* in the *Territorial Reorganization Case* already cited above.[85] To its other arguments for compelling the redrawing of the map of the Länder under *Art. 29 GG* the Government of Hesse added an appeal to the principle of *Bundestreue.* This latter was said to impose on the Federal Government a duty to introduce an appropriate bill, since the prevailing uncertainty as to what territory the Länder would finally comprise complicated the work of government and impeded the territorial organization of Land administration.

However, the Court was not disposed to accept such a claim: 'The principle of federal comity . . . constitutes or limits rights and duties within an existing legal relationship between Bund and Länder . . ., but it does not independently establish a legal relationship between them.'[86] Thus the mutual legal relations within which comity is to be observed must already exist or be created by negotiations. But the Court held that this was not the case with *Art.* 29 *GG*, which was not a part of the constitutional order whose maintenance it had declared in the *Atomic Weapons Referendum Case* to be the common duty of Bund and Länder; rather, it created a right and a duty exclusively for the Bund. It was true that Bund and Länder had in the exercise of their share of state power each to show consideration for the interests of the other part. But territorial reorganization was enjoined upon the Bund precisely not in the interests of the existing Länder, which could even be abolished, but in the interests of the whole. The Länder would simply have to live with the fact that the uncertainty of their continued existence and territorial integrity impeded their legislative and administrative activity.

The Court thus resisted the temptation to put forward an interpretation along the lines that although the duty to reorganize the federal territory was not an obligation to the Länder, nevertheless the principle of federal comity required the Bund in its approach to its general constitutional rights and duties to show due consideration for the legitimate interests of the Länder, for example for the difficulties arising for the Länder from uncertainty about their future territorial extension. The decision thus reveals a markedly more restrictive approach to federal comity than in the *Television Case*. It is interesting to note that the Court expressly added an indication of its unwillingness to be drawn into the realm of the political: the appropriate means for the Länder to press their political interest in the settlement of their territorial existence, it declared, was not application to the Constitutional Court but the political means of influence on the Federal organs, in particular through the Bundesrat as the organ designed to bring the political interests of the Länder to bear at the Federal level. It added that although it was assumed on account of the complicated nature of the subject that the bill would be introduced by the Federal Government, the latter had no monopoly of initiative regarding a territorial reorganization bill.

The Court's decision that not every duty arising from the Basic Law entails a corresponding justiciable right of another participant looks surprising in view of its finding in the *Television Case* that the guarantee of the freedom of broadcasting contained in *Art.* 5 *GG* is of such fundamental importance for the whole public, political, and constitutional life of the Länder that they have the right to demand of the Bund even by legal action that it observe the common constitutional order. It therefore felt obliged to refer to the question which it had there explicitly left open, and concluded that the right of the Länder to demand *Bundestreue* of the Bund did not extend to all provisions of the Basic Law but only to cases (such as a state-controlled broadcasting network) in which the interests of the Länder as member states of the federation were damaged. In fact the failure to carry out a constitutional directive to reorganize the federal territory could not damage the legal interests of the existing Länder as regards their incorporation in the total constitutional order. Rather, *Art.* 29 *GG* instructed the Bund to determine territorially the Länder for which the common constitutional order would then be valid.

Although it has been argued here that the Court could have used the principle of federal comity to compel a territorial reorganization, there can be little doubt that its restrictive interpretation in this case was a wise one, not least in view of the formidable political consequences of compelling a redrawing of Länder boundaries. Moreover, the practical difficulties of the Länder were not very convincing given the manifest determination of the Federal Government to postpone such a measure indefinitely. It has already been noted[87] that after further protracted efforts to secure implementation of *Art.* 29 *GG* it was finally amended in 1976 so as to remove entirely the obligation of the Bund to act: this belated constitutional adjustment may be held to vindicate the Constitutional Court's rejection of the Hessian submission, showing as it does that there was no strong and enduring tide of opinion in its favour.

At all events it can clearly be argued that *Art.* 29 *GG* has special features, so that it would be premature to deduce from this decision too radical a reassessment by the Court of the political scope of the legal doctrine of *Bundestreue*.

(viii) The *Bank Lending Case* in 1962[88] contained a brief reference to the principle of federal comity, only to dismiss it as inapplicable. Nevertheless for the purposes of the present assessment the decision *not* to draw consequences from the doctrine of *Bundestreue* may in itself be significant.

The case arose from an application by the Länder challenging a Federal law of 1961 which subjected the lending banks to the supervision of a Federal Bank Inspectorate (*Bundesaufsichtsamt für das Kreditwesen*). The latter was set up as an 'autonomous Federal higher authority' under *Art.* 87 *Abs.* 3 *GG* and was to work in close co-operation with the Bundesbank. This replaced the situation which had grown up since 1945, whereby the Länder carried out supervision of the banks, with a special committee for purposes of co-ordination. One of the submissions of the Länder was that the establishment without good reason of the Federal Bank Inspectorate violated the duty of federal comity.

The Court rejected the Länder's case on all counts. It found that *Art.* 87 *Abs.* 3 *GG* on the establishment of 'autonomous Federal higher authorities' gave the Bund an additional administrative power, which did not need to have foundation elsewhere in the Basic Law. Moreover, the Federal Bank Inspectorate met the condition, implicit in the concept of 'autonomous Federal higher authority', that it could be established only for functions which by their nature could be exercised for the whole federal area without an administrative substructure or substantive employment of the administrative authorities of the Länder; on the other hand, *Art.* 87 *Abs.* 3 *GG* did not rule out a Federal higher authority which could perform its functions only in co-operation with an already existing Federal higher authority or Federal corporate body or institution under public law, as was the case with the new Inspectorate's relationship with the Bundesbank.

The Court then turned briefly to the view of the Länder that under the principle of federal comity the Bund must not, without a compelling reason, deprive the Länder by the establishment of autonomous Federal higher authorities of functions which Land administration had exercised over a long period. Citing the *Television Judgment*, the Court recalled that the duty of *Bundestreue* acted as a check upon the exercise of Federal powers too. But the mere fact of the Bund's availing itself of a power granted to it by the Basic Law did not in itself constitute a violation of federal comity. That could be the case only if its use of the power was improper, as already laid down in the *North Rhine Westphalian Salaries Case*.[89]

The Court had really no option here but to reject the argument based on *Bundestreue*, not merely in view of the rest of the decision but also because of its virtual irrelevance. It looks indeed as if the Länder had simply thrown in the breach of comity claim as an afterthought for good measure, and perhaps because of the Court's notorious partiality to the doctrine. A finding in favour of the Länder on the basis of the requirements of federal comity would in its own way have been more sensational than the *Television Judgment*, where at least the Federal Government's lack of competence was already manifest on other grounds.

(ix) The principle of federal comity does not make another appearance until the *Hessian Water Law Case* in 1967, when it is again urged against the Bund, again only to be rapidly dismissed.[90] In this case, however, the Court's decision itself went (and unanimously) against the Bund. The question at issue, as raised by the Government of Hesse, was whether the Bund had violated *Art.* 30 *GG* and the duty of federal comity in that authorities belonging to the Federal 'Water and Shipping Administration' had issued licences and authorizations on the basis of the Water Act of the Land of Hesse and charged fees for them according to the Hessian Law on Administrative Fees. The application to Karlsruhe was made after unsuccessful requests to the Federal Ministry of Transport to desist from this practice.

In upholding Hesse's case the Court found that the Hessian Water Act, upon which the Federal authorities were relying, and the Federal framework law which it was elaborating, concerned 'water' in its significance for human use and consumption, that is under the aspect of 'water economy and land use', not in its significance as 'waterway and traffic route': in consequence, a Federal right to implement these laws could not be derived from the powers conferred by *Art.* 89 *Abs.* 2 *GG* for the administration of the federal waterways. It then demonstrated exhaustively that the relevant activities of the Federal authorities nevertheless required a legislative foundation but that such a foundation was lacking. To the extent that they were executing a Land law—something for which under *Art.* 30 and 83 *GG* the Land authorities were exclusively competent—they were acting unconstitutionally.

As an illustration of the contradictory position of the Bund, the Government of Hesse had cited its different treatment of the individual Länder: in Bavaria and Baden-Württemberg the Bund had not claimed the right to execute the corresponding provisions of Land law. The result was that, for example, the licence for the introduction of a ferry to link the Hessian with the Bavarian bank of the Main had been issued for the Bavarian part of the Main by the Regierungspräsident of Unterfranken, but for the Hessian part by the Federal administration. On such grounds, it was argued, the Bund had violated its duty of federal comity. For, since all the Länder had the same constitutional status, the Bund was not entitled to lay claim in certain Länder to a power which it ceded to the Land administration in others.

The Court, however, declared that the duty of federal comity would come into play only if a concrete constitutional relationship existed between the Bund and the Land such as gave rise to a *right* of the Bund; in the light of the duty of federal comity the Bund might not be permitted to exercise this right in a specific way or else might be required to act in a specific way on the basis of it. It cited all the applications of the doctrine up to the *Television Case* in support of this view. In the case under review, on the contrary, there was no right or power on the basis of which the Bund could take the administrative action contested by Hesse.

The view of *Bundestreue* advanced here by the Court is in conformity with its interpretation in the *Territorial Reorganization Case*, although the formulation seems to be subtly more restrictive; certainly some of the more boldly articulated decisions cited here by the Court can only with some difficulty be fitted into these specifications. And this time the Court's failure to avail itself of the principle of federal comity when it could have put it to modest use in support of its main finding does leave a slight impression of loss of faith in its doctrine and of judicial retreat.

(x) The *Broadcasting Authorities Taxation Case* of 27 July 1971[91] raises another aspect of the question of the Bund's powers in relation to broadcasting, namely its right to subject the broadcasting organizations to turnover tax. The judgment gives a valuable insight into the current state of the doctrine of *Bundestreue* as a result of the introduction of dissenting opinions.

Under the Federal Turnover Tax Act of 1967 the activity of the broadcasting organizations was deemed to be a commercial or business activity within the meaning of the Act and therefore to be liable to turnover tax. This ruling was challenged in Karlsruhe by the Government of Hesse. One of its arguments was that the radio and television licence fees assigned to the broadcasting organizations by Land law were resources of the Länder, which were under obligation to finance broadcasting. The attempt by the Bund to tax these fees thus amounted to taxation of the Länder by the Bund. This attempt and the disregarding of the Land organization of broadcasting as a 'public function' (the exercise of functions of the state being by tradition not liable to tax) constituted a violation of the constitutional principle that Bund and Länder were bound by mutual obligations of federal comity. The Federal Government denied a breach of comity on the ground that its exercise of its powers did not amount to 'misuse': its provisions did not affect the Land legislator's decision as to the organizational form of broadcasting; nor did they involve taxation of the Länder by the Bund since the licence fees were resources of the broadcasting organizations, not of the Länder; nor did the Federal tax threaten the fulfilment of tasks assigned to the Länder by the Basic Law.

The decision of the Court, reached by four votes to three, rejected the Federal case on grounds other than federal comity. In particular it found that the activity of the broadcasting organizations as regulated by the Länder was a public function: their engagement in the sphere of economic intercourse (which was also true of the state itself) did not alter this, nor were the licence fees payment for services rendered but the funds introduced by the Länder for financing the operation as a whole. Furthermore, the Bund was not entitled, on the basis of its concurrent legislative responsibility for property transfer and excise taxes under *Art.* 105 *Abs.* 2 *GG* in its earlier unamended form, to transform the operation of radio and television broadcasting by legal fiction into an activity of a commercial or business nature.

Since the Bund had in any case transgressed its powers, the majority decision saw no need to test its action against 'other constitutional norms'—a reticence which contrasts with some of its earlier decisions and most strikingly with the *Television Judgment*. But the dissenting opinion of the judges Geiger, Rinck, and Wand contains one of the most eloquent discussions of federal comity to be found anywhere.[92]

The three judges said that the Federal Government's action was quite constitutional, since despite their formal organization the broadcasting organizations lacked any specifically public-law element such as employment of civil servants, exercise of sovereign authority *vis-à-vis* the citizen, or performance of a function reserved to the state (they compete potentially with private-law companies); they were to this extent like any large concern. They also maintained that the licence fee, though determined by the Länder, was a payment by subscribers to the broadcasting organizations for receipt of the programme and the facilities provided for its reception.

But even if the Bund's measures were within its legislative competence and in themselves constitutional, the dissenting judges continued, they might still clash with the requirements of federal comity. Before proceeding to a review of the case in hand under this heading, they gave an impressive restatement of the importance and comprehensiveness of the comity principle. This principle, they declared, arises out of the inherent basic relationship between 'Federation' (*Gesamtstaat*) and member states; as a constitutional principle it is specifically federal. It cannot be detached from this context. Its function is the strengthening of the federal state, to which Bund and Länder must contribute. It keeps the egotism of the Bund and the Länder within bounds, in so far as they might have the freedom and the possibility, on the basis of the powers granted to them, 'recklessly' to give effect to their own designs and to follow only their own interests. A review of the extent of its previous applications (up to the *Television Case*) yielded the conclusion:

Thus the principle intervenes in those cases in which the interests of the Bund and the Länder are at variance in such a way that damage would be caused to the one side (and thereby indirectly to the whole) if the other side were to undertake its measures (its legislative regulation) exclusively in accordance with its own interests.

The dissenting judges argued that the principle of *Bundestreue* could also on occasion play a part in tax law; for example, if the Bund in its determination of the distribution of yield from the turnover tax one-sidedly looked only to the covering of its own expenditure, thereby making it impossible for the Länder to perform their necessary functions adequately. But they were of the opinion that in the present case the principle of *Bundestreue* was not affected. For there was no conflict of interests peculiar to the intra-federal relationship whereby the Bund could by the relevant provisions of the Federal Turnover Tax Act have prosecuted its own interests to the detriment of and in neglect of specific Land interests. The taxation of the turnover of a concern by the Bund could not violate the tax interests of the Land or Länder, which shared in the revenue from the turnover tax and did not lose or risk losing any other source of revenue through this arrangement. The Länder, they said, could not even claim any special interest in the Bund's refraining from making the broadcasting organizations liable to turnover tax, since this was not an interest of the Land in the federal state but of the broadcasting organizations themselves. Nor had the Land organized its broadcasting authorities as public law bodies in order to save them from liability to turnover tax, but rather to safeguard the provisions of *Art. 5 GG*, which were in no way threatened by the Federal measures. The judges concluded: differing general political views of the Bund and the Länder as to whether a legislative regulation (in Bund or Land) is politically right, wise, expedient, economically damaging or culturally advantageous do not in themselves establish a conflict of interests between Bund and Länder which would require to be settled by recourse to the principle of *Bundestreue* and would place the Federation or a Land under a constitutional obligation to restrain itself in the exercise of its powers and refrain from a particular measure.

Thus in this case we find, on the one hand, the majority refraining from picking up the Land Government's accusations of a breach of federal comity by the Federal Government and using it to support its own decision against the Bund; on the other hand, the dissenting judges, having come down in favour of the Federal Government, wax eloquent about the requirements of federal comity only to assert that the principle is not applicable in the case in hand. It looks as if several of the judges were not particularly anxious to press the principle even when offered an opportunity, while at least one seized an opportunity to show that it was still alive even when the tenor of his opinion prevented him from making any use of it. But despite all the rhetoric we are still without any instance since the *Television Case* of the comity principle being invoked as requiring a certain line of conduct from either Bund or Länder.

As in the earliest years, the principle of federal comity has appeared in several recent decisions concerning the salaries of officials employed by the Länder.

(xi) The first case (in 1969)[93] was actually a constitutional complaint, though it came before the Second Senate in the same way as normal federal disputes. The complaints were raised by judges of the finance courts of several Länder against their being given a lower salary rating than judges at other higher regional courts. They found both Federal and Länder Governments in approximate agreement that they were unjustified, and the Constitutional Court unanimously took the same view. It held that the special circumstance that the finance courts as higher regional courts nevertheless possess an exclusive first-instance jurisdiction and that the post of *Finanzgerichtsrat* can be a point of entry into the judicial service was a justifiable ground for a (somewhat) lower salary rating.

The issue of *Bundestreue* arose because new provisions of the Federal finance court regulations (*Finanzgerichtsordnung*) of 6 October 1965 had expressly designated the finance courts as 'higher regional courts' (*obere Landesgerichte*) and altered their organization accordingly, and the Bund had assumed that this would produce a correspondingly improved salary rating. The Court rejected the idea that the Länder were bound by the duty of federal comity to give effect to the Bund's views on salaries, since in the absence of framework regulations under *Art. 98 Abs.* 3 and *Art. 75 GG* this was the exclusive concern of the Länder. They *were* required to examine what consequences the Federal law on the organization of the finance courts had for the status of the courts and the responsibilities of the individual groups of judges, which could indirectly influence their salary classification. But that they had done.

(xii) Rather more important was the *Hessian Judicial Salaries*

Case of 1971.[94] It concerned a Land law of 1970 which effected changes in the 'salary groups' to which the judges in Hesse were assigned. This law was challenged by the Federal Government on the ground that it offended against the relevant framework law of the Bund, which assigned judges to the same salary classification as civil servants, and thereby against the provisions of *Art.* 75 *GG* concerning framework legislation. The Federal Government further contended that the Hessian law violated the principle of federal comity.

The Constitutional Court, however, agreed with the Hessian Landtag that at least since the revision of *Art.* 75 *GG* by the 22nd Amendment in 1969 it had become unquestionable that the Länder under *Art.* 98 *Abs.* 3 *GG* had the right to create a 'special' salary law for their judges. Moreover, because of the quite different criteria required for assessing the salary groups of judges and civil servants, the Federal framework provisions for civil servants' salaries could not be counted as the special framework provisions of *Art.* 98 *Abs.* 3 *GG*, and in the absence of such framework provisions the Länder's powers were unrestricted.

The Court also rebutted (by four votes to three) the arguments of the Federal Government alleging a breach of federal comity. The consideration required to be shown for the general interest had in previous decisions often concerned the financial effects of a Land law upon the burdens of the poorer Länder and on the maintenance of the total financial structure in Bund and Länder. But it could also concern effects which the Land law might have on all groups in the public service by promoting a trend towards an undesirable fragmentation of the salary system. However, the financial effects were here admitted by the Federal Government to be small (probably under 2 million DM) and would be no problem even if the other Länder were forced to follow suit. The Bund's fear that other groups in the public service might be prompted to demand special terms for themselves was in any case also unjustified since they, unlike the judges, were covered by the traditional principle of uniformity of salary structures for civil servants. The possibility that a Land might give in to such pressure was not something that need be borne in mind by Hesse under the principle of federal comity. Nor was there any obligation on Hesse, when introducing a new regulation in the public service, to 'co-ordinate' it with the other Länder and the Bund. For, the Court declared, within their exclusive legislative competence the Länder are basically free and independent; the Basic Law assumes that the subjects left to Land legislation can be treated differently from Land to Land. In any case Hesse had tried—in vain—in the Bundesrat to promote a legislative initiative corresponding to its conception of special salary terms for judges. The Länder had been unable to reach agreement, while the Federal Government wanted to postpone the question until the so-called 'reform of justice', which lay far in the future. In these circumstances the action of the Hessian legislator could not be claimed to have been lacking in federal comity.

In this case there are two dissenting opinions which cast light on the doctrine of federal comity. Judges Geller, Rupp, and Wand first argued at length that those parts of the Second Federal Act for the Revision of Salary Provisions which concerned judges' salaries did indeed count as the framework provisions which had to be observed by the Land legislator, and the Hessian Judicial Salaries Act was invalid because it conflicted with them. They then went on to maintain that even if one accepted the majority decision on the question of jurisdiction the Hessian law would still be unconstitutional as violating the requirement of federal comity. The *Housing Funds Case*[95] was cited as having established the principle that all participants in the constitutional 'covenant' are bound to co-operate in accordance with the essence of that covenant, and to strengthen it and uphold the clear interests of its members; the *North Rhine Westphalian Salaries* and *Bank Lending Judgments*[96] as authority for the requirement of mutual consideration as a restriction upon the exercise of the legislative powers of Bund and Länder. The judges then demonstrated that the Hessian law had been passed during a period in which constitutional amendments had conferred on the Bund first framework powers (1969) and later full concurrent powers (1971: *Art.* 74a *GG*) for public service salaries in the Länder. In view of this development towards an integrated approach, which had clearly been motivated by general dissatisfaction with the previous disparity of regulations in Bund and Länder, they maintained that the problems arising from the transition to 'special' laws concerning judges required a uniform decision. Their solution depended partly on the future form of the organization of the courts and the law of procedure—such as the prescribed sequence of appeal and the hierarchical system. For this reason alone, a decision could not be made in isolation in a single Land, above all since Bund and Länder had by the 22nd and 28th Amendments of the Basic Law bound themselves so strongly together in the field of salary law that virtually nothing could happen without general agreement. From this 'constitutional covenant' in the strict sense arose the duty of every member to show regard for the totality of the Bund and the Länder in the field of salary law. Failure to do so violated the duty of *Bundestreue*, even if the Land had sincerely believed it had the necessary powers, and the law concerned was thereby rendered unconstitutional. This was in no way affected by the fact that Hesse first tried to achieve its purpose by legislative initiative in the Bundesrat: indeed Hesse should then have shown due consideration for the predominant opinion of Bund and Länder that the question should be postponed until the 'reform of justice' and therefore have curbed its impatience and co-operated on future developments.

Finally, the dissenting opinion of Judge Geiger found in favour of the constitutionality of the Hessian law. He relied heavily on the implications of the actual wording of *Art. 75 Abs. 3* and *Art. 98 Abs. 3 GG*, agreeing with the Landtag that the latter provision laid a constitutional charge upon the Länder to regulate the salaries of their judges in a special law (a question left open by the majority decision): the execution of this charge could not be hindered by a simple Federal law based on the old uniform salary system for civil servants and judges. Thus to the reasons given in the main decision for rejecting the allegation of breach of federal comity he added that such a breach is impossible when a Land is carrying out the instructions of the constitution.

Thus those who decide that Hesse did have the necessary power to enact its law on judges' salaries also hold that it remained within the requirements of federal comity; while those who argue its unconstitutionality because of incompatibility with Federal framework law also assert a breach of *Bundestreue*. The question of *Bundestreue* is given fairly substantial discussion at the end of each opinion, but there is little sign of readiness to let it alter the already established tenor of the decision. The dissenting opinion of Judges Geller, Rupp, and Wand suggests how, if it had been deciding this case in its early years, the Court might well have added to its finding that the Land's power was unrestricted by Federal framework provisions a warning that this did not mean that the Land could proceed arbitrarily: it could have stressed the need to minimize variations in the attractiveness of the judicial service from Land to Land or dissatisfaction within the judicial service[97] and in general to pay due regard to the interrelation of salary provisions and the general organization of the nation-wide judicial system. That the majority decision preferred the (in itself perfectly valid) alternative of denying any obligation on Hesse to 'co-ordinate' its new public service regulations, since it was fundamentally independent within its legislative preserve, is indicative of the change from the Court's earlier judicial activism. (It is of course quite consistent with a policy of preserving the position of the Länder, a policy from which the Court seldom radically departed in the cases under review in this chapter.)

(xiii) Another case concerning the Land of Hesse in which the issue of federal comity played a significant part was the *Hessian Salary Adaptation Act Case* in 1972.[98] This law of 1971 aimed to achieve conformity with the First Federal Act for the Standardization and Reorganization of Salary Law in Bund and Länder passed on the basis of the 28th Amendment of the Basic Law (*Art.* 74a *GG*). But some of its provisions for individual groups were held by the Federal Government to be unconstitutional and with respect to some of the categories its objections were upheld by the Constitutional Court.[99]

On the other hand, the Court rejected the Federal Government's complaint of violation of the principle of federal comity. According to the past decisions of the Court, it said, such violation presupposed that the contested Land measure was 'in itself' adequately covered by a conferment of powers in the Basic Law and compatible with Federal law: if it was already invalid on these grounds, there was no room left for testing it against the principle of federal comity. But in those parts of the Hessian law which did remain within the Land's competence the Court declared that there could be no question of unjustifiable prejudice to the interests of the other Länder and of the whole. It agreed with the Government of Hesse that the financial effects were so minor as to cause no financial difficulties even if other Länder followed Hesse's example. Nor did it prejudice any reasonable standardization of Länder salary law by the Bund, provided it was not bent on 'perfectionist' detail but left the Länder the necessary freedom to make salary regulations which were imperative in conjunction with reforms of their administrative organization. In particular, it was not a breach of federal comity if the Land's measure provided an impetus for the Länder and the Bund for example to modernize their school system, enlarge the middle ranges of university staff, thin the multiplicity of names of official posts, or remove musicians from the category of civil servants (all references to individual provisions of the Hessian law). Summing up, and forsaking its usual elegant clarity, the Court said: 'The principle of federal comity is after all not a barrier by which nullities can be inhibited.'[100]

This decision seems to continue the retreat from any adventurous use of the principle of federal comity. In particular the statement that it could not even be *applied* when the measure concerned was already invalid on grounds of *ultra vires*, although following the Court's line from the *Territorial Reorganization Case* onwards, is a marked change from its behaviour in the *Television Case*. And the argument that a Land did not violate its duty of *Bundestreue* if its measure set a salutary example seems to provide a wide opportunity for restricting the range of the principle even further. The argument is reminiscent of that already criticized in the discussion of the *North Rhine Westphalian Salaries Case*, namely that behaviour of a Land which realized some of the generally recognized requirements of a Federal salary reform could not violate the principle of *Bundestreue*. In fact it goes further, since in the earlier case it was stressed that the Federal authorities themselves considered reform necessary, whereas here it is implied that it suffices if such reforms are thought desirable by public opinion or perhaps by the Court itself. It may be intended to convey that this was not a case of 'obvious misuse' of its legislative freedom by Hesse, but in effect it reinjects a political flavour into the

Court's treatment of the doctrine of federal comity, to no obvious purpose.

However, the principle of *Bundestreue* makes another appearance earlier in the decision, where the Court is considering whether *Art.* 74a *Abs.* 1 *GG,* on which the Federal law was based, is itself compatible with the prohibition in *Art.* 79 *Abs.* 3 *GG* of any amendment affecting 'the division of the Federation into Länder'. Whatever else may belong to the inviolable core of the statehood of the Länder, the Court said, it includes free disposition over their organization and its constitutional principles and the guarantee of constitutional allocation of a reasonable share of the total tax revenue in the federal state. The transfer to the Bund of a concurrent power over the whole field of salary law for Länder civil servants deprived the Land of the right of determining an essential part of the legal relationship existing exclusively between the Land and its public servants; particularly since salary regulations could have much wider consequences and could even possibly prevent the development of new posts and forms of organization in the Land and make it dependent on the Bund for reforms of its administrative structure. But the Court decided that *Art.* 74a *Abs.* 1 *GG* was nevertheless compatible with the requirements of *Art.* 79 *Abs.* 3 *GG* because the Bund's exercise of this power was governed by the constitutional duty of federal comity arising from the federal principle (*Art.* 20 *Abs.* 1 *GG*). From this it followed that irrespective of the limitations of *Art.* 72 *Abs.* 2 *GG,* whose observance could not be reviewed by the Constitutional Court,[101] the Federal provisions must be such as to leave the Länder the possibility, in the course of organizational reforms, of creating on their own responsibility posts with new functions and a salary classification corresponding to the structure of the Federal salary regulations. This restriction on the Bund's exercise of its powers is declared to be fully subject to investigation by the Constitutional Court.

If the only thing that saves a constitutional amendment from being itself unconstitutional is the fact that the exercise of the powers it bestows is substantially restricted by the requirements of federal comity, then it is clear that federal comity is still regarded as having a major role to play. Indeed it looks as if it could have a new role of justifying various transfers of powers from the Länder to the Bund which would otherwise be constitutionally dubious or even inadmissible.

(xiv) Whether or not this is the beginning of a revival of the principle of *Bundestreue* as a major determinant of the balance struck in decisions on federal matters cannot yet be judged conclusively. It will certainly be seen in the next chapter that the judgment on the special Federal aid programme for areas with structural problems is reminiscent of the earliest years in deriving from the duty of federal comity a requirement that the Federal Government conclude the relevant agreement simultaneously with all the Länder affected and an obligation upon the Länder not to refuse to agree to the proposed programme for irrelevant reasons.[102] Moreover, having decided that in spite of the necessarily supraregional nature of the task the Bund must leave each Land free to decide which investment projects should be subsidized, the Court affirms that the Länder in turn are bound by the principle of federal comity to ensure to the best of their ability that the use of the funds is in conformity with the objectives of the programme. This demonstrates a renewed willingness on the part of the Second Senate to make positive use of the doctrine.

(xv) However, little evidence of such a revival of the comity principle can be detected in the most recent instance of its application by the First Senate. This comes in the *Länder Quotas for University Admissions Case* of 1977,[103] in which the Government of Hesse was again involved, this time as applicant. For the purpose of selecting university entrants in subjects with restricted admission (*numerus clausus*) the new Federal framework law on institutions of higher education provided for the allocation to each Land of a specific quota based primarily on its proportion of the national population in the relevant age group. This criterion was challenged, however, by the Government of Hesse, which wanted the quotas to be calculated according to the proportion of total university applicants coming from each Land. It alleged discrimination against those Länder which had striven to enable as many as possible to qualify for higher education and claimed that this constituted a violation of the principle of federal comity.

On the general basic rights aspect of the diminution of the admission prospects of a proportion of the Hessian applicants, the First Senate proceeded to point out the advantages and disadvantages of each method in terms of justice and equality and held that the Federal legislator had taken sufficient account of both. Since the superior merits of neither method were capable of definite proof at this stage, it concluded that judicial self-restraint was necessary and discretion must be left to the legislature.

In the same vein, the Court denied any breach of federal comity. It cited previous judgments as showing that this principle required mutual consideration in the exercise of existing powers, especially where one side would suffer damage if the other took its measures exclusively according to its own interests. The case in hand was admitted to be a typical case of conflicting interests and conceptions in which implementation of the one point of view was bound to work to the detriment of the other. Furthermore, the method of measuring the Länder quotas would affect the policy decisions of the Länder in the educational field, which as their own preserve was exempted from Federal regulation. For, as the Court explicitly acknowledged, the population criterion necessarily benefited those Länder which for reasons of education policy wanted to keep down the number of pupils taking the university qualifying examination, whereas the applicant quota favoured Länder like Hesse which pursued the contrary policy.

Because of these effects on the educational policies of the Länder, the Court said that the Federal legislature was obliged to exercise its powers with respect to higher education in accordance with the principle of federal comity. However, it held that a finding of violation of this principle was conditional upon the obligations it imposed on one of the partners in a particular case being specifiable with sufficient certainty. The general yardstick it established was found to be insufficient for an evaluation of the inconsiderable differences between the possible solutions in the case in question. Given that the considerations in favour of one or the other system had not yet been confirmed or refuted, the small numerical difference of one-sixth between the existing combination of the applicant and population quotas in a ratio of 1:2 and the ratio of 1:1 which Hesse was prepared to accept could not be objected to on constitutional grounds; especially since the Federal legislator, by opting for a mixed quota, was trying to preserve neutrality with regard to educational policy.

In this case, therefore, the Constitutional Court first expounded the various reasons why federal comity came into play—not least the effects on the 'cultural sovereignty' of the Länder—only to conclude that it was too blunt an instrument to be able to prove that the particular solution chosen by the Federal Government did not show due consideration for the position of Hesse. It must be admitted, however, that it might be difficult to view the compromise quota system actually adopted as an obvious misuse of legislative discretion; so that to have decided otherwise would have been a remarkable instance of judicial activism.

4 Evaluation of the role of the comity principle

It is now possible to assess the extent to which the Constitutional Court has made use of the unwritten principle of federal comity as an instrument for achieving a 'desired' verdict.

Here 1961 can definitely be regarded as a watershed. The claim made in that year by Judge Geiger that the principle had attained through the decisions of the Constitutional Court a fundamental, comprehensive significance shaping the whole constitutional structure[104] looks rather far-fetched today. But at that time it had indeed enjoyed the bold application which the Court itself claims for it in the *Television Judgment*.[105] The duty of federal comity had affected the exercise of powers by determining whether a given measure for which a particular authority was competent (i.e. had discretion) must not (or must) be carried out. Thus it required that Bund and Länder assist each other within certain limits (*Finance-Equalization Case*); that they refrain from actions which would lead to unreasonable burdens on the financial resources of individual Länder (or of the Bund) or to the disruption of the financial structure of Bund and Länder (*Christmas Bonus* and *North Rhine Westphalian Salaries Cases*); that each avoid exercising its powers in such a way as to hinder the other in the exercise of its powers (*Television Case*). It had required that in the fulfilment of their common duty to maintain the constitutional order at all levels of the federal state Bund and Länder should each ensure that the other did not suffer illegitimate interference with the free exercise of its powers (*Atomic Weapons Referendum Case*). It had also established unwritten subsidiary constitutional duties of mutual information and co-operation where necessary decisions could only be taken uniformly; duties to co-operate sincerely and reach a common understanding where the law requires it (*Housing Funds Case*) and of fairness of procedure and style in negotiations which are necessary between Bund and Länder (*Television Case*).

The contrast with the years after 1961 is striking. For, although even then there were still frequent references to the general implications of the principle of federal comity, it did not, at least until 1972, have any practical effect on the import of a single decision. Instead we find emphasis on the argument that only if a concrete constitutional relationship existed between Bund and Länder entailing a right for one of them could the duty of federal comity restrict the exercise of that right; on the precondition of a conflict of interests peculiar to the interfederal relationship; on the basic freedom and independence of the Länder within their legislative competence, the Basic Law assuming that subjects left to Land legislation can be treated differently from Land to Land. This restrictive approach looks, indeed, like a retreat to the positivist tradition.

It is possible to exaggerate the change in the Court's theoretical stance after 1961. After all, even in the course of its early enthusiasm for the doctrine it conceded that in the case of legislative powers only the transgression of outermost limits or obvious misuse of discretion was to be disallowed for breach of *Bundestreue* (*North Rhine Westphalian Salaries Case*). No doubt it always assumed that there must be a specific legal relationship between Bund and Länder within which loyalty was to be observed, i.e. that the principle of *Bundestreue* could not in itself establish such a legal relationship. Certainly the Court had never maintained that the principle could call in question an explicit federal provision of the Basic Law or alter its demarcation of powers: merely that it could limit the exercise of those powers and create additional obligations. And it had stressed the legal nature of ascertainment of violation of the duty of federal comity, which, it said, did not imply political accusations of 'faithlessness' or malevolence (*Atomic Weapons Referen-*

dum Case). Indeed in some of the cases of the first decade a more purely positivist approach might not have yielded substantially different results.

Nevertheless there is a marked change in the Court's approach to the principle. For while one may justifiably maintain that up to 1961 the Court did indeed make use of federal comity to shift the weight of decisions based on the letter of the Basic Law and indeed to some extent to impose its own preferences as to the development of the federal system, there is hardly any evidence for this after the *Television Case*. The early judgments tended to make use of the principle of *Bundestreue* to mitigate the main decision in favour of the Länder and warn against over-reaction. The *Atomic Weapons Referendum Case* then (although unnecessarily) made the principle the basis of its judgment compelling the Länder to take action against their local authorities; and the *Television Case* used it to strengthen the impact of its decision against the Bund and to extend the range of demands which the Länder could constitutionally make and legally pursue in the federal system. But since that time there has not, except in the *Hessian Salary Adaptation Act Case* and most notably in the *Special Federal Aid Programme Case*, been any instance of application of the doctrine of federal comity for substantially mitigating or enhancing the impact of a decision, let alone as the foundation of the decision.

One possible explanation for this change appears to be abortive, namely that the extent to which the Court has made use of the comity principle has depended on whether its application in the case in hand would benefit the Bund or the Länder. The early applications were all restraints upon the Länder, while the most dramatic use of the principle was against the Federal Government. It could admittedly be argued that the Constitutional Court had tended consistently to favour the Länder in the earlier judgments, in that these cases (with the exception of the *Atomic Weapons Referendum Case*) were all decided in the Länder's favour and in none of them was application of the comity principle pushed so far as to sway the decision in the other direction by independently creating a sufficiently concrete or immediate obligation upon the Länder concerned. On the other hand, a total refusal to countenance the derivation of obligations from the principle of federal comity would, until the

Television Case itself, have had results even more favourable to the Länder.

The later judicial self-restraint with regard to *Bundestreue* shows similar variety. It was in the Bund's favour in the *Territorial Reorganization, Bank Lending, Hessian Water Law,* and *Broadcasting Authorities Taxation Cases* (although in the first two cases the Court could hardly have acted otherwise and in the latter two the judgment had in any case gone against the Bund on other grounds). In the salaries cases of the late sixties and early seventies, however, it benefited the Land (just as in the earlier *Concordat Case* the failure to press the doctrine of federal comity harder may have been due to a concern to protect Länder control of education). The evidence cannot therefore support allegations of wholesale partisanship in the application of federal comity.[106]

There can be little doubt (and this was admitted in interview by one of the judges) that one reason for the declining importance of the principle of federal comity after 1961 was that the Court was susceptible to public criticism. For, although the responsible quarters in both Bund and Länder took up the idea of *Bundestreue* with some enthusiasm, particularly when it suited their case in a constitutional dispute, and it even figured in the inaugural speech of President Lübke, the adventurousness of the *Television Judgment* unleashed much public censure. In addition, academic criticism tended to fasten on the doctrine of *Bundestreue* itself. The strongest attack came from Konrad Hesse in his book *Der unitarische Bundesstaat,* which was published in 1962.[107] His decisive objection was that this unwritten principle was added to the written constitution and the guaranteed unwritten principles of law without any necessity. Thus, for example, if the Court recognized a violation of *Bundestreue* in the exercise of powers only if that exercise was improper or arbitrarily transgressed the outermost limits, then the traditional principle of *Rechtsmissbrauch* was sufficient to secure the required result, and it was never necessary to adduce the comity principle. Emphasizing the contrast between the extended principle and its Smendian origins as a non-justiciable legal norm with an elastic regulatory function in the monarchical state, he argued that the fully developed federal system of the Basic Law guaranteed by comprehensive judicial review left no room for completion by such unwritten constitutional law. There were a few exceptions such as a possible obligation of the Länder to execute international treaties of the Bund (on which the Basic Law does not make a ruling), but otherwise it encouraged undue judicial regulation of political relationships. This was particularly objectionable in federal disputes with a strong party-political element, since it in effect required 'comity' from the Opposition towards the Government. It seems clear that such criticism[108] made the Court cautious in its approach to the comity principle, even if it has never made reference to the literature concerned. Even Bayer, an evident protagonist of *Bundestreue*, admitted that it was still so indeterminate in content that its application would endanger legal predictability (*Rechtssicherheit*) unless it were marked by a high degree of judicial self-restraint.[109]

However, it may also be because of the nature of the cases themselves that the principle of federal comity has had a lesser role since the *Television Judgment*. As compared with the cases of the first decade, those raising the question of *Bundestreue* since then seem to have been intrinsically less conducive to appeals to general principles, less concerned with major questions of federalism and more with tidying-up operations, important though the delineation of powers remains. In 1961 Judge Geiger expressly asserted that the partial concretization and stabilization of the federal system by means of the principle of *Bundestreue* was an important defence of a federalism threatened by the centralizing tendencies of the modern state.[110] His aims may not have coincided with the views of his less federalist colleagues; but even if one merely regarded the doctrine of federal comity as a useful reminder that there is more to federalism than a war of jurisdictions, its impact was bound in the sixties to pale before the advance of 'co-operative federalism', which took place (at least until 1969) mainly outside the constitutional framework. When the whole trend in the political arena is towards greater co-operation, as will be seen in the next chapter, there is clearly less need of legal application of the doctrine of federal comity to compel co-operation.

Another way of looking at this would be to say that the principle of *Bundestreue* is still important mainly because it has generally been well heeded since the decisions of the Constitutional Court's first decade, and it therefore no longer looms so large in the decisions themselves. This view receives some support from the general currency which the concept gained, as already mentioned. It is clearly unwise to press too far a suggestion that the principle is thus experiencing the 'problems of success' (especially as the development of co-operative federalism involved a partial capitulation by the Länder). Nevertheless the principle of federal comity developed by the Court has not been ineffective as an instrument for impressing upon both Bund and Länder and the public consciousness that the federal component of the constitutional system is to be taken seriously.

Finally, it may be recalled that the analysis of cases in this chapter was also intended to serve as a 'barometer' of the Constitutional Court's role as arbiter of federal relations. It has been shown above that the application of the comity principle has not been as one-sided as is sometimes supposed. But if one looks rather to the general outcome of the Court's decision-making in each of the cases discussed, it reveals a marked and undeniable tendency to uphold the interests of the Länder. The only clear exceptions are the *Atomic Weapons Referendum* and *Bank Lending Cases* and, in part, the *Hessian Salary Adaptation Act Case*; for the decisions against Hesse in the *Territorial Reorganization Case* and with regard to the Länder quotas for university admissions were at the same time in effect decisions to the benefit of some of the other Länder. In view of the fact that the cases reviewed in this chapter include a high proportion of the most important judgments in the federal sphere, the significance of this finding of a general tendency to rule in favour of the Länder is obvious.

CHAPTER VIII
Co-operative Federalism and the By-passing of the Court

1 Introduction

In writing about the influence of the Constitutional Court on the federal system it is easy to give the impression that all major issues and developments of federal relations come within the purview of the Court—i.e. that although questions of policy within the system may not be directly its concern, nevertheless all aspects of the form of the system, its structure and procedures, are subject to the Court's ratification. Yet increasingly it would appear that major developments in the federal system have passed the Court by.

The development of the modern state as a provider of welfare and services, with on the one hand problems of resources and planning on an ever larger scale and on the other expectations of equality of treatment, was bound to have its effect on the operation of the German federal system, as it has done elsewhere. Moreover, in a comparatively small and homogeneous country the forces pushing for ever greater uniformity in the provision of government services, co-ordinated planning for efficient use of resources, and centralized oversight of public expenditure in accordance with the needs of economic management were particularly strong. They were partly manifested in, partly encouraged by, the transformation of the political context, with the move to the SPD/CDU coalition with its centralizing propensities in 1966, followed by the SPD/FDP reform era after 1969. But in any case, as it became increasingly clear that the Länder were no longer capable of coping with all their problems unaided, unitarizing tendencies of various kinds inevitably emerged.

This situation might have been partially remedied by a radical territorial reorganization, leaving perhaps five large and viable Länder of roughly equal size and economic strength. Such a course would certainly not have been without its problems,[1] and it is not surprising if not only some of the existing Länder but also the Federal Government shrank from it. At any rate since amendment of *Art.* 29 *GG* in 1976, by which the Bund's obligation to redraw the map of the Länder was finally removed, this particular solution may be regarded as a dead duck. Undoubtedly it is possible to see in this abandonment of territorial reorganization a confirmation of the extent to which the for the most part new and artificial Länder of the Bonn Republic have been able to put down roots in the political system. Instead, however, there has been a continual, fairly irregular, but (at least until the early 1970s) basically accelerating increase of Federal power at the expense of the Länder.

The alternative approach which prevailed over that of territorial reorganization was the rapid expansion of institutionalized co-operation and co-ordination of the activities of Bund and Länder which took place under the banner of 'co-operative federalism'. The term was adopted from Anglo-Saxon federations, and especially from the United States, where it had long been familiar as connoting the break with the previous 'dual federalism' and its strict compartmentalization of Federal and State powers. There too it had been a product of the twentieth-century administrative state, and its salient feature was the development of joint programmes based on grants-in-aid, by which Federal funds were made available to the States for particular projects on condition of adherence to Federal standards and acceptance of Federal supervision of the implementation of the programmes. By this means a highly complex network of Federal–State interrelationships had evolved, with some degree of institutionalization.[2]

The notion of co-operative federalism was introduced into German constitutional terminology in the 1960s by the Report of the Troeger Commission set up by the Federal and Länder Governments to propose reforms to the financial structure.[3] Together with the 'Finance Reform' which it inspired, this report may indeed be regarded as its most prominent political expression. In the section expounding the guiding principles of the Report, the Commission concludes from the need for the federal order to adapt to changing political, economic, and social conditions that contemporary federalism can only be co-operative federalism.[4] This new form of 'intergovernmental relations' is summed up as follows:

> Co-operative federalism is an active principle of government; it achieves a balance between clear demarcation of responsibilities, without which a federal order is inconceivable, and a concentration of forces in the federal state, which guarantees the greatest efficiency in the commitment of public resources. Such an ordering of our federal state calls for the improvement of hitherto existing forms of co-operation by the creation of new institutions in a federal spirit. This must be backed up by a readiness on both sides, for the sake of the vitality of the federal idea, to make generous use of the opportunities newly opened up, wherever this is required in the interests of the public good.

Although in some of its aspects this concept of co-operative federalism may be reminiscent of the principle of federal comity,[5] it is clearly much more far-reaching in its implications. For federal comity, as a purely legal doctrine, is largely restricted to mitigating the effects of the 'competence mentality' by requiring the exercise of powers to be tempered by some consideration for the legitimate interests of the other parties in the federal system, and it quickly runs into difficulties when it tries to do more. The doctrine of co-operative federalism, on the other hand, is above all a political doctrine, answering to changes in the tasks of government to which the federal system had to be adapted—though, in view of the pervasiveness of German public law, it inevitably became the preoccupation of academic lawyers.[6] As the exposition of the concept in the Troeger Report quoted above already indicates, in the setting of the German constitutional order co-operative federalism was not to be limited to an emphasis on mutual consultation and co-ordination of governmental activities, or to legitimizing such paraconstitutional phenomena as Federal subventions, but was to extend above all to new forms of constitutionally prescribed shared functions and planned joint action of the two levels of government.

It is true, as was stressed in Chapter I, that West German federalism from its inception differed markedly from the classical federal model and incorporated a degree of intertwining of powers and possibilities of mutual influence not found in Anglo-Saxon federations. Yet the cumulative changes in the quality and the balance of Bund–Länder relations since the foundation of the Federal Republic are far from being mere adjustments of existing arrangements. Not all such developments can be subsumed under the heading of co-operative federalism. Indeed, as will be shown at once, more direct forms of unitarization are also in evidence. Nevertheless it is the vast and complex evolution of intergovernmental relations which has gone under the name of co-operative federalism that has had the most substantial impact on the character of West German federalism.

This chapter attempts an assessment of some of these changes in the operation and the balance of the federal system which have come about largely uninfluenced and uncontrolled by the Federal Constitutional Court. It raises the question whether the 'judicialization of politics', seen by many from Carl Schmitt onwards as a necessary consequence of judicial review, has in the federal sphere given way to the political resolution even of genuine constitutional issues.

2 Changes in the federal system by constitutional amendment

Given the detailed and comprehensive nature of the Basic Law, the comparative ease with which it can be amended, and the German preference for clear and explicit legal authorization, one of the most obvious ways in which changes in the balance of the federal system may be effected is by amendment of the constitutional text. Here the simple effect of the enumeration of powers may be recalled. To have a catalogue allocating powers to the Bund, and to proceed on the principle that powers can be exercised by the Bund only if put into the catalogue (all residual powers devolving on the Länder), is to provide a continuing incentive to extend the catalogue. This is also likely to be a one-way process: given the provision of *Art.* 31 *GG* that Federal law overrides Land law, there would be serious problems involved in taking powers out of the concurrent list in virtue of which Federal laws had already been enacted. It may be that extending the catalogue need not prove fatal to a federalism which assumes the desirability of Federal legislation and execution of that legislation by the States, and which provides certain guarantees in respect of financial allocations and the involvement of the States in the passing of Federal legislation. Yet too far-reaching a surrender of Land legislative powers to the Bund would pose an awkward definitional problem, as well as depriving the Länder, for all their crucial administrative powers, of the necessary political backbone and destroying most of the *raison d'être* of the Länder parliaments.[7]

Numerous modifications of the West German constitution have in fact taken place during the thirty years of its existence: the text of the Basic Law had been officially amended thirty-four times by the end of 1979. The changes have been for the most part more superficial than profound, but the majority of them have concerned the powers of or relations between Bund and Länder. Whenever new fields of activity appeared, as when the Federal Republic was permitted the use of atomic energy or the development of its own civil aviation, the powers necessarily accrued to the Federation and therefore had to be given constitutional foundation (*Art. 74 Nr.* 11a; 87c; 87d *GG*). Similarly, the creation of West German defence forces required and gave rise to a number of constitutional provisions, some of which inevitably affected relations between Bund and Länder (*Art.* 73 *Nr.* 1; 79 *Abs.* 1 *Satz* 2; 87a; 87b *GG*, etc.). The same applied to the belated incorporation in the Constitution in 1968 of the emergency powers which had devolved upon the Federal Republic when the Western Allies had given up their reserve powers. A secure constitutional basis had to be provided for legislation concerning the implementation of the equalization of burdens resulting from the Second World War (*Art.* 120a *GG*) and for the General Law on the Consequences of the War (*Art.* 135a *GG*), and clarification was later thought necessary of the distribution of costs and burdens in this area between the different levels of government (*Art.* 120 *GG*). Similarly, an amendment was needed to give the Bund explicit concurrent powers for benefits to war-disabled persons and to dependants of those killed in the war and for war graves (*Art. 74 Nr.* 10, 10a

GG). Some of these amendments were fairly insignificant, while others concerned new functions which were bound to be assigned to the Federation. Nevertheless none of them can have given much comfort to the Länder and many of them may have forestalled potential disputes which could eventually have been taken to Karlsruhe and there decided with a rather different emphasis.

Meanwhile, repeated attempts were made to improve the unsatisfactory provisions for the distribution of financial resources between the different levels of government and adjust them in the light of changed circumstances (*Art.* 106, 107 *GG*). Then during the economic recession of 1967 the Bund furnished itself by amendment of *Art.* 109 *GG* with weapons of economic management and the possibility of medium-term financial planning covering the Länder also. This was followed in 1969 by a major overhaul of Section X of the Basic Law concerning distribution of revenue and financial relations between Bund and Länder and by the introduction of a new Section VIIIa giving the Bund and Länder responsibility for co-operation in certain areas of 'joint tasks'. These elements of the so-called Finance Reform are of much greater significance and are given separate treatment below.

At the same time the Bundesrat acceded to mounting demands, based on arguments of efficiency and the need for nation-wide efforts and uniform solutions, for a series of transfers of legislative power from the Länder to the Bund which were at once more genuine than amendments which had concerned brand new fields of activity, and more far-reaching than the other earlier cessions of power. In 1969 the Bund was given concurrent power for the regulation of educational and training grants (*Art.* 74 *Nr.* 13 *GG*), for the economic viability of hospitals and the regulation of hospitalization fees (*Art.* 74 *Nr.* 19a *GG*), and for the collection of charges for the use of public highways by vehicles and the allocation of revenue therefrom (*Art.* 74 *Nr.* 22 *GG*). A general Federal responsibility was also established in the field of higher education (*Art.* 75 *Nr.* 1a *GG*). It was no doubt because it represented an encroachment upon the sacred Länder domain of education that this extension of Federal power was hedged around with restrictions. Not merely did the Bund receive a framework rather than a concurrent legislative power, that is, the right to enact no more than general or skeleton provisions; but this right of framework legislation was given only in respect of '*the general principles governing higher education*'.[8] Nevertheless it has been generally agreed that in practice this double limitation can have little special significance. Two years later the concurrent powers of *Art. 74 Nr.* 20 *GG* were extended to the protection of animals, while a special new article (74a) provided, in addition to the Federal framework responsibility under *Art.* 75 *Nr.* 1 *GG* for the conditions of public service at the sub-Federal level, a concurrent legislative power over the pay scales and pensions of non-Federal civil servants (where divergent Länder policies had long been a bone of contention).

The most recent increases in Federal powers date mainly from 1972. The addition of refuse disposal, clean air, and noise abatement to the catalogue of concurrent legislative powers (*Art.* 74 *Nr.* 24 *GG*) gave the Federation control over a considerable part of the increasingly important and politically fashionable field of the protection of the environment. It is true that the Federal Government's hopes of similar powers for the management of water resources, the protection of nature, and care of the countryside were frustrated, so that in these areas it must fall back on its framework powers under *Art.* 75 *Nr.* 3 and 4 *GG*. But all the same the reform amounted to substantial Federal annexation of territory in one of the major provinces of the Länder. A further loss of legislative power by the Länder resulted from the insertion of Federal concurrent jurisdiction over the law on fire-arms (*Art.* 74 *Nr.* 4a *GG*), which was extended to explosives in 1976. Previously the Federation had been responsible only for the economic aspects of this topic, whereas its new powers were designed to facilitate concerted initiatives for the promotion of internal security, another of the few prominent fields traditionally under the legislative control of the Länder. At the same time, and in the same area of internal security, extensions were made to the exclusive Federal legislative powers under *Art.* 73 *Nr.* 10 *GG*. These had already covered co-operation between the Federation and the Länder in matters of criminal police and of protection of the Constitution, establishment of a Federal Criminal Police Department, and international control of crime. By the extension of Federal rights for the maintenance of external and internal security it became possible to empower the authorities charged with the protection of the Constitution (*Verfassungsschutz*) to keep German and foreign radical political movements under observation in so far as they pose a threat to the free democratic basic order or the existence or security of the Federation or a Land or aspire by the use of violence to jeopardize the foreign relations of the Federal Republic.

The explicit amendments of the catalogue of powers which have taken place particularly since 1966 thus amount to a not insignificant transfer of functions to the Federal level. Admittedly they should not be overrated: except perhaps in the field of higher education, the nucleus of the Länder's legislative powers emerged relatively unscathed. Indeed in some areas the compromise arrangements extorted by the Länder could be argued to fall short of what was required for an optimal solution of national problems. Nevertheless, taken together, the surrenders of jurisdiction would be sufficient to cut the ground from beneath a constitutional court which was pursuing a strategy of shoring up the powers of the Länder whenever and wherever it found an opportunity. For they ensured that as regards some crucial shifts of power the Court obtained no such opportunity. It should be clear from the analysis in previous chapters that the Bundesverfassungsgericht has not in any case conducted such a desperate rear-guard action; a balanced assessment of its role will be offered in Chapter IX. The point to be made here is only that, regardless of the Court's policy or lack of it, it is relatively impotent in the face of willing (even if grudging) abdication of power by the Länder themselves.

3 The development of co-operative federalism

The significant changes in the pattern of federal relationships as established in 1949 which took place without reference to or control by the Constitutional Court did not always take the form of overt transfers of powers. Some could more accurately be termed paraconstitutional, while others have only recently been given constitutional recognition.

(i) *Co-operation between the Länder*

The first such development, though a unitarizing process, did not involve an extension of the power of the Federal Government; on the contrary, it was in many cases a means of forestalling it. Co-operation between the Länder arose from the need which became felt for as uniform a regulation as possible of certain areas falling within their competence. This was due not only to practical considerations of administrative expediency but also to strong public pressure to co-ordinate policy in such fields as education, where major differences in the school systems of the Länder were an obstacle to the mobility of the population. It quickly became clear that if the Länder were at all points to stand on their constitutional rights and insist on deciding each independently what was best for him, sooner or later a revision of the constitutional distribution of powers in favour of the Federation would become inevitable.

Appreciating the need for a reasonable degree of co-ordination, the Länder concluded a great variety of treaties and administrative agreements. By 1961 H. Schneider[9] claimed to have found approximately 340 such formal agreements. Significant examples include the *Königsteiner Abkommen* of 1949 on the financing of institutions of scientific research of supraregional importance, an agreement in 1964 on the financing of new institutions of higher education, treaties on grammar-school education, and treaties on broadcasting such as that of 1955 between Hamburg, Schleswig-Holstein, and Lower Saxony establishing the Norddeutscher Rundfunk and that of 1962 between all the Länder providing for the joint management of the country's second television channel. For particularly important fields the Länder institutionalized their co-operation in permanent co-ordinating bodies, even permanent ministerial bodies such as the conferences of ministers of the interior, ministers of justice, and education ministers. The fact that these bodies have taken decisions only by unanimous vote has not in general prevented them from producing a wide range of agreements on harmonizing standards and practices, and they soon became an important feature of the federal landscape.

The proliferation of such co-ordinating machinery among the member states is by no means unique to West German federalism. On the contrary, a similar evolution is observable in all developed federations,[10] demonstrating that it springs from the exigencies and interrelationships of modern activist government. However, it is arguable that (no doubt because of the relative weakness of the 'federal attitude' in West German society and the consequent impatience with local differences) consultation and co-ordination between the German Länder is unusually intense.

The assessment of these agreements and institutions of inter-Länder co-operation from a constitutional point of view was by no means undisputed. On the one hand it was pointed out that they all concerned matters belonging to the competence of the Länder, did not encroach upon Federal prerogatives, and were thus a legitimate product of a thriving modern federalism, avoiding the need to transfer more powers to the Federation. On the other hand it was argued that the constitutional regulation of the federal and the unitary elements of the system was definitive. The existence of more than one federation of the same member states with the same purpose of looking after the interests of the whole, being neither recognized nor regulated by the constitution, would give rise to conflicts and contradictions of authority, procedure, and decisions.[11] The transformation of Länder functions into joint functions by means of co-operative practices not provided for in the constitution is seen by some as thwarting the federal objective of the preservation of regional individuality.

However, those who objected to such institutionalized co-operation were often prepared to distinguish transactions of a public, legally binding nature, which were subject to the requirements of constitutional law, from internal or preparatory consultation which took place outside the constitutional framework and was therefore unobjectionable even when given an institutional form. Thus the only legitimate means of standardization in the domain of the Länder was seen as individual legislation by each Land in conformity with the law of the other Länder. The constitution did not permit the Länder to establish institutions with authority to make law binding them jointly, since this would be tantamount to the creation of a federation within the federation; it would also simply prove that the functions made over to such institutions could be satisfactorily carried out only from the centre and that the distribution of powers was in need of overhaul. On this basis at most those co-ordinating bodies could be regarded as admissible which, like the Standing Conference of Ministers of Education of the Länder, consisted of mandated representatives of the Länder and made recommendations only by unanimous vote.[12]

The question whether the creation of supraregional or centralized inter-Länder institutions for the co-ordination of functions constitutionally assigned to the Länder ran counter to the federal structure established by the Basic Law was certainly not clear-cut. As the constitution had certainly not foreseen the development of such bodies, it could be persuasively argued that it amounted to the creation of a 'third level' between Bund and Länder without any constitutional support. The argument drew some force from the earlier academic dispute as to whether West Germany was a 'two-tiered' or 'three-tiered' federal state, a dispute which had finally been resolved by the Karlsruhe Court, after some wavering, coming down in favour of the former.[13] Yet the 'third level' that had been in question at that time was not a confederal arrangement of the Länder but the concept of the *Gesamtstaat,* of which both Bund (as *Zentralstaat*) and Länder were thought to be members with equal rank and status, as opposed to the inevitably subordinate position of the Länder where the Bund represented the whole. Thus the Court's rejection of the concept of the separate *Gesamtstaat* has no bearing on the issue of inter-Länder co-operation.

Nevertheless the misgivings expressed by Adenauer as to the constitutionality of the television channel established by the Länder in the wake of the *Television Judgment* of 1961 (Zweites Deutsches Fernsehen), on the ground that it was a central administrative organization of the Länder on the Federal level, were shared by many less biased observers. Sometimes[14] the objection was similarly to the sheer deliberate frustration of the development of Federal constitutional responsibilities. Yet the Constitutional Court had in the *Television Judgment*[15] explicitly rejected the view that unwritten Federal powers were derivable merely from the supraregional nature of the task, that being precisely what the Federation was there for: on the contrary, the mere fact of joint or co-ordinated performance of a function by the Länder, regardless of the motives of such co-operation, was not a sufficient justification for a natural Federal responsibility.

Other objections have exercised lawyers at greater length, particularly the organizational form of the joint institutions.[16] There seems on the whole to be agreement that they are permissible when legally assigned to the administrative structure of one of the Länder.[17] This is the case, for example, with the College of Administrative Sciences (Hochschule für Verwaltungswissenschaften) in Speyer and the Film Censorship Office (*Filmbewertungsstelle*) in Wiesbaden. More difficult is the case of joint institutions of the Länder which do not 'belong' to the administration of either Bund or Länder, in particular those which are organized as independent public-law bodies like the Zweites Deutsches Fernsehen in Mainz. Such bodies clearly raise problems of control. Their constitutionality has not yet been pronounced upon by the Constitutional Court, although the Federal Administrative Court decided in their favour.[18] Academic opinions on the subject appear to depend partly on whether the author's sympathies are federalist or unitarist, since the institutions clearly represent advanced attempts to achieve centralized solution of problems without transfers of powers to the Federation (though the occasional federalist may object to the abandonment of that individuality of the Länder which is the *raison d'être* of federalism).

Constitutionally most dubious of all is the tendency to introduce the possibility of individual Länder being overruled in co-operative activities. This is certainly not part of the original concept as exemplified by formal agreements between the Länder or the unanimity rule prevailing in Conferences of the Minister-Presidents of the Länder or the Standing Conference of Education Ministers. On the other hand, treaties between the Länder have established bodies in which individual Länder can be overruled. One example is the commissions administering the second television channel. Another is the treaty of 1972 which set up a central office for the allocation of university places. Its administrative committee, which takes decisions on the inclusion of courses within the ambit of the central office and on criteria for uniform assessment of ability, has one representative for each Land (as well as two advisory representatives of the Federal Government), and the treaty permits decision-making by qualified majority. Such arrangements are admittedly a natural consequence of the joint 'hiving off' of such functions to public-law institutions.

Any tendency to abandon the requirement of unanimous agreement is difficult to square with the Constitutional Court's interpretation of the constitution. As early as the *Housing Funds Case* in 1952 the Court clearly laid down the principle of the separate and equal juxtaposition of the Länder, with consequent exemption from the rule of majority decision-making obtaining in the sphere of the democratic principle and commitment to the unanimity principle, whereby no Land could be outvoted by the other Länder.[19] (Perhaps not enough attention has been paid to the fact that the passage in question, even if prompted by the issue of Federal disbursement of resources 'in consultation with the Länder', appears to imply quite happily the existence of institutions—other than the Bundesrat, where majority voting is indeed the rule—in which the Länder take joint decisions.) The conclusion is clear: despite the undoubted duty of the Länder, ever more frequently emphasized, to seek consensus and co-operative solutions, the legal and practical possibility must still exist for them to go their own way. On the other hand, it can be readily appreciated that the needs of ever closer co-ordination can scarcely accommodate the possibility that any individual participant, by refusing to co-operate, may frustrate projects developed and supported by all the others. The unanimity rule may in practice lead to paralysis. As has been seen, the Court did try in the same *Housing Funds Case* to mitigate this danger by establishing a constitutional duty based on the requirements of federal comity for Bund and Länder in their relations with each other to co-operate sincerely and reach a common undertaking.[20] But the misgivings there expressed suggest that this was unlikely to be a very practical alternative to more specific regulation of day-to-day negotiations, particularly in the context of joint institutions.

Despite its doubtful constitutionality, therefore, erosion of the unanimity principle may well continue. Thus the interim report of the Commission of Inquiry into Questions of Constitutional Reform set up by the Bundestag in 1970 considered the introduction of qualified majority voting both for the proposed extended joint planning of Bund and Länder and for the whole 'third level' of independent co-ordination by the Länder acting together.[21]

In any case even without an extension of majority voting the practice of co-ordination so widely indulged in by the Länder is tantamount to a confession that even in the narrow sphere of legislative sovereignty remaining to them their autonomy has no real substance. For where is the independent decision-making power of the Länder when each of them has in practice to accede to compromises negotiated by its delegates with ten others?

Perhaps for this reason inter-Länder co-operation has not in the longer term proved entirely effective in warding off the advance of Federal influence. On the one hand, it has not prevented some of the constitutional amendments referred to above. A case in point is the conditions of service of Land officials. Although this was, within the limits of the Federal framework power, a matter for the individual Länder, both the requirements of federal comity[22] and common sense demanded mutual consideration in salary policy. The Minister-Presidents of the Länder therefore concluded an agreement in 1966 committing themselves to as uniform salary arrangements for the public service as possible. In future, changes of salary law were to be made only by mutual agreement. Yet this collaboration did not prevent the creation of a concurrent Federal power with respect to salary scales in 1971 (*Art.* 74a *GG*).

On the other hand, from the mid-1960s onwards agreements between the Länder alone have in any case become fewer and consultation with the Federal Government ever more prominent. Indeed the Federal Government was generally welcomed as a partner in co-operative undertakings, because the Länder felt they needed it. Thus the Standing Conference of Länder Ministers of the Interior, when reorganizing its mode of operation in 1972, declared itself in favour of complete integration of the Federal Government into all its activities.

(ii) *Co-ordination between Bund and Länder*

The evolution of arrangements for co-ordination and co-operation between Bund and Länder, and the controversy to which they gave rise, closely paralleled the purely inter-Länder developments.

It was no doubt inevitable, particularly in view of the peculiar character of German federalism with its horizontal division of powers whereby the implementation of most Federal legislation is carried out at Land level, that a network of consultative bodies and committees should grow up between the Federal Government and the Länder. These range from routine contacts between Federal and Länder officials, for example on the preparation of Federal legislation, to top-level meetings between the Federal Chancellor and the heads of government of the Länder.[23] If all such co-ordinative activity perhaps already belongs to a constitutional grey area, nevertheless mutual information and consultation is clearly a necessary attribute of an efficiently functioning federal system and indeed is presupposed by the doctrine of federal comity. On the other hand, the common practice of inviting Federal ministers to attend inter-Länder ministerial conferences might appear more questionable; certainly it gives the Federal Government opportunities for taking the initiative and expounding its preferences in matters of Länder concern.

However, co-operative arrangements have frequently been subject to greater and more explicit formalization.

A wide range of agreements have been concluded between the Federal and Länder Governments, both in the form of state treaties (*Staatsverträge*) and of administrative agreements (*Verwaltungsabkommen*).[24] These include interpretative agreements on disputed areas of jurisdiction under the Basic Law, such as the *Lindauer Abkommen* of 1957 on the co-operation of Federal and Länder administrations in the preparation and conclusion of international treaties;[25] doubt was cast on the constitutionality even of these, though they were generally accepted as necessary and indeed desirable on the understanding that they could not carry ultimate legal authority. But there were also agreements between Bund and Länder which affected a transfer of competence from the Bund to a Land or vice versa. An example of the former is the agreement whereby the turnover and transportation taxes, which under *Art. 108 Abs. 1 GG* should be administered by Federal authorities, were to be collected by the tax inspectors' offices of the Länder on behalf of the Federal chief revenue boards.[26] The agreement of 1957 between the Federal Government and North Rhine Westphalia on Federal performance of Land responsibilities with regard to Federal waterways belongs to the latter category.[27] Here a distinction is frequently made between a transfer of competence *quoad substantiam*, which is decisively rejected by commentators as tantamount to constitutional amendment by illegitimate means, and a transfer which is merely *quoad usum*, that is a conferment of the right to carry out functions which can be reclaimed at any time. This latter is in general also regarded as inadmissible[28] and the *Television Judgment*, for example, insisted that Federal organs could never be competent to execute Land law. But some authors[29] regard a delegation of powers *quoad usum* as implicitly permitted by the Basic Law where the intermeshing of Federal and Länder functions is such as to constitute a recognized 'collective task' (*Gesamtaufgabe*): Kölble lists among these the protection of law and order and in particular of the constitution, broadcasting (especially since clarification of the division of responsibilities by the *Television Judgment*), provision of adequate housing, promotion of economic development, and development aid.

As in the case of inter-Länder collaboration, formal agreements between Bund and Länder have also led to extensive institutionalization of co-operation. As early as 1953 the Länder Ministers of Culture joined with the Federal Minister of the Interior to set up the *Deutscher Ausschuss für das Erziehungs- und Bildungswesen* as an informal advisory and co-ordinating body to review educational developments; its work was formalized by the agreement of 1965 establishing the *Bildungsrat* ('Education Council'), though the latter has since been discontinued. Another important co-ordinating body, the *Wissenschaftsrat* ('Science Council'), was established by administrative agreement in 1957 with the task of co-ordinating the plans of Bund and Länder into an overall plan for the promotion of science and research, especially through the universities. By such means the Federal Government came increasingly to have a say in matters which, particularly in the cultural field, belonged to the heart of the domain of the Länder (though there was admittedly also a Federal power under *Art.* 74 *Nr.* 13 *GG* for the promotion of scientific research). Since such bodies had only a planning and consultative role, a persuasive legal case could be made for distinguishing them from the kind of administrative links between the two levels of government which were alien to the Basic Law (with the major exception of financial administration under *Art.* 108 *GG*) and tended to be denounced as *Mischverwaltung* ('mixed administration'). But although they had only the right to make non-binding recommendations and so did not formally affect the constitutional system of powers, the authority which their joint decisions carried and the fact that they were in practice normally complied with nevertheless amounted to a shift in the balance of influence in the federal system and to that extent an erosion of Länder autonomy.

Joint institutions of Bund and Länder have taken a variety of forms. Some are legally subordinated to one of the contracting parties, such as the College of Administrative Sciences in Speyer established by agreement between the Länder and the Federal Government on the basis of a statute of Rhineland Palatinate, the Land in which it was situated;[30] the Federal Government has one vote in its administrative council and contributes to its costs. Others are independent corporate bodies under public law, not subject to the administrative organization of any of the participants. Such institutions are by no means constitutionally uncontroversial. Yet the important point is that since they are co-operative ventures they are unlikely to be challenged before the Constitutional Court.

(iii) *Federal financing of Länder activities*

The original federal conception of the Basic Law involved, despite the possibilities of mutual influence entailed especially by the nature of the Bundesrat and by Länder execution of Federal legislation under 'Federal supervision', a fairly strict demarcation of the powers of the two levels of government. But from the start, as has already been noted, various trends began to work against this rigid separation. Nowhere was this tendency more marked than in the financial field. The regulation of finances is of particular importance in a federal system, since the ability of the member states to exploit the powers assigned to them depends substantially on possession of sufficient resources enabling them to put their designs into effect independently of influence exerted by financial pressure. The principle of separate budgets for Bund and Länder has been retained to this day. However, the initial attempt to establish in the constitution a comprehensive system of separate sources of revenue for the Federation and the member states on Anglo-Saxon lines having quickly been abandoned as unrealistic under modern conditions, a continuing struggle emerged over the Länder's share of the common sources of revenue (income and corporation tax and, more recently, also value added tax) and over the degree of 'horizontal financial equalization' between the Länder.[31]

Until the mid-sixties the Länder may be seen as having done relatively well out of the system of revenue apportionment, particularly as the shared income and corporation taxes turned out to be more buoyant than those taxes (such as the turnover tax) which were exclusive to the Bund. However, this did not prevent the Federal Government from building up a substantial reserve fund or the financially weaker Länder from running into budgetary difficulties. Then in the 1960s both Federal and Länder expenditure began to rise steeply, and this imposed serious strains on the apportionment principles, which were eventually overhauled by the Finance Reform of 1969, especially by the revision of *Art.* 106 *GG*.

Meanwhile, however, the Federal Government had begun to make use of its greater financial weight in relation to the budgets of individual Länder to make inroads into areas which constitutionally were their prerogative. It began to offer the Länder tied grants for specific purposes of its own choice which would normally have had to be financed, if at all, from the Länder's own resources, thus securing for itself a degree of influence in fields of Länder responsibility such as education and sport. That the Federal Government could choose what its financial aid should be spent on[32] might in itself seem clear enough interference in the affairs of the Länder. But its contribution was normally also made conditional on the provision of a complementary (and often equal) sum by the Land concerned (even though at the insistence of the Bundesrat measures were taken to curtail this). Since no Land government could afford (especially politically speaking) to turn down a substantial sum of Federal money, the practical consequence was that the choice of priorities for expenditure passed to the Federal Government. Federal payments and subsidies for investments carried out by third parties had by 1969 reached the figure of 5,000 million DM, or about 13 per cent of the tax revenue officially accruing to the Länder.[33] This may not be a very high proportion by international standards, but when one adds on the cost of the provision of a multiplicity of services imposed on the Länder by Federal legislation, as well as expenditure on salaries and other running costs of administration, which are a very significant element in a Land's budget, it is clear that the scope for initiating independent political programmes is severely circumscribed by the extent to which the funds at the Land's disposal are already committed.

It would be easy to exaggerate the loss of autonomy suffered in this way by the Länder. They still retained a reasonable sphere of discretion as to where to concentrate their spending efforts; through their position in the Bundesrat they have had an effective say in provisions of Federal legislation touching on revenue apportionment; and on balance they have been fairly successful in defending their interests. All the same, further substantial erosion of their freedom of action by an expansion of Federal subvention and mixed financing would seriously call in question the financial autonomy of the Länder prescribed by the constitution.

In developing this system of grants-in-aid West Germany was merely following the same path as most federal systems, in which the extension of the power of the centre has come principally via the superior financial power of the Federal authorities, who by offers of subsidies can often ensure that their policy preferences prevail and indeed reduce the weaker members of the federation to a state of dependence.[34] The scope for such developments is undoubtedly substantially less under the West German system of apportionment of common sources of revenue with adjustment related to expenditure needs than under other federal systems relying on independent sources of revenue for the different levels of government. But this makes it all the more interesting that even in a system where the member states have sacrificed the legal right to levy any major taxes or determine tax levels, in return for a greater assurance of obtaining through tax-sharing an adequate share of total financial resources and thereby avoiding financial domination by the centre, the practice of tied Federal subvention has nevertheless attained significant proportions.

That policy influence was behind the extension of Federal subsidy can be seen from the fact that at the very same time over a wide field of activity—from national parks and the breeding of Trakehner horses to grants for the education and training of young immigrants—the Länder, for all their complaints about the Federal Government's use of subsidies, actually requested Federal financial aid; while Bonn insisted that these were purely or at least primarily concerns of the Länder. Thus if a matter was of little political importance or interest, neither side was keen to pick up the bill. In practice the Federal Government was free to decide over what it did or did not want to buy influence, and it could always find a formula justifying such intervention in matters of Länder responsibility.

In several fields, such as student grants according to the so-called 'Honnef model' and the promotion of scientific research by such supraregional bodies as the Deutsche Forschungsgemeinschaft and the Max-Planck-Gesellschaft, originally formed by the inter-Länder Königstein Agreement of 1949, joint financing by Bund and Länder led to smooth and fruitful co-operation. Nevertheless, judged by the spirit of the constitution, the legal basis of the whole system of grants-in-aid was to say to the least dubious. After all, *Art.* 30 *GG*, which declares that the exercise of governmental powers and the discharge of governmental functions shall be incumbent on the Länder in so far as the Basic Law does not otherwise prescribe or permit, is scarcely reconcilable with the Federal Government's appropriating to itself a decisive policy influence in any field it chooses where substantial public expenditure is involved. Nor does the Constitutional Court's own interpretation of that article[35] give any encouragement in this direction. *Art.* 30 *GG* embraces the totality of governmental functions, and no distinction is made between administrative and financial powers and responsibilities.

More specifically, the former *Art.* 106 *Abs.* 4 *Nr.* 1 *GG* (since the Finance Reform of 1969 appearing as *Art.* 104a *Abs.* 1 *GG*) provided that the Federation and the Länder should meet separately the expenditure resulting from the discharge of their respective tasks. But how are grants-in-aid compatible with the principle that the holder of the relevant power should bear all the administrative costs? On the face of it, the Federation is thereby debarred from any expenditure within the domain of the Länder. Equally, *Art.* 109 *Abs.* 1 *GG* lays down that the Federation and the Länder shall be autonomous and independent of each other in their fiscal administration. Yet regardless of this the Federation is able by means of the conditions attached to its grants to commit large sums from the funds of the Länder and direct their application to the achievement of its own objectives. It is no wonder that Maunz sees in Federal grants-in-aid an undermining of the constitutional distribution of powers.[36]

Nevertheless, given the prevailing distribution of financial resources, Federal subsidies were indispensable for major investment projects, particularly as far as the financially weaker Länder were concerned. The result was that, despite all the uneasiness of the Land governments, the questionable legality of Federal grants-in-aid was never made an issue before the Constitutional Court. It is true that in the summer of 1959 the Court, at the instance of the Bavarian Government, declared a Federal law invalid on the ground that it had imposed on the Länder the settlement of demands for compensation amounting to 1,000 million DM, in violation of the provisions of *Art.* 120 *GG* on the burdens resulting from the War, according to which such settlement was a matter for the Bund.[37] But this case involved an attempt by the Federal Government to bind the Länder by law to pay for matters falling within its own responsibility (after all, if the Federal Government has control over policy in any case, the Länder may as well be made to pay if possible); the judgment could not be taken as a verdict upon voluntary Federal contribution to matters which are constitutionally the prerogative of the Länder. Nevertheless it is significant[38] that although as a result of the judgment the Länder were relieved of annual expenditure in the region of 400 million DM, which the Bund now had to find from its own resources, the total of Federal funds devoted to subsidization of projects in the Länder was not reduced at all. The influence gained thereby was apparently too valuable.

In the absence of judicial clarification of the constitutionality of grants-in-aid some attempts were made to justify the *status quo*, at least at the edges. On the one hand, given the widespread view that the Federation's right to assume financial responsibilities was restricted to the areas where it had administrative authority, the question of grants-in-aid became bound up with that of the scope of such authority and the possibility of implied Federal administrative powers.[39] On the other hand some argued, and not unreasonably, though certainly without explicit backing from the constitution, that the principle should be recognized that the costs of a project should not have to be borne by the Länder, who were responsible for the administration, but rather by the Bund, whose legislation had occasioned the expenditure. In fact such a practice had at least been partially followed from the start, and this area of legal and practical uncertainty was in time glossed over by unofficial acceptance of the proposition that the Länder should meet expenditure on establishments and running costs, while the main investment funds were provided by the Bund. But whatever the merits of this interpretation of the principle that the Federation and the Länder should meet separately the costs arising from the discharge of their tasks, it does not cover the relevant case where the Bund's financial contribution is based not on its power of legislative enactment but on the persuasive power of the purse alone. In a case such as the provision of funds for student grants on the *Honnef-Modell*, the Federal Government had neither administrative nor legislative rights under the Basic Law. But its financial strength enabled it to act to some degree as if it had both.

Some of the most popular areas for Federal grants-in-aid, such as hospitals, educational and training grants and the promotion of scientific research, were in the end partly or wholly transferred to the Bund by inclusion in the concurrent catalogue of powers (*Art.* 74 *Nr.* 13 and 19a *GG*: both 1969); others, such as university building, were selected to become 'joint tasks' under the new *Art.* 91a *GG*. For the rest, *Art.* 104a *Abs.* 4, inserted in the Basic Law in 1969, created a constitutional foundation, its purpose being on the one hand to give official recognition to the reality of grants-in-aid, on the other hand to limit their scope somewhat and to strengthen the influence of the Länder. Thus it

restricts Federal assistance to particularly important investments, and only where these are necessary to avert a disturbance of the overall economic equilibrium or to equalize differences of economic capacities within the federal territory or to
promote economic growth.[40] The form finally taken by *Art.*
104a *Abs.* 4 *GG* was a compromise produced by the Mediation
Committee (*Vermittlungsausschuss*) between the blanket criterion
'maintenance of the uniformity of living conditions within the
federal territory' proposed by the Bundestag and the Bundesrat's demand for an enumeration of specific subjects eligible for
Federal investment aid (to cover local transport systems, urban
renewal and local authority development). The blanket authorization had been attacked as a fundamental undermining by
financial means of the constitutional distribution of powers[41]
—particularly as the proposed formula would not prove any
more adequately justiciable than it had done as a restriction on
the Federation's concurrent legislative power in *Art.* 72 *Abs.* 2
Nr. 3 *GG*.[42] However, even if the conditions finally agreed
upon restricted the former scope of grants-in-aid somewhat
(and there might still appear to be little that they could not be
stretched to cover), the restriction could be seen as being more
than compensated for by the constitutional legitimation of
what has in most federal systems been the national government's
most potent instrument for making the member states dance to
its tune.[43]

This institutionalization of Federal grants-in-aid seemed to
have put them virtually beyond challenge before the Constitutional Court. But in the event it neither strengthened the
Federal Government's hand so much nor proved so immune
to judicial control as some had expected. Complaints were soon
heard in the Bundesrat and elsewhere[44] that the Federal Government was again exercising powers of subvention in excess of its
constitutional right to do so. These complaints applied particularly to the law of 1971 on Federal financial support for local
authority transport systems,[45] the 1971 Act for the Promotion
of Urban Building,[46] and the 1972 law on the economic viability
of hospitals.[47]

Both the Municipal Transport Finance Act and the Hospital
Finance Act appeal to two criteria of *Art.* 104a *Abs.* 4 *GG*,
namely the need to equalize differences of economic capacity

within the federal territory and to promote economic growth, as justifying Federal investment aid. Yet it is at least debatable how far they conform to either criterion: for they both provide for a continuing Federal subsidy regardless of whether the growth of the economy needs to be stimulated or restrained, while the allocation of financial aid—in one case in proportion to the population of each Land, in the other on the basis of the number of registered motor vehicles—is scarcely designed effectively to counteract inequalities in economic capacity. In view of their dubious constitutional foundation the Bundesrat passed them reluctantly, having initially insisted in particular that *Art*. 104a *GG* did not authorize the payment of grants-in-aid on a semi-permanent basis but rather if in the longer term the financial resources of the Länder were insufficient to meet their needs, appropriate changes must be made in the division of tax revenue.

In practice, however, the effects of such legislation were not as damaging to the Länder's autonomy as was claimed. The very fact that it did not seriously contribute to promoting any of the very broadly defined goals of *Art*. 104a *Abs*. 4 *GG* is itself an indication that the Federal Government was not enabled thereby to pursue a coherent national strategy through its power of subvention. On the contrary, during the 1970s hospital building by local authorities, spurred on by the availability of Federal funds, rose so steeply that it led to considerable excess capacity and a heavy burden in running costs. This was scarcely the result of centralized planning of efficient resource application: the Hospital Finance Act at any rate seems to cast the Bund in the role of paymaster with negligible influence over construction programmes or the assessment of hospital requirements at Land or local authority level. The institutionalization of grants-in-aid seems in fact to have increased the lower authorities' room for manoeuvre at the expense of that of the Federal Government.

The Act for the Promotion of Urban Building did provide the Federal Government with a degree of policy influence, though even here in the allocation of grants to the Länder it had to agree to base itself in general on the Länder's own priorities. In the event, therefore, it was this law that prompted the Bavarian Government to apply to the Constitutional Court in 1972 for a declaration of its unconstitutionality. It based its case mainly on the 'programmatic power' with accompanying rights of participation in planning granted to the Federation, which was held to be incompatible with *Art. 104a Abs. 4 GG* in conjunction with the guarantees of the residual jurisdiction of the Länder and the federal system in general contained in *Art.* 30, 83, 20 *Abs.* 1 and 79 *Abs.* 3 *GG*.

Giving judgment in 1975,[48] the Constitutional Court decided that the Promotion of Urban Building Act was susceptible of an interpretation whereby it conformed to the requirements of the Basic Law. In particular it was generous in its interpretation of the criteria of *Art.* 104a *Abs.* 4 *GG* for Federal investment aid, which it declared to be so vague as legal concepts that judicial review had to be restricted to examining whether the Federal legislature had in principle interpreted them correctly and had kept within the framework indicated by them.[49] In this regard it had no doubts about the importance of urban redevelopment as a contribution to the promotion of economic growth.

On the other hand, the Court seized the opportunity to make wide-ranging comments on the whole system of grants-in-aid. It showed itself perfectly well aware of the questionable status and the undesirable political consequences of the practice as it had developed in the past, and its approach was not the narrow legalistic one whereby such aspects of 'constitutional reality' had been dismissed as irrelevant to an alleged formal conformity with the constitutional text. The vital influence of financial arrangements in the federal structure was explicitly recognized: subventions from the Federal budget for responsibilities of the Länder made the latter dependent on the Federation and thereby affected their autonomy; therefore, the Court declared:

A federal order must guarantee in principle that financial subsidies from the Federal budget to the Länder remain the exception and their provision is legally regulated in such a way that they do not become a means of exerting influence over the freedom of decision of the member states in the fulfilment of the tasks incumbent on them.[50]

This danger the Court viewed as greatest when the national government decided whether and how to give financial aid, the Länder were dependent on Federal funds, and the Federal decision at the same time committed a substantial part of the budget of the Länder because the granting of the Federal subvention was conditional upon their financial participation. Now that the uncontrolled and unsatisfactory development of grants-in-aid had been put on a constitutional basis and legally circumscribed, apart from the special cases of the joint tasks, by *Art.* 104a *Abs.* 4 *GG*, the latter could not be taken to authorize an encroachment upon the freedom of the Länder to carry out their own responsibilities autonomously: otherwise it would conflict with the federal structure and the principles of *Art.* 83 ff., 30 *GG*, which were restricted only by the mutual obligation of federal comity. In particular the requirement that the Länder accept certain conditions or controls as a prerequisite for receiving the investment aid would amount to a crucial alteration of the federal structure which would violate the basic principle of *Art.* 84 *GG*. Moreover, the Court insisted that *Art.* 104a *Abs.* 4 *GG* could constitute no more than a modification of the general provision of *Art.* 104a *Abs.* 1 *GG*, whereby the Federation and the Länder meet separately the expenditure resulting from the discharge of their separate tasks. Therefore it could not be resorted to as a substitute for an appropriate redistribution of the joint taxes or a proper regulation of financial equalization under *Art.* 107 *Abs.* 1 and 2 *GG*.

Despite its subsequent generous interpretation of the limitations of *Art.* 104a *Abs.* 4, the Court affirms the general principle that the powers granted by that clause are not an instrument of direct or indirect manipulation of investment in order to promote general economic, monetary, planning, or structural objectives of the Bund in the Länder. Beyond the objectives of *Art.* 104a *Abs.* 4 *Satz* 1 *GG* these Federal subsidies do not permit the exercise of influence from the political point of view of the Federal Government over the performance of the Länder. The Court points to the availability of other constitutional instruments for these purposes. The only function of the 'financial aid' clause is to supplement the attempts made via vertical and horizontal financial equalization to balance the distribution of tax revenue against the genuine needs of Bund and Länder, and to do so by the provision of grants for specified important tasks which the Länder have proved unable to accomplish from their own resources alone.

The Constitutional Court further protected the fundamental

planning and administrative powers of the Länder by limiting
the extent to which the Federal legislation regulating the kinds
of investments to be promoted could go into detail and at the
same time laying down that this legislation, which was subject
to the safeguard of requiring the consent of the Bundesrat,
should contain everything of importance to the Länder and not
leave it to administrative orders or discretionary decisions of a
Federal ministry, let alone to mere administrative practice. It is
the Länder that decide whether in their sphere of jurisdiction
an investment project shall be carried out and partly financed
by the Federation. Thus Federal aid depends on the presenta-
tion of suitable investment projects by the Länder and the
Bund cannot infringe upon their powers either directly by
selecting measures which it regards as more or less worthy of
support or indirectly by laying down narrower criteria of selection than simply the kind of investment to be promoted. The
Court points out that where the Constitution has not granted
the Bund the appropriate substantive jurisdiction, rights of
participation in planning, administration, and decision-
making of whatever kind in the domain of the Länder offend
against the constitutional prohibition of so-called 'mixed administration' (*Mischverwaltung*):[51] it is indeed precisely in this
that the distinction between the joint tasks of *Art.* 91a and b *GG*
and all other fields is to be found. The attachment to the
payment of Federal grants of conditions designed directly or
indirectly to commit the Länder in their planning discretion, to
a degree beyond that sanctioned by *Art.* 104a *Abs.* 4 *GG,* to the
political interests and purposes of the Bund, is (in contrast to
the practice prevailing before the constitutional reform) no
longer possible.

This judgment delivered by the Federal Constitutional
Court in 1975 shows little sign of judicial self-restraint, but
rather appears to relish the opportunity afforded at last to
intervene in the crucial financial sphere and cover as many
aspects of the question of grants-in-aid as it can. It was not
disposed to quarrel with the Promotion of Urban Building Act
as a worthy example of Federal investment aid, but nevertheless made it clear that it was both competent and determined to
act as a watch-dog over future developments. To this end the
judgment lays down a wide variety of guidelines and restric-

tions to provide clarification, as far as is possible, of a field which remains ill defined and extremely complex. It is tempting to regard the Second Senate as endeavouring to restore the balance in the wake of the constitutional legitimation of grants-in-aid by developing to the utmost the safeguards that had been built into it. At all events the Bavarian application had at last given the Court another opportunity to establish a broad range of principles in the federal sphere which might prove capable of exerting a real influence on a particularly intractable aspect of political reality.

The willingness of the Bavarian Government to stand up for its constitutional rights in the face of the Federal spending power by seeking legal remedy in Karlsruhe was in fact confirmed in a case which reached judgment in the following year.[52] The object of its challenge was an exceptional Federal programme of economic aid for areas with special structural problems. This programme had been devised in early 1974 in response to rapidly rising unemployment in some areas of the Federal Republic, including well above average unemployment in certain parts of Bavaria. It thus constituted financial assistance within the meaning of *Art.* 104a *Abs.* 4 *GG.*

It was stipulated in the relevant clause, however, that the details, especially concerning the kinds of investments to be promoted, must be regulated by Federal legislation requiring the consent of the Bundesrat, or by administrative arrangements based on the Federal budget. The Constitutional Court underlined that only by these means was it possible to assure the constitutionally guaranteed right of the Länder to exercise decisive influence over the provisions concerning the conditions and procedure for the granting of aid. Yet it agreed with the Bavarian Government that no administrative agreement had been concluded. Such an agreement was provided for as an alternative to a law requiring the consent of the Bundesrat in cases where swift action was called for. But because it was functionally equivalent to a statute, and from considerations of legal clarity and the position of the Länder in the federal structure, it must be formalized. Not only must it be in written form (which was not in fact the case), but, as laid down in the *Financial Subsidies Case*, such laws or administrative agreements must contain all that is of importance to the Länder.

This was held to include, as a minimum, (a) provisions for the selection of the investment projects to be subsidized, in so far as the Länder are not given general grants on a quota basis but specific grants linked to the promotion of particular projects; (b) stipulation of the amount of the Federal share in the costs of the investment aid; (c) a uniform criterion of apportionment for the Federal Government—subject to general agreement with the Länder—to observe in the absence of clearly established or calculable Länder quotas when the sum of the Federal funds applied for by the Länder is in excess of that provided for in the Federal budget. The Court concluded that an informal agreement could scarcely meet these requirements.

This finding was then supported by further considerations. The possibility of tacit administrative agreements was rejected on the ground that the existence of such agreements could only be deduced from the behaviour of the parties in implementing the programme: this would conflict with the normative function of such agreements. It would also endanger the right of the Länder, deriving from the federal organization of the Federal Republic, to enjoy the same opportunities of influencing the content of the norms as in the case of laws requiring Bundesrat consent. For, if the declarations of the parties concluding the agreement were not made explicitly, the Bund might be able to exploit its financial strength and, by unilaterally laying down guidelines for the grants and the procedure to be followed, put the Länder—which were generally unable for political reasons to refuse the financial aid—into a position in which their behaviour might be interpreted as effective acceptance of the proffered compact.

The Court then invoked the duty of federal comity. If the Federal Government was not to violate this duty, it could only conclude such an agreement simultaneously with all the Länder affected as equal partners. In view of the fundamental requirement of unanimous assent for the agreement to be valid,[53] all the Länder must be given the chance to examine in advance the appropriateness and necessity of the programme and its compatibility with the relevant legal norms. This was sufficiently guaranteed only if the text were put down on paper.

Having decided that there was no constitutional basis for the special aid programme because the Bavarian Government had not expressly and in writing accepted the Federal Government's offer to conclude an administrative agreement, the Constitutional Court turned its attention to the content and the mode of implementation of the aid programme. It found these in conflict with *Art.* 104a *Abs.* 4 *GG* in as much as the Federal Government reserved to itself, instead of the Länder, the right to decide on individual applications from local authorities—even if only on those applications which were passed on to it by the Länder. This offended against the constitutional prohibition of 'mixed administration'. Referring explicitly to its judgment in the *Financial Subsidies Case*, the Court stressed that the inalienability of the powers which were constitutionally apportioned between Bund and Länder must not be infringed by the Länder's allowing the Federal Government within a relationship of financial aid to exercise powers which it did not otherwise possess. Within such a context Bund and Länder were not prevented from concluding an administrative agreement about an individual project. But this did not mean that the Bund could share in the decision: only the Land could decide what investment project was to be subsidized, the Federal Government being entitled merely to review whether the general conditions for granting aid were fulfilled and funds were available for a Federal subsidy.

The Court further held that a Federal right of participation was not 'intrinsically implicit' or derivable 'by association' either. It was true that grants designed to avert a disturbance of the overall economic equilibrium were *ipso facto* of supra-regional significance and in their intended effects need not be restricted to the territory of a single Land. But the Court saw no need to consider whether the overall economic objective of such aid programmes could be better achieved if decisions about the allocation of Federal subsidies were principally in the hands of a central authority. For it cited the *Boiler* and *Youth Welfare Judgments* as having established that such considerations of expediency were not capable of generating a Federal administrative power.[54] This would be possible only where there was from the start no prospect of achieving the goal in question if the aid programme were implemented entirely by the Länder. But there was no question of that in the case in hand.

Finally, the Federal Government was found to have violated

Art. 104a *Abs.* 4 *GG* by according the grants applied for not to Bavaria but directly to its local authorities (or associations of local authorities). Where financial aid was provided by the Federal Government for promoting investments by local authorities, the partners in the federal state must remain Bund and Länder, with the latter being responsible for allocating the funds to the municipal investors.

In these two judgments in Bavaria's favour the Constitutional Court thus made a detailed and determined attempt to tackle one of the problems posing the greatest threat to the balance of power between Bund and Länder. Both are unmistakably federalist in tone and substance, emphasizing the limitations to the spending power conferred on the Bund by *Art.* 104a *Abs.* 4 *GG* and trying to preserve the Länder's independent power of decision as a reality. In the process the Court had recourse to several items in its arsenal of interpretative aids. It confirmed its refusal to deduce implicit Federal powers from the sheer supraregional nature of a task; it revived its use of the principle of federal comity primarily as an instrument for safeguarding the rights of the Länder; and it showed a renewed willingness to draw practical conclusions from the fundamental nature of the federal order. These two cases therefore show a new judicial activism at one of the most vulnerable points in the federal system.

How far the Court's efforts will help to curb the proliferation of grants-in-aid is still an open question. Certainly what has been dubbed the *Angebotsdiktatur* of the Federal Government, i.e. the power to make offers that cannot be refused, has been restricted. But so long as appropriations are made in the Federal budget for investment subsidies the competition for them will continue among the Länder, even if this means neglecting other objectives which could be given priority in Länder budgets but for which there is no Federal money. Nevertheless it is significant that such an important federal question, which had for long been left to the vagaries of political practice, did eventually, like the issue of the extent of the Bundesrat's absolute veto power over amendments of Federal legislation,[55] come under the scrutiny of the Karlsruhe judges. Had it done so sooner, before the constitutional authorization of Federal subventions by the passage of the Finance Reform, the Court's scope for regulating and curtailing the practice, and perhaps indirectly compelling a major shift of the allocation of tax revenue in favour of the Länder, would have been considerably greater.

(iv) *Financial planning and co-ordination between Bund and Länder*

Perhaps an even more important aspect of the Finance Reform of 1967–9 than the constitutional legitimation of grants-in-aid was the provisions for imposing common objectives on the budgetary measures of Bund and Länder and enabling their co-ordination as an instrument for the management of the economy. The amended *Art.* 109 *Abs.* 2 and 4 *GG* commits both levels of government jointly to the preservation as far as possible of overall economic equilibrium. The co-ordination of fiscal management is promoted by the authorization of Federal legislation placing restrictions on the raising of loans by public bodies, including Land governments (since carried out by the *Konjunkturrat* or 'Trade Cycle Council').[56] Moreover, the whole system of Federal medium-term financial planning necessarily involves increased co-operation with the Länder, which has taken place on a voluntary basis, though again not without complaints of Federal domination. *Art.* 109 *Abs.* 3 *GG* as amended in 1969 establishes a legislative power of the Federation to lay down principles applicable to both Bund and Länder governing financial planning for several years ahead. On the basis of this the Council for Financial Planning (*Finanzplanungsrat*), in which both Bund and Länder are represented and the Federal Finance Minister presides, has played a co-ordinating role based on the five-year programmes of expenditure and revenue which all are required to present. As so often, the Federal Government is in the best position to take the initiative. Given the principle of separate budgets for Bund and Länder (*Art.* 109 *Abs.* 1 *GG*), the financial planning takes the form of separate plans for Bund and Länder. But in view of its manifest advantages pressure can be expected to mount against federalist resistance to 'integrated' financial planning. In any case the extension of Federal powers in this field effects a transformation of original federal principles by providing for congruence or co-ordination of budgetary law, fiscal administration, and financial planning based primarily on the Federal Government's conception of political priorities.

The necessity of many of the co-ordinative measures is scarcely open to dispute. The fact cannot be ignored that the economic field forms a basic unity, and therefore the federal system would be bound to break down without wide-ranging co-ordination for the promotion of economic stability and the pursuit of economic growth through long-term planning. In particular the economic recession of 1966–7 highlighted the deficiencies in the co-ordination of the economic and financial policy of the different levels of government. The results of the informal agreement to endeavour to bring financial policy into line with the needs of economic stability were that in 1965 the Länder exceeded the rate of growth of public expenditure agreed with the Federation by up to 100 per cent, thereby frustrating any attempt at a coherent overall economic policy. The Länder were thus partly themselves to blame for the developments leading to the establishment of the Trade Cycle Council and the Council for Financial Planning as organs of co-operative federalism under Federal direction.[57]

But if the trend away from autonomy of financial decision-making towards mere participation is backed by substantial economic arguments and by threats that its hindrance would provoke an explosive centralizing shift in the whole federal system of powers, it scarcely does justice to the independent power of authoritative political action and self-government of the member states which is both on various grounds a political desideratum and, more important, a constitutional imperative. The potential created for the wielding of influence by the Federal Finance Ministry over the financial policy and administration of the Länder is great.

The alterations made in the federal sphere by the Finance Reform were heralded as an evolution in line with contemporary needs in that they made possible the mobilization of combined strength through co-operative federalism. But what actually lay behind the fine language was not so much greater mutual dependence as a general erosion of the independence of the Länder in favour of the Federation under pressure of social and economic circumstances.[58]

Maunz[59] comes to the conclusion that these legal forms of

co-operative federalism, developed over the years out of the relations between Bund and Länder and partly accepted, partly even striven for, by the latter, are not inroads into the heart of the federal structure but rather a natural evolution. Yet it can be held that the traditional federal structure *has* been decisively, even if in part indirectly, altered by the totality of measures both strengthening Federal rights and squeezing the financial power of the Länder. (The corresponding additions to the power of the Bundesrat are far from being an adequate substitute.) It is at least open to argument whether the foundations on which a true co-operative federalism can be built are not undermined by the fact that the prerequisite of independent partners with full decision-making authority is not fulfilled.

(v)   *The institutionalization of 'joint tasks'*

The ever more widespread *ad hoc* co-operative activity of Bund and Länder received the *imprimatur* of constitutional law in 1969 with the introduction of 'joint tasks' in *Art.* 91a and b *GG*. Apart from the institution of joint planning, their essence consists in joint financing by Bund and Länder of projects falling within the competence of the latter. To the extent that they bring about a shift of financial responsibility towards the Federal Government they are thus open to some of the same comments as the institutionalization of Federal subsidies to the Länder by *Art.* 104a *Abs.* 4 *GG*. The joint tasks pose a long-term threat to the financial autonomy of the Länder since they increase the proportion of the Länder budgets that is already earmarked by planning agreement and by on-going programmes of expenditure. This means that they are no longer able to finance adequately other areas of Länder activity such as protection of the environment against pollution. The natural result is that the Federation should fill the gap with new legislative powers or more joint tasks, thus having a claim on an increased share of taxes while the Länder are saddled with the subsidiary expenditure, especially on staff.

On the face of it the threat to Länder autonomy posed by the joint tasks is not as great as has here been made out. In particular the provision that the inclusion of a project in the overall planning shall require the consent of the Land in whose territory it is to be carried out may seem to provide a significant guarantee. But in practice the Länder are constrained on the contrary to try to get a project included in the overall planning in order to obtain the Federal participation in investment which goes with it. As a result of the basic imbalance in the distribution of total revenue, even the richer Länder are in no position to turn down their share of the proposed Federal investment in the joint project—a situation already familiar from elsewhere. Although it is still theoretically open to a Land to go its own way when the conditions laid down in *Art.* 91a for participation by the Federation obtain, this is practically a dead letter.

As for the planning undertaken by Bund and Länder together under the aegis of joint tasks, it is of course no free co-ordinative planning without obligation by advisory or pre-paratory bodies, but rather a kind of institutionalized inte-grated planning and decision-making by planning committees consisting of representatives of the Federal and Länder gov-ernments, the products of which are directly legally binding on the governments concerned. To this extent it is a completely new phenomenon in a federal system. Moreover, the position of the Federation as representing the interests of the whole and its right to make or withhold offers of financial contribution would seem to ensure for it the dominant role.

Above all the organization of the planning committees is hardly designed to protect the Länder from central guidance. The relevant Federal minister takes the chair. As against the Bund's uniform bloc of eleven votes there are the single votes of eleven individual Länder pursuing sometimes quite different interests, which are not cast unanimously but are variously susceptible to Federal influence according to their party-political colouring or their dependence upon financial aid. Thus, although decisions of the planning committees require the at first sight substantial margin of three-quarters of the votes, in fact the Federal Government needs to carry only a bare majority of the Länder with it in order to have its way. This is a major departure from the unanimity rule which prevails in inter-Länder commissions. Equally, there is no chance of the Federal Government being itself overruled. Yet the subjects included in the catalogue of joint tasks are still described in *Art.* 91a *GG* as 'responsibilities of the Länder'!

In these circumstances what is surprising is that the Federal Government's position within the field of joint tasks is not in practice more dominant. On the contrary, its attempts to achieve planning according to uniform rational criteria have generally been frustrated by the competing interests of the Länder. Both the ratios adopted for the apportionment of resources among the Länder and other criteria such as the definition of development areas tended to be based initially on previously existing practice and were scarcely adapted thereafter to changing needs, maintenance of the status quo being evidently the easiest way to reach a degree of consensus. With few exceptions, the Federal Government has therefore had limited influence over the basic elements of the framework plans, apart from determining the overall amount of the resources devoted to them, while it has had no control over the Länder's internal allocation of funds to particular kinds of project.[60] Being confronted in the planning committees by all the Länder at once has put the Federal Government in a weaker position to push through its own policy priorities than when it could exert its full weight in bilateral dealings with individual Länder.

The fact remains, however, that in terms of the autonomy of the individual Land the system of joint planning and financing is far from being an adequate substitute for independent policy-making with sufficient resources of its own. Moreover, even worse sufferers than the Länder governments are the Länder parliaments. The shift towards joint decision-making in the planning committees, where only the executives are represented, reduces the parliamentary responsibility of the Länder governments and presents the Landtage with *faits accomplis* and the certainty of being in very bad odour if they upset the carefully constructed edifice.[61] In purely legal terms, of course, the decisions bind only the Länder governments and *Art.* 91a *Abs.* 4 *GG* expressly declares that provision of funds shall be subject to appropriation in the budgets of the Federation and the Länder (i.e. by their parliaments). But a refusal to make any provision for expenditure on a particular project, with the consequent loss of Federal investment aid, is politically as unthinkable for the parliaments as for the governments of the Länder.

The threat to the federal order posed by the system of joint tasks is mitigated by the fact that *Art.* 91a *GG* contains only a restricted list of subjects eligible for such joint planning, while the subordinate legislation required to put the joint tasks into effect must, to the satisfaction of the Länder governments as represented in the Bundesrat, define them in detail and mark them off clearly from functions which are to remain entirely in the hands of the Länder. Yet a closer look at the subjects covered by the joint tasks reveals the extent of this invasion of Länder powers by the Federation. The general planning principles of the Act for the furtherance of university construction[62] make clear that the joint task 'expansion and construction of institutions of higher education' covers not merely bricks and mortar but also the internal structure and functions of such institutions. When taken in conjunction with the recently added Federal framework power over 'the general principles of higher education' (*Art.* 75 *Nr.* 1a *GG*) and the provision of *Art.* 91b *GG* for co-operation between Bund and Länder in educational planning and research, this opens the way for far-reaching Federal influence over the whole field of higher education. Similarly, the joint tasks 'improvement of regional economic structures' and 'improvement of the agrarian structure and of coastal preservation' cover fields of major political importance. They are seen by Seeger[63] as designed to promote a development in the course of which the economic and agriculture ministries of the Länder are bound in the end to become subordinate branches of the Federal ministries. This rather provocatively expressed view is clearly not shared by all.[64] But Frido Wagener has more recently drawn attention to the effects of joint planning between relevant Federal and Länder departments as producing a vertical congruence of interests which is used to strengthen the department's position *vis-à-vis* its competitors for resources at the same level of government.[65] Such vertical inter-departmental fraternization (*'vertikale Ressortkumpanei'*) is bound to be prejudicial to the independent unity and cohesion of the Länder administrations.

Thus any significant expansion of joint tasks, for example into the rest of the educational field or protection of the environment, must seriously jeopardize that minimum of independent decision-making power of the member-states which is generally regarded as the *sine qua non* of a federal system and which can never be totally compensated for by extensive administrative powers or by even increased participation in bodies where decisions are taken by simple or qualified majority. Voices were indeed quickly raised suggesting additions to the catalogue of *Art.* 91a *GG*, and *Nr.* 1 did undergo an extension. But it was not long before some Länder Prime Ministers, concerned at the curtailment of the Länder's freedom of action caused by the operation of the joint tasks, began to call for their major overhaul. Complaints of excessive Federal intervention were particularly insistent with regard to expansion and construction of institutions of higher education.[66] In consequence demands have arisen for rectification of the blurring of responsibilities implied by joint tasks and for the restoration of clear lines of demarcation. Criticism of its interim report of 1972 also led the Commission of Inquiry into Constitutional Reform to adopt in its final report [67] a much more sober view of the possibilities of integrated planning. Indeed, in view of the complexity of the processes of concerting plans for joint tasks, executing them, and referring them back for modification, it is not even clear that they have made the contribution to the rationalization and efficiency of government that was expected of them and so justified the watering down of the original system of federal separation of powers. This is not to deny that the rational fulfilment of certain important tasks of Bund and Länder does demand extensive co-ordination of the planning of the different levels of government. But it is illustrative of the disillusionment which can be detected with the practical operation of joint tasks, as with other aspects of co-operative federalism.[68]

There is wide recognition, therefore, that the joint tasks represent a further significant erosion of the political autonomy of the Länder. The previously clear boundary-lines between the activities of Bund and Länder have been blurred and their financial responsibilities have become almost inextricably entangled. Yet the whole process has passed the Constitutional Court by. Admittedly, since the joint tasks, like the various additions to the category of concurrent powers, have been given a clear constitutional foundation, an objection to them in constitutional law could be based only on the claim that the limits of *Art.* 79 *Abs.* 3 *GG* ('Amendments of this Basic Law affecting the division of the Federation into Länder, the participation on principle of the Länder in legislation, or the basic principles laid down in Articles 1 and 20, shall be inadmissible'), and the thereby protected principle of *Art.* 20 *GG* that the Federal Republic of Germany is a federal state, had been transgressed.[69]

But even supposing that one of the Länder had objected to the system of joint tasks strongly enough to take the matter to Karlsruhe, how could the Constitutional Court have reacted in the face of such a problem? It would be remarkable if it did not accept ever more erosion of the powers of the Länder in the name of natural development of the constitutional system and shrink back from the momentous pronouncement that such development now meant that the 'Federal Republic' was no longer a federal state. The Court's comparative self-restraint in federal questions since the furore caused by the *Television Judgment* makes this even more likely. The day might indeed come when it would no longer be possible to delude oneself or anyone else that one had a genuine federal system (though by then it would be less feasible than ever to put the clock back); but that day is still some way off. The institutions of co-operative federalism may amount to an alteration of the basic federal structure of the constitution, characterized as it has been by a separation of functions between Bund and Länder. But the lack of a constitutional definition of federalism has already been noted, and it is probable that although this vagueness could theoretically be exploited in either direction by a determined court (and the *Financial Subsidies Case* demonstrated what could be achieved by the Bundesverfassungsgericht in an apparently restricted field of manoeuvre), it will in practice facilitate swimming with the tide of events.

If, therefore, the institutions and practices of co-operative federalism are by no means immune from review by the Constitutional Court, it must nevertheless be concluded that the forces which promote their adoption are much less amenable to either constitutional litigation or judicial control than a jealous insistence on jurisdictional 'territory' would be.

CHAPTER IX

The Influence of the Constitutional Court on the West German Federal System

1 The policy of the Court in federal judgments

Despite the tendency, in a climate of co-operative federalism, for major developments in the federal system to pass the Court by, rulings of the Bundesverfassungsgericht have been sought and given over a wide range of federal issues and have affected in detail the relations between Bund and Länder. A broad survey of the Court's decisions has been provided under various headings in the course of this study. Beyond these, federal judgments have ranged, in the realm of taxation, from the validation of Länder taxes on juke-boxes, pin-tables, and other entertainments[1] to that of special Federal imposts on the wine trade or road freight traffic or on incomes in accordance with the requirements of the economy;[2] from the disallowance of a special local import tax for Heligoland to that of a Land tax on the sale of ice-cream.[3] Judgments on social matters have included confirmation of Federal provisions for family allowances, for employers' contributions to employees' pension insurance and for accident insurance.[4] Other decisions of the Court have covered a variety of subjects, from the assignment to Federal or Länder jurisdiction of provisions of Reich laws on explosives and weapons to the denial that existing law on casinos fell within the competence of the Federation;[5] from the constitutionality of Land legislation for the expropriation of Hamburg's dikes to confirmation of Federal road traffic provisions;[6] from the Federal law on the dissemination of literature harmful to young people to the power to prohibit the importation of films for reasons of public order and security.[7]

The importance for the federal system of some of these cases taken individually may appear to be slight. Yet the cumulative effect is substantial, and the foregoing examination of judgments affecting the balance of powers between Bund and Länder has revealed that the Court's opportunities of influence have by no means been insignificant.[8] It remains to sum up the direction of that influence.

A uniform and single-minded policy in federal judgments has not emerged. However, the analysis of specific areas of federal adjudication, individual articles interpreted and applied, and the use of particular instruments of constitutional exegesis and amplification, has achieved a substantial clarification, differentiation, and revision of the original inconclusive picture. Thus, even if the Court's attitude to the requirement in *Art. 72 Abs.* 2 *GG* that there should be a need for the exercise of Federal concurrent legislative powers has been one of extreme self-restraint and so consistently favoured the Bund, this is not the case with the other areas covered by Chapter V. The resolution of issues of how far Federal concurrent legislation has 'occupied the field' has upheld Länder interests on the whole, and the demarcation of the framework power has done so fairly unequivocally, while the tally of cases relating to the powers of the Bundesrat is at most inconclusive.

In its approach to broad construction and implied powers as discussed in Chapter VI the stance taken up by the Court has been of unmistakable benefit to the Länder. Although it has at times accepted an extensive interpretation, particularly of the economic power, it has placed reasonably consistent emphasis on the presumption in favour of the Länder derived from *Art.* 30, 70, and 83 *GG*. Likewise, the very modest invocation of powers 'by virtue of association' and 'from the intrinsic nature of the matter concerned' must work to the advantage of the Länder in a situation where only Federal powers are enumerated and the residue automatically belongs to the Länder.

In so far as the Court has derived practical consequences from the 'federal principle' or the essential nature of the federal state, this has had an undoubted and inherent tendency to uphold the position of the Länder against possible Federal encroachment, even if it has sometimes been used to stress the need for co-operation and accommodation. The evidence from the application of the doctrine of federal comity, however, was found in Chapter VII to be rather more ambivalent. Although its early use was generally to mitigate the impact of decisions in favour of the Länder, it was invoked to dramatic effect against the Federal Government in the *Television Case*. The subsequent minimization of the doctrine has been shown not to have been obviously to the benefit of either level of government in the cases concerned. On the other hand, it may be surmised that during the centralizing period of the 1960s a zealous application of the federal comity principle would more naturally have tended to require the Federal authorities to exercise their increasing powers with due regard for the legitimate interests of the Länder than to compel the Länder to still further submission to the alleged needs of the whole. If so, to play it down probably indicated an attitude of acquiescence, or at least prudent resignation, towards the unitarizing trend. The more so since it was on the whole the federalists who in the early 1960s had taken such pride in the development of the doctrine. The signs of a revival of positive use of the comity principle in the 1970s, though significant, could not be said to amount as yet to an identifiable trend in the opposite direction. On the other hand, consideration of the actual outcome in all of the often highly important cases analysed in relation to federal comity showed a marked preponderance of decisions in favour of the Länder. And these included rulings of such consequence as the narrow construction of the Federal foreign affairs power in the *Concordat Case*.

Finally, it may be noted that similar results would be achieved if attention were turned specifically to other aspects of federal relations which have not been given separate treatment in their own right. In the field of administrative powers, for example, the Court has recognized the principle that the legislative competence of the Federation forms the outermost limit of its administrative powers and has refused to countenance any inference of legislative powers from administrative responsibilities. It has also been seen that the principle that all residual powers accrue to the Länder, which is laid down in *Art. 30 GG* and specifically repeated with regard to the execution of Federal laws in *Art. 83 GG*, was interpreted by the Court as applying equally to administration of a non-implementory kind: thus the Federal Government in principle requires constitutional authorization for any kind of administrative activity. Admittedly, this position was somewhat weakened by the acceptance that in cases where smooth and complete execution of Federal laws could not be guaranteed by Länder administration the possibility of tacit constitutional authorization of Federal execution could be considered. But Chapter VI found a general disinclination to acknowledge implied administrative, any more than legislative, powers.

Again, if the Court's decision-making in relation to the financial arrangements of the federal system is singled out, a similar generally federalist tendency is discernible. Such cases have been predominantly concerned with legislative powers for the imposition of taxes and levies. Thus the general principle of *Art. 70 Abs. 1 GG,* whereby every Federal legislative power must have explicit constitutional foundation, was applied to the taxation field; so that the Länder were left not merely with concurrent powers for local excise taxes but also with the right to legislate in respect of any other taxes so long as the Basic Law had not conferred legislative authority on the Bund.[9] On the other hand, in the sphere of concurrent powers of taxation the Court took a stricter line than with other concurrent legislation, considering any use of a Federal power to levy a particular kind of tax as an exhaustive regulation which prevented the Länder from subjecting the same object to a similar tax.[10] But there was no objection to the Länder's introducing taxes which pursued secondary purposes in fields normally reserved to the Bund, provided that their primary purpose was to raise public revenue. Finally, when the amended version of *Art.* 105 *GG* reduced the Länder's preserve in the field of tax legislation from the beginning of 1970 to local excise taxes which are not identical with taxes imposed by Federal legislation, the Court did not submit meekly to the trend of constitutional amendment. In interpreting the term 'identical' (*Gleichartig*),[11] it assumed that the amendment had not intended to interfere with the power of the Länder to regulate the traditional local excise taxes, i.e. at any rate those which had generally existed at the time of its promulgation. Such taxes were therefore *a priori* not identical with taxes imposed by Federal legislation. This reference to the presumed intention of the legislator where the text of the new constitutional provision in fact gave no hint of such a meaning was presumably motivated by the wish to preserve at least a modicum of fiscal autonomy for the Länder.

Other financial aspects of federal relations have seldom been dealt with by the Constitutional Court. But the two recent judgments on the issue of grants-in-aid which were reviewed in Chapter VIII provide evidence of renewed judicial activism with a pronounced federalist flavour.

The outcome of this survey is a scarcely overwhelming but nevertheless substantial correction of the findings obtained by the quantification of judgments in Chapter II. For, although the trend is far from uniform, if the decision-making of the Court is weighed against both the legal and the political possibilities open to it and constraints upon it the balance is clearly in favour of reinforcing the position of the Länder.

This conclusion is in harmony with the preponderant opinion of the judges interviewed that the decisions of the Court had been unmistakably federalist in their tenor and tone. It is perhaps significant that the one judge who felt that the Court decided '*in dubio* pro-Bund' was a member of the more unitarist First Senate. It has been seen that, whereas at the outset there were many convinced federalists in the Second Senate, this influence has declined, and along with it the rhetoric and eloquence of the federalist line of its early judgments, so that the pro-Länder position is generally more temperate now. Yet a comparison with the Court's approach to the autonomy of the local authorities is instructive. Here the contrary tendency is apparent to that shown towards the Länder, for the case of the local authorities has normally been rejected.[12] The Court could have taken a similar line in relation to the federal system. But in practice attempts by the Bund to achieve a widening of its allotted powers by other means than explicit constitutional amendment have generally been given a frosty reception. To this extent the decisions of the Court, or at least of the Second Senate, have revealed, not a clear and conscious long-term strategy, which it would be unrealistic to expect, but a continuing, though by no means blind, inclination to uphold the federal element of the constitutional order and so protect the interests of the Länder.

2 The impact of the Court's decisions

There has been little sign in Germany of a disposition to do other than submit to and comply with the decisions of the Constitutional Court. Even in the case of the *Television Judgment*, in spite of Adenauer's assertion that it was 'false', there was no attempt at defiance, and the same is true of more recent controversial judgments such as that on the abortion reform.[13] A conflict on the Rooseveltian model is unthinkable in Germany. Even the kind of situation which arose in Canada during the long-drawn-out dispute between the Federal and Provincial Governments over off-shore oil rights seems improbable in the German context: here the Federal Government, having eventually procured a favourable ruling from the Supreme Court on all counts, nevertheless felt obliged to make a new compromise offer to the Provinces, so that the judicial verdict became little more than a political bargaining counter.[14]

However, although there may be almost automatic compliance, and the Court would not be alone in its indignation at any attempt to overturn the effects of a decision by legislation, the impact of judgments may vary both in intensity and in duration. The response of the Federal Government to the *Abortion Judgment*, for instance, was to produce a new bill having as minimal regard to the Court's strictures as it seemed likely to get away with. Other decisions, though initially observed, have later been overtaken by changes in the social or political environment, and perhaps consequently of the views of the parties concerned.

When it comes to assessing the effects of the decisions of the Bundesverfassungsgericht in the federal sphere and their lasting influence, some differentiation is necessary. As those judgments which went in favour of the Bund were in conformity with the general trend towards the expansion of Federal power, it is not surprising that they have remained effective and unchallenged. If this is true also of many decisions in favour of the Länder, one reason is that many concern relatively minor questions or activities and it is not difficult for the Bund to live with them. Other federalist decisions, however, are more far-reaching in their effects, and it might be expected that some of these would in time be overturned, ignored, or eroded.

Yet this has occurred only to a limited extent. Certainly some judgments have been rendered void by constitutional amendment. Thus the various instances of defence and reinforcement of the autonomous powers of the Länder regarding the salaries of public officials[15] were overtaken by the insertion into the Basic Law of a wider Federal responsibility for pay scales in the form of *Art.* 74a *GG* in 1971. Similarly, the decision in the *Residence Tax Case*[16] whereby *Art.* 105 *GG* left the Länder free to invent and regulate such taxes as it did not assign to the sphere of Federal legislation was rendered obsolete by the reform of this constitutional provision in 1969. In addition to such direct invalidation by constitutional means, it has been shown, for instance, in Chapter VIII that the unanimity rule in inter-Länder decision-making, so strongly emphasized by the Court in the early years, has gradually been eroded. Again, an example of federalist judicial doctrine being ignored is provided by the Federal Hunting Act (*Bundesjagdgesetz*) based on the framework legislative authority of *Art.* 75 *Nr.* 3 *GG*. Despite the Court's strict circumscription of Federal action under *Art.* 75 *GG* by the requirement that room be left for substantial regulation by the Länder, the Federal Hunting Act is exhaustive—the work of a lobby well represented in all parties.

On the other hand, decisions in favour of the Länder may also be found which have had a significant and lasting impact on the distribution of powers in the federal system. Among these must be included the early legal opinion[17] which held that the Federal concurrent powers for land law, housing, and other matters under *Art.* 74 *Nr.* 18 *GG* could not be interpreted extensively to give general jurisdiction over building law: the Bund has remained largely excluded from this field. The Federal Building Act of 1960 kept clear of those aspects, such as those concerning public safety, which the Federal Constitutional Court had reserved to the Länder, though there was Bund–Länder co-operation on the drawing up of model building regulations which were generally followed by the Länder.

A more striking example is the *Television Judgment*, whose abrupt and dramatic termination of the prolonged uncertainty arising from Federal claims to broadcasting powers has had a powerful and lasting effect both on the development of broadcasting in West Germany and on relations between Bund and

Länder over a wider field. It is true that the emphasis on the overall cultural sovereignty of the Länder, to which the *Television Judgment* gave a considerable boost, was relatively short-lived, so that by the late 1960s the Länder were prepared to relinquish some of their powers in the hitherto sacrosanct educational domain. But it is scarcely a coincidence that broadcasting is one of the few fields of importance remaining almost exclusively in the hands of the Länder. Indeed the aspect of the *Television Judgment* which has been under serious discussion in recent years as arguably threatened by technical progress is not the federal demarcation of powers but the observations on the requirements of *Art.* 5 *GG* (freedom of expression) and the maintenance of the monopoly of the public law corporations.[18]

The impact of the *Federal Waterways Judgment* of 1962[19] has been of similarly long duration. Its restriction of the Federal authorities to regulation of the transport functions of the Federal waterways has prevented them ever since from introducing comprehensive measures to solve the problem of water pollution. For it meant that a constitutional amendment would be required to give the Bund the necessary powers. But in 1972, when various powers for the protection of the environment were being transferred to the Federal level, the Bundesrat refused the transformation of the framework responsibilities for protection of nature, care of the countryside and water management into concurrent powers, and further attempts by the Federal Government to obtain full water management powers were frustrated by the refusal of the Opposition CDU/CSU to supply the necessary two-thirds majority. So the Bund still has only a framework power, although the Federal Water Management Act as amended in 1976 contains a large number of individual regulations in full detail.[20]

However, influential though these major decisions in favour of the Länder have been, it is arguable that the cumulative effect of the many more minor demarcations of powers and clarifications of the rights and duties of the two levels of government is at least as important in its impact on the development of the West German federal system. For the submission of such issues to judicial resolution, their frequency, and the evident vigilance of the Constitutional Court against even relatively modest infringements of the dispositions of the Basic Law, especially from a Federal quarter, contrast with the greater recourse to political accommodation between governments and parliaments under earlier German constitutions and the consequent greater ease of Federal encroachment into the domain of the Länder. They have ensured that questions of constitutional powers play an important role in public affairs, sometimes inhibiting legislative and administrative intentions, and that neither level of government is tempted to a careless or wanton attitude to the boundaries of its legitimate sphere of action. As is often the case with institutions of control, the impact is not limited to the individual cases actually decided but includes the deterrent effect on behaviour of awareness of the ultimate possibility of recourse to judicial decision. In the circumstances of West Germany such a force must work above all to restrain aggrandizement by the central government. It is safe to assume that without the influence of the Constitutional Court, both by the tenor of its judgments and by its emphasis of the need for constitutional propriety, the Bund would have reached its present position much sooner.

3 The Court in the context of German federalism

The role of a court in the live political process is necessarily limited, but certain features of West German federalism particularly affect the Constitutional Court's scope for interpretation. In spite of the multiplicity of federal cases and the appreciable impact of certain of the Court's decisions, it has already been noted that, with evident exceptions, the points which are referred to Karlsruhe for adjudication tend to be relatively 'narrow'. A variety of factors combine to produce this effect. Foremost among them is the presence of a constitution which in terms of its specification of powers is 'rigid', thorough and fairly precise. By comparison with some federal constitutions, on the other hand, it is flexible as far as amendment is concerned. Many of the more substantial problems which arise can therefore be solved by amending the constitutional text.

The nature of the constitution which it is called upon to interpret, together with the fact that it is set in a legal tradition directed more strongly towards the written law, has also ensured that the Court has not practised the breadth of interpretation that is common in the United States. But other features of the federal system and of West German society have played their part too in determining the compass of the Court's adjudicatory role.

In the first place it should be recalled that West German federalism, in contrast not only to certain contemporary counterparts but also to its German antecedents, is not on the whole a means of combining communities marked by sharp ethnic or cultural differences or a strong sense of separate identity. Rather, it is 'organizational', a cutting up of powers concerned especially with decentralization of political decision-making, diversity of initiatives, and government tailored to regional needs. This greatly reduces the likelihood that the Court will be confronted by explosive issues, unless they spring from party-political rivalry.

Furthermore, the federal comity doctrine may be seen as mirroring a pervasive quality of German politics, the desire to avoid and contain sharp conflict. So long as there is sufficient over-arching consensus on political goals, there is little objection to meticulous judicial resolution of rather narrow issues. Indeed this may be regarded as a convenient means of disposing of sources of friction (and perhaps of evading political responsibility). Even after the much emphasized pressure for uniformity of living conditions had taken its firm hold over West German federalism, there was still room for such detailed demarcation of responsibilities and clarification of permissible procedures, particularly in view of the fact that a majority of federal cases reach the Constitutional Court by reference from another court. But such cases are normally unlikely to be laden with drama.

Again, there is in Germany no intrinsic relationship between civil rights and federalism of the kind which is often taken for granted by American commentators on their own political system. This is clearly due to the lack of any identifiable geographical pattern for the violation of basic rights. Thus another source of piquancy, and indeed animosity, in federal relations is lacking. However, a less obvious but still significant impact of basic rights on the operation of the federal system may be mentioned. The vast majority of cases dealt with by the Constitutional Court concern the catalogue of basic rights, and the progressive refinement of this catalogue and its requirements by the decisions of the Court has a cumulative unitarizing effect, in that the consequences drawn concerning admissible or obligatory action by the State are binding on all the Länder alike and restrict the room for independent approaches.[21]

Finally, it could be argued that in conformity with the character of modern government, whereby it is no longer possible to take the eighteenth-century view of governing as being virtually synonymous with law-making, the conferment of implementing responsibilities on the Länder itself compensates for much of the rigidity and precision of the enumeration of legislative powers. This could reduce the Court's potential function as a contributor of the necessary flexibility. On the other hand, the horizontal distribution of powers works strongly against 'peculiar institutions' and in favour of uniform Federal legislation, including general administrative rules. The Court's operations are necessarily confined within this given framework. A similar effect may be attributed to the relative homogeneity and consistency of principles characterizing public law in Germany, which tends to limit the possibilities of diversity inherent in the federal structure.[22]

All these factors operating to limit the scope of the Constitutional Court's role of federal adjudication were present before the rise of co-operative federalism. Inevitably, the latter restricted this scope still further. For even if given the opportunity to do so, a court cannot attempt for long to reverse a clear political trend. By doing so it would risk exhausting the reservoir of public respect and destroying the consensus in favour of judicial resolution of political issues on which its influence and above all the assurance of compliance with its decisions depend. At most it can attempt to modify or retard such a process.

In the case of West German federalism, as the number of fields which can be regulated by a Land without reference to other Länder's interests grew ever smaller,[23] there was a continuous decline in the areas where political sentiment or a feeling for the point of a federal system made people seek legal arguments for assigning them to the Länder. Public opinion demanded in general even stronger federal powers. The lack of much real federalist feeling in the population made the Länder reluctant to overtax it and compelled them to self-restraint in insisting on the letter of their constitutional rights. Although in the early years after 1949 they did fight hard to protect their prerogatives, their success can now be seen to have been comparatively short-lived. For though the trend of centralization may be held up at some points by the Constitutional Court, it can, if strong and urgent enough, break through somewhere else, whether in the form of constitutional amendment in the Bund's favour or of paraconstitutional vehicles of co-ordination and co-operation. When the Länder in recognition of reality themselves agree to surrender powers or to pool their efforts in joint institutions, the possibility of defending their rights by recourse to the Constitutional Court seems to lose much of its relevance.

To a certain degree, the Constitutional Court has been obliged to swim with the tide, to recognize the reality of co-operative federalism and the forces of unitarization. This has already been observed, for example, in the much more modest use of the principle of federal comity since the *Television Case*. In general, the trend of the Court's judgments after 1961 suggests a degree of realism, receptiveness towards prevailing opinions, and appreciation of the problems facing modern society which would be incompatible with a policy of intransigent defence of Länder positions. Indeed on occasion its willingness to sacrifice sacred cows of the Länder has been surprising, as witness the *Numerus Clausus Judgment* of 1972.[24] An institution concerned primarily, in the federal sphere, with the definition of the powers of the two levels of government has had to contend with the increasing realization that in tackling the complex and interrelated problems of modern government a rigid demarcation of jurisdictions is inadequate and constricting.

However, if the increase of pragmatic co-operation during the 1960s had the effect that the Constitutional Court was less often brought into Bund–Länder conflicts than previously, a situation never arose like that in Canada, where in the off-shore oil controversy the Federal Government's eventual abandonment of 'negotiation' to seek vindication of its strong legal claim by the Supreme Court could be branded as a 'violation of co-operative federalism'.[25] The appearance during the 1970s of such cases as the Bavarian challenges to Federal behaviour in relation to grants-in-aid and the issue of the Bundesrat's veto power in relation to the Pensions Insurance Act shows, moreover, that the trend against constitutional litigation need not continue, particularly in circumstances of increased party-political polarization. For the political structure of federalism has friction, and the risk of conflict, built into it. However much the practice of co-operative federalism may subject the federal division of powers to *ad hoc* agreement and co-ordination by the governments concerned, the ultimately competitive nature of the federal relationship is not removed, and if negotiation leads only to deadlock, appeal to an independent arbiter can be not merely more efficient in producing a settlement but perhaps also less damaging to intergovernmental relations.

Much depends on the political climate in which the federal system has to function. Public pressure in Germany has been predominantly in the direction of uniformity and therefore of centralized decision-making. But as the (admittedly dissimilar) example of Canada, including English Canada, and the moves towards decentralization or regionalization in several European countries show, there can well be a reversal of this attitude. In fact, evidence from opinion polls indicates that a majority of the population is already opposed to further increases in the powers of central government.

New federal impulses have indeed begun to make themselves felt during the 1970s, though admittedly linked with political antitheses of the kind already noted in Chapter IV and stressed by K. Hesse as the foundation of federal disputes. To some extent the south-German Länder have developed into a conservative counterweight to stronger social-democratic tendencies in northern Germany. It is natural that the role of the Christian-Democratic Länder governments in the Bundesrat should go hand in hand with a determination to defend a distinctive political identity and scope for autonomous action at Länder level. Indeed it may be due to these Opposition blocking tactics based on positions of power in the Länder, and to the loss of impetus thereby caused to the reforming ardour of the SPD/FDP coalition, that the centralizing tendency of the late 1960s has arguably affected the operation of the federal system less than was expected or feared. It has been seen that

Bavaria has become a spear-head of new politically motivated constitutional challenges to the Bund (as in the cases of the Basic Treaty with East Germany and abortion reform), so that the Constitutional Court is by no means left out of these ideologically coloured federal antagonisms.

If such developments do not spring from pure federal sources, that does not prevent them from breathing new life into federal structures and relations.[26] In these circumstances disillusionment on the part of at least some Länder with the effects of co-operative federalism is clearly likely to be intensified, and this could lead to a major constitutional case calling into question much of the network of Bund–Länder co-operation which still leads a shady existence on the periphery of the constitution. Indeed the possibility cannot be excluded of the Court being faced at some stage with a crucial challenge based on an alleged threat to the federal nature of the state, which would require of the judges either considerable political courage or all their skill of creative interpretation.

The Constitutional Court thus necessarily retains a vital 'reserve' or 'potential' role in the federal system. But even apart from this, opportunities remain for the exercise of a formative influence at some points in the complex interplay of Bund and Länder. There is in any case a continuing place for the relatively routine aspects of delimitation of powers and review of legislation. Particularly in a political culture so imbued with legalism as the German, the stabilizing effect on intergovernmental relations of the common subjection to norms susceptible of independent adjudication should not be underestimated. It may not be possible nowadays seriously to entertain the view put forward in the early 1960s that West German federalism is a function of the umpiring role of the Court. But in the future, as in the past, the judgments of the Federal Constitutional Court may be expected to play a significant, indeed essential, part in the arbitration of the federal relationship.

Notes

NOTES TO CHAPTER I

1 *Art.* 20 *Abs.* 1 *GG*: = Article 20, Paragraph 1 of the Basic Law (*Grundgesetz*).
2 The best overall account of the West German federal system is by N. Johnson, 'Federalism and Decentralization in the Federal Republic of Germany': *Commission on the Constitution*, Research Paper I (London, HMSO, 1973).
3 K. C. Wheare, *Federal Government* (London, OUP, 4th edn. 1963), p. 26.
4 K. Hesse, *Der unitarische Bundesstaat* (Karlsruhe, Müller, 1962). The paradox is largely resolved by the discussion of concepts in Chapter VII, §3, below.
5 See W. S. Livingston, 'A Note on the Nature of Federalism', *Political Science Quarterly*, lxvii (1952), 81–95.
6 M. J. C. Vile, *The Structure of American Federalism* (London, OUP, 1961), p. 3.
7 Cf. the definition given by W. H. Riker, *Federalism: Origins, Operation, Significance* (Boston, Little Brown, 1964), p. 11.
8 In fact only the Bavarian parliament refused to ratify.
9 They range from North Rhine Westphalia with approximately 17 million inhabitants to Bremen with about 700,000. In surface area the differences are even greater: Bavaria covers 70,547 sq. km, Bremen only 404 sq. km.
10 M. Usteri, *Theorie des Bundesstaates* (Zurich, Polygraphischer Verlag, 1954).
11 W. J. M. Mackenzie and B. Chapman, 'Federalism and Regionalism', *Modern Law Review*, xiv (1951), 182–94 (p. 187).
12 P. H. Merkl, 'Executive-Legislative Federalism in West Germany', *A.P.S.R.* liii (1959), 732–41.
13 G. Sawer, 'Federalism in West Germany', *Public Law* (1961), 26–44.
14 A. V. Dicey, *Introduction to the Study of the Law of the Constitution* (London, Macmillan, 10th edn. 1959), p. 144.

15 Ibid., p. 175.

16 Ibid., p. 179.

17 D. R. Reich, 'Court, Comity and Federalism in West Germany', *Midwest Journal of Political Science*, vii (1963), 197–228, at p. 200.

18 For more extensive general information on the Constitutional Court the best sources in English are E. McWhinney, *Constitutionalism in Germany and the Federal Constitutional Court* (Leyden, Sythoff, 1962) and, more recently, D. P. Kommers, *Judicial Politics in West Germany* (Beverly Hills/London, Sage, 1976).

19 *Bundesverfassungsgerichtsgesetz* = *BVerfGG*.

20 It follows that the Federal Constitutional Court is not the only court concerned with legal relations between Bund and Länder. Thus its jurisdiction with respect to all obligations arising directly under the Basic Law includes issues pertaining to the constitutional right and duty of the Länder to execute Federal legislation; but questions concerning the correct application of a Federal law by the Länder are the preserve of the Federal Administrative Court (Bundesverwaltungsgericht). (The dividing-line is admittedly not always clear.) Similarly, the Federal Constitutional Court adjudicates in disputes about the conclusion of or compliance with state treaties between Bund and Länder or between two or more Länder; but for administrative agreements between the same parties, which are in practice much more common, it is the Federal Administrative Court that is competent.

21 The procedure is laid down in detail in the Federal Constitutional Court Act: *BVerfGG* §§5 ff.

22 See Ch. II, §3.

23 See esp. the so-called 'Status-Denkschrift' of the Bundesverfassungsgericht of 27 June 1952, *JöR* N.F. vi (1957), 109–221.

NOTES TO CHAPTER II

1 The federal aspects of its work have, however, received less attention than e.g. those concerning basic rights.

2 See the Bibliographical Note, pp. 310 ff.

3 *Entscheidungen des Bundesverfassungsgerichts*, issued by the members of the Court (Tübingen, Mohr, 1952–   ); abbr. = *BVerfGE*. No account could be taken of decisions published after the middle of 1979.

4 This linguistic usage is another indication of the centralized nature of German federalism: whereas in most federations the term 'federalist' normally denotes one who is a supporter of the power of the centre (the opposite being perhaps a 'States'-

righter'), in Germany the term is used on the contrary to mean the opposite of 'unitarist'. The reason is no doubt that a proponent of federalism in Germany sees the most likely threat to his preferred form of government not in its disintegration into a loose confederation or indeed its complete break-up, but in its absorption into a unitary state.

5 *BVerfGE* 8, 274; 28, 66. See Ch. V, §4.

6 See the Index of Cases. The constitutional provisions in question receive mention on numerous other occasions also, but this is always more or less incidental or perfunctory.

7 *BVerfGE* 1, 283; 4, 60; cf. also 45, 297.

8 *Judicial Politics in West Germany*, p. 147.

9 'Fünf gehen, fünf kommen, einer bleibt', *FAZ*, 6 Nov. 1975.

10 H. Laufer, *Verfassungsgerichtsbarkeit und politischer Prozess* (Tübingen, Mohr, 1968), p. 235, suggests that one reason why Gebhard Müller, who in 1951 was Staatspräsident of Württemberg-Hohenzollern and already in the running for the Presidency of the Bundesverfassungsgericht, did not appear on the short list was that at that time representatives of federalist tendencies could not reckon with the votes of the SPD in the Bundestag's Electoral Committee.

11 In 'Richter—besser als ihr Ruf', *Nürnberger Nachrichten*, 14 Oct. 1971.

12 *Süddeutsche Zeitung*, 12 Jan. 1966.

NOTES TO CHAPTER III

1 'Wesen und Entwicklung der Staatsgerichtsbarkeit', *VVDStRL* v (1929), 2–29 (at p. 28).

2 'Das Reichsgericht als Hüter der Verfassung', repr. in *Verfassungsrechtliche Aufsätze* (Berlin, Duncker & Humblot, 1958), pp. 63–100.

3 See O. L. Brintzinger, 'Aufgaben und Grenzen der Verfassungsgerichtsbarkeit', *Neue Politische Literatur*, x (1965), 133–44.

4 Declarations by the Court of the compatibility or incompatibility of a law with the constitution or its invalidation even have statutory force and must be published in the Federal Law Gazette (*Bundesgesetzblatt*): *BVerfGG* §31.

5 See G. Leibholz, 'Der Status des Bundesverfassungsgerichts', *JöR* N.F. vi (1957), 109–221 (at pp. 120 ff.).

6 H. Triepel, *Streitigkeiten zwischen Reich und Ländern* (Tübingen, Mohr, 1923), pp. 15–29.

7 328 US 549 (1946).

8 369 US 186 (1962).

9 *Pacific States Telephone & Telegraph Co.* v. *Oregon*, 223 US 118 (1912).
10 See F. A. von der Heydte (ed.), *Der Kampf um den Wehrbeitrag* (Munich, Isar, 2 vols. 1952–3).
11 *BVerfGE* 2, 1; 5, 85.
12 See below, esp. p. 67.
13 This was the case e.g. with the first application by the SPD on the rearmament issue: *BVerfGE* 1, 396.
14 See Ch. V, §2 for a striking example in the federal sphere which does in fact amount to a refusal to apply detailed stipulations of the constitution.
15 'Significant Developments in German Legal Philosophy since 1945', *A. J. Comp. Law*, iii (1954), 379–96.
16 This problem of the approach to the genesis, ascertainment and development of the law was given thorough treatment, in all its complexity, in 1956 by J. Esser, *Grundsatz und Norm in der richterlichen Fortbildung des Privatrechts* (Tübingen, Mohr, 2nd edn. 1964).
17 *BVerfGE* 1, 299 (p. 312); 8, 274 (p. 307); 10, 20 (p. 51).
18 *BVerfGE* 11, 126 (at p. 130). A classic successive application of all these methods occurs in the *Television Judgment* (*BVerfGE* 12, 205: Part D) in relation to the scope of the Federal legislative competence for 'postal and telecommunication services' under *Art. 73, Nr. 7 GG*.
19 This solution is proposed by H. H. Klein, 'Die Bedeutung des Sachzusammenhangs für die Verfassungsauslegung' (Heidelberg Univ. Jur. Diss. 1960), esp. pp. 40 ff.
20 *BVerfGE* 1, 299 (p. 312).
21 *BVerfGE* 12, 205 (pp. 230 ff.).
22 *BVerfGE* 2, 347 (pp. 374 f.).
23 *BVerfGE* 1, 351.
24 Other examples of departure from the Court's own recognized rules of interpretation are cited by K. Hesse, *Grundzüge des Verfassungsrechts der Bundesrepublik Deutschland* (Karlsruhe, Müller, 11th edn. 1978), pp. 24 f.
25 Thirty-four in the first twenty-seven years of its existence.
26 The 16th Amendment of 1913 conferred on the Congress the power to levy income tax, which had been held to be unconstitutional by the Supreme Court in 1895.
27 See *BVerfGE* 2, 380 (p. 401); 3, 407 (p. 422); 7, 342 (p. 351).
28 Amongst the numerous writings on this subject see especially P. Wittig, 'Politische Rücksichten in der Rechtsprechung des Bundesverfassungsgerichts', *Der Staat*, viii (1969), 137–58, and

the further literature cited there; also H. Laufer, 'Verfassungs-gerichtsbarkeit als politische Kontrolle'.

29 H.-H. Lammers–W. Simons (eds.), *Die Rechtsprechung des Staatsgerichtshofes für das Deutsche Reich* (Berlin, Stilke, 1929–39), i. 352.

30 *BVerfGE* 1, 208 (p. 259).

31 Speech reprinted in *Das Bundesverfassungsgericht*, ed. by the Court (Karlsruhe, Müller, 1963), pp. 1–4.

32 *BVerfGE* 2, 143 (p. 181).

33 *BVerfGE* 4, 157 (pp. 168 ff.).

34 See O. Bachof, 'Der Verfassungsrichter zwischen Recht und Politik', in *Summum ius, summa iniuria* (Tübingen, Mohr, 1963), pp. 41–57.

35 *BVerfGE* 8, 274. See also pp. 147 ff. for those aspects of the case concerning the requirement of the Bundesrat's consent.

36 See W. Weber, 'Zur Gültigkeit des Preisgesetzes', *DÖV* x (1957), 33–6.

37 See F. Gräber, 'Zur Frage der Zustimmungsgesetze', *DÖV* xii (1959), 893–6; H. Ridder, 'Preisrecht ohne Boden', *AöR* lxxxvii (1962), 311–35.

38 O. Bachof, op. cit.

39 *Bundesanzeiger*, No. 232, p. 1.

40 *BVerfGE* 32, 145.

41 *BVerfGE* 16, 130.

42 *BVerfGE* 21, 12. In fact the decision was quickly followed by the replacement of the offending turnover tax by value added tax.

43 'Man hat nie eine rechtliche Meinung, weil man eine Begründung hat, sondern man hat eine Begründung, weil man eine rechtliche Meinung hat.'

44 O. Bachof, 'Der Verfassungsrichter zwischen Recht und Politik', *Summum ius, summa iniuria*, p. 46.

45 See E. McWhinney, *Constitutionalism in Germany*, for an account of the development of the Court's jurisprudence during its first decade.

46 D. P. Kommers, 'The Federal Constitutional Court in the West German Political System', in J. B. Grossman and J. Tanenhaus (eds.), *Frontiers of Judicial Research* (New York, Wiley, 1969), pp. 73–132 (at p. 113).

47 H. G. Rupp, 'The Federal Constitutional Court and the Constitution of the Federal Republic of Germany', *Saint Louis University Law Journal*, xvi (1972), 365.

48 See the references in H. Laufer, 'Verfassungsgerichtsbarkeit als politische Kontrolle', in *Probleme der Demokratie heute = Politische*

Vierteljahresschrift, Sonderheft 2 (Opladen, Westdeutscher Verlag, 1971), pp. 226–40, at pp. 232–3, with footnotes.

49 See *BVerfGE* 2, 266 (p. 282); 8, 71 (p. 77); 12, 46 (pp. 49 f.); 19, 1 (p. 5); 22, 180 (pp. 217 f.); 33, 52 (p. 65); 39, 96 (pp. 106 ff.) etc.

50 *BVerfGE* 36, 1. See below, p. 67.

NOTES TO CHAPTER IV

1 See *FAZ*, 21 Jan. 1975.

2 *BVerfGE* 1, 14; 5, 34; 13, 54; 49, 10 and 49, 15 related to these issues.

3 But not always: cf. some of the Constitutional Court's applications of the principle of 'federal comity' in Ch. VII, §3.

4 See Ch. V, §4.

5 See below, pp. 61 f. and 176 ff.

6 *BVerfGE* 6, 309; 8, 104 and 122; 3, 52; 4, 115; 32, 199; 34, 9.

7 Cf. *BVerfGE* 42, 103 as an isolated example.

8 The only clear examples among the thirty-four cases discussed in this chapter are the *Boiler Case* (*BVerfGE* 11, 6) and the *Bank Lending Case* (*BVerfGE* 14, 197). The *Hessian Water Law Case*, the *Television Case*, and the *Youth Welfare Case* also concern administrative powers in one way or another (*BVerfGE* 21, 312; 12, 205; 22, 180).

It is worth adding in this context that the ability of the Bund to include or provide for administrative regulations in Federal legislation (mainly via *Art.* 84 *GG*) and to exert paraconstitutional influence on Länder administration has even led some commentators to declare the power of Federal supervision of Länder administration enshrined in *Art.* 84 and 85 *GG* to be virtually redundant: cf. R. Herzog, 'Zwischenbilanz im Streit um die bundesstaatliche Ordnung', *Juristische Schulung*, vii (1967), 193–200.

9 For a detailed treatment of this complex field see R. Kunze, *Kooperativer Föderalismus in der Bundesrepublik* (Stuttgart, Fischer, 1968).

10 'Streitigkeiten zwischen Bund und Ländern sind heute bekanntlich in aller Regel nicht mehr echte föderalistische Streitigkeiten, sondern Streitigkeiten zwischen politischen Richtungen innerhalb des Gesamtstaates, die im Gewande der föderalistischen Streitigkeiten verfassungsgerichtlich ausgetragen werden.' *Der unitarische Bundesstaat*, p. 9.

11 *Art.* 93 *Abs.* 1 *Nr.* 3 *GG*; §13 *Nr.* 7 *BVerfGG*.

12 *Art.* 93 *Abs.* 1 *Nr.* 2 *GG*; §13 *Nr.* 6 *BVerfGG*.

13 A 'federal' dispute may also occasionally be initiated (a) as an

Organklage between the Bundesrat and another Federal organ (*Art.* 93 *Abs.* 1 *Nr.* 1 *GG*; §13 *Nr.* 5 *BVerfGG*)—cf. *BVerfGE* 24, 148; (b) as an 'other public-law dispute between the Federation and the Länder . . .' (*Art.* 93 *Abs.* 1 *Nr.* 4 *GG*; §13 *Nr.* 8 *BVerfGG*)—cf. the *Housing Funds Case, BVerfGE* 1, 299; or (c) as a dispute about the continuation of law in force as Federal law (§13 *Nr.* 14 *BVerfGG*)—cf. the *Small-Arms Case, BVerfGE* 8, 143. But the constitutional dispute and abstract judicial review account for the overwhelming majority of applications.

14 Apart from three suits which either were withdrawn or became devoid of application.

15 Most of the cases surveyed in this chapter are also discussed in the chapters devoted to the decision-making of the Court (Chs. V–VII). The relevant passages are cited in the Index of Cases.

16 *BVerfGE* 1, 14.

17 *BVerfGE* 3, 52.

18 *BVerfGE* 4, 115.

19 *BVerfGE* 11, 6.

20 Source: E. W. Sante (ed.), *Geschichte der Deutschen Länder: 'Territorien Ploetz'* (Würzburg, Ploetz, 1971), ii. 695.

21 *BVerfGE* 13, 54. The Constitutional Court ruled that neither Hesse nor the *Heimatbünde* had any standing in the case.

22 *BVerfGE* 21, 312.

23 *BVerfGE* 1, 117.

24 *BVerfGE* 5, 25.

25 *BVerfGE* 7, 305.

26 *BVerfGE* 8, 174.

27 *BVerfGE* 9, 305.

28 *BVerfGE* 10, 20.

29 *BVerfGE* 10, 285.

30 See pp. 160 f. below.

31 *BVerfGE* 14, 197.

32 *BVerfGE* 15, 1.

33 *BVerfGE* 26, 338.

34 *BVerfGE* 31, 314.

35 See below, pp. 61 f.

36 *BVerfGE* 32, 199.

37 *BVerfGE* 34, 9.

38 *BVerfGE* 39, 96; the judgment went in Bavaria's favour.

39 *BVerfGE* 41, 291.

40 *BVerfGE* 6, 309.

41 On this general issue see especially Wheare, *Federal Government*, Ch. IX.

42 Notably by challenging the Petersberg Agreement concluded by Adenauer with the representatives of the Western occupying powers (*BVerfGE* 1, 351) and in several attempts to secure a ruling against the constitutionality of the abortive European Defence Community Treaty. See also p. 33 above and pp. 65–6 (esp. n. 51).

43 *BVerfGE* 8, 104; 8, 122.

44 *BVerfGE* 12, 205.

45 'Der Fernsehstreit I und II', in *Zur politischen Praxis in der Bundesrepublik* (Munich, Piper, 2nd edn. 1967), i. 213–21.

46 *BVerfGE* 22, 180.

47 *BVerfGE* 37, 363.

48 Quoted in the *Süddeutsche Zeitung*, 16 Aug. 1974.

49 *BVerfGE* 48, 127.

50 See pp. 108 ff. below.

51 Nor is this because such litigation has normally been undertaken by one-third of the members of the Bundestag. Of these too there is only a handful: *BVerfGE* 1, 396; 4, 157; 20, 150; 25, 308; 39, 1 (in common with several Länder Governments: see below); also the application concerning the *Deutschlandvertrag* and the European Defence Community Treaty of 1952 (1 *BvF* 4/53), which did not reach decision, and the challenging of the 1973 Bremen Law on the Training of Lawyers (2 *BvF* 1/74, later changed to 2 *BvF* 2/78). For an accurate picture it would be necessary to add several suits brought in the form of *Organstreitigkeiten* by the parliamentary parties, especially that of the SPD, in the early 1950s.

52 *BVerfGE* 8, 51; 20, 56. The history of these cases is recounted in detail by Laufer, *Verfassungsgerichtsbarkeit und politischer Prozess*, pp. 504 ff.

53 The SPD-led coalitions in Hamburg and North Rhine Westphalia also declared their support for Hesse's case.

54 In reality the SPD was not united on the issue. Its Federal leadership was not ill disposed towards subsidization and in fact went along with it soon afterwards.

55 *BVerfGE* 30, 1.

56 *BVerfGE* 35, 171; 35, 246.

57 *BVerfGE* 35, 193; 35, 257.

58 *BVerfGE* 36, 1. See also p. 42 above.

59 The highly controversial decision of the Constitutional Court declared the legalization of abortion on demand during the first twelve weeks of pregnancy to be invalid: *BVerfGE* 39, 1.

60 *BVerfGE* 43, 291.

NOTES TO CHAPTER V

1 *Art.* 93 *Abs.* 1 *Nr.* 4a *GG;* §13 *Nr.* 8a *BVerfGG.*
2 *Art.* 100 *Abs.* 1 *GG;* §13 *Nr.* 11 *BVerfGG.*
3 In fact the German term *konkurrierend* means 'competing' rather than 'concurrent'. On this question of concurrence and its relation to that of 'paramountcy' (*Art.* 31 *GG*: 'Federal law shall override Land law') see the comparative remarks by G. Sawer, *Modern Federalism* (London, Watts, 1969), pp. 168 f.
4 Cf. its upholding of Bavarian provisions concerning wages for work on public holidays (*BVerfGE* 2, 232) and of several Länder laws on employees' annual holidays (*BVerfGE* 7, 342). Each of these constituent parts of the concurrent field of labour law (*Art.* 74 *Nr.* 12 *GG*) was found to have undergone only partial Federal regulation.
5 *BVerfGE* 7, 244.
6 *Schankerlaubnissteuer: BVerfGE* 13, 181.
7 *BVerfGE* 20, 238; 21, 106. Cf. also the disallowance of building law provisions of Baden-Württemberg and North Rhine Westphalia: *BVerfGE* 29, 11; 31, 141.
8 *BVerfGE* 36, 193; 36, 314: see below, p. 132.
9 *BVerfGE* 34, 9: see also pp. 196 ff. below. A criticism of this judgment is provided by P. König, 'Beginn der Sperrwirkung für die Länder bei konkurrierender Gesetzgebung', *NJW* xxvi (1973), 1825–9.
10 *Erstes Gesetz zur Vereinheitlichung und Neuregelung des Besoldungsrechts in Bund und Ländern* (*BGBl.* i. 208).
11 *BVerfGE* 32, 319.
12 Cf. also the *Bavarian Administrative Appeals Case* of 1973: *BVerfGE* 35, 65.
13 See e.g.—as early as 1962—K. Hesse, *Der unitarische Bundesstaat*, p. 15.
14 But by no means universally: cf. the references in M. Gruson, *Die Bedürfniskompetenz* (Berlin, Duncker & Humblot, 1967), p. 92 n. 401.
15 *BVerfGE* 1, 14 (pp. 35 f.).
16 The *Chimney-Sweeps Case: BVerfGE* 1, 264 (pp. 272 f.); the *First Shop-Closing Case: BVerfGE* 1, 283.
17 *Gesetz über die Gewährung von Straffreiheit: BVerfGE* 2, 213 (pp. 224 f.).
18 *BVerfGE* 4, 115 (p. 127).
19 The *Platow Amnesty Case: BVerfGE* 10, 234 (pp. 245 f.).
20 *Ladenschlussgesetz: BVerfGE* 13, 230; 13, 237.

21 See U. Scheuner, 'Struktur und Aufgabe des Bundesstaates in der Gegenwart', *DÖV* xv (1962), 641–8; id., 'Wandlungen im Föderalismus der Bundesrepublik', *DÖV* xix (1966), 513–20 (at p. 517). This conception, or rather misconception, of a clause which was devised as a constraint upon Federal legislative activity might qualify as an interesting instance of mutation of a constitutional norm: see p. 35 above.

22 *BVerfGE* 3, 407 (p. 421); see Ch. VI below.

23 *BVerfGE* 15, 1 (pp. 17 f.); see Ch. VI below.

24 Cf. the Court's repetition of the principle of self-restraint in relation to the question of a need for Federal legislation in the judgment on the Federal Railway Crossings Act: *BVerfGE* 26, 338 (pp. 382 f.).

25 *BVerfGE* 34, 9 (p. 21).

26 pp. 38 f.

27 Quoted by Gruson, *Die Bedürfniskompetenz*, p. 91.

28 See Ch. VII below.

29 *Schlussbericht der Enquête-Kommission Verfassungsreform*, BT Drucksache 7/5924.

30 Ibid., p. 123.

31 Ibid., pp. 131 f.

32 *BVerfGE* 4, 115.

33 See Ch. VII, §3 below.

34 *BVerfGE* 7, 29; 8, 186 (pp. 192 ff.).

35 *BVerfGE* 18, 159.

36 *BVerfGE* 30, 90.

37 *BVerfGE* 25, 142.

38 *BVerfGE* 38, 1.

39 See Ch. VI, §5.

40 Cf. also e.g. *BVerfGE* 51, 43.

41 *BGBl* i. 1110.

42 *BGBl* i. 1025.

43 On this subject in general see E. Friesenhahn, 'Die Rechtsentwicklung hinsichtlich der Zustimmungsbedürftigkeit von Gesetzen und Verordnungen des Bundes', in *Der Bundesrat als Verfassungsorgan und politische Kraft*—Beiträge zum 25jährigen Bestehen des Bundesrates der Bundesrepublik Deutschland, ed. by the Bundesrat (Bad Honnef/Darmstadt, Neue Darmstädter Verlagsanstalt, 1974), pp. 251–76.

44 *BVerfGE* 1, 76.

45 *BVerfGE* 8, 274 (pp. 294 f.). See also pp. 37 f. above.

46 Cf. the similar argument at *BVerfGE* 24, 194 (p. 200). Whether it would really be so impracticable to single out those clauses

requiring consent may be doubted. After all, the Constitutional Court itself did not balk at the task of determining which individual sections of laws were to be declared invalid. See also the discussion of *BVerfGE* 37, 363 below.

47 Whereas at the outset approximately 10 per cent of bills were treated as requiring consent, by 1971 the proportion had risen to 55–60 per cent according to H. Laufer, *Der Bundesrat: Untersuchungen über Zusammensetzung, Arbeitsweise, politische Rolle und Reformprobleme*, Schriftenreihe der Bundeszentrale für politische Bildung, Bonn, 1972. M. Schweitzer, 'Die Zustimmung des Bundesrats zu Gesetzen', *Der Staat*, xv (1976), 169–84, puts the figure at exactly 55 per cent to the end of 1973.

48 *BVerfGE* 10, 20.

49 *Gesetz über das Kreditwesen*: *BVerfGE* 14, 197. See also, in relation to federal comity, pp. 185 ff. below.

50 *BVerfGE* 24, 184.

51 *BVerfGE* 28, 66.

52 *BVerfGE* 26, 338 (p. 399).

53 *BVerfGE* 24, 184 (p. 201).

54 This is not to suggest that there had never before been voting along party lines. The SPD did so sometimes in the early 1950s, as on the EDC Treaty. But it could never muster a purely party-political majority. On the Bundesrat as an instrument of Opposition see H. Laufer, 'Der Bundesrat als Instrument der Opposition?', *ZParl* i. (1969/70), 318–41; id., *Der Bundesrat*, Schriftenreihe der Bundeszentrale für politische Bildung, Bonn, 1972; also the discussion between politicians and professors of law on the political character and role of the Bundesrat in *ZParl* vii (1976), 291–316.

55 *BVerfGE* 37, 363.

56 The Court here cites Friesenhahn, 'Zustimmungsbedürftigkeit von Gesetzen und Verordnungen', in *Der Bundesrat als Verfassungsorgan und politische Kraft*, pp. 251–76.

57 See Ch. VII, §2 below.

58 *BVerfGE* 8, 274 (pp. 294 f.).

59 *BVerfGE* 24, 184 (p. 197).

60 *BVerfGE* 28, 66 (p. 77).

61 In practice it may not always be easy to disentangle procedural provisions from the rest, as indeed the Court's own discussion of the Pensions Insurance Amendment Act suggests.

62 At p. 383.

63 Admittedly the result of the Bundesrat's veto power, only partially constricted by this judgment, has been not so much a

political impasse as extensive co-determination by the Opposition based on its positions of power in the Länder: see below, p. 111.

64 *BVerfGE* 39, 1; see also p. 68.

65 *BVerfGE* 48, 127.

66 Cf. p. 64 above.

67 See the statistics in *Der Bundesrat als Verfassungsorgan und politische Kraft*, pp. 479–83.

68 According to Gerhard Jahn, the Parliamentary Manager of the SPD, the frequency of reference to the Mediation Committee had risen to every sixth bill by the Seventh Bundestag: see his contribution, 'Tendenzen zum "Parteienbundesstaat" seit 1969', to the debate in *ZParl* vii (1976), at p. 293.

69 Part of the reason for this must lie in the comparative rarity of recourse to the Constitutional Court in the administrative field by the interested parties: see above, pp. 46 f.

70 *BVerfGE* 32, 145: see above, pp. 38 f.

71 *BVerfGE* 11, 105 (pp. 124 f.).

72 See below, p. 233.

73 For such an overall view of the Court's work in relation to administrative powers see H. H. Klein, 'Verwaltungskompetenzen von Bund und Ländern in der Rechtsprechung des Bundesverfassungsgerichts', in *Bundesverfassungsgericht und Grundgesetz*, ed. by C. Starck (Tübingen, Mohr, 1976), ii. 277–99.

NOTES TO CHAPTER VI

1 Art.I, Section 8, Clause 18. See e.g. B. Schwartz, *A Commentary on the Constitution of the United States*: Part I, The Powers of Government (New York/London, Macmillan, 1963), pp. 91–6.

2 Section 51.

3 Various instances are quoted by G. Sawer (ed.), *Cases on the Constitution of the Commonwealth of Australia* (Sydney, Law Book Co. of Australasia, 1948), esp. Ch. VI. On broad construction of Federal powers in general a useful account is provided by G. Sawer, 'The Record of Judicial Review', in Sawer (ed.), *Federalism: an Australian Jubilee Study* (Melbourne, Cheshire, 1952), pp. 211–54.

4 In Canada, decisions have often revolved around the general Dominion power 'to make laws for the peace, order and good government of Canada' (Section 91, opening paragraph). See e.g. M. Fletcher, 'Judicial Review and the Division of Powers in Canada', in J. P. Meekison (ed.), *Canadian Federalism: Myth or Reality* (Toronto, Methuen, 1968), pp. 140–58.

5 *The Federalist*, No. 44.
6 4 Wheat 316 (1819).
7 *Art.* 73 *GG.*
8 *Art.* 74 *GG.*
9 *BVerfGE* 11, 6.
10 *BVerfGE* 12, 205 (pp. 228 f., 244 ff.).
11 *Gesetz zur Reinhaltung der Bundeswasserstrassen: BVerfGE* 15, 1 (p. 17).
12 *BVerfGE* 16, 64.
13 Cited at p. 77 of the judgment.
14 See §4 below. There were no doubt political limits to the extent that the Federal Government, or indeed other Länder, could in practice tolerate far-reaching new taxation measures by an individual Land: *Art.* 105 and 106 *GG* were amended accordingly in 1969.
15 *BVerfGE* 22, 180 (pp. 216 f.).
16 See §5 below.
17 *BVerfGE* 26, 246.
18 On the other hand the decision positively encourages the Bund to regulate the whole professional activity of the engineer, as the only way of putting through its provisions concerning the title *Ingenieur* constitutionally.
19 *BVerfGE* 26, 281.
20 For a more recent example, see *BVerfGE* 42, 20. Appeal is there made to the presumption in favour of the Länder in order to justify the decision that the regulation of property relations on the public roads of the Länder, and of liability in case of damage to such public property, falls under the Länder's powers for public highways and not under the property or other concepts of the civil code, assigned to the Federation by *Art.* 74 *Nr.* 1 *GG.*
21 T. Maunz, G. Dürig, and R. Herzog, *Grundgesetz: Kommentar* (Munich/Berlin, Beck, 4th edn. 1976), *Rdnr.* 13 at *Art.* 30.
22 T. Maunz, *Deutsches Staatsrecht* (Munich, Beck, 22nd edn. 1978), p. 241; Maunz–Dürig, *Grundgesetz, Rdnr.* 30 at *Art.* 70.
23 Cf. M. Bullinger, *Die Mineralölfernleitungen* (Stuttgart, Kohlhammer, 1962), pp. 55 f.; H. -J. Rinck, 'Zur Abgrenzung und Auslegung der Gesetzgebungskompetenzen von Bund und Ländern', in *Festschrift für Gebhard Müller*, ed. by T. Ritterspach and W. Geiger (Tübingen, Mohr, 1970), pp. 289–300.
24 *BVerfGE* 15, 126 (p. 139). It is perhaps significant that this pronouncement came from the First Senate.
25 *Art.* 74 *Nr.* 11 *GG.*
26 *BVerfGE* 4, 7.

27 *Apothekenstoppgesetze: BVerfGE* 5, 25.

28 *BVerfGE* 1, 264 (pp. 271 f.).

29 *BVerfGE* 8, 143, analysed below in relation to *Sachzusammenhang.*

30 *BVerfGE* 41, 344.

31 *Art. 74 Nr.* 1 *GG.*

32 Both types of implied or inherent power are discussed by Kisker, *Kooperation im Bundesstaat* (Tübingen, Mohr, 1971), pp. 20–34, in the context of a search for Federal means of co-ordinating Länder spheres of activity. See also H. H. Klein, 'Die Bedeutung des Sachzusammenhangs für die Verfassungsauslegung' (Heidelberg Univ. Jur. Diss. 1960).

33 On this see esp. N. Achterberg, 'Die Annex-Kompetenz', *DÖV* xix (1966), 695–701.

34 *Grundgesetz: Kommentar, Rdnr.* 32 at *Art.* 70.

35 Ibid., *Rdnr.* 31 at *Art.* 70, with footnote 4.

36 e.g. H. v. Mangoldt/F. Klein, *Das Bonner Grundgesetz* (Berlin/ Frankfurt, Vahlen, 2nd edn. 1957–74), Vol. ii, *Anm.* III 4 c on *Art.* 70. Cf. M. Bullinger, 'Ungeschriebene Kompetenzen im Bundesstaat', *AöR* xcvi (1971), 237–85 (at pp. 243 f.).

37 *BVerfGE* 3, 407.

38 'Ein sogenannter Sachzusammenhang vermöchte vielmehr eine Zuständigkeit nur dann zu stützen, wenn eine dem Bund ausdrücklich zugewiesene Materie verständigerweise nicht geregelt werden kann, ohne dass zugleich eine nicht ausdrücklich zugewiesene andere Materie mitgeregelt wird, wenn also ein Übergreifen in nicht ausdrücklich zugewiesene Materien unerlässliche Voraussetzung ist für die Regelung einer der Bundesgesetzgebung zugewiesenen Materie' (p. 421).

39 *BVerfGE* 12, 205 (p. 237).

40 *Art. 73 Nr. 7 GG.*

41 Op. cit., *AöR* 96 (1971), 246.

42 See e.g. the *'Ingenieur' Judgment: BVerfGE* 26, 246 (pp. 256 f.). The *Midwife Law Judgment (BVerfGE* 17, 287) might also be considered in this connection.

43 *BVerfGE* 26, 281 (p. 300).

44 Cf. H. Triepel, 'Die Kompetenzen des Bundesstaates und die geschriebene Verfassung', in *Staatsrechtliche Abhandlungen, Festgabe für Paul Laband* (Tübingen, Mohr, 1908), ii. 247–335 (pp. 285 ff.).

45 *BVerfGE* 3, 407 (pp. 430 ff.).

46 *BVerfGE* 8, 143.

47 *BVerfGE* 9, 185.

48 *BVerfGE* 7, 29; see also p. 89 above.

49 *BVerfGE* 36, 193. An exactly equivalent judgment in relation to the Hamburg Press Act appears at *BVerfGE* 36, 314.
50 *Strafprozessordnung*: §53 *Abs.* 1 *Nr.* 5.
51 Cf. *Art.* 70 *Abs.* 2 *GG.*
52 *BVerfGE* 7, 29 (p. 40).
53 *BVerfGE* 48, 367.
54 *BVerfGE* 16, 64; see pp. 118 f. above.
55 *BVerfGE* 4, 74.
56 *BVerfGE* 15, 1 (pp. 20 ff.).
57 *BVerfGE* 22, 180 (pp. 212 f.); see also pp. 119 f. above.
58 *BVerfGE* 23, 113.
59 *BVerfGE* 26, 246 (pp. 257 f.); see p. 120 above.
60 See the references in Bullinger, *Die Mineralölfernleitungen*, pp. 71 ff.
61 *BVerfGE* 11, 89 (pp. 96 f.).
62 G. Anschütz and R. Thoma (eds.), *Handbuch des deutschen Staatsrechts* (Tübingen, Mohr, 1930–2), i. 367.
63 *BVerfGE* 3, 407 (p. 422).
64 *BVerfGE* 12, 205 (pp. 242, 250 ff.).
65 *BVerfGE* 15, 1 (p. 24).
66 *BVerfGE* 24, 246 (p. 257). A more recent instance of refusal to consider an intrinsically implicit power based on the sheer supraregional nature of the task is found in the judgment on the exceptional Federal aid programme, which is discussed in the context of grants-in-aid at pp. 234 ff.
67 *BVerfGE* 3, 407 (pp. 427 f.).
68 *BVerfGE* 22, 180 (pp. 216 ff.).
69 *BVerfGE* 11, 6 (pp. 17 f.); see above, pp. 116 f. (The term *Natur der Sache* is not in fact used in this judgment.) On the question of implied powers in the administrative sphere see J. Kölble, 'Zur Lehre von den—stillschweigend—zugelassenen Verwaltungszuständigkeiten des Bundes', *DÖV* xvi (1963), 660–73.
70 It occurs in a judgment which already contains a generous application of the doctrine of *Sachzusammenhang*: see pp. 135 f. above.
71 *BVerfGE* 15, 1 (p. 22).
72 *BVerfGE* 33, 303 (pp. 356 ff.).
73 On this see esp. R. Scholz, 'Ausschliessliche und konkurrierende Gesetzgebungskompetenz von Bund und Ländern in der Rechtsprechung des Bundesverfassungsgerichts', in *Bundesverfassungsgericht und Grundgesetz*, ed. by C. Starck (Tübingen, Mohr, 1976), ii 252–76 (at pp. 265 f.).
74 See p. 125 above. Among other recent examples of this appar-

ently growing tendency on the Court's part cf. *BVerfGE* 33, 52; 41, 205; 42, 20.

NOTES TO CHAPTER VII

1 Emphasis added.
2 A useful history of the theory of federalism in Germany is provided by E. Deuerlein, *Föderalismus: Die historischen und philosophischen Grundlagen des föderativen Prinzips* (Munich, List, 1972).
3 See p. 1 above.
4 H. Triepel, *Unitarismus und Föderalismus im Deutschen Reiche* (Tübingen, Mohr, 1907), pp. 9 ff.
5 Ibid., p. 21. It is in this sense that the title of Hesse's book, *Der unitarische Bundesstaat*, avoids being a contradiction in terms.
6 Even if the epithets *Föderalist* and *Unitarier* are freely attached to individual judges in private and by the press; see Ch. II, §3.
7 'Der Bundesstaatsbegriff', *Zeitschrift für die gesamte Staatswissenschaft*, xxviii (1872), 185–256.
8 Cf. A. Haenel, *Studien zum Deutschen Staatsrechte* (Leipzig, Haessel, 1873), i. 240 ff.
9 *Das Staatsrecht des Deutschen Reiches* (Tübingen, Mohr, 5th edn. 1911), i. 102–7.
10 O. Mayer, 'Republikanischer und monarchischer Bundesstaat', *AöR*, xviii (1903), 337–73.
11 H. Nawiasky, *Der Bundesstaat als Rechtsbegriff* (Tübingen, Mohr, 1920).
12 U. Scheuner, 'Struktur und Aufgabe des Bundesstaates in der Gegenwart', *DÖV* xv (1962), 641–8; id., 'Wandlungen im Föderalismus der Bundesrepublik', *DÖV* xix (1966), 513–20 (p. 514).
13 The collapse of the totalitarian regime in 1945 called forth a spate of political pleas on behalf of federalism which drew their inspiration from various sources, notably the subsidiarity principle of Catholic social doctrine: see the bibliography compiled by E. Deuerlein, *Föderalismus*. But the influence of this source of federalist sentiment was short-lived. Moreover, there has been widespread agreement amongst jurists that the primarily social orientation of the doctrine of subsidiarity disqualifies it as a foundation for the constitutional concept of federalism.
14 See e.g. the formulations in Maunz, *Deutsches Staatsrecht*, 22nd edn., pp. 216 ff.; also the discussion of the so-called 'three-tiered *Bundesstaat*', below.
15 This is explicitly contested by Maunz, op. cit., pp. 223–6, who attempts to sketch such a theory.

16 References at note 12 above. For the latter characteristics Scheuner cites E. McWhinney, *Federal Constitution-Making for a Multinational World* (Leyden, Sythoff, 1966).

17 'Föderalismus als nationales und internationales Ordnungsprinzip', *VVDStRL* xxi (1964).

18 'Eine weitere Grundlage der Verfassung ist das *bundesstaatliche* Prinzip (*Art.* 20, 28, 30 *GG*). Die Länder sind als Glieder des Bundes Staaten mit eigener—wenn auch gegenständlich beschränkter—nicht vom Bund abgeleiteter, sondern von ihm anerkannter staatlicher Hoheitsmacht': *BVerfGE* 1, 14 (p. 34).

19 *The Finance-Equalization Case: BVerfGE* 1, 117.

20 Since 1969, 25 per cent of the Länder's share of VAT may be so used.

21 The current amended provisions on horizontal financial equalization are to be found in *Art.* 107 *Abs.* 2 *GG*.

22 *BVerfGE* 1, 299.

23 Ibid., pp. 310 f.

24 Ibid., pp. 314 f.

25 See below, pp. 164 f.

26 Cf. also the language employed in the *North Rhine Westphalian Salaries Case*, discussed below in relation to federal comity (pp. 166 ff.).

27 Published under the title 'Die wechselseitige Treuepflicht von Bund und Ländern' in A. Süsterhenn (ed.), *Föderalistische Ordnung* (Koblenz, Rhenania, 1961), pp. 113–28.

28 H. Kelsen, *Allgemeine Staatslehre* (Berlin, Gehlen, 1925), pp. 199 f.

29 H. Nawiasky, *Allgemeine Staatslehre*, Part III (Einsiedeln/ Cologne, Benzinger, 1956), pp. 159 ff.

30 *Deutsches Staatsrecht*, 10th edn. 1961, pp. 159 f. However, in the 11th edition the following year (at p. 164) Maunz starts to disengage himself from this position, with reference to the *Territorial Reorganization Judgment* of the Constitutional Court. That judgment's rejection of the three-tier theory is explicitly endorsed in later editions.

31 *BVerfGE* 1, 14 (p. 51).

32 *BVerfGE* 6, 309, at pp. 340, 361 ff.; see also below, pp. 168 ff. Cf. *BVerfGE* 12, 205 (p. 255).

33 *BVerfGE* 13, 54; see also in relation to federal comity, pp. 183 ff.

34 See p. 44 above.

35 'Die wechselseitige Treuepflicht', p. 116.

36 See e.g. J. H. Kaiser, 'Die Erfüllung der völkerrechtlichen Verträge des Bundes durch die Länder', *Zeitschrift für ausländisches öffentliches Recht und Völkerrecht*, xviii (1957/8), 526–58 (esp.

pp. 531 ff.). On the other hand the Court's virtual recantation was later deplored in emphatic terms by H. H. Rupp, 'Einige wichtige Entscheidungen in der Rechtsprechung des Zweiten Senats des Bundesverfassungsgerichts', in *Das Bundesverfassungsgericht 1951–1971*, ed. by the Court (Karlsruhe, Müller, 1971), pp. 121–58 (at pp. 129 f.).

37 See e.g. the 'federalist' interpretation of *Art. 80 Abs. 1 GG* in the *Milk Products Case: BVerfGE* 11, 77 (pp. 85 ff.). Cf. also *BVerfGE* 18, 407 (pp. 417 ff.).

38 *BVerfGE* 10, 285 (p. 296).

39 *BVerfGE* 6, 309; see esp. pp. 168 ff. below.

40 See e.g. pp. 100 and 117 above.

41 However, the *Financial Subsidies Case* of 1975 (*BVerfGE* 39, 96), which was concerned with the thorny problem of grants-in-aid, seems to indicate a newly activist approach to the invocation of the federal principle, and it finds an echo in the 1976 judgment on the special Federal aid programme (*BVerfGE* 41, 291): see below, pp. 231 ff.

42 It is proposed to use the term 'federal comity' as a translation of both *Bundestreue* ('federal fidelity') and *bundesfreundliches Verhalten* ('federal-friendly behaviour'), a distinction no longer being made between the two terms. Other terms with similar meaning have also appeared occasionally.

43 'Das Reich hat die feste Basis in der Bundestreue der Fürsten.' Both quotations are found in O. Mayer, op. cit., *AöR* xviii (1903), at pp. 365 and 370.

44 *Unitarismus und Föderalismus*, esp. p. 29.

45 'Ungeschriebenes Verfassungsrecht im monarchischen Bundesstaat', in *Festgabe für Otto Mayer zum 70. Geburtstag* (Tübingen, Mohr, 1916), pp. 245–70.

46 H. -W. Bayer, *Die Bundestreue*, pp. 63 f.

47 *BVerfGE* 1, 299; see above, pp. 154 ff.

48 The word used is *Bündnis* ('alliance'), and the phrase could also mean 'all the parties to the constitutional compact'.

49 Here the debt to Smend is explicitly acknowledged (p. 315).

50 Cf. the *Television Case* below.

51 *BVerfGE* 3, 52.

52 *BVerfGE* 1, 117.

53 One could conceivably have been provoked by the tendency of Länder expenditure to frustrate Federal countercyclical economic policy prior to the recession of 1966–7. See below, p. 239.

54 *BVerfGE* 4, 115.

55 See pp. 86 ff. above.

56 Cf. the *Atomic Weapons Referendum Case* discussed below.

57 *BVerfGE* 6, 309. See also p. 161 above.

58 *Constitutionalism in Germany*, pp. 46 ff.

59 *Attorney-General for Canada* v. *Attorney-General for Ontario*, [1937] A. C. 326. For details of the situation in the English-speaking federations see Wheare, *Federal Government*, Ch. IX.

60 At p. 362.

61 'Es muss dem Einvernehmen von Bund und Ländern auf dem Boden der Gleichordnung überlassen bleiben, im Falle einer Spannungslage zwischen Bundes- und Landesinteressen einen tragbaren Ausgleich zu schaffen.'

62 See Geiger, 'Die wechselseitige Treuepflicht', p. 114.

63 The *Concordat Judgment* was in fact the object of academic criticism, notably by J. H. Kaiser, op. cit., *Z. ausl. öff. R. u. VR.* xviii (1957/8), 526–58. Kaiser asserts a right of the Federal authorities to intervene in the exclusive field of the Länder for the implementation of treaties in so far as the Länder cannot or will not carry them into effect. In place of the inflexible tying of the treaty power to the relevant legislative competence, which he argues was demonstrably not the intention of the framers of the Basic Law, he urges that an adequate 'implied limitation' on the Bund's comprehensive foreign affairs power can be derived from the principle of federal comity.

64 *Schlussbericht der Enquête-Kommission Verfassungsreform*, BT Drucksache 7/5924, pp. 232 ff.

65 *BVerfGE* 8, 122.

66 See pp. 60 f.

67 *BVerfGE* 8, 104.

68 'Gegen diesen Grundsatz kann sowohl durch ein Tun als auch durch ein Unterlassen verstossen werden.'

69 'Was nach Landesrecht im Verhältnis zur Gemeinde eine im Ermessen der Landesregierung liegende *Befugnis* ist, kann nach Bundesverfassungsrecht im Verhältnis zum Bund *Pflicht* des Landes werden.'

70 *BVerfGE* 1, 117.

71 *BVerfGE* 1, 299.

72 *Der unitarische Bundesstaat*, p. 7.

73 *BVerfGE* 12, 205.

74 See pp. 117 f. and 139 f. above.

75 At p. 249 of the judgment.

76 'Die bisherige Rechtsprechung lässt erkennen, dass sich aus diesem Grundsatz sowohl konkrete, über die in der bundesstaat-

lichen Verfassung ausdrücklich normierten verfassungsrecht-
lichen Pflichten hinausgehende, zusätzliche Pflichten der
Länder gegenüber dem Bund und zusätzliche Pflichten des
Bundes gegenüber den Ländern entwickeln lassen als auch konkrete Beschränkungen in der Ausübung der dem Bund und den
Ländern im Grundgesetz eingeräumten Kompetenzen ergeben'
(p. 255).

77 'Auch das *procedere* und der Stil der Verhandlungen, die zwischen
dem Bund und seinen Gliedern und zwischen den Ländern im
Verfassungsleben erforderlich werden, stehen unter dem Gebot
bundesfreundlichen Verhaltens.'

78 'Die wechselseitige Treuepflicht', p. 121.

79 See e.g. O. Schulmeister, 'Mehr als "Fernsehurteil" ', *Wort und
Wahrheit*, xvi (1961), 247–50; F. Gehrung, 'Karlsruhe und
danach: Der Bund als Vertriebener', *Politische Welt*, xxxi (1961),
4–5.

80 'Gedanken zum Fernseh-Urteil des Bundesverfassungsgerichts',
AöR lxxxvi (1961), 361–404, at p. 369.

81 Op. cit., p. 121.

82 Cf., in addition to Zeidler, H. Spanner, 'Zur Rechtskontrolle des
bundesfreundlichen Verhaltens', *DÖV* xiv (1961), 481–6; Hesse,
Der unitarische Bundesstaat, pp. 7 f.

83 Op. cit., p. 123.

84 Op. cit., *Midwest Journal of Political Science*, vii (1963), 223.

85 See pp. 157 ff.

86 At p. 75 of the judgment.

87 See p. 44.

88 *BVerfGE* 14, 197; see also pp. 97 f. above.

89 *BVerfGE* 4, 115 (p. 140).

90 *BVerfGE* 21, 312.

91 *BVerfGE* 31, 314.

92 Ibid., pp. 354–7.

93 *BVerfGE* 26, 116 (esp. p. 137).

94 *BVerfGE* 32, 199.

95 *BVerfGE* 1, 299 (p. 315).

96 *BVerfGE* 4, 115 (p. 140); *BVerfGE* 14, 197 (p. 215).

97 Cf. the *North Rhine Westphalian Salaries Case* above, pp. 166 ff.

98 *BVerfGE* 34, 9.

99 See also pp. 75 f.

100 'Der Grundsatz der Bundestreue ist schliesslich keine Schranke,
mit der man Nichtigkeiten inhibieren kann' (p. 45).

101 See above, p. 83.

102 *BVerfGE* 41, 291: see pp. 234 ff. The comity principle also makes

a brief appearance in the *Financial Subsidies Case* (*BVerfGE* 39, 96, at p. 125).

103 *BVerfGE* 43, 291: see also pp. 68 f. above.
104 'Die wechselseitige Treuepflicht', p. 123.
105 See the quotation above, p. 178.
106 E. Bauschke, 'Bundesstaatsprinzip und Bundesverfassungs-gericht' (Berlin Univ. Rechtswiss. Diss. 1970), p. 123, does see the application of *Bundestreue* as being in its effect 'preponder-antly directed against the Bund'. However, this conclusion seems to be based purely on the principal outcome of each case in which the issue of federal comity arose.
107 At pp. 6 ff.
108 Hesse's criticism was anticipated by Spanner, op. cit., *DÖV* xiv (1961), who however did not reject *Bundestreue* as an implied constitutional principle, objecting only to its too extensive appli-cation as leading the Court too far into the realm of politi-cal value judgements. It was echoed e.g. by Scheuner, op. cit., *DÖV* xv (1962), though again in a more qualified form, and by E. W. Fuss, 'Die Bundestreue—ein unentbehrlicher Rechtsbe-griff?', *DÖV* xvii (1964), 37–42. Although still urging great cau-tion in its application, Hesse appears now to accept that the principle of federal comity, as a general requirement of co-operation, mutual consultation and co-ordination between Bund and Länder, is a constitutional norm which is 'immanent' in the Basic Law: cf. *Grundzüge des Verfassungsrechts*, 11th edn., pp. 108 ff.
109 *Die Bundestreue*, p. 125.
110 'Die wechselseitige Treuepflicht', pp. 126–7.

NOTES TO CHAPTER VIII

1 The literature on this issue of *Neugliederung* is substantial: see the sample bibliography in Laufer, *Der Föderalismus der Bundesrepublik Deutschland* (Stuttgart, Kohlhammer, 1974), pp. 161 f. To this should certainly be added two articles by P. Feuchte: 'Neu-gliederung: Versagen von gestern, Chance von morgen', *DÖV* xxi (1968), 456–65; and 'Wege und Umwege zu einer neuen Struktur', in *Festschrift für Gebhard Müller*, pp. 59–76. See also the various contributions to the discussion in *DÖV* xxvii (1974), 1–20.
2 See e.g. Vile, *Structure of American Federalism*, pp. 160 ff., 193 f.
3 Kommission für die Finanzreform, *Gutachten über die Finanzreform in der Bundesrepublik Deutschland*, (Stuttgart, Kohlhammer, 2nd edn. 1966).
4 *Tz.* 73–7.

5 Bauschke tries to expand the comity principle into a general duty of federal co-operation: 'Bundesstaatsprinzip und Bundesverfassungsgericht', pp. 131 ff.
6 See e.g. the excellent discussions by Scheuner, op. cit., *DÖV* xix (1966); id., 'Kooperation und Konflikt', *DÖV* xxv (1972), 585–91; K. Hesse, 'Aspekte des kooperativen Föderalismus in der Bundesrepublik', in *Festschrift für Gebhard Müller*, pp. 141–60. The most thorough treatment is by Kisker, *Kooperation im Bundesstaat*, whose bibliography includes an impressive number of articles which had already sprung up on the subject by 1971.
7 The need to preserve an adequate sphere of independent Länder legislative power is duly emphasized in the final report of the Commission of Inquiry into Constitutional Reform (*Enquête-Kommission Verfassungsreform*): BT Drucksache 7/5924, esp. p. 123.
8 Emphasis added.
9 'Verträge zwischen Gliedstaaten im Bundesstaat', *VVDStRL* xix (1961), 1–85.
10 See e.g. Vile, *Structure of American Federalism*, pp. 166 ff.
11 See C. Heinze, ' "Kooperativer Föderalismus" und die Umbildung der Verfassung', in *Festschrift für Ernst Forsthoff zum 70. Geburtstag*, ed. by R. Schnur (Munich, Beck, 1972), pp. 119–38.
12 See F. Klein, 'Verfassungsrechtliche Grenzen der Gemeinschaftsaufgaben', in *Gemeinschaftsaufgaben zwischen Bund, Ländern und Gemeinden*, Schriftenreihe der Hochschule Speyer Vol. 11 (Berlin, Duncker & Humblot, 1961), pp. 125–74, at pp. 157 ff.
13 See pp. 156 ff. above.
14 As in the case of Kölble, 'Gemeinschaftsaufgaben der Länder und ihre Grenzen', *NJW* xv (1962), 1081–5.
15 *BVerfGE* 12, 205 (pp. 250 ff.).
16 The most thorough criticism of the various forms of inter-Länder co-operation is undertaken by Kisker, *Kooperation im Bundesstaat*, esp. pp. 116–54.
17 See W. Geiger, *Missverständnisse um den Föderalismus* (Berlin, De Gruyter, 1962), pp. 26 f.
18 *BVerwGE* 22, 299 ff.; 23, 194 ff.
19 *BVerfGE* 1, 299 (p. 315); see pp. 154 ff. above.
20 See pp. 164 f. above.
21 *Zwischenbericht der Enquête-Kommission für Fragen der Verfassungsreform*, BT Drucksache 6/3829, pp. 51–4. Although the Commission's final report at the end of 1976 substantially modifies this ambitious approach to joint planning, it actually proposes that Bund–Länder planning should require only the consent of the

Bund and of a majority of the Länder, on the ground that otherwise the Opposition could frustrate any real planning: BT Drucksache 7/5924, pp. 176 f.

22 See esp. pp. 166 ff. above (*North Rhine Westphalian Salaries Case*).

23 They are documented in detail by Renate Kunze, *Kooperativer Föderalismus in der Bundesrepublik.*

24 See esp. R. Grawert, *Verwaltungsabkommen zwischen Bund und Ländern in der Bundesrepublik Deutschland* (Berlin, Duncker & Humblot, 1967).

25 See p. 171. On problems and developments in co-operation in international negotiations see H. von Meibom, 'Die Mitwirkung der Länder im Bereich der auswärtigen Gewalt', *NJW* xxi (1968), 1607–10.

26 See pp. 38 f. above.

27 *NRW GVBl.* 1957, p. 255.

28 Cf. J. Kölble, 'Gemeinschaftsaufgaben zwischen Bund und Ländern sowie zwischen den Ländern', in *Gemeinschaftsaufgaben zwischen Bund, Ländern und Gemeinden*, Schriftenreihe Speyer Vol. 11, pp. 17–62 (at pp. 27 f.).

29 e.g. Kölble, op. cit., p. 33; B. Tiemann, 'Gemeinschaftsaufgaben von Bund und Ländern in verfassungsrechtlicher Sicht' (Munich Univ. Jur. Diss. 1969), pp. 112 f.

30 *GVBl.* 1950, p. 265.

31 See also pp. 152 ff. above. The complex financial arrangements of German federalism are well described by N. Johnson, 'Federalism and Decentralization in the Federal Republic of Germany', Part I, Section VII (= §§73–91).

32 After the fashion of the recognized 'spending power' in the USA.

33 *Finanzbericht*, Federal Ministry of Finance.

34 That such a development was not a novel phenomenon in Germany either is shown, for example, by the complaint of the Bavarian Government in the 'Denkschrift über die fortschreitende Aushöhlung der Eigenstaatlichkeit der Länder unter der Weimarer Verfassung' of 1926 that the Reich was acting on the principle that he who pays calls the tune and by attaching conditions to the funds which it made available for a multiplicity of purposes was gaining a far-reaching influence over a wide range of administrative fields. (*Drucksachen des Reichsrats*, 1926 *Nr.* 98, *Druckschrift*, pp. 4, 12.)

35 See *BVerfGE* 12, 205 (pp. 243 ff.), and in general Ch. VI, esp. §2.

36 Maunz–Dürig–Herzog, *Grundgesetz, Rdnr.* 14 under *Art.* 30 *GG*. On the other hand Tiemann agrees with the view of the Federal Government that these considerations are more political than

legal, since the Länder retain freedom of decision as to whether to accept the subventions. He also points to the difficulty of deciding at what point influence exerted through conditions attached to grants-in-aid becomes such as to impair the financial autonomy of the Länder: 'Gemeinschaftsaufgaben von Bund und Ländern in verfassungsrechtlicher Sicht', pp. 157 f.

37 *BVerfGE* 9, 305.

38 As pointed out by W. Henle, 'Die Förderung von Landesaufgaben aus Bundesmitteln', in *Gemeinschaftsaufgaben zwischen Bund, Ländern und Gemeinden*, Schriftenreihe Speyer Vol. 11, pp. 63–77.

39 See A. Köttgen, *Fondsverwaltung in der Bundesrepublik* (Stuttgart, Kohlhammer, 1965), pp. 42 ff. The question of implied Federal powers is discussed in Ch. VI above.

40 The Federal Government had argued for the inclusion of this provision on the basis of the importance of public investment, the greater part of which took place at the level of the Länder and local authorities, as an instrument for steering the economy and the consequent need to legalize and facilitate the supplementary use of Federal funds for such purposes: *Troeger-Gutachten, Tz.* 119.

41 See J. Seeger, 'Finanzierung von Länderaufgaben durch den Bund', *DÖV* xxi (1968), 781–8; F. Heubl, 'Die gegenwärtige Lage unserer föderativen Struktur', *BayVBl* xiv (1968), 113–17.

42 See Ch. V, §2.

43 For a more legalistic view, whereby the competences and autonomy of the Länder may be politically but not legally impaired by a clause enabling the Federation to make grants to the Länder to assist them in the performance of their tasks on their own responsibility, see Tiemann, 'Gemeinschaftsaufgaben', pp. 285–8.

44 See especially G. Holch, 'Die Finanzhilfen des Bundes nach *Art.* 104a *Abs.* 4 *GG*', *DÖV* xxvi (1973), 115–21.

45 *Gemeindeverkehrsfinanzierungsgesetz: BGBl.* i. 239, revised in 1972, *BGBl.* i. 501.

46 *Städtebauförderungsgesetz: BGBl.* i. 1125.

47 *Krankenhausfinanzierungsgesetz: BGBl.* i. 1009.

48 *BVerfGE* 39, 96.

49 Here it referred to its earlier decision, *BVerfGE* 13, 230, on *Art.* 72 *Abs.* 2 *Nr.* 3 *GG*: see pp. 80 f. above.

50 The resurgence of the general nature of federalism as a source of specific conclusions concerning what is admissible in the West German federal system (see Ch. VII, §2 above) is most striking here.

51 Although the Court here refers to its earlier decision in the

Transportation Tax Administration Case, BVerfGE 32, 145 (p. 156), the import of its judgment is quite different: see pp. 38 f., 112.

52 *BVerfGE* 41, 291.

53 The Court recalled, however, that the unanimity principle was not called into question if a Land refused its assent to the proposed aid programme for irrelevant reasons and thereby offended against the duty of federal comity; but it found that there was no question of that in Bavaria's case. Reference was made to the decisions in the *Housing Funds, Television*, and *Financial Subsidies Cases*.

54 See pp. 116 and 119 above.

55 See pp. 102 ff. above.

56 The Act for the Promotion of Stability and Growth in the Economy, passed in 1967 under the auspices of the new *Art.* 109 *GG*, authorized the Federal Government, if economic circumstances so required, after consulting with the Länder in the *Konjunkturrat* and securing the consent of the Bundesrat, to make ordinances restricting the permissible rates of spending of both Bund and Länder.

57 Despite their successes they were not able totally to curb such prodigality, particularly on the part of Länder Governments unsympathetic to the political aims of the Federal Government: see A. Zunker, 'Finanzplanung und Bundeshaushalt' (Freiburg Univ. Wirtschaftswiss. Diss. 1971), pp. 171–6.

58 There seems, significantly, to be a clear change of tone in the final report of the Commission on Constitutional Reform in 1976.

59 'Die Verfassungsmässigkeit der Finanzreform', *NJW* xxi (1968), 2033–5.

60 See F. W. Scharpf, B. Reissert, F. Schnabel, *Politikverflechtung: Theorie und Empirie des kooperativen Föderalismus in der Bundesrepublik* (Kronberg/Taunus, Scriptor, 1976), pp. 71–132.

61 See H. C. F. Liesegang and R. Plöger, 'Schwächung der Parlamente durch den kooperativen Föderalismus?', *DÖV* xxiv (1971), 228–36. G. Kisker, *Kooperation im Bundesstaat*, pp. 290 f., suggests that constitutional objections may therefore be raised on the basis of the democratic as well as the federal principle and sees an *oligarchischer Bundesstaat* emerging.

62 *Hochschulbauförderungsgesetz:* Section 2.

63 Op. cit., *DÖV* xxi (1968), 781–8.

64 See Tiemann, 'Gemeinschaftsaufgaben', p. 261.

65 F. Wagener, 'Milderungsmöglichkeiten nachteiliger Folgen vertikaler Politikverflechtung', in J. J. Hesse (ed.), *Politikverflechtung*

im föderativen Staat (Baden-Baden, Nomos, 1978), pp. 149–65, at pp. 155 f.

66 See e.g. P. Feuchte, 'Hochschulbau als Gemeinschaftsaufgabe', *Die Verwaltung*, v (1972), 199–222.

67 BT Drucksache 7/5924, pp. 163 ff.

68 Cf. the remarks of Reissert/Schnabel, op. cit. (n. 60), esp. pp. 232 f., about 'over-entanglement' (*Überverflechtung*) of the policy-making processes: what is often the sole benefit of Federal involvement, viz. an increase in the general level of investment, could have been achieved simply by a direct redistribution of financial resources from Bund to Länder.

69 On the significance of *Art. 79 Abs*. 3 *GG* as a barrier to excessive transfers of powers to the Bund see esp. P. Lerche, *Aktuelle föderalistische Verfassungsfragen* (Munich, Bayerische Staatskanzlei, 1968), pp. 43–7; K. Hesse, 'Bundesstaatsreform und Grenzen der Verfassungsänderung', *AöR* xcviii (1973), 1–52.

NOTES TO CHAPTER IX

1 *BVerfGE* 14, 76; 31, 8; 31, 119; 40, 52; 40, 56; 42, 38.

2 *BVerfGE* 37,1; 38, 61; 29, 402; 32, 333; 36, 66.

3 *BVerfGE* 8, 260; 16, 306.

4 *BVerfGE* 11, 105; 14, 312; 23, 12; 36, 383.

5 *BVerfGE* 13, 367; 33, 206; 28, 119.

6 *BVerfGE* 24, 367; 27, 18.

7 *BVerfGE* 31, 113; 33, 52.

8 It has not been possible to cover *every* issue with which the Court has been concerned in the federal sphere. Another question of some interest would, for instance, be the extent of the influence of certain norms of the Federal Constitution (*e.g. Art*. 28 *GG*) on the constitutions of the Länder. But those issues which have been treated seem to be the most prominent or significant.

9 See pp. 118 f. above.

10 Cf. pp. 73 f.

11 *BVerfGE* 40, 56; cf. also *BVerfGE* 42, 38.

12 Cf. the review of the relevant judgments by W. Weber, 'Selbstverwaltungskörperschaften in der Rechtsprechung des Bundesverfassungsgerichts', in *Bundesverfassungsgericht und Grundgesetz*, ed. by C. Starck (Tübingen, Mohr, 1976), ii. 331–63.

13 Some Länder, such as Bremen, seem to have ignored the judgment (*BVerfGE* 35, 79) whereby professors must have a majority on university bodies taking decisions on academic matters. But in January 1976 the new Federal Framework Law on Univer-

sities (*Hochschulrahmengesetz*) did comply with this requirement, thus binding the Länder.

14 See N. Caplan, 'Offshore mineral rights: anatomy of a federal–provincial conflict', *Journal of Canadian Studies*, v (1970), 50–61.

15 Cf. *BVerfGE* 3, 52; 4, 115; 26, 116; 32, 199.

16 *BVerfGE* 16, 64: see pp. 118 f. above.

17 *BVerfGE* 3, 407.

18 Even with this judgment, however, a certain amount of 'erosion' can be observed. Although the Constitutional Court specifically applied the criteria of *Art.* 30 and 83 *GG* (the need for explicit constitutional foundation for any Federal exercise of governmental powers) to the creation of a private company, the Federal Government has established a number of administrative bodies under private law to carry out public functions. This can be a way round the constitutional restrictions on the establishment of Federal administrative authorities.

19 *BVerfGE* 15, 1.

20 See R. Riegel, 'Die neuen Vorschriften des Wasserhaushaltsgesetzes', *NJW* xxix (1976), 783–7. Reactions to this situation vary. Some deplore the frustration for more than a decade of any Federal attempt to solve a problem which can only be solved nationally or indeed internationally, when it was not clear that constitutional amendment was necessary at all. Again, W. Weber, *Die Gegenwartslage des deutschen Föderalismus* (Göttingen, Vandenhoeck & Ruprecht, 1966), p. 21, complained that in the fields of civil service and water law, both of which had been subjected to framework regulation, an incoherent jumble of complex legislation had developed which was of benefit to neither Bund nor Länder. But others see Federal framework law and Land law as dovetailing well, point to close co-ordination between the Länder without central direction, and point out that the Federal powers under the disallowed law had in any case applied only to inland waterways used for general traffic, whereas pollution could equally originate elsewhere.

21 This effect is noted by Scheuner, op. cit., *DÖV* xix (1966), 519.

22 Cf. Johnson, 'Federalism and Decentralization in the Federal Republic of Germany', §6.

23 One judge called this the *Strohdächerbereich* ('sphere of thatched roofs').

24 See p. 143 above. Admittedly that judgment was a product of the traditionally less federalist-minded First Senate.

25 See N. Caplan, 'Some factors affecting the resolution of a

federal-provincial conflict', *Canadian Journal of Political Science*, ii (1969), 173–86. This case suggests interesting differences in the conception of co-operative federalism, which was of course being appealed to here for propaganda purposes on an issue where the will to co-operate was nonexistent.

26 See on this subject G. Lehmbruch, *Parteienwettbewerb im Bundesstaat* (Stuttgart, Kohlhammer, 1976).

Appendix

Excerpts from the Basic Law
of the Federal Republic of Germany

Provisions relating particularly to the federal system

(The text is that of the official translation published by the Press and Information Office of the Federal Government in Bonn, as amended up to and including 23 August 1976.)

II. THE FEDERATION AND THE CONSTITUENT STATES (LAENDER)

Article 20 (Basic principles of the Constitution—Right to resist)

(1) The Federal Republic of Germany is a democratic and social federal state.

Article 28 (Federal guarantee of Laender constitutions)

(1) The constitutional order in the Laender must conform to the principles of republican, democratic and social government based on the rule of law, within the meaning of this Basic Law. In each of the Laender, counties (Kreise), and communes (Gemeinden), the people must be represented by a body chosen in general, direct, free, equal, and secret elections. In the communes the assembly of the commune may take the place of an elected body.

(2) The communes must be guaranteed the right to regulate on their own responsibility all the affairs of the local community within the limits set by law. The associations of communes (Gemeindeverbaende) shall also have the right of self-government in accordance with the law and within the limits of the functions assigned to them by law.

(3) The Federation shall ensure that the constitutional order of the Laender conforms to the basic rights and to the provisions of paragraphs (1) and (2) of this Article.

Article 29* (Reorganization of the federal territory)

(1) The federal territory may be reorganized to ensure that the Laender by their size and capacity are able effectively to fulfil the functions incumbent upon them. Due regard shall be given to regional, historical and cultural ties, economic expediency, regional policy, and the requirements of town and country planning.

(2) Measures for the reorganization of the federal territory shall be introduced by federal laws which shall be subject to confirmation by referendum. The Laender thus affected shall be consulted.

(3) A referendum shall be held in the Laender from whose territories or partial territories a new Land or Land with redefined boundaries is to be formed (affected Laender). The referendum shall decide whether the affected Laender shall remain in their existing state or whether the new Land or Land with redefined boundaries shall be formed. The referendum shall be in favour of the formation of a new Land or Land with redefined boundaries if in its future territory and the whole of the territories or partial territories of an affected Land whose incorporation is to be modified in the same sense a majority vote for the modification. It shall not be in favour if in the territory of one of the affected Laender a majority reject the modification; such rejection shall, however, be of no consequence if in one part of the territory whose incorporation in the affected Land is to be modified a majority of two-thirds approve of the modification, unless in the entire territory of the affected Land a majority of two-thirds reject the modification.

(4) If in an integral settlement and economic agglomeration, the parts of which lie in several Laender and which has a population of at least one million, one-tenth of those of its population entitled to vote in Bundestag elections petition by popular initiative for the incorporation of that area in one Land, a decision shall be taken within two years by means of a federal law as to whether such reorganization shall be carried out pursuant to paragraph (2) of this Article or to the effect that a referendum shall be held in the affected Laender.

(5) The referendum shall establish whether a modification to be proposed in the law meets with approval. The law may submit different but no more than two proposals for the referendum. If a majority approve of such a proposed modification a decision shall be taken by means of a federal law within two years as to whether the

---

* As amended by federal law of 23 August 1976 (Federal Law Gazette I p. 2381).

reorganization shall take place pursuant to paragraph (2) of this Article. If a proposal which has been made the subject of a referendum meets with approval in accordance with the third and fourth sentences of paragraph (3) of this Article, a federal law providing for the formation of the proposed Land shall be enacted within two years after the referendum and shall no longer be subject to confirmation by referendum.

(6) Referendums shall be decided by the majority of votes cast if they make up at least one-quarter of the population entitled to vote in Bundestag elections. Other details with regard to referendums and initiatives (Volksentscheide, Volksbegehren, Volksbefragungen) shall be regulated by a federal law; such federal law may also provide that initiatives may not be repeated within a period of five years.

(7) Other modifications of the territory of the Laender may be effected by state agreements between the Laender concerned or by a federal law with the approval of the Bundesrat if the territory which is to be the subject of reorganization does not have more than 10,000 inhabitants. The details shall be regulated by a federal law requiring the approval of the Bundesrat and the majority of the members of the Bundestag. It must make provision for the affected communes and districts to be heard.

Article 30 (Functions of the Laender)
The exercise of governmental powers and the discharge of governmental functions shall be incumbent on the Laender in so far as this Basic Law does not otherwise prescribe or permit.

Article 31 (Priority of federal law)
Federal law shall override Land law.

Article 32 (Foreign relations)
(1) Relations with foreign states shall be conducted by the Federation.
(2) Before the conclusion of a treaty affecting the special circumstances of a Land, that Land must be consulted in sufficient time.
(3) In so far as the Laender have power to legislate, they may, with the consent of the Federal Government, conclude treaties with foreign states.

Article 35 (Legal, administrative and police assistance)
(1) All federal and Land authorities shall render each other legal and administrative assistance.

Article 37 (Federal enforcement)
(1) If a Land fails to comply with its obligations of a federal character imposed by this Basic Law or another federal law, the Federal Government may, with the consent of the Bundesrat, take the necessary measures to enforce such compliance by the Land by way of federal enforcement.
(2) To carry out such federal enforcement the Federal Government or its commissioner shall have the right to give instructions to all Laender and their authorities.

IV. THE COUNCIL OF CONSTITUENT STATES (BUNDESRAT)

Article 50 (Function)
The Laender shall participate through the Bundesrat in the legislation and administration of the Federation.

Article 51 (Composition)
(1) The Bundesrat shall consist of members of the Land governments which appoint and recall them. Other members of such governments may act as substitutes.
(2) Each Land shall have at least three votes; Laender with more than two million inhabitants shall have four, Laender with more than six million inhabitants five votes.
(3) Each Land may delegate as many members as it has votes. The votes of each Land may be cast only as a block vote and only by members present or their substitutes.

IVa.* THE JOINT COMMITTEE

Article 53a
(1) Two-thirds of the members of the Joint Committee shall be deputies of the Bundestag and one-third shall be members of the Bundesrat. The Bundestag shall delegate its deputies in proportion to the sizes of its parliamentary groups; such deputies must not be members of the Federal Government. Each Land shall be represented by a Bundesrat member of its choice; these members shall not be bound by instructions. The establishment of the Joint Committee and its procedures shall be regulated by rules of procedure to be adopted

* Inserted by federal law of 24 June 1968 (Federal Law Gazette I p. 710).

by the Bundestag and requiring the consent of the Bundesrat.
(2) The Federal Government must inform the Joint Committee
about its plans in respect of a state of defence. The rights of the
Bundestag and its committees under paragraph (1) of Article 43 shall
not be affected by the provision of this paragraph.

VII. LEGISLATIVE POWERS OF THE FEDERATION

Article 70 (Legislation of the Federation and the Laender)
(1) The Laender shall have the right to legislate in so far as this Basic
Law does not confer legislative power on the Federation.
(2) The division of competence between the Federation and the
Laender shall be determined by the provisions of this Basic Law
concerning exclusive and concurrent legislative powers.

Article 71 (Exclusive legislation of the Federation, definition)
In matters within the exclusive legislative power of the Federation the
Laender shall have power to legislate only if, and to the extent that, a
federal law explicitly so authorizes them.

Article 72 (Concurrent legislation of the Federation, definition)
(1) In matters within concurrent legislative powers the Laender shall
have power to legislate as long as, and to the extent that, the Federation does not exercise its right to legislate.
(2) The Federation shall have the right to legislate in these matters to
the extent that a need for regulation by federal legislation exists
because:
1. a matter cannot be effectively regulated by the legislation of individual Laender, or
2. the regulation of a matter by a Land law might prejudice the
   interests of other Laender or of the people as a whole, or
3. the maintenance of legal or economic unity, especially the maintenance of uniformity of living conditions beyond the territory of
   any one Land, necessitates such regulation.

Article 73 (Exclusive legislation, catalogue)
The Federation shall have exclusive power to legislate in the following
matters:
1. *foreign affairs as well as defence including the protection of the
   civilian population;

* As amended by federal laws of 26 March 1954 (Federal Law Gazette I p. 45) and 24
June 1968 (Federal Law Gazette I p. 711).

2. citizenship in the Federation;
3. freedom of movement, passport matters, immigration, emigration, and extradition;
4. currency, money and coinage, weights and measures, as well as the determination of standards of time;
5. the unity of the customs and commercial territory, treaties on commerce and on navigation, the freedom of movement of goods, and the exchanges of goods and payments with foreign countries, including customs and other frontier protection;
6. federal railroads and air transport;
7. postal and telecommunication services;
8. the legal status of persons employed by the Federation and by federal corporate bodies under public law;
9. industrial property rights, copyrights and publishers' rights;
10. *co-operation of the Federation and the Laender in matters of
    (a) criminal police,
    (b) protection of the free democratic basic order, of the existence and the security of the Federation or of a Land (protection of the constitution) and
    (c) protection against efforts in the federal territory which, by the use of force or actions in preparation for the use of force, endanger the foreign interests of the Federal Republic of Germany,
    as well as the establishment of a Federal Criminal Police Office and the international control of crime.
11. statistics for federal purposes.

Article 74 (Concurrent legislation, catalogue)

Concurrent legislative powers shall extend to the following matters:
1. civil law, criminal law and execution of sentences, the organization and procedure of courts, the legal profession, notaries, and legal advice (Rechtsberatung);
2. registration of births, deaths, and marriages;
3. the law of association and assembly;
4. the law relating to residence and establishment of aliens;
4a. **the law relating to weapons and explosives;
5. the protection of German cultural treasures against removal abroad;
6. refugee and expellee matters;
7. public welfare;

---

* As amended by federal law of 28 July 1972 (Federal Law Gazette I p. 1305).
** Inserted by federal law of 28 July 1972 (Federal Law Gazette I p. 1305) and amended by federal law of 23 August 1976 (Federal Law Gazette I p. 2383).

8. citizenship in the Laender;
9. war damage and reparations;
10. *benefits to war-disabled persons and to dependants of those killed in the war as well as assistance to former prisoners of war;
10a. **war graves of soldiers, graves of other victims of war and of victims of despotism;
11. the law relating to economic matters (mining, industry, supply of power, crafts, trades, commerce, banking, stock exchanges, and private insurance);
11a. ***the production and utilization of nuclear energy for peaceful purposes, the construction and operation of installations serving such purposes, protection against hazards arising from the release of nuclear energy or from ionizing radiation, and the disposal of radioactive substances;
12. labour law, including the legal organization of enterprises, protection of workers, employment exchanges and agencies, as well as social insurance, including unemployment insurance;
13. ****the regulation of educational and training grants and the promotion of scientific research;
14. the law regarding expropriation, to the extent that matters enumerated in Articles 73 and 74 are concerned;
15. transfer of land, natural resources and means of production to public ownership or other forms of publicly controlled economy;
16. prevention of the abuse of economic power;
17. promotion of agricultural and forest production, safeguarding of the supply of food, the importation and exportation of agricultural and forest products, deep sea and coastal fishing, and preservation of the coasts;
18. real estate transactions, land law and matters concerning agricultural leases, as well as housing, settlement and homestead matters;
19. measures against human and animal diseases that are communicable or otherwise endanger public health, admission to the medical profession and to other health occupations or practices, as well as trade in medicines, curatives, narcotics, and poisons;
19a. †the economic viability of hospitals and the regulation of hospitalization fees;

---

* As amended by federal law of 16 June 1965 (Federal Law Gazette I p. 513).
** Inserted by federal law of 16 June 1965 (Federal Law Gazette I p. 513).
*** Inserted by federal law of 23 December 1959 (Federal Law Gazette I p. 813).
**** As amended by federal law of 12 May 1969 (Federal Law Gazette I p. 363).
† Inserted by federal law of 12 May 1969 (Federal Law Gazette I p. 363).

20. *protection regarding the marketing of food, drink and tobacco, of necessities of life, fodder, agricultural and forest seeds and seedlings, and protection of plants against diseases and pests, as well as the protection of animals;

21. ocean and coastal shipping as well as aids to navigation, inland navigation, meteorological services, sea routes, and inland waterways used for general traffic;

22. **road traffic, motor transport, construction and maintenance of long-distance highways as well as the collection of charges for the use of public highways by vehicles and the allocation of revenue therefrom;

23. non-federal railroads, except mountain railroads;

24. ***disposal of waste, keeping the air pure, and combating noise.

Article 74a**** (Wider competence of Federation for pay scales)

(1) Concurrent legislation shall further extend to the pay scales and pensions of members of the public service whose service and loyalty are governed by public law, in so far as the Federation does not have exclusive power to legislate pursuant to item 8 of Article 73.

(2) Federal laws enacted pursuant to paragraph (1) of this Article shall require the consent of the Bundesrat.

(3) Federal laws enacted pursuant to item 8 of Article 73 shall likewise require the consent of the Bundesrat, in so far as they prescribe for the structure and computation of pay scales and pensions, including the appraisal of posts, criteria or minimum or maximum rates other than those provided for in federal laws enacted pursuant to paragraph (1) of this Article.

(4) Paragraphs (1) and (2) of this Article shall apply mutatis mutandis to the pay scales and pensions for judges in the Laender. Paragraph (3) of this Article shall apply mutatis mutandis to laws enacted pursuant to paragraph (1) of Article 98.

Article 75† (General provisions of the Federation, catalogue)

Subject to the conditions laid down in Article 72 the Federation shall have the right to enact skeleton provisions concerning:

---

* As amended by federal law of 18 March 1971 (Federal Law Gazette I p. 207).
** As amended by federal law of 12 May 1969 (Federal Law Gazette I p. 363).
*** As amended by federal law of 14 April 1972 (Federal Law Gazette I p. 593).
**** As inserted by federal law of 18 March 1971 (Federal Law Gazette I p. 206).
† As amended by federal law of 12 May 1969 (Federal Law Gazette I p. 363).

1. *the legal status of persons in the public service of the Laender, communes, or other corporate bodies under public law, in so far as Article 74a does not provide otherwise;
1a. **the general principles governing higher education;
2. the general legal status of the press and the film industry;
3. hunting, protection of nature, and care of the countryside;
4. land distribution, regional planning, and water management;
5. matters relating to the registration of changes of residence or domicile (Meldewesen) and to identity cards.

Article 76 (Bills)

(1) Bills shall be introduced in the Bundestag by the Federal Government or by members of the Bundestag or by the Bundesrat.

(2) *** Bills of the Federal Government shall be submitted first to the Bundesrat. The Bundesrat shall be entitled to state its position on such bills within six weeks. A bill exceptionally submitted to the Bundesrat as being particularly urgent by the Federal Government may be submitted by the latter to the Bundestag three weeks later, even though the Federal Government may not yet have received the statement of the Bundesrat's position; such statement shall be transmitted to the Bundestag by the Federal Government without delay upon its receipt.

(3) ****Bills of the Bundesrat shall be submitted to the Bundestag by the Federal Government within three months. In doing so, the Federal Government must state its own view.

Article 77 (Procedure concerning adopted bills—Objection of the Bundesrat)

(1) Bills intended to become federal laws shall require adoption by the Bundestag. Upon their adoption they shall, without delay, be transmitted to the Bundesrat by the President of the Bundestag.

(2) †The Bundesrat may, within three weeks of the receipt of the adopted bill, demand that a committee for joint consideration of bills, composed of members of the Bundestag and members of the Bundesrat, be convened. The composition and the procedure of this committee shall be regulated by rules of procedure to be adopted by the Bundestag and requiring the consent of the Bundesrat. The members of the Bundesrat on this committee shall not be bound by instructions. If the consent of the Bundesrat is required for a bill to become a

* As amended by federal law of 18 March 1971 (Federal Law Gazette I p. 206).
** Inserted by federal law of 12 May 1969 (Federal Law Gazette I p. 363).
*** As amended by federal law of 15 November 1969 (Federal Law Gazette I p. 1177).
**** As amended by federal law of 17 July 1969 (Federal Law Gazette I p. 817).
† As amended by federal law of 15 November 1968 (Federal Law Gazette I p. 1177).

law, the convening of this committee may also be demanded by the Bundestag or the Federal Government. Should the committee propose any amendment to the adopted bill, the Bundestag must again vote on the bill.

(3) *In so far as the consent of the Bundesrat is not required for a bill to become a law, the Bundesrat may, when the proceedings under paragraph (2) of this Article are completed, enter an objection within two weeks against a bill adopted by the Bundestag. This period shall begin, in the case of the last sentence of paragraph (2) of this Article, on the receipt of the bill as re-adopted by the Bundestag, and in all other cases on the receipt of a communication from the chairman of the committee provided for in paragraph (2) of this Article, to the effect that the committee's proceedings have been concluded.

(4) If the objection was adopted with the majority of the votes of the Bundesrat, it can be rejected by a decision of the majority of the members of the Bundestag. If the Bundesrat adopted the objection with a majority of at least two-thirds of its votes, its rejection by the Bundestag shall require a majority of two-thirds, including at least the majority of the members of the Bundestag.

Article 78 (Conditions for passing of federal laws)

A bill adopted by the Bundestag shall become a law if the Bundesrat consents to it, or fails to make a demand pursuant to paragraph (2) of Article 77, or fails to enter an objection within the period stipulated in paragraph (3) of Article 77, or withdraws such objection, or if the objection is overridden by the Bundestag.

Article 79 (Amendment of the Basic Law)

(1) This Basic Law can be amended only by laws which expressly amend or supplement the text thereof. In respect of international treaties the subject of which is a peace settlement, the preparation of a peace settlement, or the abolition of an occupation regime, or which are designed to serve the defence of the Federal Republic, it shall be sufficient, for the purpose of clarifying that the provisions of this Basic Law do not preclude the conclusion and entry into force of such treaties, to effect a supplementation of the text of this Basic Law confined to such clarification**.

(2) Any such law shall require the affirmative vote of two-thirds of the members of the Bundestag and two-thirds of the votes of the Bundesrat.

* As amended by federal law of 15 November 1968 (Federal Law Gazette I p. 1177).
** Second sentence inserted by federal law of 26 March 1954 (Federal Law Gazette I p. 45).

(3) Amendments of this Basic Law affecting the division of the Federation into Laender, the participation on principle of the Laender in legislation, or the basic principles laid down in Articles 1 and 20, shall be inadmissible.

Article 80 (Issue of ordinances having force of law)

(1) The Federal Government, a Federal Minister or the Land governments may be authorized by a law to issue ordinances having the force of law (Rechtsverordnungen). The content, purpose, and scope of the authorization so conferred must be set forth in such law. This legal basis must be stated in the ordinance. If a law provides that such authorization may be delegated, such delegation shall require another ordinance having the force of law.

(2) The consent of the Bundesrat shall be required, unless otherwise provided by federal legislation, for ordinances having the force of law issued by the Federal Government or a Federal Minister concerning basic rules for the use of facilities of the federal railroads and of postal and telecommunication services, or charges therefor, or concerning the construction and operation of railroads, as well as for ordinances having the force of law issued pursuant to federal laws that require the consent of the Bundesrat or that are executed by the Laender as agents of the Federation or as matters of their own concern.

VIII. THE EXECUTION OF FEDERAL LAWS AND THE FEDERAL ADMINISTRATION

Article 83 (Execution of federal laws by the Laender)

The Laender shall execute federal laws as matters of their own concern in so far as this Basic Law does not otherwise provide or permit.

Article 84 (Land administration and Federal Government supervision)

(1) Where the Laender execute federal laws as matters of their own concern, they shall provide for the establishment of the requisite authorities and the regulation of administrative procedures in so far as federal laws consented to by the Bundesrat do not otherwise provide.

(2) The Federal Government may, with the consent of the Bundesrat, issue pertinent general administrative rules.

(3) The Federal Government shall exercise supervision to ensure that the Laender execute the federal laws in accordance with applicable law. For this purpose the Federal Government may send com-

missioners to the highest Land authorities and with their consent or, if such consent is refused, with the consent of the Bundesrat, also to subordinate authorities.

(4) Should any shortcomings which the Federal Government has found to exist in the execution of federal laws in the Laender not be corrected, the Bundesrat shall decide, on the application of the Federal Government or the Land concerned, whether such Land has violated applicable law. The decision of the Bundesrat may be challenged in the Federal Constitutional Court.

(5) With a view to the execution of federal laws, the Federal Government may be authorized by a federal law requiring the consent of the Bundesrat to issue individual instructions for particular cases. They shall be addressed to the highest Land authorities unless the Federal Government considers the matter urgent.

Article 85 (Execution by Laender as agents of the Federation)

(1) Where the Laender execute federal laws as agents of the Federation, the establishment of the requisite authorities shall remain the concern of the Laender except in so far as federal laws consented to by the Bundesrat otherwise provide.

(2) The Federal Government may, with the consent of the Bundesrat, issue pertinent general administrative rules. It may regulate the uniform training of civil servants (Beamte) and other salaried public employees (Angestellte). The heads of authorities at the intermediate level shall be appointed with its agreement.

(3) The Land authorities shall be subject to the instructions of the appropriate highest federal authorities. Such instructions shall be addressed to the highest Land authorities unless the Federal Government considers the matter urgent. Execution of the instructions shall be ensured by the highest Land authorities.

(4) Federal supervision shall extend to conformity with law and appropriateness of execution. The Federal Goverment may, for this purpose, require the submission of reports and documents and send commissioners to all authorities.

Article 86 (Direct federal administration)

Where the Federation executes laws by means of direct federal administration or by federal corporate bodies or institutions under public law, the Federal Government shall, in so far as the law concerned contains no special provision, issue pertinent general administrative rules. The Federal Government shall provide for the establishment of the requisite authorities in so far as the law concerned does not otherwise provide.

Article 87*(Matters of direct federal administration)

(1) The foreign service, the federal finance administration, the federal railroads, the federal postal service, and, in accordance with the provisions of Article 89, the administration of federal waterways and of shipping shall be conducted as matters of direct federal administration with their own administrative substructures.

**Federal frontier protection authorities, central offices for police information and communications, for the criminal police and for the compilation of data for the purposes of protection of the constitution and protection against efforts in the Federal territory which, by the use of force or actions in preparation for the use of force, endanger the foreign interests of the Federal Republic of Germany may be established by federal legislation.

(2) Social insurance institutions whose sphere of competence extends beyond the territory of one Land shall be administered as federal corporate bodies under public law.

(3) In addition, autonomous federal higher authorities as well as federal corporate bodies and institutions under public law may be established by federal legislation for matters in which the Federation has the power to legislate. If new functions arise for the Federation in matters in which it has the power to legislate, federal authorities at the intermediate and lower levels may be established, in case of urgent need, with the consent of the Bundesrat and of the majority of the members of the Bundestag.

VIIIa. JOINT TASKS***

Article 91a*** (Definition of joint tasks)

(1) The Federation shall participate in the discharge of the following responsibilities of the Laender, provided that such responsibilities are important to society as a whole and that federal participation is necessary for the improvement of living conditions (joint tasks):

1. expansion and construction of institutions of higher education including university clinics;
2. improvement of regional economic structures;
3. improvement of the agrarian structure and of coast preservation.

---

* Inserted by federal law of 19 March 1956 (Federal Law Gazette I p. 111) and amended by federal law of 24 June 1968 (Federal Law Gazette I p. 711).
** As amended by federal law of 28 July 1972 (Federal Law Gazette I p. 1305).
*** Inserted by federal law of 12 May 1969 (Federal Law Gazette I p. 359).

(2) Joint tasks shall be defined in detail by federal legislation requiring the consent of the Bundesrat. Such legislation should include general principles governing the discharge of joint tasks.

(3) Such legislation shall provide for the procedure and the institutions required for joint overall planning. The inclusion of a project in the overall planning shall require the consent of the Land in which it is to be carried out.

(4) In cases to which items 1 and 2 of paragraph (1) of this Article apply, the Federation shall meet one-half of the expenditure in each Land. In cases to which item 3 of paragraph (1) of this Article applies, the Federation shall meet at least one-half of the expenditure, and such proportion shall be the same for all the Laender. Details shall be regulated by legislation. Provision of funds shall be subject to appropriation in the budgets of the Federation and the Laender.

(5) The Federal Government and the Bundesrat shall be informed about the execution of joint tasks, should they so demand.

Article 91b* (Co-operation of Federation and Laender in educational planning and in research)

The Federation and the Laender may pursuant to agreements co-operate in educational planning and in the promotion of institutions and projects of scientific research of supraregional importance. The apportionment of costs shall be regulated in the pertinent agreements.

IX. THE ADMINISTRATION OF JUSTICE

Article 92** (Court organization)

Judicial power shall be vested in the judges; it shall be exercised by the Federal Constitutional Court, by the federal courts provided for in this Basic Law, and by the courts of the Laender.

Article 93 (Federal Constitutional Court, competency)

(1) The Federal Constitutional Court shall decide:

1. on the interpretation of this Basic Law in the event of disputes concerning the extent of the rights and duties of a highest federal organ or of other parties concerned who have been vested with rights of their own by this Basic Law or by rules of procedure of a highest federal organ;

---

* Inserted by federal law of 12 May 1969 (Federal Law Gazette I p. 359).
** As amended by federal law of 18 June 1968 (Federal Law Gazette I p. 657).

2. in case of differences of opinion or doubts on the formal and material compatibility of federal law or Land law with this Basic Law, or on the compatibility of Land law with other federal law, at the request of the Federal Government, of a Land government, or of one-third of the Bundestag members;

3. in case of differences of opinion on the rights and duties of the Federation and the Laender, particularly in the execution of federal law by the Laender and in the exercise of federal supervision;

4. on other disputes involving public law, between the Federation and the Laender, between different Laender or within a Land, unless recourse to another court exists;

4a. *on complaints of unconstitutionality, which may be entered by any person who claims that one of his basic rights or one of his rights under paragraph (4) of Article 20, under Article 33, 38, 101, 103, or 104 has been violated by public authority;

4b. *on complaints of unconstitutionality, entered by communes or associations of communes on the ground that their right to self-government under Article 28 has been violated by a law other than a Land law open to complaint to the respective Land constitutional court;

5. in the other cases provided for in this Basic Law.

(2) The Federal Constitutional Court shall also act in such other cases as are assigned to it by federal legislation.

Article 94 (Federal Constitutional Court, composition)

(1) The Federal Constitutional Court shall consist of federal judges and other members. Half of the members of the Federal Constitutional Court shall be elected by the Bundestag and half by the Bundesrat. They may not be members of the Bundestag, the Bundesrat, the Federal Government, nor of any of the corresponding organs of a Land.

(2) The constitution and procedure of the Federal Constitutional Court shall be regulated by a federal law which shall specify in what cases its decisions shall have the force of law*. Such law may require that all other legal remedies must have been exhausted before any such complaint of unconstitutionality can be entered, and may make provision for a special procedure as to admissibility.

* Inserted by federal law of 29 January 1969 (Federal Law Gazette I p. 97).

X. FINANCE

Article 104a* (Apportionment of expenditure, Financial assistance)

(1) The Federation and the Laender shall meet separately the expenditure resulting from the discharge of their respective tasks in so far as this Basic Law does not provide otherwise.

(2) Where the Laender act as agents of the Federation, the Federation shall meet the resulting expenditure.

(3) Federal laws to be executed by the Laender and involving the disbursement of funds may provide that such funds shall be contributed wholly or in part by the Federation. Where any such law provides that the Federation shall meet one-half of the expenditure or more, the Laender shall execute it as agents of the Federation. Where any such law provides that the Laender shall meet one-quarter of the expenditure or more, it shall require the consent of the Bundesrat.

(4) The Federation may grant the Laender financial assistance for particularly important investments by the Laender or communes or associations of communes, provided that such investments are necessary to avert a disturbance of the overall economic equilibrium or to equalize differences of economic capacities within the federal territory or to promote economic growth. Details, especially concerning the kinds of investments to be promoted, shall be regulated by federal legislation requiring the consent of the Bundesrat, or by administrative arrangements based on the federal budget.

(5) The Federation and the Laender shall meet the administrative expenditure incurred by their respective authorities and shall be responsible to each other for ensuring proper administration. Details shall be regulated by a federal law requiring the consent of the Bundesrat.

Article 105 (Customs duties, Monopolies, Taxes—legislation)

(1) The Federation shall have exclusive power to legislate on customs matters and fiscal monopolies.

(2) **The Federation shall have concurrent power to legislate on all other taxes the revenue from which accrues to it wholly or in part or where the conditions provided for in paragraph (2) of Article 72 apply.

* Inserted by federal law of 12 May 1969 (Federal Law Gazette I p. 359).
** As amended by federal law of 12 May 1969 (Federal Law Gazette I p. 359).

(2a) *The Laender shall have power to legislate on local excise taxes as long and in so far as they are not identical with taxes imposed by federal legislation.

(3) Federal laws relating to taxes the receipts from which accrue wholly or in part to the Laender or communes or associations of communes shall require the consent of the Bundesrat.

Article 106** (Apportionment of tax revenue)

(1) The yield of fiscal monopolies and the revenue from the following taxes shall accrue to the Federation:
1. customs duties,
2. excise taxes in so far as they do not accrue to the Laender pursuant to paragraph (2) of this Article, or jointly to the Federation and the Laender in accordance with paragraph (3) of this Article, or to the communes in accordance with paragraph (6) of this Article,
3. the road freight tax,
4. the capital transfer taxes, the insurance tax and the tax on drafts and bills of exchange,
5. non-recurrent levies on property, and contributions imposed for the purpose of implementing the equalization of burdens legislation***,
6. income and corporation surtaxes,
7. charges imposed within the framework of the European Communities.

(2) Revenue from the following taxes shall accrue to the Laender:
1. property (net worth) tax,
2. inheritance tax,
3. motor-vehicle tax,
4. such taxes on transactions as do not accrue to the Federation pursuant to paragraph (1) of this Article or jointly to the Federation and the Laender pursuant to paragraph (3) of this Article,
5. beer tax,
6. taxes on gambling establishments.

(3) Revenue from income taxes, corporation taxes and turnover taxes shall accrue jointly to the Federation and the Laender (joint taxes) to the extent that the revenue from income tax is not allocated to the communes pursuant to paragraph (5) of this Article. The

---

* Inserted by federal law of 12 May 1969 (Federal Law Gazette I p. 359).
** As amended by federal laws of 23 December 1955 (Federal Law Gazette I p. 817), of 24 December 1956 (Federal Law Gazette I p. 1077), and of 12 May 1969 (Federal Law Gazette I p. 359).
*** i.e., contributions imposed on persons having suffered no war damage and used to indemnify persons having suffered such damage.

Federation and the Laender shall share equally the revenues from income taxes and corporation taxes. The respective shares of the Federation and the Laender in the revenue from turnover tax shall be determined by federal legislation requiring the consent of the Bundesrat. Such determination shall be based on the following principles:

1. The Federation and the Laender shall have an equal claim to coverage from current revenues of their respective necessary expenditures. The extent of such expenditures shall be determined within a system of pluri-annual financial planning;

2. the coverage requirements of the Federation and of the Laender shall be co-ordinated in such a way that a fair balance is struck, any overburdening of taxpayers precluded, and uniformity of living standards in the federal territory ensured.

(4) The respective shares of the Federation and the Laender in the revenue from the turnover tax shall be apportioned anew whenever the relation of revenues to expenditures in the Federation develops substantially differently from that of the Laender. Where federal legislation imposes additional expenditures on, or withdraws revenue from, the Laender, the additional burden may be compensated by federal grants under federal laws requiring the consent of the Bundesrat, provided such additional burden is limited to a short period. Such laws shall lay down the principles for calculating such grants and distributing them among the Laender.

(5) A share of the revenue from income tax shall accrue to the communes, to be passed on by the Laender to their communes on the basis of income taxes paid by the inhabitants of the latter. Details shall be regulated by a federal law requiring the consent of the Bundesrat. Such law may provide that communes shall assess communal percentages of the communal share.

(6) Revenue from taxes on real property and businesses shall accrue to the communes; revenue from local excise taxes shall accrue to the communes or, as may be provided for by Land legislation, to associations of communes. Communes shall be authorized to assess the communal percentages of taxes on real property and businesses within the framework of existing laws. Where there are no communes in a Land, revenue from taxes on real property and businesses as well as from local excise taxes shall accrue to the Land. The Federation and the Laender may participate, by assessing an impost, in the revenue from the trade tax. Details regarding such impost shall be regulated by a federal law requiring the consent of the Bundesrat. Within the framework of Land legislation, taxes on real property and businesses as well as the communes' share of revenue from income tax may be taken as a basis for calculating the amount of such impost.

(7) An overall percentage, to be determined by Land legislation, of

the Land share of total revenue from joint taxes shall accrue to the communes and associations of communes. In all other respects Land legislation shall determine whether and to what extent revenue from Land taxes shall accrue to communes and associations of communes.

(8) If in individual Laender or communes or associations of communes the Federation causes special facilities to be established which directly result in an increase of expenditure or a loss of revenue (special burden) to these Laender or communes or associations of communes, the Federation shall grant the necessary compensation, if and in so far as such Laender or communes or associations of communes cannot reasonably be expected to bear such special burden. In granting such compensation, due account shall be taken of third-party indemnities and financial benefits accruing to the Laender or communes or associations of communes concerned as a result of the institution of such facilities.

(9) For the purpose of this Article, revenues and expenditures of communes and associations of communes shall be deemed to be Land revenues and expenditures.

Article 107* (Financial equalization)

(1) Revenue from Land taxes and the Land share of revenue from income and corporation taxes shall accrue to the individual Laender to the extent that such taxes are collected by revenue authorities within their respective territories (local revenue). Federal legislation requiring the consent of the Bundesrat may provide in detail for the delimitation as well as the manner and scope of allotment of local revenue from corporation and wage taxes. Legislation may also provide for the delimitation and allotment of local revenue from other taxes. The Land share of revenue from the turnover tax shall accrue to the individual Laender on a per-capita basis; federal legislation requiring the consent of the Bundesrat may provide for supplemental shares not exceeding one-quarter of a Land share to be granted to Laender whose per-capita revenue from Land taxes and from the income and corporation taxes is below the average of all the Laender combined.

(2) Federal legislation shall ensure a reasonable equalization between financially strong and financially weak Laender, due account being taken of the financial capacity and financial requirements of communes and associations of communes. Such legislation shall specify the conditions governing equalization claims of Laender entitled to equalization payments and equalization liabilities of Laender

* As amended by federal laws of 23 December 1955 (Federal Law Gazette I p. 817) and of 12 May 1969 (Federal Law Gazette I p. 359).

owing equalization payments as well as the criteria for determining the amounts of equalization payments. Such legislation may also provide for grants to be made by the Federation from federal funds to financially weak Laender in order to complement the coverage of their general financial requirements (complemental grants).

Article 108*(Fiscal administration)

(1) Customs duties, fiscal monopolies, excise taxes subject to federal legislation, including the excise tax on imports, and charges imposed within the framework of the European Communities, shall be administered by federal revenue authorities. The organization of these authorities shall be regulated by federal legislation. The heads of authorities at the intermediate level shall be appointed in consultation with the respective Land governments.

(2) All other taxes shall be administered by Land revenue authorities. The organization of these authorities and the uniform training of their civil servants may be regulated by federal legislation requiring the consent of the Bundesrat. The heads of authorities at the intermediate level shall be appointed in agreement with the Federal Government.

(3) To the extent that taxes accruing wholly or in part to the Federation are administered by Land revenue authorities, those authorities shall act as agents of the Federation. Paragraphs (3) and (4) of Article 85 shall apply, the Federal Minister of Finance being, however, substituted for the Federal Government.

(4) In respect of the administration of taxes, federal legislation requiring the consent of the Bundesrat may provide for collaboration between federal and Land revenue authorities, or in the case of taxes under paragraph (1) of this Article for their administration by Land revenue authorities, or in the case of other taxes for their administration by federal revenue authorities, if and to the extent that the execution of tax laws is substantially improved or facilitated thereby. As regards taxes the revenue from which accrues exclusively to communes or associations of communes, their administration may wholly or in part be transferred by Laender from the appropriate Land revenue authorities to communes or associations of communes.

(5) The procedure to be applied by federal revenue authorities shall be laid down by federal legislation. The procedure to be applied by Land revenue authorities or, as envisaged in the second sentence of paragraph (4) of this Article, by communes or associations of communes, may be laid down by federal legislation requiring the consent of the Bundesrat.

* As amended by federal law of 12 May 1969 (Federal Law Gazette I p. 359).

(6) The jurisdiction of fiscal courts shall be uniformly regulated by federal legislation.

(7) The Federal Government may issue pertinent general administrative rules which, to the extent that administration is incumbent upon Land revenue authorities or communes or associations of communes, shall require the consent of the Bundesrat.

Article 109*(Separate budgets for Federation and Laender)

(1) The Federation and the Laender shall be autonomous and independent of each other in their fiscal administration.

(2) The Federation and the Laender shall take due account in their fiscal administration of the requirements of overall economic equilibrium.

(3) **By means of federal legislation requiring the consent of the Bundesrat, principles applicable to both the Federation and the Laender may be established governing budgetary law, responsiveness of the fiscal administration to economic trends, and financial planning to cover several years ahead.

(4) With a view to averting disturbances of the overall economic equilibrium, federal legislation requiring the consent of the Bundesrat may be enacted providing for:

1. maximum amounts, terms and timing of loans to be raised by public administrative entities, whether territorial (Gebietskoerperschaften) or functional (Zweckverbaende), and

2. an obligation on the part of the Federation and the Laender to maintain interest-free deposits in the German Federal Bank (reserves for counterbalancing economic trends).

Authorizations to enact pertinent ordinances having the force of law may be issued only to the Federal Government. Such ordinances shall require the consent of the Bundesrat. They shall be repealed in so far as the Bundestag may demand; details shall be regulated by federal legislation.

Article 123 (Continued validity of old law and old treaties)

(1) Law in force before the first meeting of the Bundestag shall remain in force in so far as it does not conflict with this Basic Law.

(2) Subject to all rights and objections of the interested parties, the treaties concluded by the German Reich concerning matters which, under this Basic Law, shall be within the competence of Land legislation, shall remain in force, if they are and continue to be valid in accordance with general principles of law, until new treaties are

---

* As amended by federal law of 8 June 1967 (Federal Law Gazette I p. 581).
** As amended by federal law of 12 May 1969 (Federal Law Gazette I p. 357).

concluded by the agencies competent under this Basic Law, or until they are in any other way terminated pursuant to their provisions.

Article 124 (Old law affecting matters subject to exclusive legislation)

Law, wherever applicable*, affecting matters subject to the exclusive legislative power of the Federation, shall become federal law.

Article 125 (Old law affecting matters subject to concurrent legislation)

Law, wherever applicable*, affecting matters subject to the concurrent legislative power of the Federation, shall become federal law:
1. in so far as it applies uniformly within one or more zones of occupation;
2. in so far as it is law by which former Reich law has been amended after 8 May 1945.

Article 126 (Disputes regarding continued validity of old law)

Disputes regarding the continuance of law as federal law shall be decided by the Federal Constitutional Court.

* i.e., Land or zonal law.

Bibliographical Note

A. Works in German

The literature in German both on the federal system and even more on the Bundesverfassungsgericht is positively voluminous. Yet, covering though it does a field which is clearly of direct interest to at least two disciplines, it is overwhelmingly of a legal nature.

Thus there is a wide range of legal dissertations on federal topics, mostly dealing with highly detailed aspects, many of them concerned with procedural questions, many of them rather arid and with much less concern for political realities than for the technicalities of juridical construction. To this may be added a vast store of articles and monographs on specific aspects of the federal system, usually also taking account of the decisions of the Constitutional Court, many of which, although purely legal in their approach, have an important clarificatory value for the student of politics. By way of example, mention may be made of the discussion of unwritten powers in M. Bullinger, 'Ungeschriebene Kompetenzen im Bundesstaat', *AöR* 96 (1971), 237–85, and the same author's monograph, *Die Mineralölfernleitungen* (Stuttgart, Kohlhammer, 1962); the work on federal comity by H.-W. Bayer, *Die Bundestreue* (Tübingen, Mohr, 1961); and the analysis of co-operation under the federal constitution by G. Kisker, *Kooperation im Bundesstaat* (Tübingen, Mohr, 1971). There are also numerous juridical discussions of prominent cases decided by the Court, such as the *Concordat Case* and the *Television Case*.

Fortunately, there are also a number of contributions by legal scholars which show an excellent grasp of the political as well as the legal implications of the subject and are in the best tradition of German *Staatslehre*. Here articles and essays by Geiger, K. Hesse, and Scheuner deserve particular attention (the first a judge at the Bundesverfassungsgericht for twenty-six years from its inception, the second since 1975): these are listed below in the select bibliography.

Special mention must also be made of Hesse's short monograph, *Der unitarische Bundesstaat* (Karlsruhe, Müller, 1962), and of Werner Weber's collected essays: *Spannungen und Kräfte im westdeutschen Verfassungssystem* (Berlin, Duncker & Humblot, 3rd edn. 1970).[1] These contributions, though excellent, are generally rather brief. But they are all the more valuable in view of the striking dearth of political studies of West German federalism. O. Nyman, *Der westdeutsche Föderalismus* (Stockholm, Almqvist & Wiksell, 1960), is useful though now rather out of date, while H. Laufer, *Der Föderalismus der Bundesrepublik Deutschland* (Stuttgart, Kohlhammer, 1974), gives the most essential information on most aspects but does not go into any depth. To these general titles may be added the valuable analysis of the historical and philosophical bases of the federal principle by E. Deuerlein, *Föderalismus* (Munich, List, 1972). Among more specialised works, apart from a number of studies of the role of the Bundesrat, mention may be made of R. Kunze, *Kooperativer Föderalismus in der Bundesrepublik* (Stuttgart, Fischer, 1968). A welcome upsurge of academic interest during the 1970s in interconnections and interaction between politics at Federal and Land level is evidenced by some of the contributions to *Politikverflechtung zwischen Bund, Ländern und Gemeinden*, Schriftenreihe der Hochschule Speyer Vol. 55 (Berlin, Duncker & Humblot, 1975); by F. W. Scharpf, B. Reissert and F. Schnabel, *Politikverflechtung: Theorie und Empirie des kooperativen Föderalismus in der Bundesrepublik* (Kronberg/Taunus, Scriptor Verlag, 1976); and by J. J. Hesse (ed.), *Politikverflechtung im föderativen Staat* (Baden-Baden, Nomos, 1978). The same period saw the publication of G. Lehmbruch's perceptive and enlightening book on party competition in the federal state: *Parteienwettbewerb im Bundesstaat* (Stuttgart, Kohlhammer, 1976). Nevertheless, comprehensive studies of the operation of West German federalism are still far to seek, a more detailed and specialised investigation of the resolution of conflicts in the federal system at least equally so.

The situation is similar when approached from the direction of the Constitutional Court. There are multitudinous discussions of the Bundesverfassungsgericht, of judicial review and of the relationship between law and politics. An excellent and exhaustive catalogue is provided by the staff of the Court's own library: J. Mackert and F. Schneider, *Bibliographie zur Verfassungsgerichtsbarkeit des Bundes und der Länder* (Tübingen, Mohr, 2 vols., 1971 and 1976). Most of these publications are, understandably, written from a legal point of view,

---

1 The perceptive article by G. Kisker, 'Kooperation zwischen Bund und Ländern in der Bundesrepublik Deutschland', DÖV **xx** (1977), 689–96, also falls into this category.

though this does not prevent many of them from being of considerably wider interest. But often relatively little attention is paid to federal cases. Among the most notable exceptions may be cited a number of the contributions to the major collection of essays published on the occasion of the twenty-fifth anniversary of the Federal Constitutional Court under the title *Bundesverfassungsgericht und Grundgesetz*, ed. by C. Starck (Tübingen, Mohr, 2 vols., 1976). For an investigation from a purely legal angle of federalist and unitarist tendencies in the decision-making of the Court see E. Bauschke, 'Bundesstaatsprinzip und Bundesverfassungsgericht' (Berlin Univ. Rechtswiss. Diss. 1970).

Political studies of the Constitutional Court are thin on the ground. The most prominent is the substantial work by H. Laufer, *Verfassungs-gerichtsbarkeit und politischer Prozess* (Tübingen, Mohr, 1968); see also the same author's essay 'Verfassungsgerichtsbarkeit als politische Kontrolle', in *Probleme der Demokratie heute. = Politische Viertel-jahresschrift*, Sonderheft 2 (Opladen, Westdeutscher Verlag, 1971), pp. 226–40. Otherwise there are only the modest essays by R. Wildenmann, *Die Rolle des Bundesverfassungsgerichts und der Deutschen Bundesbank in der politischen Willensbildung* (Stuttgart, Kohlhammer, 1969), and, from a radical left-wing standpoint, O. Massing, 'Recht als Korrelat der Macht', in G. Schäfer and C. Nedelmann (eds.), *Der CDU-Staat* (Munich, Suhrkamp, 3rd edn. 1972), i. 211–58; idem, 'Das Bundesverfassungsgericht als Instrument sozialer Kontrolle', in *Probleme der Demokratie heute*, pp. 180–225. Mention may also be made of the specialized dissertation by W. Billing on the method of electing Constitutional Court judges: *Das Problem der Richterwahl zum Bundesver-fassungsgericht* (Berlin, Duncker & Humblot, 1969); and of the socio-logical study of Federal judges by J. Feest, 'Die Bundesrichter', in W. Zapf (ed.), *Beiträge zur Analyse der deutschen Oberschicht* (Munich, Piper, 2nd edn. 1965), pp. 95–113.

B. Works in English

Works in English in this field are few in number but in general highly useful. Valuable analyses of the Constitutional Court, its organiza-tion, composition, methods, general trends in decision-making, and impact have been provided by E. McWhinney, *Constitutionalism in Germany and the Federal Constitutional Court* (Leyden, Sythoff, 1962), and D. P. Kommers, *Judicial Politics in West Germany* (Beverly Hills/London, Sage, 1976). See also the latter's essay on 'The Federal Constitutional Court in the West German Political System', in J. B. Grossman and J. Tanenhaus (eds.), *Frontiers of Judicial Research* (New

York, Wiley, 1969), pp. 73–132. On the other hand, Kommers himself points out that he has not sought critically to examine judicial policy in any substantive field of German constitutional law, fully warranted though such a treatment would be.

As far as the federal system is concerned, good introductions are supplied by P. H. Merkl, 'Executive-Legislative Federalism in West Germany', *A.P.S.R.* liii (1959), 732–41, and by G. Sawer, 'Federalism in West Germany', *Public Law* (1961), 26–44, the latter with considerable reference to the decisions of the Constitutional Court. But both are only articles, and neither is very recent. They may be supplemented by Taylor Cole, 'New dimensions of West German Federalism', in *Comparative Politics and Political Theory*, essays written in honour of Charles Baskervill Robson, ed. by E. L. Pinney (Chapel Hill, Univ. of North Carolina Press, 1966), pp. 99–122. There are also one or two more specialized articles, such as D. R. Reich, 'Court, Comity and Federalism in West Germany', *Midwest Journal of Political Science*, vii (1963), 197–228, which gives an account of the relevant Constitutional Court decisions during the first decade. On the role of the Bundesrat E. L. Pinney, *Federalism, Bureaucracy and Party Politics in Western Germany* (Chapel Hill, Univ. of North Carolina Press, 1963) is still useful. The most illuminating general account in either language of the operation of the West German federal system is the memorandum prepared by Nevil Johnson for the Commission on the Constitution in 1973: 'Federalism and Decentralization in the Federal Republic of Germany': *Commission on the Constitution*, Research Paper I (London, HMSO, 1973). However, it is little concerned with the umpiring of the federal system by the Constitutional Court.

Additional Select Bibliography

A. Works in German

1. Works relating to earlier German constitutions

ANSCHÜTZ, G. and R. THOMA (eds.), *Handbuch des deutschen Staatsrechts* (Tübingen, Mohr, 1930–2).

HAENEL, A., *Studien zum Deutschen Staatsrechte* (Leipzig, Haessel, 1873).

LABAND, P., *Das Staatsrecht des Deutschen Reiches* (Tübingen, Mohr, 5th edn. 1911).

LAMMERS, H.-H. and W. SIMONS (eds.), *Die Rechtsprechung des Staatsgerichtshofes für das Deutsche Reich* (Berlin, Stilke, 1929–39).

MAYER, O., 'Republikanischer und monarchischer Bundesstaat', *AöR* xviii (1903), 337–72.

NAWIASKY, H., *Der Bundesstaat als Rechtsbegriff* (Tübingen, Mohr, 1920).

SCHMITT, C., 'Das Reichsgericht als Hüter der Verfassung', repr. in *Verfassungsrechtliche Aufsätze* (Berlin, Duncker & Humblot, 1958), pp. 63–100.

SEYDEL, M. von, 'Der Bundesstaatsbegriff', *Zeitschrift für die gesamte Staatswissenschaft*, xxviii (1872), 185–256.

SMEND, R., 'Ungeschriebenes Verfassungsrecht im monarchischen Bundesstaat', in *Festgabe für Otto Mayer zum 70. Geburtstag* (Tübingen, Mohr, 1916), pp. 245–70.

TRIEPEL, H., *Unitarismus und Föderalismus im Deutschen Reiche* (Tübingen, Mohr, 1907).

——, 'Die Kompetenzen des Bundesstaates und die geschriebene Verfassung', in *Staatsrechtliche Abhandlungen. Festgabe für Paul Laband* (Tübingen, Mohr, 1908), ii. 247–335.

——, *Streitigkeiten zwischen Reich und Ländern* (Tübingen, Mohr, 1923).

——, 'Wesen und Entwicklung der Staatsgerichtsbarkeit', *VVDStRL* v (1929), 2–29.

2. General works on West German constitutional law

HESSE, K., *Grundzüge des Verfassungsrechts der Bundesrepublik Deutschland* (Karlsruhe, Müller, 11th edn. 1978).

LEIBHOLZ, G. and H.-J. RINCK, *Grundgesetz für die Bundesrepublik Deutschland: Kommentar an Hand der Rechtsprechung des Bundesverfassungsgerichts* (Cologne, Schmidt, 5th edn. 1975).

MANGOLDT, H. von and F. KLEIN, *Das Bonner Grundgesetz* (Berlin/Frankfurt, Vahlen, 2nd edn. 1957–74).

MAUNZ, T., *Deutsches Staatsrecht* (Munich, Beck, 22nd edn. 1978).

MAUNZ, T., G. DÜRIG and R. HERZOG, *Grundgesetz: Kommentar* (Munich/Berlin, Beck, 4th edn. 1976).

3. Judicial review in general and the Federal Constitutional Court

BACHOF, O., 'Der Verfassungsrichter zwischen Recht und Politik', in *Summum ius, summa iniuria*. Ringvorlesung, gehalten von Mitgliedern der Tübinger Juristenfakultät im Rahmen des Dies academicus WS 1962/63 (Tübingen, Mohr, 1963), pp. 41–57.

Das BUNDESVERFASSUNGSGERICHT, ed. by the Court (Karlsruhe, Müller, 1963).

ERMACORA, F., *Verfassungsrecht durch Richterspruch. Weiterbildung des Rechts durch die Rechtsprechung der Verfassungsgerichte* (Karlsruhe, Müller, 1960).

ESSER, J., *Grundsatz und Norm in der richterlichen Fortbildung des Privatrechts* (Tübingen, Mohr, 2nd edn. 1964).

FRIESENHAHN, E., 'Wesen und Grenzen der Verfassungsgerichtsbarkeit', *Zeitschrift für Schweizer Recht*, lxxiii (1954), 129–62.

——, *Die Verfassungsgerichtsbarkeit in der Bundesrepublik Deutschland* (Cologne, Heymann, 1963).

FROWEIN, J. A., H. MEYER and P. SCHNEIDER (eds.), *Das Bundesverfassungsgericht im dritten Jahrzehnt. Symposium zu Ehren von Ernst Friesenhahn zum 70. Geburtstag* (Frankfurt, Metzner, 1973).

GEIGER, W., 'Zur Lage unserer Verfassungsgerichtsbarkeit', in *Festgabe für Theodor Maunz zum 70. Geburtstag*, ed. by H. Spanner et al. (Munich, Beck, 1971), pp. 117–43.

HESSE, K., 'Grenzen der Verfassungswandlung', in *Festschrift für Ulrich Scheuner zum 70. Geburtstag*, ed. by H. Ehmke et al. (Berlin, Duncker & Humblot, 1973), pp. 123–41.

JELLINEK, H., 'Die Weiterentwicklung des Grundgesetzes durch die Rechtsprechung des Bundesverfassungsgerichts', *JöR* N.F. xvi (1967), 183–206.

JORDAN, K. E., 'Zur Verwendung des Stilarguments in der Bundesrepublik Deutschland', *Politische Vierteljahresschrift*, vii (1966), 97–118.

KLEIN, F., *Das Bundesverfassungsgericht und die richterliche Beurteilung politischer Fragen* (Münster, Aschendorff, 1966).

KLEIN, H. H., *Bundesverfassungsgericht und Staatsraison* (Frankfurt/Berlin, Metzner, 1968).

KRÜGER, H., 'Verfassungswandlung und Verfassungsgerichtsbarkeit', in *Staatsverfassung und Kirchenordnung. Festgabe für Rudolf Smend zum 80. Geburtstag*, ed. by K. Hesse et al. (Tübingen, Mohr, 1962), pp. 151–70.

LEIBHOLZ, G., 'Das Spannungsverhältnis von Politik und Recht und die Integrationsfunktion des Bundesverfassungsgerichts', in D. Stolte and R. Wisser (eds.), *Integritas* (Tübingen, Wunderlich, 1966), pp. 211–23.

SPANNER, H., 'Probleme der Verfassungsgerichtsbarkeit', Österreichische Juristen-Zeitung, xxiii (1968), 337–43.

'Der STATUS des Bundesverfassungsgerichts', Denkschrift (with introduction by Gerhard Leibholz), in *Jahrbuch des öffentlichen Rechts der Gegenwart*, N.F. vi (1957), 109–221.

VOIGT, L., 'Entscheidungen gegen den klaren Wortlaut des Gesetzes' (Göttingen Univ. Jur. Diss. 1967).

WITTIG, P., 'Politische Rücksichten in der Rechtsprechung des Bundesverfassungsgerichts', *Der Staat*, viii (1969), 137–58.

4. *Problems of the federal system*

ACHTERBERG, N., 'Die Annex-Kompetenz', *DÖV* xix (1966), 695–701.

BARBARINO, O., 'Zur Revision des Grundgesetzes: Planerische und finanzielle Aspekte des Bund-Länder-Verhältnisses unter besonderer Berücksichtigung der Gemeinschaftsaufgaben', *DÖV* xxvi (1973), 19–23.

BROHM, W., *Landeshoheit und Bundesverwaltung: Vorfragen der Planung im Bundesstaat* (Baden-Baden, Nomos, 1968).

Der *BUNDESRAT als Verfassungsorgan und politische Kraft*—Beiträge zum 25-jährigen Bestehen des Bundesrates der Bundesrepublik Deutschland, ed. by the Bundesrat (Bad Honnef/Darmstadt, Neue Darmstädter Verlagsanstalt, 1974).

DAGTOGLOU, P., 'Streitigkeiten zwischen Bund und Ländern im Bereich der Gesetzgebung', *DÖV* xxiv (1971), 35–42.

ENQUÊTE-KOMMISSION für Fragen der Verfassungsreform, Zwischenbericht. BT Drucksache 6/3829.

ENQUÊTE-KOMMISSION *Verfassungsreform, Schlussbericht.* BT Drucksache 7/5924.

ERHARDT, M., 'Bundeskompetenzen für die Kulturfinanzierung', *AöR* xcv (1970), 135–7.

'FEHLENTWICKLUNG im Verhältnis von Bundesrat und Bundestag?', Papers and Discussion at the Deutsche Vereinigung für Parlamentsfragen, *ZParl* vii (1976), 291–316.

FEUCHTE, P., 'Neugliederung: Versagen von gestern, Chance von morgen', *DÖV* xxi (1968), 456–65.

——, 'Wege und Umwege zu einer neuen Struktur', in *Festschrift für Gebhard Müller*, ed. by T. Ritterspach and W. Geiger (Tübingen, Mohr, 1970), pp. 59–76.

——, 'Hochschulbau als Gemeinschaftsaufgabe', *Die Verwaltung*, v (1972), 199–222.

——, 'Die bundesstaatliche Zusammenarbeit in der Verfassungswirklichkeit der Bundesrepublik Deutschland', *AöR* xcviii (1973), 473–528.

'FÖDERALISMUS als nationales und internationales Ordnungsprinzip', Verhandlungen der Tagung der Deutschen Staatsrechtslehrer zu Münster (Westfalen) 1962, *VVDStRL* xxi (1964).

GEIGER, W., 'Die wechselseitige Treuepflicht von Bund und Ländern', in A. Süsterhenn (ed.), *Föderalistische Ordnung* (Koblenz, Rhenania, 1961), pp. 113–28.

——, *Missverständnisse um den Föderalismus* (Berlin, De Gruyter, 1962).

——, 'Föderalismus in der Verfassungsordnung der Bundesrepublik Deutschland', in *Zur Struktur der deutschen Verwaltung*, Schriftenreihe der Hochschule Speyer, Vol. 33 (Berlin, Duncker & Humblot, 1967), pp. 12–35.

GORONCY, R., 'Der Mitwirkungsbereich des Bundes bei den Gemeinschaftsaufgaben nach Art. 91a und 91b des Grundgesetzes', *DÖV* xxiii (1970), 109–14.

GRAWERT, R., *Verwaltungsabkommen zwischen Bund und Ländern in der Bundesrepublik Deutschland* (Berlin, Duncker & Humblot, 1967).

GRUSON, M., *Die Bedürfniskompetenz* (Berlin, Duncker & Humblot, 1967).

HEINZE, C., ' "Kooperativer Föderalismus" und die Umbildung der Verfassung', in *Festschrift für Ernst Forsthoff zum 70. Geburtstag,* ed. by R. Schnur (Munich, Beck, 1972), pp. 119–38.

HEMPEL, W., *Der demokratische Bundesstaat* (Berlin, Duncker & Humblot, 1969).

HENLE, W., 'Die Förderung von Landesaufgaben aus Bundesmitteln', in *Gemeinschaftsaufgaben zwischen Bund, Ländern und Gemeinden,*

Schriftenreihe der Hochschule Speyer, Vol. 11 (Berlin, Duncker & Humblot, 1961), pp. 63–77.

HERZOG, R., 'Zwischenbilanz im Streit um die bundesstaatliche Ordnung', *Juristische Schulung*, vii (1967), 193–200.

HESSE, K., 'Aspekte des kooperativen Föderalismus in der Bundesrepublik', in *Festschrift für Gebhard Müller*, ed. by T. Ritterspach and W. Geiger (Tübingen, Mohr, 1970), pp. 141–60.

——, 'Bundesstaatsreform und Grenzen der Verfassungsänderung', *AöR* xcviii (1973), 1–52.

HOLCH, G., 'Die Finanzhilfen des Bundes nach Art. 104a Abs. 4 GG', *DÖV* xxvi (1973), 116–21.

KAISER, J. H., 'Die Erfüllung der völkerrechtlichen Verträge des Bundes durch die Länder', *Zeitschrift für ausländisches öffentliches Recht und Völkerrecht*, xviii (1957/8) 526–58.

KEWENIG, W.,'Kooperativer Föderalismus und bundesstaatliche Ordnung', *AöR* xciii (1968), 433–84.

KISKER, G., 'Kooperation zwischen Bund und Ländern in der Bundesrepublik Deutschland', *DÖV* xxx (1977), 689–96.

KLEIN, F., 'Verfassungsrechtliche Grenzen der Gemeinschaftsaufgaben', in *Gemeinschaftsaufgaben zwischen Bund, Ländern und Gemeinden*, Schriftenreihe der Hochschule Speyer, Vol. 11 (Berlin, Duncker & Humblot, 1961), pp. 125–74.

KLEIN, H. H., 'Die Bedeutung des Sachzusammenhangs für die Verfassungsauslegung' (Heidelberg Univ. Jur. Diss. 1960).

KÖLBLE, J., 'Gemeinschaftsaufgaben zwischen Bund und Ländern sowie zwischen den Ländern', in *Gemeinschaftsaufgaben zwischen Bund, Ländern und Gemeinden*, Schriftenreihe der Hochschule Speyer, Vol. 11 (Berlin, Duncker & Humblot, 1961), pp. 17–62.

——, ' "Gemeinschaftsaufgaben" der Länder und ihre Grenzen', *NJW* xv (1962), 1081–5.

——, 'Zur Lehre von den—stillschweigend—zugelassenen Verwaltungszuständigkeiten des Bundes', *DÖV* xvi (1963), 660–73.

KÖNIG, P., 'Beginn der Sperrwirkung für die Länder bei konkurrierender Gesetzgebung', *NJW* xxvi (1973), 1825–9.

KÖTTGEN, A., *Fondsverwaltung in der Bundesrepublik* (Stuttgart, Kohlhammer, 1965).

KOMMISSION für die Finanzreform, *Gutachten über die Finanzreform in der Bundesrepublik Deutschland, erstattet im Auftrage des Bundeskanzlers und der Ministerpräsidenten der Länder* = 'Troeger-Gutachten' (Stuttgart, Kohlhammer, 2nd edn. 1966).

LAUFER, H., 'Der Bundesrat als Instrument der Opposition?', *ZParl* i (1969/70), 318–41.

——, 'Der Bundesrat, Untersuchungen über Zusammensetzung,

Arbeitsweise, politische Rolle und Reformprobleme', *Schriftenreihe der Bundeszentrale für politische Bildung*, Bonn, 1972.

LERCHE, P., *Aktuelle föderalistische Verfassungsfragen* (Munich, Bayerische Staatskanzlei, 1968).

LIESEGANG, H. C. F. and R. PLÖGER, 'Schwächung der Parlamente durch den kooperativen Föderalismus?', *DÖV* xxiv (1971), 228–36.

MAUNZ, T., 'Pflicht der Länder zur Uneinigkeit?', *NJW* xv (1962), 1641–5.

——, 'Die Verfassungsmässigkeit der Finanzreform', *NJW* xxi (1968), 2033–5.

——, 'Die Abgrenzung des Kulturbereichs zwischen dem Bund und den Ländern', in *Festschrift für Gebhard Müller*, ed. by T. Ritterspach and W. Geiger (Tübingen, Mohr, 1970), pp. 257–74.

MEIBOM, H. von, 'Die Mitwirkung der Länder im Bereich der auswärtigen Gewalt', *NJW* xxi (1968), 1607–10.

NEUGLIEDERUNG des Bundesgebiets: Contributions to the discussion in *DÖV* xxvii (1974), 1–20.

NEUNREITHER, K. H., *Der Bundesrat zwischen Politik und Verwaltung* (Heidelberg, Quelle & Meyer, 1959).

PATZIG, W., 'Der kooperative Föderalismus', *Deutsches Verwaltungsblatt*, lxxxi (1966), 389–96.

RIEGEL, R., 'Die neuen Vorschriften des Wasserhaushaltsgesetzes', *NJW* xxix (1976), 783–7.

RINCK, H.-J., 'Zur Abgrenzung und Auslegung der Gesetzgebungskompetenzen von Bund und Ländern', in *Festschrift für Gebhard Müller*, ed. by T. Ritterspach and W. Geiger (Tübingen, Mohr, 1970), pp. 289–300.

RUDOLF, W., *Bund und Länder im aktuellen deutschen Verfassungsrecht* (Bad Homburg v. d. Höhe, Gehlen, 1968).

SCHEUNER, U., 'Struktur und Aufgabe des Bundesstaates in der Gegenwart', *DÖV* xv (1962), 641–8.

——, 'Wandlungen im Föderalismus der Bundesrepublik', *DÖV* xix (1966), 513–20.

——, 'Kooperation und Konflict', *DÖV* xxv (1972), 585–91.

SCHMID, C., 'Bund und Länder', in R. Löwenthal and H.-P. Schwarz (eds.), *Die Zweite Republik* (Stuttgart, Seewald, 1974), pp. 244–60.

SCHMIDT, J., 'Der Bundesstaat und das Verfassungsprinzip der Bundestreue' (Würzburg Univ. Jur. Diss. 1966).

SCHMIDT, W., 'Das Verhältnis von Bund und Ländern im demokratischen Bundesstaat des Grundgesetzes', *AöR* lxxxvii (1962), 253–96.

SCHNEIDER, H., 'Verträge zwischen Gliedstaaten im Bundesstaat', *VVDStRL* xix (1961), 1–85.

SCHWEIZER, M., 'Die Zustimmung des Bundesrates zu Gesetzen', *Der Staat*, xv (1976), 169–84.

SEEGER, J., 'Finanzierung von Länderaufgaben durch den Bund', *DÖV* xxi (1968), 781–8.

SPANNER, H., 'Zur Rechtskontrolle des bundesfreundlichen Verhaltens', *DÖV* xiv (1961), 481–6.

STERN, K., 'Föderative und unitarische Aspekte im deutschen Rundfunkwesen', in *Rundfunkrecht und Rundfunkpolitik*, Schriftenreihe des Instituts für Rundfunkrecht an der Universität zu Köln, Vol. V (Munich, Beck, 1969), pp. 26–51.

TIEMANN, B., 'Gemeinschaftsaufgaben von Bund und Ländern in verfassungsrechtlicher Sicht' (Munich Univ. Jur. Diss. 1969).

WEBER, W., *Die Gegenwartslage des deutschen Föderalismus* (Göttingen, Vandenhoeck & Ruprecht, 1966).

ZUNKER, A., 'Finanzplanung und Bundeshaushalt' (Freiburg Univ. Wirtschaftswiss. Diss. 1971).

5. *Commentaries on individual judgments*

ESCHENBURG, T., 'Der Fernsehstreit I und II', in *Zur politischen Praxis in der Bundesrepublik* (Munich, Piper, 2nd edn. 1967), i. 213–21.

GRÄBER, F., 'Zur Frage der Zustimmungsgesetze', *DÖV* xii (1959), 893–6.

KLEIN, F., 'Die Gesetzgebungszuständigkeit des Bundes im Rundfunksendewesen nach dem Fernseh-Urteil des Bundesverfassungsgerichts', in *Persönlichkeit und Technik im Lichte des Urheber-, Film-, Funk- und Fernsehrechts: Ehrengabe für Ernst Hirsch*, ed. by G. Roeber (Baden-Baden, Verlag für Angewandte Wissenschaften, 1963), pp. 249–84.

NAWIASKY, H., 'Die volle Bedeutung des bundesverfassungsgerichtlichen Fernsehurteils in föderalistischer Sicht', *Zeitschrift für Politik*, viii (1961), 135–8.

RIDDER, H., 'Finanzausgleich und Grundgesetz: Bemerkungen zum Urteil des Bundesverfassungsgerichts vom 20.2.1952 (BVerfGE 1, 117)', *AöR* lxxviii (1952/3), 237–42.

——, 'Preisrecht ohne Boden', *AöR* lxxxvii (1962), 311–35.

SCHMUCK, H., 'Reinhaltung der Bundeswasserstrassen', *DÖV* xvii (1964), 73–8.

WEBER, W., 'Zur Gültigkeit des Preisgesetzes', *DÖV* x (1957), 33–6.

ZEIDLER, K., 'Gedanken zum Fernseh-Urteil des Bundesverfassungsgerichts', *AöR* lxxxvi (1961), 361–404.

B. Works in English

1. Works on federalism of general or comparative interest

BIRCH, A. H., 'Approaches to the study of federalism', *Political Studies*, xiv (1966), 15–33.

CAPLAN, N., 'Some factors affecting the resolution of a federal–provincial conflict', *Canadian Journal of Political Science*, ii (1969), 173–86.

——, 'Offshore mineral rights: anatomy of a federal–provincial conflict', *Journal of Canadian Studies*, v (1970), 50–61.

FLETCHER, M., 'Judicial Review and the Division of Powers in Canada', in J. P. Meekison (ed.), *Canadian Federalism: Myth or Reality* (Toronto, Methuen, 1968), pp. 140–58.

FRIEDRICH, C. J., *Trends of Federalism in Theory and Practice* (London, Pall Mall, 1968).

LIVINGSTON, W. S., 'A Note on the Nature of Federalism', *Political Science Quarterly*, lxvii (1952), 81–95.

——, *Federalism and Constitutional Change* (Oxford, Clarendon Press, 1956).

MACKENZIE, W. J. M. and B. CHAPMAN, 'Federalism and Regionalism', *Modern Law Review*, xiv (1951), 182–94.

MACMAHON, A. W. (ed.), *Federalism, mature and emergent* (New York, Doubleday, 1955).

MCWHINNEY, E., *Comparative Federalism: States' Rights and National Power* (Toronto, University of Toronto Press, 1962).

——, *Federal Constitution-Making for a Multinational World* (Leyden, Sythoff, 1966).

RIKER, W. H., *Federalism: Origins, Operation, Significance* (Boston, Little Brown, 1964).

SAWER, G., 'The Record of Judicial Review', in G. Sawer (ed.), *Federalism: an Australian Jubilee Study* (Melbourne, Cheshire, 1952), pp. 211–54.

——, *Modern Federalism* (London, Watts, 1969).

SCHWARTZ, B., *A Commentary on the Constitution of the United States: Part I, The Powers of Government* (New York/London, Macmillan, 1963).

VILE, M. J. C., *The Structure of American Federalism* (London, OUP, 1961).

WHEARE, K. C., *Federal Government* (London, OUP, 4th edn. 1963).

2. *Judicial review in Germany and the Federal Constitutional Court*

BLAIR, P. M., 'Law and Politics in Germany', *Political Studies*, xxvi (1978), 348–62.

BODENHEIMER, E., 'Significant Developments in German Legal Philosophy since 1945', *A.J. Comp. Law*, iii (1954), 379–96.

COLE, T., 'The West German Federal Constitutional Court: An Evaluation after six years', *Journal of Politics*, xx (1958), 278–307.

——, 'Three Constitutional Courts: a comparison', *A.P.S.R.* iii (1959), 963–84.

HAHN, H. J., 'Trends in the jurisprudence of the German Federal Constitutional Court', *A.J. Comp. Law*, xvi (1968), 570–9.

MEHREN, A. T. von, 'Constitutionalism in Germany—The first decision of the new Constitutional Court', *A.J. Comp. Law*, i (1952), 70–94.

NAGEL, H., 'Judicial Review in Germany', *A.J. Comp. Law*, iii (1954), 233–41.

RUPP, H. G., 'Judicial Review in the Federal Republic of Germany', *A.J. Comp. Law*, ix (1960), 29–47.

——, 'The Federal Constitutional Court and the Constitution of the Federal Republic of Germany', *Saint Louis University Law Journal*, xvi (1972), 359–83.

3. *Federalism in Germany*

BRAUNTHAL, G., 'Federalism in Germany: the Broadcasting Controversy', *Journal of Politics*, xxiv (1962), 545–61.

BRECHT, A., *Federalism and Regionalism in Germany* (London/Toronto/New York, O.U.P., 1945).

LEIBHOLZ, G., 'The Federal Constitutional Court in Germany and the South-West Case', *A.P.S.R.* xlvi (1952), 723–31.

NEUNREITHER, K. H., 'Federalism and West German bureaucracy', *Political Studies*, vii (1958/9), 233–45.

WELLS, R. H., *The States in West German Federalism. A study of federal—state relations, 1949–1960* (New York, Bookman, 1961).

Index of Cases

The following table includes those cases decided by the Federal Constitutional Court which deal with federal issues as defined on p. 17. A short list of other cases cited which have a bearing on the federal system is further appended.

Cases explicitly cited in the text are supplied with English titles. Bold page numbers refer to discussions of cases in their own right.

General Index